Teach Yourself
ORACLE8™
DATABASE
DEVELOPMENT
in 21 days

Teach Yourself

ORACLE8™

DATABASE

DEVELOPMENT

in 21 days

David Lockman

SAMS
PUBLISHING

201 West 103rd Street
Indianapolis, Indiana 46290

To Joanne: Without you, there would be no joy.

To Josh, Michael, and Daniel: The man upstairs loves you.

Copyright © 1997 by Sams Publishing

FIRST EDITION

International Standard Book Number: 0-672-31078-3

Library of Congress Catalog Card Number: 97-65457

2000   99   4   3   2

Interpretation of the printing code: the rightmost double-digit number is the year of the book's printing; the rightmost single-digit, the number of the book's printing. For example, a printing code of 97-1 shows that the first printing of the book occurred in 1997.

Composed in AGaramond and MCPdigital by Macmillan Computer Publishing

Printed in the United States of America

Trademarks

President, Sams Publishing   Richard K. Swadley
Publishing Manager   Rosemarie Graham
Director of Marketing   Kelli S. Spencer
Product Marketing Manager   Wendy Gilbride
Assistant Marketing Managers   Jennifer Pock, Rachel Wolfe

Acquisitions Editor
Steve Straiger

Development Editor
Marla Reece

Software Development Specialist
John Warriner

Production Editors
Deborah Frisby
Kristi Hart

Copy Editors
Margo Catts
Howard Jones
Bonnie Lawler

Indexer
Benjamin Slen

Technical Reviewers
Byron Pearce
Kelly Leigh

Editorial Coordinators
Mandi Rowell
Katie Wise

Technical Edit Coordinator
Lorraine E. Schaffer

Resource Coordinator
Deborah Frisby

Editorial Assistants
Carol Ackerman
Andi Richter
Rhonda Tinch-Mize

Cover Designer
Tim Amrhein

Book Designer
Gary Adair

Copy Writer
David Reichwein

Production Team Supervisors
Brad Chinn
Charlotte Clapp

Production
Jeanne Clark
Lana Dominguez
Shawn Ring
Becky Stutzman

Overview

Contents

Acknowledgments

Without the help of many people at Sams Publishing, I would not have been able to complete this book. Many thanks to Steve Straiger, acquisitions editor; Marla Reece, development editor; Kristi Hart, production editor, and Byron Pearce, technical editor.

I would also like to acknowledge some special colleagues: David Lerner, Anita Talbot, and George Krestyn.

Special thanks to Barry Cooper for keeping me informed about the progress of the Lakers during the season while I was too busy to pay attention.

To my family, what can I say? Thank you for not questioning my sanity during the past few months. Joanne, thank you for teaching Bo to sing while I was busy. And to Josh, Michael, and Daniel: I promise that we'll be out fishing for yellowtail and bonito in the near future.

About the Author

David Lockman

When he's not fishing for trout or bass, David Lockman provides guidance to organizations on the use of Oracle products. He has participated in the design and implementation of client/server applications for a variety of industries. He is the author of *Developing Personal Oracle7 for Windows 95 Applications*, Second Edition, published by Sams Publishing.

At Oracle Corporation, he was employed as a managing consultant. He was responsible for a consulting group that supported a broad range of projects, including the migration of large legacy databases to Oracle, performance tuning, and applications development.

You can reach David vie e-mail at `dlockman@earthlink.net`.

Tell Us What You Think!

As a reader, you are the most important critic and commentator of our books. We value your opinion and want to know what we're doing right, what we could do better, what areas you'd like to see us publish in, and any other words of wisdom you're willing to pass our way. You can help us make strong books that meet your needs and give you the computer guidance you require.

Do you have access to CompuServe or the World Wide Web? Then check out our CompuServe forum by typing **GO SAMS** at any prompt. If you prefer the World Wide Web, check out our site at http://www.mcp.com.

 NOTE

> If you have a technical question about this book, call the technical support line at 317-581-4669.

As the team leader of the group that created this book, I welcome your comments. You can fax, e-mail, or write me directly to let me know what you did or didn't like about this book—as well as what we can do to make our books stronger. Here's the information:

Fax: 317-581-4669

E-mail: enterprise_mgr@sams.mcp.com

Mail: Rosemarie Graham
          Comments Department
          Sams Publishing
          201 W. 103rd Street
          Indianapolis, IN 46290

Introduction

Welcome to *Teach Yourself Oracle8 Database Development in 21 Days*! This book explores the use of the Oracle database and related Oracle tools in the application development process. During a three-week period, you will be introduced to the various facets of database development including logical database design, physical database design, and the use of Structured Query Language (SQL), a standard language for interfacing with a relational database.

In addition, you will learn about PL/SQL, Oracle's procedural language extension to SQL. With PL/SQL, you can embed application logic within an Oracle database. Once you've learned the basics of PL/SQL, you'll spend five lessons on Developer/2000, a suite of application-development tools, including Oracle Forms, Reports, Graphics, and Procedure Builder. Another two lessons focus on a different application-development tool: Oracle Power Objects. You'll also learn about Oracle database security and performance tuning; following that lesson is an overview of two Oracle products that you might use during application development: Designer/2000 and Database Designer. The final lesson delves into three areas: the Oracle Web Application Server, Developer/2000 for the Web, and Oracle's Network Computing Architecture.

In addition to the 21 lessons, there are two Bonus Days: the first day discusses the use of Powerbuilder with an Oracle database, and the second day discusses new features of Oracle8 that are of particular interest to database designers and application developers.

Assumptions

You'll get the most out of this book if you have the following level of experience:

☐ Some knowledge of a programming language, such as BASIC or C

☐ Familiarity with the Windows or Windows 95 environment

☐ Previous experience with a database, such as Microsoft Access, dBASE, FoxPro, Paradox, or even Excel

The best way to learn any new subject is to practice and experiment. To follow the examples presented in each lesson, as well as each quiz and exercise, you'll need access to the following:

☐ An Oracle database. The type of Oracle database isn't crucial; it could be either the Universal Server, the Workgroup Server, or Personal Oracle. If you are accessing an Oracle server, you'll obviously need reliable network access to the database. Ideally, the Oracle database should be running version 7.1 or higher of the Oracle RDBMS.

☐ Developer/2000 or Power Objects. Five lessons address the components of Developer/2000, release 1.3: Oracle Forms, Reports, Graphics, and Procedure Builder. Two other lessons focus on Power Objects 2.0. To follow the sample applications presented in these lessons, you definitely will want to have the appropriate version of these tools to practice with.

☐ A PC running Windows 95. However, although the examples in the book are presented in a Windows 95 environment, you could also use Windows NT for many of these examples.

About the CD-ROM

The CD-ROM contains a file, named `flugle.dmp`, which contains the sample database discussed throughout the book. By loading this file into an Oracle database, you can follow the examples that are presented in each lesson. A file on the CD-ROM, `readme.txt`, contains directions for loading `flugle.dmp` into an Oracle database.

In addition, there is a folder for each lesson which contains the script files for the code listings presented in each lesson. Each folder may also contain other files that are applicable to the Oracle tool discussed in that lesson.

How To Use This Book

This book has been designed as a 21-day teach-yourself training course complete with chapter quizzes, exercises, and examples that you can try out on your own. It is expected that you can complete one chapter each day of the week for three weeks. However, you should work at your own rate. If you think you can complete two or more chapters a day, go for it! Also, if you think that you should spend more than one day on a certain chapter, spend as much time as you need.

Each week begins with a Week at a Glance section and ends with a Week in Review section. Each day ends with a Q&A section containing questions and answers related to that day's material. There also is a Workshop at the end of the day. A Quiz tests your knowledge of the day's concepts, and one or more exercises put your new skills to use. We urge you to complete these sections to reinforce your new knowledge.

Conventions Used in This Book

This book contains special features to help highlight important concepts and information.

NOTE

A Note presents interesting pieces of information related to the surrounding discussion.

TIP

A Tip offers advice or teaches you an easier way to do something.

WARNING

A Warning advises you about potential problems and helps you steer clear of disaster.

 The New Term icon is added to paragraphs in which a new term is defined. The new term also is italicized so you can find it easily.

 The Input icon identifies a code snippet or listing in which you must type some or all the code yourself.

 The Output icon identifies information that represents Oracle output in a code snippet or listing.

 The Input/Output icon identifies a code snippet or listing that contains code that you must type and code that is output by Oracle. Input is presented in boldface type, and output is presented in regular type.

 The Analysis icon identifies the explanation and purpose of the listing just presented.

At A Glance

During Week 1, you'll learn about many fundamental concepts that are used throughout the book. In fact, the first four days of the week focus on concepts. Beginning on Day 4, you'll begin to learn the specifics of using the Oracle database. Here's a day-by-day summary of Week 1.

☐ **Day 1, "Exploring the World of Relational Databases"**
This lesson discusses the historical development of the relational database. You'll be introduced to some of the products developed by Oracle Corporation. You'll also learn about the architecture of client/server computing.

☐ **Day 2, "Guidelines for Developing an Oracle Application"**
The focus of this lesson is on the standard methodology used to develop an Oracle application. In addition to technical issues, the lesson also addresses organizational questions.

☐ **Day 3, "Logical Database Design"**
In this lesson, you will learn about the theory behind relational databases. The lesson also discusses the database design for the sample database that is discussed throughout the book.

☐ **Day 4, "Implementing Your Logical Model: Physical Database Design"**
Using what you learned during Day 3, this lesson discusses how to construct an Oracle database. You'll learn how to create tables, indexes, and other database objects.

☐ **Day 5, "Introduction to Structured Query Language (SQL)"**
The focus of this lesson is the use of SQL in retrieving data from an Oracle database.

☐ **Day 6, "Using SQL to Modify Data"**
In this lesson, you'll learn how to use SQL to modify the contents of a table.

☐ **Day 7, "Taking Advantage of SQL Built-In Functions"**
This lesson discusses many of the built-in functions that can be used in an SQL statement. You'll see many examples of string, numeric, and other functions that provide tremendous flexibility.

Day 1

Exploring the World of Relational Databases

In 1970 the *Communications of the ACM*, a respected computer science journal, published a paper entitled "A Relational Model of Data for Large Shared Data Banks." Authored by Dr. E. F. Codd, a member of the IBM San Jose Research Laboratory, the paper provided a theoretical and mathematical foundation for the concept of a relational database. It is difficult to point to another single article in the field of computer science that has had as great an influence on vendors, practitioners, and users as Codd's contribution.

 NEW TERM A *relational database* is an information system that presents information as rows contained in a collection of tables, each table possessing a set of one or more columns.

In his paper, Codd described the elements of a relational database: relations, attributes, domains, and the relational operators. Codd's paper described a data storage system that possessed three characteristics that were sorely needed at that time:

☐ **Logical data independence:** This desirable characteristic means that changes made to an attribute (column)—for example, an increase or decrease in size—have no perceivable effect on other attributes for the same relation (table). Logical data independence was attractive to data processing organizations because it could substantially reduce the cost of software maintenance.

☐ **Referential and data integrity:** Unlike other database systems, a relational database would relieve the application software of the burden of enforcing integrity constraints. Codd described two characteristics that would be maintained by a relational database—referential and data integrity. These characteristics are discussed in detail throughout this book.

☐ **Ad hoc query:** This characteristic would enable the user to tell the database which data to retrieve without indicating how to accomplish the task.

It's important to understand the limitations of database systems that existed at that time. The average user—unless he or she were a programmer—could not retrieve data satisfying certain criteria unless a program were written to meet those needs. To simply increase the width of an existing field, such as zipcode, from five to nine characters, maintenance programmers would have to modify countless programs just to adjust field offsets. Many of these programs might not even contain a direct reference to zipcode, but the effect of increasing the width of a field rippled through these older database systems.

Some time passed before a commercial product actually implemented some of the features of the relational database that Codd described. During the early 1980s, the relational database became the foundation for decision support systems. The power of the relational database made it possible for business users to analyze data through interactive queries and reports without the need for programmers. In the late 1980s, continuing advancements in both hardware and relational technology increased the acceptance of the relational database in transaction processing systems.

NOTE

Today's relational databases implement a number of extremely useful features that Codd did not mention in his original article. However, as of this writing, no commercially available database fully implements Codd's rules for relational databases.

Today, the relational database is at the core of the information systems for many organizations, both public and private, both large and small. Today many vendors sell relational database management systems (RDBMS); some of the more well-known vendors are Oracle, Sybase, IBM, Informix, Microsoft, and Computer Associates. Of these vendors, Oracle has emerged as the leader. The Oracle RDBMS engine has been ported to more platforms than any other database product. Because of Oracle's multiplatform support, many application software vendors have made Oracle their database platform of choice.

NEW TERM *RDBMS* (Relational Database Management System) is the software provided by a vendor such as Oracle Corporation that manages a relational database. An RDBMS supports the use of declarative statements which describe the rules that the data must satisfy. This feature is referred to as *declarative integrity*. An RDBMS is the principal component in a client/server architecture, which is discussed later in this lesson.

Structured Query Language (SQL)

Structured Query Language (SQL) is a non-procedural language; unlike C or COBOL, in which you must describe exactly how to access and manipulate data, SQL specifies what to do. Internally, Oracle determines how to perform the request. SQL exists as an American National Standards Institute (ANSI) and International Standards Organization (ISO) standard as well as an industry standard. Oracle's implementation of SQL adheres to Level 2 of the ANSI X3.135-1989/ISO 9075-1989 standard with full implementation of the Integrity Enhancement Feature. As with other database vendors, Oracle provides many extensions to ANSI SQL.

NEW TERM *Structured Query Language* (SQL) is the official and de facto standard language for interfacing with a relational database.

In addition, Oracle's implementation of SQL adheres to the U.S. government standard as described in the Federal Information Processing Standard Publication (FIPS PUB) 127, entitled *Database Language SQL*.

The Oracle Product Line

As the world's leading vendor of relational database software, Oracle Corporation supports its flagship product, the Oracle RDBMS, on more than 90 platforms. The Oracle RDBMS is available in the following three configurations:

☐ **Oracle Universal Server** can support many users on highly scalable platforms such as Sun, HP, Pyramid, and Sequent. Various options are available only with this configuration. The Oracle Universal Server is available for a wide variety of operating systems and hardware configurations. Oracle WebServer—an integrated system for dynamically generating HTML output from the content of an Oracle database—also is included with the Universal Server.

- **Oracle Workgroup Server** is designed for workgroups and is available on NetWare, Windows NT, SCO UNIX, and UnixWare. The Oracle Workgroup Server is a cost-effective and low-maintenance solution for supporting small groups of users. Oracle WebServer also is available as an option with the Oracle Workgroup Server.
- **Personal Oracle** is a Windows-based version of the Oracle database engine that offers the same functionality that exists in the Oracle Universal Server and the Oracle Workgroup Server. Even though Personal Oracle cannot function as a database server by supporting multiple users, it still provides an excellent environment for experimentation and prototyping.

Oracle Universal Server

The Oracle Universal Server includes several optional components:

- **The Distributed Option** allows several Oracle databases on separate computers to function as a single logical database. For example, a database transaction can modify several different databases through a mechanism called *two-phase commit* which guarantees that the required changes are either made successfully in all of the databases or they are all undone.
- **The Replication Option** allows an Oracle database to propagate changes in an Oracle database to other databases.
- **The Context Option** extends the ability of users to search the contents of an Oracle database for specific keywords and themes.
- **The Spatial Data Option** allows a database designer to designate the creation of special indexes that support sophisticated spatial, temporal, and other queries.

Oracle Workgroup Server

The Oracle Workgroup Server is designed to serve a smaller group of users than the Oracle Universal Server. For example, a typical Oracle Workgroup Server installation might consist of a high-end Pentium server running Microsoft NT and supporting up to 25 users. The Workgroup Server automatically configures itself so that database administration tasks are minimized.

Personal Oracle

Personal Oracle provides almost all of the same features that the Oracle8 Server provides on larger platforms. As a result, you can use Personal Oracle to build a working database application that you can later port to a multiuser version of the Oracle8 Server. You can use Personal Oracle to build all the tables, indexes, views, sequences, and other database objects that would exist in a production-quality database application. At the present time, Personal Oracle is available on three platforms—Windows 3.11, Windows 95, and Windows NT.

Personal Oracle provides a tool called the Navigator, an intuitive graphical tool for managing the objects in a Personal Oracle database as well as remote Oracle databases. You can use the Navigator to define remote connections with which you can manipulate a remote Oracle database, whether it is on a UNIX, NT, or other system.

Other Oracle Products

In addition to the Oracle RDBMS, Oracle Corporation also builds and markets a family of other software products:

☐ **Developer/2000** is a family of tools that support the development of client/server applications. Each of these tools is supported in three different GUI environments: Windows, Mac, and Motif. You will be learning about Developer/2000 in the lessons on Days 12 through 16. Developer/2000 includes:

　☐ Oracle Forms is an enterprise tool for building forms-based applications that are well-integrated with the Oracle database.

　☐ Oracle Reports is a report writer that can tackle the most complex reporting requirements. These reports can be previewed on a screen before being printed.

　☐ Oracle Graphics is a tool for generating presentation graphics from database queries.

　☐ Oracle Procedure Builder is used for the development, maintenance, and testing of software written in a language named PL/SQL, which can be stored and executed from an Oracle database.

New Term PL/SQL is a programming language, developed by Oracle Corporation, that provides procedural extensions to the SQL language. PL/SQL modules exist within an Oracle database to enforce business rules, handle exceptions, and provide functionality that can be invoked from other application development tools.

☐ **Power Objects** is another application development environment that is supported in the Windows and Mac environments. The Power Objects user interface is closer to Visual Basic than Oracle Forms. Power Objects also provides object-oriented features such as inheritance.

New Term *Inheritance* is the mechanism that allows the instances of a class to derive all the properties and methods of the class.

☐ **Designer/2000** is a family of tools that support the development of complex applications that may span many organizations within an enterprise. Each tool supports different roles within the development organization—analyst, database designer, application designer, and programmer. The Designer/2000 components support the development of logical models, automatic generation of databases, design of business functions, and the generation of application objects such as Oracle Forms applications, Visual Basic programs, and Web applications.

- [ ] **Database Designer** is an entity-relationship diagramming tool that generates an Oracle database from a model. Database Designer is a single-user design tool; it is closely related to one of the components of Designer/2000.

- [ ] **Precompilers such as Pro*C** are software development tools that enable you to embed SQL statements in a program written in a 3GL (third-generation language) such as C, FORTRAN, or COBOL. The appropriate Oracle precompiler translates embedded SQL statements into Oracle library function calls. The translated program can be built as required by the language and operating system.

What Is Client/Server Computing?

In this lesson, you explore both the development of the client/server computing architecture and its future. Most of the application development tools that are discussed in this book support the client/server computing architecture. So, without further delay, let's define what client/server computing architecture is.

NEW TERM   *Client/server computing architecture* consists of one or more computers, designated as the client machines, running an application program which communicates with a remote computer, designated as the server machine, which services requests from the client machines.

NEW TERM   In the basic model of client/server architecture, a relational database management system (RDBMS) resides on the server machine. The application program that resides on the client machine interfaces with another software layer, called *middleware*, that is responsible for communicating requests and their results between the application program and the RDBMS.

The client/server architecture offers several advantages over previous computing architectures:

- [ ] It supports a heterogeneous mix of client machines. In today's environment, users may be using Windows 3.11, Windows 95, Windows NT, a Mac, or a UNIX workstation, all of which can be supported by the same server.

- [ ] Computing responsibilities are sensibly allocated between client and server. The client machine is responsible for controlling the user interface—displaying information, validating input, and providing meaningful feedback—typically while the server platform is dedicated as a database server.

- [ ] It is independent of networking protocol, server platform operating system, and client platform operating system. This independence results in a tremendous amount of flexibility in selecting hardware and software components for a new system or in implementing a client/server application on existing hardware.

With the client/server architecture, the burden of supporting different networking protocols (such as TCP/IP, SPX/IPX, and Named Pipes) and operating systems (such as Windows, Mac, UNIX, and others) rests on the shoulders of various software vendors: the RDBMS vendors such as Oracle, Sybase, Microsoft, and Informix; tool vendors such as Oracle, Powersoft, and Microsoft; and other third-party vendors that supply components such as ODBC drivers for specific platforms and RDBMSs.

The Origins of Client/Server Computing

To appreciate the advantages of the client/server architecture, it is necessary to recall the previous computing architecture. Before the introduction of the PC, a computer system was typically composed of a mainframe computer accessed by many "dumb" terminals. A dumb terminal had no memory of its own and no processing capability; every character displayed on the terminal screen was controlled by a program on the mainframe. This architecture had a number of implications:

- [ ] The mainframe computer was responsible for everything: storing and retrieving data, arranging the user interface on all terminals, and validating user input. As the number of active terminals increased, the I/O burden on the mainframe computer also increased. Hardware solutions such as terminal concentrators and multiplexers usually were required to manage the workload.

- [ ] The users were completely dependent on the mainframe computer. When the mainframe computer was "down," all computing ceased; a dumb terminal was worthless without the computer to which it was attached. However, in the 1970s, "smart" terminals were introduced which had local memory and limited processing power that could be harnessed by a clever software developer.

- [ ] An application program was responsible for "painting" the terminal screen, accepting requests from each user such as a menu pick, validating user input, and managing data storage. With so many responsibilities, a typical application program was quite complex.

Because of the cost of computer hardware and the technical expertise required to make it function, the computer resources of most large organizations were centrally controlled by a single group, usually called the Data Processing (DP) department. Due to the complexity of application programs, there was a significant backlog for developing new applications, typically measured in years. Very quickly, the introduction of the PC changed everything.

The Birth of the PC

In August of 1981, IBM introduced the IBM 5150 PC Personal Computer. Of course, the IBM PC wasn't the world's first personal computer, but there is no question that IBM gave legitimacy to the value of a personal computer. By today's standards, the first PC was quite modest—based on a 4.77 MHz Intel 8088 processor, it included 64KB of RAM, a monochrome display, and a 5.25-inch floppy disk drive for permanent storage.

One of the first programs written for the PC was a terminal emulator which allowed the PC to mimic an IBM 3270 or DEC VT100 terminal. Of course, compared with the cost of a dumb terminal, the first PC was quite expensive. However, a number of office automation programs, such as WordStar (word processor) and VisiCalc (the first spreadsheet program), became very popular. As a result, a PC could serve dual purposes:

- ☐ It could function as a terminal with the advantage of being able to record a log of the terminal session that could be printed or incorporated into a document.

- ☐ It could function autonomously with an off-the-shelf program that substantially increased the productivity of its user.

PC Databases

Also in 1981, Ashton-Tate introduced dBASE II, a single-user database program for the PC. At the time, most DP departments had a significant backlog for new applications development. In addition, developing a new mainframe-based application—and operating it—was an expensive and complex proposition. The development and operational expenses included sizable charges for computer time and permanent data storage. The PC offered the user an attractive alternative—the purchase of a PC and the dBASE program and the development of a customized dBASE program that he had control over.

LAN Databases

As the popularity of the PC exploded, organizations with multiple PCs needed a convenient, cost-effective method for the machines to communicate with each other and share expensive resources such as mass storage, modems, and printers. The Local Area Network (LAN)—a combination of Network Interface Cards (NICs), cables, and software drivers—filled this requirement. With the acceptance of the LAN by the marketplace, users wanted a database that could be shared by multiple PCs. Multiuser versions of dBASE and other file management systems, such as Paradox and FoxPro, were quickly released.

During this time, many single-user and multiuser applications were developed by both software vendors and in-house programmers. Applications based on these tools offered tremendous benefits, including an excellent return on investment when compared with similar mainframe-based applications. However, there were some negative aspects to this phenomenon:

- ☐ **Uneven quality of developed software:** Because these tools were relatively easy to use, a novice could construct an application that was poorly designed. Although it may have met the initial requirements, the application was constructed so that future modifications to it required a sizable effort. Also, the concept of software

development was new for many of these organizations; because they had little experience with the software development methodology and lifecycle, many important steps, such as documenting requirements and design, were ignored, making it difficult to maintain the program when the original developers were no longer available.

☐ **Perceived loss of power by the DP department:** Most people will argue that loss of power and authority of the DP department was a positive aspect to the proliferation of PC applications. Some DP departments were proactive; they recognized the value of the PC revolution and guided their user community in that direction. However, many DP departments viewed all of this as a serious political and economic threat and reacted by establishing standards that, while reasonable, were used as a tactic to reassert control.

☐ **"Islands of automation":** A legitimate complaint of the DP department was that valuable corporate data was tied up in separate, PC-based databases that weren't able to share information.

The Emergence of the Relational Database

As the PC-based databases were growing during the mid to late 1980s, another dramatic shift was occurring in the DP department: a rapid increase in the use of the relational database. For the first few years, relational databases were used primarily to build decision support systems (DSS). For example, a marketing department could load a relational database with information about product-line sales for several sales regions. Using SQL, a marketing analyst could pose queries against the database that required little or no programming.

Middleware

NEW TERM   In the mid 1980s, the relational database vendors recognized the value of separating the processing for an application between two machines: a client machine that would be responsible for controlling the user interface and a server machine that would host the relational database management system. To achieve this, a category of software, called *middleware*, was invented.

Each RDBMS vendor created two middleware components: a proprietary client driver and a corresponding proprietary server driver. Each network protocol and client or server operating system required a specific implementation by the RDBMS vendor. But the development of middleware provided some serious advantages to application developers: middleware made it possible for an application program running on client machines, each running a different operating system, to communicate with a database on a server machine, running yet a different operating system. Oracle's middleware product is named SQL*Net.

NEW TERM   A *two-tier architecture* is a client/server computing architecture that consists of client machines communicating directly with a database server (see Figure 1.1).

Figure 1.1.

Two-tier architecture.

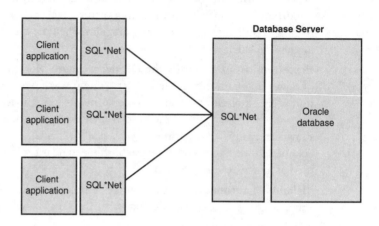

A *three-tier architecture* is a client/server computing architecture consisting of client machines communicating with an application server. The application server may contain an Oracle database in which stored program units, written in PL/SQL, are invoked by the client application program. These stored program units communicate with the database server, which resides on a separate machine. The three-tier architecture is commonly used to balance the processing load of the server machines (see Figure 1.2).

Figure 1.2.

Three-tier architecture.

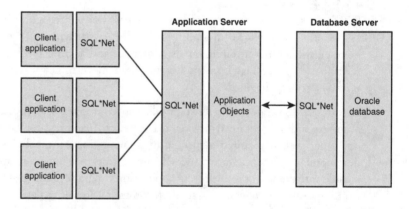

Application Development Tools

At first, most client/server applications were constructed with third-generation languages (3GLs) such as FORTRAN, C, or COBOL, that called RDBMS library routines. However, some RDBMS vendors, such as Oracle, saw the need for a tool that would streamline the development of database applications.

NEW TERM As a result, a new category of development software was created: fourth-generation languages (4GLs), whose name correctly implies that these tools were a higher level of abstraction than 3GLs. Today, 4GLs are commonly referred to as *application development environments.*

Initially, 4GLs generated a character-based user interface. However, with the acceptance of the Windows platform and widespread availability of VGA and SVGA graphics display adapters, the 4GL vendors began to support graphical user interfaces (GUIs) such as Windows, Mac, and Motif. In the early 1990s, these tools generated applications that were quite slow and buggy. Since then, many improvements have been achieved, both in operating system software (for example, the upgrade from Windows 3.11 to Windows 95) and hardware performance so that it is feasible to build reliable, well-performing applications.

The "Fat" Client versus the "Thin" Client

By 1996, the development of client/server applications was a mature technology. Organizations understood how to use application development environments, such as Oracle Forms and PowerBuilder, to construct an application. But for a large organization, the administration of a client/server application was not a trivial exercise:

- [ ] Different versions of the application had to be built for each client platform.
- [ ] If the application was upgraded, the software had to be distributed to all client machines.
- [ ] If a new user wanted to add an application program to her computer, the correct version of middleware had to be installed and configured for that machine.

A widely-referenced study by the Gartner Group indicated that the average annual cost to *administer* a PC was $12,000. Essentially, many managers viewed these problems as a financial and administrative nightmare—and they looked for a way out.

At the same time, two events were taking place that could not be ignored:

- [ ] The exponential acceptance of the Internet and the World Wide Web
- [ ] The introduction and adoption of the Java programming language by hardware and software vendors

The explosion in the use of the World Wide Web and Web browsers led RDBMS vendors, such as Oracle, to develop tools that would support the dynamic display of database content on the Web. Simultaneously, the Java language—platform-independent, object-oriented, distributed, and secure—appealed to software vendors, long interested in writing software once and deploying it on a variety of computer hardware and operating system platforms. With these two movements, many software vendors began advocating the "thin" client model: a user interface, based on a Web browser in which a Java applet is downloaded by a server to be executed on the client machine. The traditional client/server architecture was referred to as the "fat" client model because the client required a typically large executable for the application program (for example, `mybigapp.exe`), multiple libraries (such as DLLs), as well as the middleware drivers (such as SQL*Net).

The arguments in support of the thin client model are

- ☐ It significantly reduces the administrative costs for client machines.
- ☐ Applications are written once and can be deployed everywhere.
- ☐ Updates to applications are made on one machine: the server.
- ☐ Portability: Instead of being tied to a particular client machine, an application "follows" the authorized user.

However, there are concerns about the viability of the thin client model:

- ☐ Because all application software is downloaded from a server, the thin client model increases the load on the network.
- ☐ Because Java is a byte-code interpreted language, it is not as fast as other languages; performance may be an issue.

CORBA

In 1989, the Object Management Group (OMG) was established by representatives from hardware manufacturers, software vendors, researchers, and software practitioners. The OMG's goal was to promote the use of object-based software. To this end, the OMG developed a conceptual foundation called the Object Management Architecture. From this foundation, a specification was developed for the Common Object Request Broker Architecture, commonly referred to as CORBA.

The CORBA specification describes several components:

- ☐ An Object Request Broker (ORB) that supports requests and responses between objects in a heterogeneous, distributed environment.
- ☐ Object Services, which is a set of basic services that support the use and implementation of objects.
- ☐ Common Facilities, which is a set of services that applications may share.
- ☐ Application Objects, which are vendor- or developer-supplied objects with a defined interface.

NEW TERM In support of the CORBA 2.0 specification, Oracle has unveiled an architecture named the *Network Computing Architecture* (NCA). Oracle's latest version of Oracle WebServer, version 3.0, is aligned with the vision of the Network Computing Architecture. You'll be learning more about NCA in Day 21, "Oracle: The Next Generation."

The Challenge to Client/Server Computing: The Network Computer

For some time, Oracle CEO Larry Ellison has complained that PCs are too expensive and complex for the average user. His vision is a device called a *network computer* that would cost less than the typical PC and be far simpler to administer because all of its software would be downloaded via a Web browser.

In 1996, Oracle Corporation established a subsidiary company, Network Computer, Incorporated. The mission of this subsidiary is to license its network computer design to hardware manufacturers and promote the development of applications for the device.

The Purpose of This Book

This book is designed to serve readers who fit into the following categories:

- ☐ You are familiar with databases such as dBASE or FoxPro but haven't worked with Oracle or other SQL-based database products.
- ☐ You have some experience with SQL but want to learn more about its use in an Oracle database.
- ☐ You are familiar with 3GLs such as COBOL but you don't have experience in the client/server environment and want to learn about application development environments such as Developer/2000 or Power Objects.

To illustrate the concepts presented in the book, you will see many examples based on the design of a database for a small college. The examples based on this database are augmented with other specific examples, depending on the topic under discussion. The CD-ROM contains this sample database as well as relevant files from each of the chapters in the book. Refer to the Introduction of this book for more information about the CD-ROM.

When you have finished reading this book, you'll be familiar with the following languages, tools, and issues:

- ☐ **SQL:** the de facto industry and ANSI standard language for interacting with relational databases. You'll learn more about SQL on Days 4 through 8.
- ☐ **PL/SQL:** Oracle's procedural language extensions to SQL, used for writing database triggers and stored procedures and functions. Days 9 through 11 provide a solid introduction to PL/SQL.

☐ **Developer/2000:** You should be able to develop a basic Oracle Forms application, build a master-detail report with Oracle Reports, and use Procedure Builder to modify a database trigger or package. You'll spend five lessons, Days 12 through 16, learning about Developer/2000.

☐ **Power Objects:** You will be able to develop a Power Objects application with data entry, query, and reporting capabilities; you'll spend two lessons, Days 17 and 18, on the use of Power Objects.

To get the most from this book, at a minimum you should have an Oracle database available to you—either Personal Oracle7, an Oracle Workgroup Server, or an Oracle Universal Server—and SQL*Plus. However, you'll probably need to have Developer/2000 and Power Objects to follow the lessons dealing with these tools.

Summary

The crucial ideas about client/server computing introduced in this lesson are as follows:

☐ The theoretical foundation for relational databases began in 1970.

☐ Structured Query Language (SQL) is an official standard language for communicating with a relational database.

☐ There are three configurations of the Oracle Relational Database Management System (RDBMS): the Oracle Universal Server, the Oracle Workgroup Server, and Personal Oracle.

☐ The client/server architecture supports a variety of client platforms, server platforms, and networking protocols.

☐ The client/server architecture requires the use of a software layer called middleware, whose function is to support protocol-independent communication between the client machine and the server machine.

☐ A two-tier architecture consists of a client machine communicating directly with a database server.

☐ A three-tier architecture consists of a client machine communicating with an application server. The application server, in turn, communicates with the database server.

☐ The popularity of the World Wide Web and the Java programming language are piquing the interest of many software developers in a thin client model: a Web browser which downloads Java applets, as required.

What Comes Next?

On Day 2, "Guidelines for Developing an Oracle Application," you learn about some of the basic steps that are required to build an Oracle application, such as gathering user requirements.

Q&A

Q Oracle Corporation has released Oracle8. Are SQL, PL/SQL, and the Oracle development tools still supported in Oracle8?

A Absolutely. Oracle8 supports SQL, PL/SQL, and the Oracle development tools. Rather than replacing features that are currently found in the Oracle RDBMS, Oracle8 will eventually expand existing capabilities with user-defined datatypes, inheritance, a built-in Java Virtual Machine, and many other features.

Q What kind of support for Java is Oracle planning to provide?

A Oracle has embraced the use of Java, both internally and for its customers. The Oracle8 RDBMS will eventually include a Java Virtual Machine. Oracle WebServer 3.0 allows Java applets to invoke PL/SQL stored program units. And the current release of Developer/2000—1.4W—supports the generation of Java applets from Oracle Forms and Reports.

Q What application-development environments are discussed in this book?

A You learn about three application-development environments: Developer/2000, which includes Oracle Forms, Oracle Reports, and Oracle Graphics; Oracle Power Objects; and PowerBuilder.

Workshop

The purpose of the Workshop is to allow you to test your knowledge of the material discussed in the lesson. See if you can correctly answer the questions in the quiz and complete the exercise before you continue with tomorrow's lesson.

Quiz

1. Name two advantages that relational databases offer over file management systems.
2. Name three advantages of the client/server computing architecture when compared to the mainframe computing architecture.
3. What is the name of the Oracle middleware product?
4. What is a "fat" client? What is a "thin" client?

Exercise

As I mentioned, this book uses a sample database for a small college. Start thinking about what kinds of information you think the college will want to store and retrieve. Ask yourself what kinds of questions a student, a professor, or an administrator might ask of the database. Jot down how you might organize this information. You'll return to this information on Day 3, "Logical Database Design."

Day 2

Guidelines for Developing an Oracle Application

The effort to develop a new Oracle application depends on many factors. Many excellent books have been written on the general topic of application development. In this lesson, you examine some of the considerations that come into play during the development of an Oracle database application.

NOTE In this lesson, the term *users* is meant to include all the stakeholders in the application—end users, managers, suppliers, customers, operations staff, and other developers.

Lessons Learned

The sad reality of applications development is that the failure rate is surprisingly high; the majority of new applications do not go into production. As an applications developer, it is important for you to understand why this is the case and what its implications are on the development process. If you religiously follow the suggestions in this lesson—or any other source—there is no guarantee that you will be successful in implementing the new application. If you haven't already discovered it, there is no silver bullet when it comes to software development!

In an ideal world, the steps for developing a new application consist of:

- ☐ Gathering requirements
- ☐ Designing the application
- ☐ Building the application
- ☐ Testing the application
- ☐ Deploying the application
- ☐ Maintaining the application

In reality, these steps are rarely followed in a serial fashion. Instead, a more common approach is for the sequence to be repeated several times, with the application getting closer and closer to implementing the "true requirements" (see Figure 2.1).

Let's delve into each of these steps a bit further.

NOTE Every project has a set of roles that include: project manager, business process analyst, database designer, application designer, programmer, technical writer, database administrator, system administrator, and trainer. On a very small project, all of these roles may fall on your shoulders. On a large project, an entire team of people may be responsible for a particular area, such as training. The important thing to remember is that *someone* has to be responsible for each of these areas for the project to be successful.

Figure 2.1.

Application develop-
ment cycle.

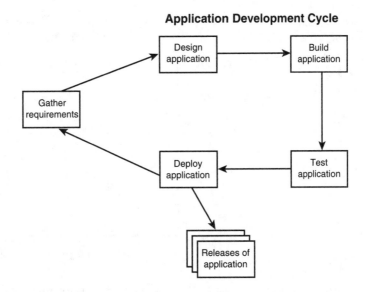

Application Development Cycle

Gathering Requirements

The starting point for developing a new application is the task of gathering requirements. The task of defining the requirements of a new application is assumed to be necessary, straightforward, and obvious by everyone who has an influence on the new application. Gathering requirements is an art, not a science, and there are pitfalls every step of the way:

☐ **Human communication:** Obtaining requirements always involves some sort of human communication—either talking, listening, reading, or writing. Because human language is imprecise, it is subject to interpretation. This interpretation applies to both others and to you, the application developer.

☐ **Politics:** The development of a new application is fraught with political danger. One set of users may specify a requirement, whereas a different set of users may demand a conflicting requirement. It is up to you to work with these individuals and determine who is correct, whose voice matters, and who really needs to be satisfied at the end of the project. The risk of an application development project is proportional to the number of organizations that are involved in its development (see Figure 2.2).

☐ **Constant change:** Very often, you'll be developing a new application in an environment where the requirements are changing. If you're lucky, someone will even remember to tell you what is changing, the reasons for the change, and the implications on the existing requirements. You'll find it quite challenging to come up with an architecture that will meet these changing requirements.

Figure 2.2.
Risk and its relation-
ship to organizational
complexity.

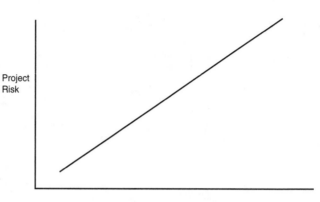

**Relationship Between Project Risk
and Organizational Complexity**

You'll want to gather several types of requirements for your application:

☐ **Functional requirements:** These describe both high-level and low-level requirements that are to be satisfied by the application. An example of a high-level
requirement might be "The Flugle College Information System shall allow instructors to assign grades to their students."

☐ **Data requirements:** These requirements describe the information that must be
managed by the application. These requirements are crucial to the development of
a logical data model that helps implement the functional requirements. For
instance, a data requirement could be "The Flugle College Information System
shall maintain information about the courses that are offered by each department."

☐ **Performance requirements:** These requirements describe the performance that the
entire system, including the application, must satisfy. For example, a performance
requirement could be "The Flugle College Information System shall be capable of
supporting 120 simultaneous users while providing a response time of less that two
seconds to register a student for a class."

There are many ways to keep track of requirements. Of course, you can take detailed notes.
You also can build a requirements database and generate documentation from that. Or you
could use components in Designer/2000 or other Computer Aided Software Engineering
(CASE) tools. However, the method that you use to gather and document requirements is
a function of several items:

☐ **Application complexity:** Is the application being developed for a small group of
users or for a major division of a large organization?

- **Budget:** Is the application being funded on a shoestring, or have vice presidents signed off on the funding for this major task?

- **Number of people assigned to the development of the application:** Are you the only full-time person working to develop the application (with others providing time on an as-needed basis), or are there dozens of people who are involved in the development of the application?

- **Visibility:** Is the application to be developed unknown outside a small team, or are upper-level managers going to be promoted or asked to resign based on the successful implementation of the application?

The answers to these questions will determine how structured you should be in gathering requirements and reviewing your understanding of the requirements with the stakeholders—end users, managers, and other developers. If your project has straightforward requirements, a modest budget, and a small staff, you may want to adapt an informal methodology for gathering and reviewing requirements: you still will want to document everything but without a formal review and signoff process. However, if your project has complex requirements, a significant budget, and a large staff, you should anticipate a formal process for requirements gathering, analysis, review, and signoff; if you don't see such a process in place, you may be witnessing a failure it its initial stage.

Designing and Building the Application

Someone once said that when designing a system, ten thousand decisions are made and rarely recorded. There are many major aspects to designing an application:

- **Develop a logical data model:** If there is no existing database for the application, a logical data model will be needed; you'll learn more about this on Day 3, "Logical Database Design." This is probably the most important step in the design process. No matter how small the project, you really should try to use an entity-relationship modeling tool such as the Entity-Relationship Diagrammer in Designer/2000, the Oracle Database Designer, or LogicWorks' ERwin; on Day 19, "An Overview of Oracle Database Security and Tuning," you'll see how Database Designer can be used to construct a logical data model. Such tools will enable you to graphically construct a model of the information to be managed by the application. The big advantage of these tools is that they will generate an Oracle database from the model. They also provide a central repository for documenting the data that the application will manipulate.

- **Choose development tools:** Unless this decision is made for you, you'll need to look at the client machines that need to be supported (for example, Windows, Mac, or Motif) and the preferences of other developers. Of course, you also should factor in your experience with various development tools. You also need to consider the installed base of users when selecting development tools; a superior product with a smaller installed base of users is a less attractive choice than a good product with a very large installed base of users. If you have decided to use a tool that you haven't used before, be sure that you allocate enough time to become thoroughly proficient with it; you don't want to discover its shortcomings halfway through a project.

☐ **Implement the functionality that the users need:** In general, it's better to schedule more releases of the application to the users rather than fewer. Each release will incorporate a little more of the functionality that the users are expecting. Each release will give the users an opportunity to provide feedback on what you've given them; it also will give you the opportunity to incorporate their feedback in the next release. Through this process, the end users "buy into" the project; over time, they become stakeholders. This is crucial; if the users don't accept the final delivery of the application, it is doomed to failure.

☐ **Make use of reusable components:** When feasible, try to design a set of reusable components. Needless to say, the degree of reusability will depend on the development tools that you are using. If the tools are not object-oriented, the reusable components will consist of form and report templates, libraries, and header files. If the tools support object-oriented development, the reusable components will consist of ancestor classes from which a working application can be constructed. During Day 18, "Developing an Application with Oracle Power Objects," you'll see how you can create classes in Power Objects to simplify the maintenance of an application. Although reusability is a lofty goal, be judicious in how much time and energy you invest.

☐ **Use a configuration management (CM) tool:** No matter how modest your application development effort is, you should plan on using some form of configuration management. At a minimum, you will want to keep a backup, either on tape or removable disk, of each release of your application. For medium-sized or large projects, this is not sufficient; plan on using a multiuser CM tool that supports version control. The items that you should keep under CM include: source-code files, SQL scripts for creating and populating the Oracle database, PL/SQL source code, design documents, test data sets, training material, and text files for producing online help.

☐ **Identify user roles and privileges:** In designing your application, identify the major roles that users will assume when using the system. You should implement these roles at two levels: at the database level and at the application level—both are important. You should specify the privileges—create, read, update, and delete (often referred to as *CRUD*)—that should be granted to each role for each database table, view, or other object. Depending on the application development tool you use, you should be able to associate a user's login to his or her role, and in turn associate that role with the menu items that should be enabled for that role.

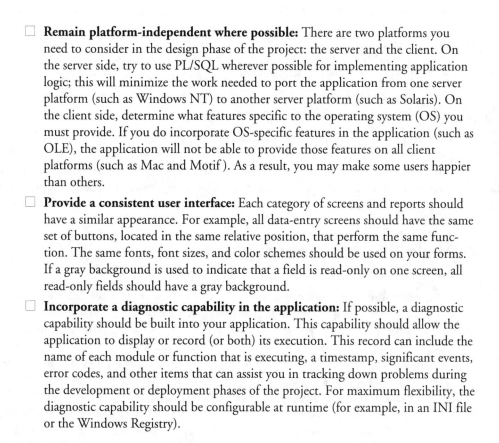

☐ **Remain platform-independent where possible:** There are two platforms you need to consider in the design phase of the project: the server and the client. On the server side, try to use PL/SQL wherever possible for implementing application logic; this will minimize the work needed to port the application from one server platform (such as Windows NT) to another server platform (such as Solaris). On the client side, determine what features specific to the operating system (OS) you must provide. If you do incorporate OS-specific features in the application (such as OLE), the application will not be able to provide those features on all client platforms (such as Mac and Motif). As a result, you may make some users happier than others.

☐ **Provide a consistent user interface:** Each category of screens and reports should have a similar appearance. For example, all data-entry screens should have the same set of buttons, located in the same relative position, that perform the same function. The same fonts, font sizes, and color schemes should be used on your forms. If a gray background is used to indicate that a field is read-only on one screen, all read-only fields should have a gray background.

☐ **Incorporate a diagnostic capability in the application:** If possible, a diagnostic capability should be built into your application. This capability should allow the application to display or record (or both) its execution. This record can include the name of each module or function that is executing, a timestamp, significant events, error codes, and other items that can assist you in tracking down problems during the development or deployment phases of the project. For maximum flexibility, the diagnostic capability should be configurable at runtime (for example, in an INI file or the Windows Registry).

Testing the Application

You should plan to test the application at every stage of development. It's important to define what is meant by testing. Perhaps it's stretching the term, but testing can be considered to include the following:

☐ Verifying that the logical data model is complete, correct, and consistent

☐ Obtaining the users' approval of the general user interface, menu structure, and flow of control

☐ Loading representative data, either legacy data or new data, into the Oracle database to validate the data model, constraints, and sizing assumptions

☐ Verifying that PL/SQL program units perform as intended (PL/SQL is a programmatic extension to the SQL language that you'll learn about in detail in later lessons)

In addition to the previous items, you need to plan for specific types of tests:

☐ Typical (and atypical) test cases to verify that the application will accept legal inputs, reject invalid inputs and choices, and produce the correct results

☐ Performance tests that will simulate various usage loads, such as the number of concurrent users changing student records

If you are building an application that needs to run on several different client machines (such as Windows 3.11, Windows 95, and Mac), be sure that someone makes these computers available to you during testing, deployment, and maintenance. Otherwise, you will have a very hard time reproducing, diagnosing, and fixing reported bugs. Also, be sure that these machines are representative of the users' machines, in terms of processor speed, memory, and available disk space.

Deploying the Application

There are several issues that you'll need to consider during deployment:

☐ **Installing the application:** If you're installing the application for a small group of users who are geographically close, you may have the luxury of installing the software yourself. If there are many users or they are geographically scattered, you must plan on a more automated way to install the software. There are several choices. You can produce a set of installation disks (or a CD-ROM) that automates the installation. You can use a file server, accessible by all users for the installation. Or, you could establish a Web site from which the users can download the software and follow a set of directions. In all cases, the installation will consist of two major tasks. The first is to create a directory on the user's machine, copy all the necessary files to that directory, and configure the environment. The second is to install and configure the SQL*Net product, assuming that it isn't already installed.

☐ **Training the users:** Somehow, time must be allocated for training the end-users in the use of the application. The training can be instructor-led or computer-based (CBT). Some managers may argue that the end-users don't have time available for formal training. However, one way or another, the users will need time to learn to use the software.

☐ **Providing online help:** After receiving training, users still will have questions about the use of the software. An effective way of providing answers to these questions is by supplying a help file that works with the application program to provide context-sensitive help.

Maintaining the Application

You've come a long way. You've gathered requirements, designed, built, tested, and deployed the application—now what? Expect feedback from the users—both positive (hopefully) and negative (if it helps, view it as constructive criticism). The user feedback probably will include requests for additional capabilities (such as "How long would it take for you to put together a report that looks like this?") as well as bug reports (such as "When I press F5, the screen goes blank."). If you don't receive any feedback, that is a bad sign—it may mean that very few people are actually using the software.

The feedback should be categorized by both criticality and scope. The fixes for critical bugs can be incorporated in an emergency release, perhaps containing only the files that need to be replaced. However, a regular release or upgrade schedule should be used to incorporate less critical bug fixes and new features.

Summary

In this lesson, you learned about the major phases of developing an Oracle application:

- ☐ Gathering requirements
- ☐ Designing the application
- ☐ Building the application
- ☐ Testing the application
- ☐ Deploying the application
- ☐ Maintaining the application

What Comes Next?

On Day 3, you will delve into the concepts of relational database theory: entities, attributes, domains, and relationships. You also will be introduced to the concepts of data and referential integrity, as well as some of the normal forms.

Q&A

Q What issues should I be concerned with if the new application is replacing an existing system?

A There are a number of political and technical issues that you need to consider. Any existing application will have its proponents and detractors. You'll want to have lots of discussions with both groups to understand the advantages and disadvantages of the existing application.

In designing the new application, try not to be constrained by the functionality of the existing application; you certainly don't want to simply "rewrite" the application using a current software development tool (in reengineering jargon, this is commonly referred to as "paving the cow path"). As much as possible, try to incorporate the developers/maintainers of the legacy application in the new development; they probably have a lot of ideas on how the system could be improved, and they are likely to be threatened by the development of a new application. Don't be critical of the legacy application; its designers and developers probably did the best they could with the resources that were available to them.

In planning for the transition from the legacy application to the new application, consider a phased approach in which the legacy system continues to operate while functional elements of the new system are deployed. Do not underestimate the effort that will be required to migrate the legacy data to the new Oracle database.

Workshop

The purpose of the Workshop is to allow you to test your knowledge of the material discussed in the lesson. See if you can correctly answer the questions in the quiz and complete the exercises before you continue with tomorrow's lesson.

Quiz

1. True or false? If you use an application-development tool that supports object-oriented development, there is a greater chance of implementing a successful application.

2. Name three types of requirements that are needed when designing a system.

3. True or false? You shouldn't begin developing software until you have a complete set of requirements.

Exercises

1. What types of risks might exist during the development of an Oracle application?

2. What factors could contribute to these risk categories?

3. What steps could be taken to mitigate these risk categories?

Day 3

Logical Database Design

The foundation of any database application is a logical data model. Like any model, a logical data model is an idealization of a real system. A model is only as useful as it is accurate. Like any real enterprise, a logical data model is dynamic rather than static. It needs to evolve as the enterprise upon which it is based changes.

NEW TERM A *logical data model* is a representation of both the data elements used by an enterprise and the relationships between those data elements.

One of the most common methods used for developing a logical data model is entity-relationship modeling. *Entities* are people, places, objects, or concepts. Each entity is described by a set of attributes. In the sample database, the college registrar views an instructor as a set of attributes, such as instructor ID, last name, first name, and department. A department administrator views an instructor with a different set of attributes for the same instructor; for instance, the instructor's current position. As you can see, business requirements are what drives the data model. Entities don't exist in a vacuum—you define relationships between entities. These relationships are used to enforce business rules.

For example, in the sample application—an information system for a small college—a class must be taught by one—*and only one*—instructor.

Why bother to develop a logical data model—why not just jump right into database design? By developing a logical data model, you are forced to focus on an organization's data and its internal relationships without initially worrying about implementation details such as a column's datatype. You can think of the logical data model at a higher level of abstraction than you can think of the database design.

Relational Database Theory

No book that deals with relational database systems can be considered complete unless it discusses the basic concepts of relational database theory. In a nutshell, those concepts are as follows:

- ☐ Every entity has a set of attributes that describe the entity. For example, an entity named Course would describe the courses offered at a college.

- ☐ A row is a single instance of attribute values. For example, a row in the Course entity would describe a single course offered by the college.

- ☐ Some of an entity's attributes uniquely identify each row in that entity. This set of attributes is called the *primary key*. For the entity that describes students, the Student ID attribute is the primary key because it uniquely identifies each student.

- ☐ None of the attributes that compose the primary key can be null.

- ☐ A foreign key is an attribute in one entity whose values must exist as the primary key in another entity.

- ☐ Entities are related to one another.

- ☐ The order of the rows in an entity is arbitrary.

- ☐ The order of the attributes in an entity is arbitrary.

A Table Is Rows and Columns

From a practitioner's perspective, an entity is implemented as a database table. An entity's attributes are implemented as a table's *columns*. A single set of attribute or column values is known as a *row*. The terms *row* and *record* are used interchangeably.

NEW TERM   A *column* in a database table represents an entity's attributes.

NEW TERM   A *row* is a single set of entity attributes or column values in a database table.

NEW TERM   A *record* is the same as a row—it is a single set of entity attributes or column values.

NOTE

> You cannot determine what tables are stored in an Oracle database by looking at a directory in the file system: the Oracle RDBMS manages the internal structure of its data files. With a file management system such as dBASE, each "table" is stored as a separate file in a directory.

The Order of Rows Is Arbitrary

A key tenet of relational database theory is that a table has no implied ordering. The only way to know the order in which rows will be retrieved from a table is to specify the order. The concept of no implied order is powerful because it enables you to think abstractly about tables and, for the most part, to ignore the physical implementation of a database's structures.

The Order of Columns Is Arbitrary

As with a table's rows, a table's columns have no implied ordering. If you use SQL*Plus to describe a table, SQL*Plus returns the columns in the order in which they were created. You can, however, specify any order for retrieving columns. You also can modify a column's definition without affecting any of the other columns. For example, you can increase the width of a column without having to modify any of your existing table definitions or SQL statements. Taking care of the physical details related to the change is the job of the Oracle relational database management system (RDBMS). A relational database is said to provide *logical data independence* because column definitions are independent from one another.

Data Integrity

According to relational theory, every entity has a set of attributes that uniquely identify each row in that entity. Relational theory also states that no duplicate rows can exist in a table, which is really just another way of saying that every table must have a primary key. This concept is referred to as *data integrity*. For example, the Social Security number for each current employee is unique.

Primary Key

Every entity has a set of attributes that uniquely define an instance of that entity. This set of attributes is referred to as the primary key. The primary key may be composed of a single attribute—a student is uniquely identified by a Student ID—or of several attributes—a course is uniquely identified by both the Department ID and the Course ID. Sometimes, the attributes that compose the primary key are obvious, and other times they are not. To test your understanding of the primary key, you must look at existing data. However, you also must interview people who understand the way in which the organization operates. Don't rely solely on existing data to validate your understanding of the primary key.

 A *primary key* is the set of attributes that uniquely define a row.

No Part of the Primary Key Is Null

A basic tenet of relational theory is that no part of the primary key can be null. If you think about that idea for a moment, it seems intuitive. The primary key must uniquely identify each row in an entity; therefore, if the primary key (or a part of it) is null, the primary key wouldn't be able to identify anything. For example, a course that has no Course ID cannot be identified or processed in any way.

Referential Integrity

Tables are related to one another through foreign keys. A *foreign key* is one or more columns for which the set of possible values is found in the primary key of a second table. Referential integrity is achieved when the set of values in a foreign key column is restricted to the primary key that it references or to the null value. Once the database designer declares primary and foreign keys, enforcing data and referential integrity is the responsibility of the RDBMS.

 A *foreign key* is one or more columns whose values must exist in the primary key of another table.

Relationship

The association between two entities is defined by a relationship. In a relationship, one entity is identified as the parent and the other entity is identified as the child. A relationship is defined by the following characteristics:

- ☐ **Identifying or non-identifying:** An identifying relationship is one in which the primary key of the parent forms a portion of the primary key of the child. A non-identifying relationship is one in which the primary key of the parent entity is not part of the primary key of the child entity.

- ☐ **Cardinality:** A relationship's cardinality is defined by the number of rows in the child entity that a single row in the parent entity must have. Examples of cardinality are zero, one, or more. For example, an instructor who is engaged in basic research may teach zero or more classes. However, a department must offer one or more courses or it ceases to be a department.

NEW TERM *Cardinality* describes the number of rows in a child entity that a single row in a parent entity may have. The cardinality of a relationship between a parent entity and a child entity may be mandatory—for example, a row in a parent entity must have one and only one row in a child entity. Or, the cardinality may be less restrictive—for example, a row in a parent entity may have zero or more rows in a child entity.

☐ **Mandatory or optional:** A relationship is mandatory when a row in the parent entity must have some number of rows in the child entity. A relationship is optional when a row in the parent entity can exist without related rows in the child entity.

☐ **Integrity rules:** These rules define what action should be taken when a row in the parent or child entity is changed in some way. There are six possibilities: a row in the parent entity is added, changed, or removed, or a row in the child entity is added, changed, or removed. For each of these possibilities, there are several possible actions—restrict the action, set the key value in the parent or child entity to null, cascade the operation to the child entity, or set the key value in the parent or child entity to a default value.

The Concept of the Null Value

A major difference between a relational database and older database technologies is the concept of the null value. In a non-relational database, a special value indicates the absence of a value in a character or numeric field.

NEW TERM The word *null* indicates that a value for a column or expression is either not applicable or has not been assigned.

In a relational database, a null value for a column represents different concepts:

☐ A value for this column is not applicable for the row in question.

☐ The column has not yet been assigned a value.

A relational database enables you to set the value of a column to null or to test a column to see if it is null.

Normalization

It's very easy to create a table in an Oracle database. You can choose from a variety of tools to accomplish this—SQL*Plus, SQL Worksheet, and others; you'll learn more about these tools beginning on Day 4, "Implementing Your Logical Model: Physical Database Design." However, it's crucial that you take the time to study the optimal design for your application's database.

A facet of relational database theory comes into play in this discussion. Normalization theory is the study of relations (tables), attributes (columns), and the dependency of attributes upon one another. The goals of normalization include the following:

- ☐ Minimizing redundant data
- ☐ Avoiding update anomalies
- ☐ Reducing inconsistent data
- ☐ Designing data structures for easier maintenance

Because this is theory, you need to understand some essential terminology. Table 3.1 breaks these terms into three categories—theoretician, analyst, and developer. As you read about databases, whether the material is academically or commercially oriented, you'll come across terms that are easily exchanged. As you read the material in this lesson, you'll see these terms used interchangeably. You can use whichever terms you prefer, as long as you use them appropriately and understand what they represent. For example, a professor of computer science may write about relation XYZ; an application developer may refer to the same *thing* as table XYZ.

Table 3.1. Orientation of database terminology.

Theoretician	Analyst	Developer
Relation	Entity	Table
Attribute	Attribute	Column
Tuple	Row	Row/Record

Normalization theory describes the desired arrangements of tables and columns as Normal Forms. This chapter discusses the First, Second, and Third Normal Forms, which are often cited as 1NF, 2NF, and 3NF. Although these terms sound theoretical and abstract, they are actually quite intuitive. Other Normal Forms—Boyce-Codd, 4th, and 5th Normal Forms—address more complex normalization issues. Those topics are beyond the scope of this book.

Normalization Rule 1: All Columns Should Contain a Single Piece of Information

An entity (table) is in First Normal Form (1NF) if all of its attributes are atomic. The term *atomic* implies that each attribute consists of a single fact about the entity. For instance, if an entity is used to store employee information, you would not use a single attribute, Dependents, to store the names of an employee's dependents. Some employees may have no dependents, whereas others may have many dependents.

Normalization Rule 2: All Columns Depend Only on the Primary Key

For an entity to be in Second Normal Form (2NF), all of its columns must depend on the primary key only. Put simply, this rule means that a table must not contain *extraneous* information. For example, in addition to other information, the Class table identifies each course and the instructor for that course. The instructor is identified by the column Instructor ID. The primary key for the table is the Class ID. If the Class table also contained the instructor's position, the table would not be in 2NF; the instructor's position depends on Instructor ID only, not on the primary key.

Normalization Rule 3: All Columns Depend on the Primary Key and Nothing But the Primary Key

To be in Third Normal Form (3NF), a table's columns must be entirely dependent on the primary key. The key word in that last sentence is *entirely*. Each column in the table must be dependent on the entire primary key, not just a portion of it.

For example, the Course table identifies each course and the department that offers it. The primary key consists of the Department ID and the Course ID; both columns are necessary to uniquely define a row in the table. If the Course table also contained a column for storing the department chairperson, the table would not be in 3NF; the department chairperson depends only on the Department ID, not on the entire primary key. So it can be said that Department Chairperson is dependent on part of the primary key, but it is not wholly dependent on the primary key.

You'll sometimes see this concept referred to as the *derived column*. In the previous example, Department Chairperson can be derived from Department ID. According to relational theory, a table should not contain any derived columns. In practice, tables frequently contain derived columns.

Applying Normalization to Database Design

Normalization theory discusses normal forms beyond the Third Normal Form (3NF), but I won't delve into that topic here. However, I would like to discuss the application of normalization theory. If you read articles about relational database technology, you will encounter what can be called "the great debate." Relational purists say that all tables must be in at least 3NF, although practitioners argue that to achieve acceptable performance, you must *denormalize* a database—in other words, reduce the database design from 3NF to 2NF. My position is somewhere in the middle. Here are my recommendations.

Do	Don't

DO ensure that your design is in 3NF.

DON'T make any assumptions about poor performance. Generate realistic test data, and characterize the performance of your database.

DO try to solve performance problems with hardware improvements rather than with database design compromises. Realize that, in the long run, better hardware is usually less expensive than a denormalized database design.

DON'T denormalize your tables unless you fully understand the trade-offs that you are making—improved query performance for more data redundancy, more complicated update logic, and more difficulty in augmenting the database design during the application's life cycle.

> **NEW TERM**   A *schema* is the set of database objects—tables, columns, primary keys, foreign keys, and other objects—that implement a logical data model.

Entity Relationship Diagramming Tools

To assist you in the development of a logical data model, you should seriously consider obtaining an entity relationship (ER) modeling tool such as Designer/2000, Oracle Data Designer, LogicWorks ERwin, or Sybase S-Designer. All of these tools are available for Windows NT or Windows 95. Briefly, these tools enable you to construct an entity-relationship diagram by selecting objects from a toolbar and drawing relationships between them.

The advantages of these tools are as follows:

- ☐ They simplify the process of creating a diagram.
- ☐ They automatically generate the SQL statements that actually create the tables, constraints, indexes, and other objects that build the desired database.
- ☐ They enable you to document each entity, attribute, relationship, and constraint. These tools also produce reports that can be shared with other developers, users, and analysts to obtain feedback on the accuracy of the logical data model.

Figure 3.1.
*Using Oracle Data-
base Designer to
develop a data model.*

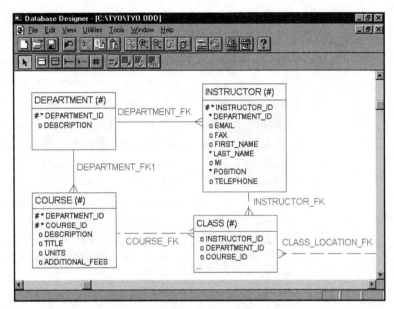

The Sample Application Database

The example used throughout this book is a database for a small, fictitious college. In 1884, Reginald Flugle, a wealthy manufacturer of cuff links and tie pins in the northern high desert of Southern California provided a sizable endowment to a small, dust-ridden college. Until now, the administration of Flugle College has been a paper-based system. The college dean has awarded you a contract to develop a computerized information system based on a client/server architecture.

Requirements

The high-level requirements for the Flugle College Information System (or FCIS as it will be known), include the following:

☐ Store, maintain, and retrieve information about students

☐ Store, maintain, and retrieve information about instructors

☐ Store, maintain, and retrieve information about each department

☐ Store, maintain, and retrieve information about offered courses

☐ Store, maintain, and retrieve information about course scheduling

☐ Enable students to schedule classes via touch-tone phone

☐ Prepare and print course catalog each semester

Using these high-level requirements, the following are the entities needed to support the information needs of Flugle College:

- ☐ The Student table contains information about each student at the college.
- ☐ The Department table contains information about each department at the college.
- ☐ The Instructor table contains information about each instructor at the college.
- ☐ The Course table describes each course that is offered by the college.
- ☐ The Class Location table identifies each classroom that is available for a class.
- ☐ The Schedule Type table identifies each type of class schedule—for example, a schedule that consists of two meetings each week.
- ☐ The Schedule Type Details table contains details about a particular schedule type, such as which days and at what times the meetings are held.
- ☐ The Class table contains information about each scheduled class, such as the course, instructor, and schedule. A class is the offering of a course during a particular semester.
- ☐ The Student Schedule table identifies the classes for which a student has enrolled.

The next sections look at each table in greater detail.

The Student Table

The purpose of the Student table is to maintain information about each student at Flugle College. Each student is identified by a Student ID—the table is defined so that two students cannot have the same Student ID. In addition to the student's name, address, and other pertinent information, the Student table also contains an attribute named Year which indicates the year of a student—for example, freshman. In this respect, the sample database may be somewhat unrealistic; it's probably more important to keep track of a student's accumulated units than the year they are in. Another note: this table doesn't indicate the student's status—for example, active, leave of absence, inactive. There is no attribute to indicate if a student has received a degree. Nevertheless, the attributes shown in the following Student table list provide sufficient realism for our purposes.

Student

Student ID
Last Name
First Name
Middle Initial
Street Address
City
State
Zipcode

Telephone
Fax
Email
Year in School
Primary key: Student ID

The Department Table

By creating the Department table, you are ensuring that other tables refer to a department in a consistent manner. The Department table list displays the simple structure of the Department table. The primary key for the Department table is the Department ID.

Department
Department ID
Description
Primary key: Department ID

The Instructor Table

Information about each instructor is kept in the Instructor table, as shown in the following list. The primary key for the table is Instructor ID. There also is one foreign key—Department ID—which points to the Department table.

Instructor
Instructor ID
Department ID (foreign key to Department table)
Last Name
First Name
Middle Initial
Position
Telephone
Fax
Email
Primary key: Instructor ID

In the Flugle database, each instructor is assigned to a single department, which is identified by Department ID. Of course, in a real college or university, you wouldn't want to impose such an artificial limitation.

The Course Table

Each department offers a series of courses. Because it's possible for two departments to offer a course with the same number, the primary key for the Course table includes both the Course ID and the Department ID. In addition to the primary key attributes, the following list contains the attributes for a course—a title, description, a number of units, and additional fees that may be required.

Course

Department ID (foreign key to Department table)
Course ID
Title
Description
Units
Additional Fees
Primary key: Course ID

As an alternative, the primary key for the Course table could consist solely of the Course ID attribute. But that would require that Course ID be unique across all departments. This requirement could be satisfied if a Course ID concatenated the Department ID with the Course ID—for example, BIO101 for Biology 101. However, the drawback to this approach is that it is a violation of First Normal Form—namely, Course ID now contains two pieces of information, department and course. Although this is a real drawback, in practice you will find many examples of primary key values that are composed in this manner.

The Class Location Table

With this table, a college administrator will be able to determine the appropriate location for a class, based on the seating capacity. The primary key for the Class Location table consists of both the class building and the class room, as shown in the following list. In a real application, you might want to know more about the class location—such as the availability of other amenities such as projection screens or microphones.

Class Location

Class Building
Class Room
Seating Capacity
Primary key: Class Building, Class Room

The Schedule Type Table

The purpose of this table is to describe different types of class schedules. An example of a schedule type is three meetings per week. The primary key for this table is Schedule ID. The following contains a description of the Schedule Type table.

Schedule Type

Schedule ID
Description
Primary key: Schedule ID

The Schedule Type Details Table

The Schedule Type Details table contains the details about a particular schedule type, such as the day, starting time, and duration for each meeting of a class with this schedule type. For example, if schedule ID T10 consists of three meetings per week at 10:00 AM, there will be three rows in the Schedule Type Details table. One row will have an entry for Monday at 10:00, another row will have an entry for Wednesday at 10:00, and the final row will have an entry for Friday at 10:00. Because duration is specified for each row, the table can accommodate a schedule type in which the duration could be different, depending upon which day the meeting was held. The following describes the structure of the Schedule Type Details table.

Schedule Type Details
___

Schedule ID (foreign key to Schedule Type table)
Day
Starting Time
Duration
Primary key: Schedule ID, Day

The Class Table

The Class table contains the specifics of each course offered by the college during a particular semester. You can think of a class as an *instantiation* of a course—therefore, the Class table must include the Course ID and the Department ID. The following list outlines the structure of the Class table. Each class must have a location and a schedule. And, of course, each class must be taught by an instructor.

Class
___

Class ID
Department ID (foreign key to Course table)
Course ID (foreign key to Course table)
Instructor ID (foreign key to Instructor table)
Schedule ID (foreign key to Schedule Type table)
Class Building (foreign key to Class Location table)
Class Room (foreign key to Class Location table)
Semester
School Year
Primary key: Class ID

The Student Schedule Table

The Student Schedule table is designed to serve two purposes. First, it records the grade that a student has received for each class. Second, for classes that have not yet been completed, it identifies which course is part of a student's current schedule. In a more realistic database, you would probably want to separate the classes that a student has completed from a student's current schedule. The primary key of the table is composed of both Student ID and Class ID. The following describes the structure of the Student Schedule table.

Student Schedule

Student ID (foreign key to Student table)
Class ID (foreign key to Class table)
Grade
Date Grade Assigned
Primary key: Student ID, Class ID

Oracle Terminology: Connection, User, and Session

Before you learn how to create a table during the lesson on Day 4, you need to feel comfortable with the terminology used in this book, in the various Oracle tools, and in the Oracle documentation. Two terms—*database connection* and *database user*—merit special attention.

 A *database connection* is an Oracle user who has supplied a username and password to an Oracle database and is able to submit SQL statements to the Oracle database.

 A *database user* is an individual or automatic process that has a unique name and password that is recognized by a specific Oracle database.

Database Connection

To *connect* to Oracle means to supply a valid username and password that is accepted by the Oracle database. A user can connect to an Oracle database using any of the Oracle tools. A user also can establish an Oracle connection with a third-party tool such as PowerBuilder. The terms *Oracle session, Oracle connection,* and *database connection* are often substituted for one another. They all refer to the same thing—the tasks performed by a database user from the time the user successfully connects to an Oracle database until the time the same user disconnects.

An important characteristic of a database connection is whether it is *local* or *remote.* The term *local connection* indicates that the program used by the user to connect to an Oracle database resides on the same machine where the Oracle database is located. The term *remote connection* indicates that the program used by the user to connect to an Oracle database resides on one machine and the Oracle database resides on a different machine.

Database User

Every database connection is established on behalf of a database user. The terms *table owner*, *Oracle user*, and *Oracle account* are used interchangeably. A *table owner* is the database user that owns a table. A table owner is always an Oracle user, but an Oracle user may or may not own any tables of his or her own. An example should help explain this concept.

Let's look at the sample database. An Oracle account named FLUGLE owns all the tables for the college information system. Sally Jensen is the biology department administrator and has an Oracle account named JENSENS. However, even though Sally Jensen has access to all the tables owned by the FLUGLE account, she owns no tables of her own.

Every table that exists in an Oracle database must have an owner. A sensible approach is to create an owner that corresponds to the organization rather than to any individual in the organization. If you think about it, an organization's data—information that members of the organization create, modify, and use—doesn't belong to any one person. Also, given the dynamics of organizations, people come and go, but the organization remains.

In the sample application, instead of making an individual the owner of the Oracle tables, you are going to create a new user named FLUGLE and have that Oracle account own all of the tables in the application.

Connecting to an Oracle Database

Before you create a new Oracle user, you'll have to know how to connect to an Oracle database. Most Oracle tools provide a dialog window for establishing a connection to an Oracle database. The dialog window prompts you for three items:

- ☐ The Oracle database user you'll be using for your connection
- ☐ The user password
- ☐ A database name or connect string

If you're using Personal Oracle, you don't have to enter a database name. If you're trying to connect to an Oracle database on a server, you'll generally have to specify the database name.

Creating a New User

As a first step in setting up the sample database, you will create an Oracle user, FLUGLE, which will own all of the database objects in the application database. This section looks at two different ways to accomplish this. If you're using Personal Oracle for Windows 95, you'll see how to use the Navigator to create the new user. If you're using an Oracle server—either Workgroup Server or Universal Server—you'll see how the same task can be performed using Security Manager, a component of Oracle Enterprise Manager.

Creating a New User with the Personal Oracle Navigator

First, invoke the Navigator from the Personal Oracle for Windows 95 program group. To see the existing users in the local database, just double-click the User folder. A list of the existing users is displayed on the right side of the main window. To create the FLUGLE user, select the User folder and right-click New. The Navigator displays a window, prompting you for the username, the password, and the password confirmation. (See Figure 3.2.)

Figure 3.2.

Creating the FLUGLE *user with the Navigator.*

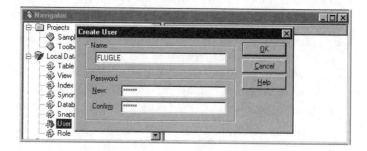

Click OK. The FLUGLE user is displayed in the list of existing users in the Local Database. (See Figure 3.3.)

Figure 3.3.

The FLUGLE *user is displayed in the list of users in the Local Database.*

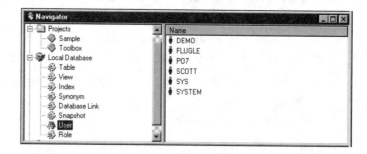

You'll want to assign an existing database role to the FLUGLE user—RESOURCE. This role enables the FLUGLE Oracle account to create new tables and other database objects. To assign this role, select the FLUGLE user and right-click Properties. A window with two tab folders will appear; select the Role/Privilege tab. Select the Roles radio button. Select the role named RESOURCE and click <. The role will be assigned to FLUGLE. (See Figure 3.4.)

Figure 3.4.
Granting the
RESOURCE *role to*
the FLUGLE *user.*

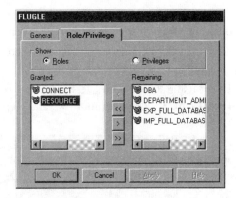

Creating a New User with Security Manager

As an alternative to the Personal Oracle Navigator, this section leads you through the steps of creating a user with Security Manager, a component of Oracle Enterprise Manager. To initially use Security Manager, you need to connect to the Oracle database using an account with DBA privileges. For this purpose, use the SYSTEM account to initially connect to the Oracle database.

1. To invoke Security Manager, select it from the Oracle Enterprise Manager program group. A dialog window displays, prompting you for username, password, and service. Enter SYSTEM, MANAGER, and FCIS into the respective fields as shown in Figure 3.5.

Figure 3.5.
Connecting to the
Oracle Server with
Security Manager.

NOTE

This example specifies the service or database as FCIS. You can create this database alias by using the SQL*Net Easy Configuration utility, as described in Day 1, "Exploring the World of Relational Databases." If you are using an Oracle server, please ask your DBA for the node and instance names that you should use when creating a new database alias with the SQL*Net Easy Configuration utility.

2. To create the new user, click the Users folder and either click the + button on the toolbar, or select User | Create from the menu.

3. As shown in Figure 3.6, enter **FLUGLE** in the User field and **FLUGLE** in the Password and Confirm Password fields.

4. If you're using Personal Oracle, enter **USER_DATA** for the Default Tablespace and **TEMPORARY_DATA** for the Temporary Tablespace.

Figure 3.6.

Adding the FLUGLE *user with Security Manager.*

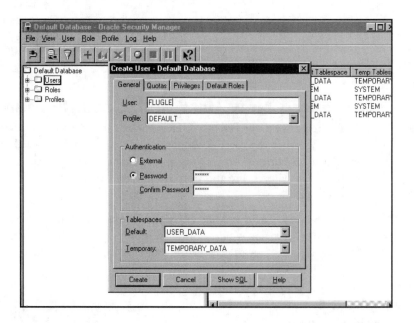

Before you actually create the FLUGLE user, you'll grant the RESOURCE role to the FLUGLE user so that the user can create tables and other database objects.

1. Click the Privileges folder.

2. In the list of roles displayed at the bottom of the dialog window, select RESOURCE, and click the Add button (see Figure 3.7). The FLUGLE user will be created—you should see it displayed on the right side of the Security Manager window.

3. To close Security Manager, select File | Exit from the menu.

3

Figure 3.7.
Granting the
RESOURCE *role to the*
FLUGLE *user with*
Security Manager.

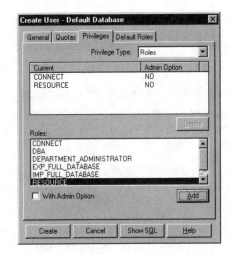

Oracle Datatypes

As a bridge to the lesson on Day 4, it's time to look at some basic facts about the datatypes available for use in an Oracle database. Every column in an Oracle database must be defined by one of these datatypes. With Oracle8, you can define your own datatype in addition to using a predefined datatype. The predefined datatypes for four categories of data are examined in the following sections:

- ☐ Numbers
- ☐ Strings
- ☐ Date and time information
- ☐ Large strings and BLOBs (Binary Large OBjects)

Numbers

Oracle offers several datatypes for storing numbers; each is suited for a different purpose.

NUMBER	Stores general numbers.
DECIMAL	Stores fixed-point numbers and enables Oracle to be compatible with other relational databases—specifically SQL/DS and DB2.
FLOAT	Stores floating-point numbers and enables Oracle to be compatible with the ANSI FLOAT datatype.

The NUMBER datatype offers the greatest flexibility for storing numeric data. It accepts positive and negative integers and real numbers, and has from 1 to 38 digits of precision.

SYNTAX

The syntax for specifying the NUMBER datatype when defining a column is

NUMBER (*precision, scale*)

The variables are defined as follows:

precision is the maximum number of digits to be stored

scale is used to indicate the position of the decimal point number of digits to the right (positive) or left (negative) of the decimal point. The scale can range from –84 to 127.

Oracle can store from 1 to 38 digits of precision for a number. The number of bytes required to store a number in an Oracle database depends on how many digits are used to express the number.

If you limit the precision, Oracle limits the values that can be stored in the column to the defined precision. For instance, suppose you define a table named Number_Digits_Demo that contains two columns:

Record_No   Defined as int

Value   Defined as number(4)

If you store a value in the Value column that exceeds its specified number of digits, Oracle returns an error as shown in Listing 3.1.

INPUT/
OUTPUT   **Listing 3.1. Oracle enforces numeric precision.**

```
SQL> insert into number_digits_demo
  2  (record_no, value)
  3  values
  4  (101, 9999);
1 row created.

SQL> insert into number_digits_demo
  2  (record_no, value)
  3  values
  4  (101, 10000);
(101, 10000)
      *
ERROR at line 4:
ORA-01438: value larger than specified precision allows for this column.
```

Take a look at a different example involving numeric precision and scale. Suppose you have a table named Scale_Precision_Demo with two columns:

Record_No   Defined as int

Value   Defined as number(6,2)

In the number column, the precision is 6 and the scale is 2. In other words, out of a total of six digits of precision, Oracle reserves two digits to the right of the decimal point, leaving a maximum of four digits to the left of the decimal point. Also, the column cannot store more than six digits of precision for any number.

As Listing 3.2 illustrates, the number 1234.5 can be stored in the number column. However, the number 12345.1 can't be stored because it contains five digits to the left of the decimal point. Similarly, the number 12345, even though it has only five digits of precision, can't be stored in the column because it has five digits to the left of the decimal point.

INPUT/OUTPUT **Listing 3.2. Oracle enforces numeric precision and scale.**

```
SQL> insert into scale_precision_demo
  2  (record_no, value)
  3  values
  4  (901, 1234.5);
1 row created.

SQL> insert into scale_precision_demo
  2  (record_no, value)
  3  values
  4  (901, 12345.1);
(901, 12345.1)
       *
ERROR at line 4:
ORA-01438: value larger than specified precision allows for this column

SQL> insert into scale_precision_demo
  2  (record_no, value)
  3  values
  4  (901, 12345);
(901, 12345)
       *
ERROR at line 4:
ORA-01438: value larger than specified precision allows for this column
```

Strings

To store strings, you can choose from several datatypes:

    CHAR
    VARCHAR
    VARCHAR2
    LONG

The bulk of many databases is character data; the advantages and disadvantages of each datatype are explained in the following paragraphs.

The CHAR datatype stores fixed-length character strings of up to 255 characters. If you don't specify a length, a CHAR column stores a single character.

You shouldn't use the VARCHAR datatype unless you have an older Oracle database that you're supporting. (Oracle warns that the VARCHAR datatype may not be supported in future releases.) The VARCHAR2 datatype was introduced with Oracle and is meant to replace VARCHAR. If you're building a new Oracle application, you won't have any reason to use the VARCHAR datatype.

VARCHAR2 stores up to 2,000 characters in a single column. If you absolutely must store more than that, you need to consider using the LONG datatype.

You can store 2GB of characters in a LONG column. However, you cannot use any of Oracle's built-in functions or operators with LONG columns. The best way to think of a LONG column is as a very large black box. You cannot search the contents of this box unless the box is emptied.

Follow these guidelines to choose an appropriate datatype for a column that will store character data.

☐ You can use CHAR to define columns that will store a single character.

☐ Use VARCHAR2 to store variable strings that contain up to 2,000 characters.

☐ Use LONG to store more than 2,000 characters in a column.

If you're trying to store more than 2,000 characters, don't create multiple VARCHAR2 columns to store the data. Assembling, searching, or manipulating the contents of multiple columns is impractical.

Using the CHAR Datatype

Because the CHAR datatype stores fixed-length columns, use it when you're defining columns that will contain a single character. Using the CHAR datatype to store larger strings isn't efficient because you will waste storage space.

Using the VARCHAR2 Datatype

Because it stores variable-length strings, the VARCHAR2 datatype is the preferred datatype for storing strings. This datatype can store up to 2,000 characters. However, the Oracle RDBMS is efficient; it will allocate only the storage that is needed to store each column value. On Day 7, "Taking Advantage of SQL Built-in Functions," you will analyze the many ways to use Oracle's built-in string functions and operators.

Date and Time Information

One of Oracle's strengths is its DATE datatype. The DATE datatype should really be named DATETIME because it provides storage for both date and time information. Oracle always allocates a fixed 7 bytes for a DATE column, even if you're using a DATE column to store date information only or time information only.

Oracle has quite a few built-in functions specifically for manipulating DATE values and expressions. You'll see some examples of these functions on Day 7. The DATE datatype enables you to store dates in the range of January 1, 4712 B.C., to December 31, 4712 A.D. Oracle uses the default format of *DD-MMM-YY* for entering and displaying dates.

Large Strings

As mentioned earlier, you must use Oracle's LONG datatype to store more than 2,000 characters in a single column. A LONG column can accommodate up to 2GB of characters. As with the VARCHAR2 datatype, the Oracle RDBMS is also efficient in its use of the LONG datatype; it will allocate only the storage that is needed to store each column value. However, you will face a number of restrictions on the use of LONG columns in SQL. You can't use Oracle functions or operators to search or modify the contents of a LONG column. If you try to search a LONG column, Oracle returns error. In a sense, you can think of a LONG column as a large container into which you can store or retrieve data—but not manipulate it.

NOTE

> Remember: You can have only one LONG column per table.

BLOBs

As you're probably aware, most databases provide for the storage of binary large objects (BLOBs). BLOBs include documents, graphics, sound, video—actually, any type of binary file you can think of. The Oracle LONG RAW datatype is designed for BLOB storage.

When you want to associate a BLOB with a "normal" row, two choices are available to you:

- [ ] Store the BLOB in an operating system file (such as an MS-DOS file) and store the directory and filename in the associated table
- [ ] Store the BLOB itself in a LONG RAW column

Some developers are more comfortable with the first method. They think that the BLOB is more readily available if it's stored in the file system, instead of in the Oracle database. They reason that they gain very little by storing a BLOB in a table column if the Oracle database can't (or shouldn't) manipulate the BLOB.

However, other developers see an advantage in centralizing all data storage in the Oracle database. They argue that this approach provides greater portability; removing references to a directory and filename leaves fewer OS-specific issues to deal with.

A column defined as LONG RAW can accommodate up to 2GB for each row. Like LONG columns, LONG RAW columns have a number of limitations. For example, you cannot use any of the built-in functions with a LONG RAW column.

The RAW Datatype

Oracle also provides the RAW datatype, which can accommodate up to 255 bytes of binary data. Because of this storage restriction, a RAW column is less useful than a LONG RAW column.

Summary

As discussed in this lesson, try to follow these steps when designing a logical data model:

1. Begin with a logical data model.
2. Identify each entity in the system that you're modeling.
3. Identify a primary key for each entity.
4. Determine the foreign keys you need to create.

Keep the following concepts in mind when you work with Oracle datatypes:

☐ Every column in a table must have an Oracle datatype.

☐ Use NUMBER to store numeric data.

☐ Use CHAR to store single characters.

☐ Use VARCHAR2 to store strings that contain up to 2,000 characters. VARCHAR2 supports Oracle built-in functions and operators.

☐ Use LONG when you must store very large text strings.

☐ Use DATE to store all date and time information.

☐ Use LONG RAW to store BLOBs of up to 2GB.

What Comes Next?

On Day 4, you learn how to actually build the tables and other structures that implement a logical data model.

Q&A

Q Won't performance be a problem if all of the tables of an application are in Third Normal Form?

A It is a mistake to assume that the performance of a database application will always be substandard if its tables are in Third Normal Form. It's better to start out with a design in Third Normal Form—or higher—and then identify any areas where performance may be a problem.

3

Q In an Oracle database, how many columns can a table contain?

A A table can contain up to 254 columns.

Workshop

The purpose of the Workshop is to enable you to test your knowledge of the material discussed in the lesson. See if you can correctly answer the questions in the quiz and complete the exercises before you continue with tomorrow's lesson.

Quiz

1. True or false? If an attribute that isn't part of the primary key is a foreign key, it must be mandatory; it cannot allow a null value.

2. Will the Student Schedule table handle the situation in which a student needs to repeat a course? Why or why not?

3. What characteristic of a relational database will prevent a class from being deleted from the Class table if there are rows in the Student Schedule table that contain the Class ID to be deleted?

4. From an entity-relationship perspective, there is a relationship between the Class and Instructor tables. Is it identifying or non-identifying?

5. True or false? If you create the proper index for a table, its rows will always be retrieved in the ascending order of the indexed columns.

Exercises

1. Suppose you want to identify the instructor who is the head of a department. Can you think of at least two ways of doing this? What are the strengths and weaknesses of each approach?

2. The Student Schedule table currently holds both current classes and previous classes that a student has taken. Propose an alternate design using two tables—one table contains the current schedule and the second table contains classes that the student has previously taken. Identify each attribute in the two tables. What are the advantages of this design?

Day 4

Implementing Your Logical Model: Physical Database Design

The previous lesson, Day 3, "Logical Database Design," discussed the elements of a data model while ignoring the implementation of this model in a "real" database. In this lesson, you will examine how a logical data model is actually implemented in an Oracle database. This lesson is about another subset of SQL: Data Definition Language (DDL). DDL consists of SQL statements used to create, modify, and discard database objects.

 DDL stands for Data Definition Language which consists of those statements in the SQL language that are responsible for creating or modifying database structures such as tables, views, and indexes.

If you're involved in developing many database applications, you definitely should consider the use of a Windows-based database design tool such as Oracle's Designer/2000 or Database Designer, LogicWorks's ERwin, or Sybase's S-Designer. These products enable you to graphically define a logical model and to generate the correct SQL statements for creating a database.

Even if you're using a database design tool, you should acquire a working knowledge of the Oracle toolset. There are many tools that provide a SQL interface to an Oracle database. Two examples are SQL*Plus and SQL Worksheet, a component of Oracle Enterprise Manager. These tools enable you to enter SQL statements to create tables, indexes, and other database objects. Most of the examples in this lesson use SQL*Plus. Figure 4.1 illustrates how you execute a SQL statement with SQL Worksheet.

Figure 4.1.

Using SQL Worksheet to execute a SQL statement.

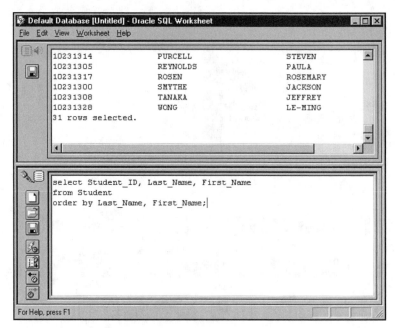

The other alternative is to use a tool such as the Personal Oracle8 Navigator or Oracle Schema Manager that provides a graphical interface for manipulating an Oracle database. If you're using Personal Oracle8 for Windows 95, take advantage of the Navigator's intuitive interface for creating and modifying tables (see Figure 4.2). Unlike SQL*Plus or SQL Worksheet, the Navigator doesn't require a knowledge of SQL. The Navigator "packages" your inputs and submits them to the Oracle database engine. These tools are ideal for users who aren't familiar with SQL and don't want to learn the language. The Navigator can be used both with Personal Oracle8 and remote Oracle database engines.

4

Figure 4.2.
Using the Personal Oracle Navigator to create and modify tables.

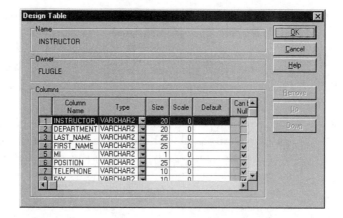

Basics of the CREATE TABLE Statement

Because of its many options and clauses, the SQL statement CREATE TABLE can be rather complex.

Here's a simplified version of its syntax:

```
CREATE TABLE table_name (
column_name1 datatype [NOT NULL],
...
column_nameN datatype [NOT NULL]);
```

The variables are defined as follows:

table_name is the name for the table.

column_name1 through column_nameN are valid column names.

datatype is a valid Oracle datatype specification.

The CREATE TABLE statement can be directly invoked from SQL*Plus or SQL Worksheet. The Personal Oracle8 Navigator or Schema Manager, a component of Oracle Enterprise Manager, package the user's entries and indirectly invoke the CREATE TABLE statement. The examples in this lesson were prepared with SQL*Plus.

Naming a Table

Oracle has several restrictions on table names:

☐ Each table owned by an Oracle account must have a unique name.

☐ A table name cannot exceed 30 characters in length.

☐ A table name must begin with an alphabetic character.

☐ A table name can contain the letters A through Z, the digits 0 through 9, and the characters $, #, and _ (underscore).

☐ A table name cannot be an SQL reserved word. (You can view a complete list of the reserved words in the Oracle8 Server *SQL Reference Manual*. If you've installed the Oracle documentation on your PC, you'll find the document as `C:\Orawin95\Doc\A32538_1.pdf`).

☐ You can use uppercase and lowercase characters in naming tables; Oracle is not case sensitive as long as table or column names are not enclosed in double quotes. The use of double quotes is a syntax that is supported by Oracle. However, you will never have a reason to use double quotes directly. Some third-party tools take advantage of this syntax (such as PowerBuilder), but this is transparent to the developer.

☐ A table name should be descriptive. Do not use excessive abbreviations when naming tables and other database objects. Many application development tools, such as PowerBuilder or Oracle Forms, provide a point-and-click interface for selecting a table. Because no typing is involved, a long table name is just as easy to select as a short table name.

Do	Don't

DO use descriptive words when naming a table.

DO use a singular term for the table name.

DON'T use cryptic codes or numbers in your table name.

DON'T use the phrase TABLE or TBL when naming a table; it's redundant.

Naming a Column

Here are some considerations for naming columns:

☐ Within a single table, a column name must be unique. However, you may use the same column name in different tables.

☐ Like other database objects, a column name can be up to 30 characters long.

☐ The column name must begin with an alphabetic character.

☐ The column name can contain the letters A through Z, the digits 0 through 9, and the characters $, #, and _ (underscore). The name cannot include spaces.

☐ A column name cannot be an SQL reserved word.

☐ As with tables, be descriptive in naming a column. Descriptive column names help users understand the definition of each column.

☐ An Oracle table may have up to 254 columns.

Examples of Creating Tables

This section starts with a simple example. You will construct a CREATE TABLE statement to create the table that contains the departments that exist at Flugle College, as shown in Listing 4.1.

INPUT/OUTPUT **Listing 4.1. Creating the Department table.**

```
SQL> Create table Department
  2  (Department_ID     Varchar2(20) NOT NULL,
  3   Department_Name   Varchar2(25));

Table created.
```

Some aspects of the statement's syntax deserve special mention:

☐ Parentheses frame the list of columns.

☐ In mandatory columns, the phrase NOT NULL follows the column's datatype specification.

☐ Where applicable, column widths are enclosed in parentheses after the datatype.

As an option, you can explicitly specify that a column is optional by specifying NULL after the datatype specification, as illustrated in Listing 4.2.

INPUT/OUTPUT **Listing 4.2. Creating the Student table.**

```
SQL> create table Student
  2  (Student_ID     Varchar2(20)  NOT NULL,
  3   Last_Name      Varchar2(25)  NOT NULL,
  4   First_Name     Varchar2(25)  NOT NULL,
  5   MI             Varchar2(1)   NULL,
  6   Year           Varchar2(25)  NULL,
  7   Street_Address Varchar2(25)  NULL,
  8   City           Varchar2(25)  NULL,
  9   State          Varchar2(2)   NULL,
 10   Zipcode        Varchar2(9)   NULL,
 11   Telephone      Varchar2(10)  NULL,
 12   Fax            Varchar2(10)  NULL,
 13   Email          Varchar2(100) NULL);

Table created.
```

4

As I mentioned, Oracle's implementation of SQL is not case sensitive (which isn't true of all vendors) as long as table and column names are not enclosed in double quotes. Listing 4.3 provides an example of the Student table in which the table and column names are enclosed in double quotes. However, Oracle will not recognize the table or column names unless they are always placed in double quotes.

Listing 4.3. Enclosing table and column names in double quotes.

INPUT/
OUTPUT

```
SQL> create table "student"
  2  ("student_id"      Varchar2(20)   NOT NULL,
  3   "last_name"       Varchar2(25)   NOT NULL,
  4   "first_name"      Varchar2(25)   NOT NULL,
  5   "mi"              Varchar2(1),
  6   "year"            Varchar2(25),
  7   "street_address"  Varchar2(25),
  8   "city"            Varchar2(25),
  9   "state"           Varchar2(2),
 10   "zipcode"         Varchar2(10),
 11   "telephone"       Varchar2(10),
 12   "fax"             Varchar2(10),
 13   "email"           Varchar2(100));

Table created.

SQL> describe student

Object does not exist.

SQL> describe "student"
```

Name	Null?	Type
student_id	NOT NULL	VARCHAR2(20)
last_name	NOT NULL	VARCHAR2(25)
first_name	NOT NULL	VARCHAR2(25)
mi		VARCHAR2(1)
year		VARCHAR2(25)
street_address		VARCHAR2(25)
city		VARCHAR2(25)
state		VARCHAR2(2)
zipcode		VARCHAR2(10)
telephone		VARCHAR2(10)
fax		VARCHAR2(10)
email		VARCHAR2(100)

Identifying the Primary Key

A table's primary key is the set of columns that uniquely identifies each row in the table.

Here's another look at the CREATE TABLE syntax:

```
CREATE TABLE table_name (
column_name1 datatype [NOT NULL],
...
column_nameN datatype [NOT NULL],
[Constraint constraint_name]
[Primary key (column_nameA, column_nameB, ... column_nameX)]);
```

The variables are defined as follows:

> *table_name* is the name for the table.
>
> *column_name1* through *column_nameN* are valid column names.
>
> *datatype* is a valid Oracle datatype specification.
>
> *constraint_name* is an optional name that identifies the primary key constraint.
>
> *column_nameA* through *column_nameX* are the table's columns that compose the primary key.

Although the primary key clause of the CREATE TABLE statement is an essential concept in relational database theory, in practice its use is optional. Using the Department table again, Listing 4.4 shows how the primary key is declared during table creation.

INPUT/ OUTPUT

Listing 4.4. Declaring the primary key during table creation.

```
SQL> create table Department
  2 (Department_ID Varchar2(20),
  3  Department_Name   Varchar2(25),
  4 Constraint PK_Department
  5 Primary Key (Department_ID));

Table created.
```

ANALYSIS Notice that I do not use the NOT NULL constraint to specify that the Department ID is a mandatory column. By default, Oracle forces all columns that comprise the primary key to be mandatory.

Primary keys are subject to several restrictions. First, a column that is part of the primary key cannot be null. Second, a column that is defined as LONG or LONG RAW cannot be part of the primary key. Third, the maximum number of columns in the primary key is 16. You can circumvent this last restriction through the use of a surrogate key—an artificial value that can be guaranteed to uniquely identify all rows in a table.

Identifying Foreign Keys

Now that you know how to specify the primary key in the CREATE TABLE statement, you are
ready to declare your foreign keys.

The following CREATE TABLE syntax includes primary and foreign key declarations:

```
CREATE TABLE table_name (
column_specification1,
...
column_specificationN,
[Constraint constraint_name Foreign key (column_nameF1,...column_nameFN)
references referenced_table (column_nameP1,...column_namePN),]
[Constraint constraint_name Primary key

(column_nameA, column_nameB, ... column_nameX)]);
```

The variables are defined as follows:

   table_name is the name for the table.

   column_specification1 through column_specificationN are valid column specifications (described below in detail).

   constraint_name is the constraint name that you want to assign to the foreign key.

   referenced_table is the name of the table referenced by the foreign key declaration.

   column_nameF1 through column_nameFN are the columns that compose the foreign key.

   column_nameP1 through column_namePN are the columns that compose the primary key
   in referenced_table.

   column_nameA through column_nameX are the table's columns that compose the primary key.

The syntax for a column_specification follows.

```
column_name datatype [DEFAULT default_value]
[CONSTRAINT constraint_name] [NULL]¦[NOT NULL]¦[UNIQUE]¦CHECK (condition)
```

The variables are defined as follows:

   column_name is a valid Oracle column name.

   datatype is a valid Oracle datatype specification.

   default_value is a legal default value assigned to the column on an insert.

   constraint_name is a legal constraint name to be assigned to the constraint.

   condition is a valid Oracle Boolean condition that must be true for a value to be
   assigned to a column.

NEW TERM   A *constraint* is a mechanism which ensures that the values of a column or a set of columns satisfy a declared condition.

For the Course table, you need to declare a primary and foreign key as demonstrated in Listing 4.5.

INPUT/ OUTPUT

Listing 4.5. Declaring primary and foreign keys during table creation.

```
SQL> create table Course
  2 (Course_ID       Varchar2(5),
  3  Department_ID   Varchar2(20) NOT NULL,
  4  Title           Varchar2(60) NOT NULL,
  5  Description     Varchar2(2000),
  6  Units           Number,
  7  Additional_Fees Number,
  8  Constraint PK_Course
  9  Primary key (Course_ID, Department_ID),
 10  Constraint FK_Course_Department_ID
 11  Foreign key (Department_ID) references Department (Department_ID));

Table created.
```

4

> **TIP**   Even though it's optional, I recommend that you use constraint names when declaring a primary or foreign key or check constraint. If you don't explicitly declare a constraint name, Oracle automatically generates a constraint and assigns it a rather cryptic name. If you want to drop the foreign key, you'll have to look up the Oracle-generated constraint name. You'll save yourself some grief by declaring a constraint in the first place.

The columns in the referenced table must actually compose the primary or unique key of the referenced table. If they don't, Oracle will not create the foreign key. In the following example, let's assume that you have not yet created the foreign key for the Course table. First, let's drop the primary key from the Department table. When you try to create the Course table, Oracle will determine that Department_ID is not defined as the primary key for the Department table; the CREATE TABLE statement will fail, as illustrated in Listing 4.6.

Listing 4.6. Unable to declare a foreign key because there is no associated primary key.

```
SQL> alter table Department drop primary key;

Table altered.

SQL> create table Course
  2  (Course_ID       Varchar2(5),
  3   Department_ID   Varchar2(20) NOT NULL,
  4   Title           Varchar2(60) NOT NULL,
  5   Description     Varchar2(2000),
  6   Units           Number,
  7   Additional_Fees Number,
  8   Constraint PK_Course
  9   Primary key (Course_ID, Department_ID),
 10   Constraint FK_Course_Department_ID
 11   Foreign key (Department_ID) references Department (Department_ID));

Foreign key (Department_ID) references Department (Department_ID))
                                                              *
ERROR at line 11:
ORA-02270: no matching unique or primary key for this column-list
```

Constraining a Column's Value with the CHECK Clause

A powerful feature of SQL is the capability to specify rudimentary data validation for a column during table creation. SQL accomplishes this task with an optional CHECK clause, which can be specified for each column. The CHECK clause is a Boolean condition that is either TRUE or FALSE. If the condition evaluates to TRUE, the column value is accepted by Oracle; if the condition evaluates to FALSE, Oracle will return an error code.

Listing 4.7 presents an example in which you will modify the definition of the Instructor table so that the table allows an instructor's position to be one of three values—ASSISTANT PROFESSOR, ASSOCIATE PROFESSOR, or PROFESSOR.

Listing 4.7. Declaring a check constraint on a column.

```
SQL> create table Instructor
  2  (Instructor_ID   varchar2(20),
  3   Department_ID   varchar2(20)  NOT NULL,
  4   Last_Name       varchar2(25)  NOT NULL,
  5   First_Name      varchar2(25),
  6   MI              varchar2(1),
  7   Position        varchar2(25) constraint CK_Instructor
  8   check (Position in ('ASSISTANT PROFESSOR', 'ASSOCIATE PROFESSOR',
  9                       'PROFESSOR')),
 10   Telephone       varchar2(10),
```

4

```
11   Fax                 varchar2(10),
12   Email               varchar2(100),
13   constraint PK_Instructor Primary Key (Instructor_ID),
14   constraint FK_Instructor_Instructor_ID
15   Foreign Key (Department_ID) references Department (Department_ID));

Table created.
```

If you attempt to add an instructor to the table whose position is not one of the three legal values, Oracle returns an error code indicating that a check constraint has been violated, as shown in Listing 4.8.

INPUT/OUTPUT **Listing 4.8. CHECK constraint is enforced.**

```
SQL> insert into Instructor
  2  (Instructor_ID, Department_ID, Last_Name, First_Name, Position)
  3  values
  4  ('C2222', 'PSYCH', 'MENCKEN', 'H.', 'CURMUDGEON');

insert into Instructor
*
ERROR at line 1:
ORA-02290: check constraint (TYO2.CK_INSTRUCTOR) violated
```

ANALYSIS Because CURMUDGEON is not a valid instructor position, the attempt to insert the row fails. This is an example of how a CHECK constraint enforces data integrity.

Establishing a Default Value for a Column

By using the DEFAULT clause when defining a column, you can establish a default value for that column. This default value is used for a column whenever a row is inserted into the table without specifying the column in the INSERT statement.

For example, suppose that most students live in the city of Springfield. As a result, you want to be sure that if a student is added to the Student table and his or her city isn't specified, its default value will be SPRINGFIELD. Listing 4.9 illustrates how you would modify the CREATE TABLE statement to achieve this result. After the default value has been established, a row that is inserted into the Student table without specifying a value for City will be set to a default value of SPRINGFIELD.

INPUT/OUTPUT **Listing 4.9. Specifying a default value for a column.**

```
SQL> create table Student
  2  (Student_ID     Varchar2(20),
  3   Last_Name      Varchar2(25)   NOT NULL,
```

continues

Listing 4.9. continued

```
 4   First_Name    Varchar2(25)  NOT NULL,
 5   MI            Varchar2(1),
 6   Year          Varchar2(25),
 7   Street_Address Varchar2(25),
 8   City          Varchar2(25) Default 'SPRINGFIELD',
 9   State         Varchar2(2),
10   Zipcode       Varchar2(9),
11   Telephone     Varchar2(10),
12   Fax           Varchar2(10),
13   Email         Varchar2(100),
14   Constraint PK_Student Primary Key (Student_ID));

Table created.

SQL> insert into Student
  2  (Student_ID, Last_Name, First_Name, Year)
  3  values
  4  ('109850', 'CARSON', 'RICARDO', 'JUNIOR');

1 row created.

SQL> select Student_ID, Last_Name, City
  2  from Student
  3  where
  4  Student_ID = '109850';

STUDENT_ID           LAST_NAME                CITY
------------------   ----------------------   -------------------------
109850               CARSON                   SPRINGFIELD
```

Using ALTER TABLE to Modify the Table Definition

At times, you'll find it necessary to modify a table's definition. The ALTER TABLE statement serves this purpose. This statement changes the structure of a table, not its contents. Using ALTER TABLE, the changes you can make to a table include the following:

☐ Adding a new column to an existing table

☐ Increasing or decreasing the width of an existing column

☐ Changing an existing column from mandatory to optional or vice versa

☐ Specifying a default value for an existing column

☐ Specifying other constraints for an existing column

SYNTAX

Here are the four basic forms of the ALTER TABLE statement:

```
ALTER TABLE table_name
ADD (column_specification | constraint ,...
     column_specification | constraint);

ALTER TABLE table_name
MODIFY (column_specification | constraint ,...
        column_specification | constraint);

ALTER TABLE table_name
DROP PRIMARY KEY;

ALTER TABLE table_name
DROP CONSTRAINT constraint;
```

The variables are defined as follows:

> table_name is the name for the table.
>
> column_specification is a valid specification for a column (column name and datatype).
>
> constraint is a column or table constraint.

The first form of the statement is used for adding a column, the primary key, or a foreign key to a table.

The second form of the statement is used to modify an existing column. Among other things, you can increase a column's width or transform it from mandatory to optional.

The third and fourth forms of the ALTER TABLE statement are used for dropping a table's primary key and other constraints.

In the next few pages, I demonstrate the use of this statement with several examples.

Changing a Column Definition from NOT NULL to NULL

Although you can freely change a column from mandatory to optional, you should think about why the change is necessary. Is this attribute really optional, or are you working with a test data set that isn't representative of realistic application data?

Listing 4.10 displays a table named demo_table. The ALTER TABLE statement is used to change the definition of the Record_No column to be mandatory.

4

Listing 4.10. Changing a column from optional to mandatory.

```
SQL> describe demo_table

Name                               Null?     Type
-------------------------------    --------  ----
  RECORD_NO                        NOT NULL  NUMBER(38)
  DESCRIPTION                                VARCHAR2(40)
  CURRENT_VALUE                    NOT NULL  NUMBER

SQL> alter table demo_table modify (current_value number null);

Table altered.

SQL> describe demo_table

Name                               Null?     Type
-------------------------------    --------  ----
  RECORD_NO                        NOT NULL  NUMBER(38)
  DESCRIPTION                                VARCHAR2(40)
  CURRENT_VALUE                              NUMBER
```

Changing a Column Definition from NULL to NOT NULL

If a table is empty, you can define a column to be NOT NULL. However, if a table isn't empty, you can't change a column to NOT NULL unless every row in the table has a value for that particular column. Listing 4.11 shows how Oracle will respond if you attempt to make the current_value column mandatory. However, if you ensure that current_value has a non-null value for each row in the table, you'll be able to set the current_value to NOT NULL.

Listing 4.11. Attempt to change a column to be mandatory.

```
SQL> alter table demo_table modify (current_value number not null);
alter table demo_table modify (current_value number not null)
                               *
ERROR at line 1:
ORA-01449: column contains NULL values; cannot alter to NOT NULL

SQL> update demo_table
  2  set current_value = record_no + 100;

4 rows updated.

SQL> select current_value from demo_table;

CURRENT_VALUE
-------------
          121
          122
```

```
                123
                124

SQL> commit;

Commit complete.

SQL> alter table demo_table modify (current_value number not null);

Table altered.
```

ANALYSIS Initially, all the rows in the table have a null value for the CURRENT_VALUE column; as a result, the column cannot be modified to be mandatory. To modify the column so that it is mandatory, all the rows must have a value for CURRENT_VALUE. Arbitrarily, you update all the rows in the table so that the CURRENT_VALUE column is assigned the value of the RECORD_NO column plus 100. Then, the column can be modified so that it is defined as NOT NULL.

Increasing a Column's Width

You can use the ALTER TABLE statement to increase the width of a character column. The example shown in Listing 4.12 demonstrates its use. Initially, the width of the Description column is 40 characters. To increase the width of the Description column from 40 to 50 characters, the column definition is modified with the ALTER TABLE statement.

INPUT/ OUTPUT **Listing 4.12. Increasing a column's width.**

```
SQL> describe demo_table
 Name                            Null?     Type
 ------------------------------- --------- ----
 RECORD_NO                       NOT NULL  NUMBER(38)
 DESCRIPTION                               VARCHAR2(40)
 CURRENT_VALUE                   NOT NULL  NUMBER

SQL> alter table demo_table modify (description varchar2(50));

Table altered.

SQL> describe demo_table
 Name                            Null?     Type
 ------------------------------- --------- ----
 RECORD_NO                       NOT NULL  NUMBER(38)
 DESCRIPTION                               VARCHAR2(50)
 CURRENT_VALUE                   NOT NULL  NUMBER
```

Decreasing a Column's Width

In the course of designing a database application, you may find that you erred in sizing a column: you specified a larger size than a column actually requires. Initially, you might not think that having a larger-than-required column is a problem because it doesn't prevent the column from accommodating the data. But it is a problem because it indicates that your data model is inaccurate. If you want to "do the right thing," you need to reduce the size of the column so that the column definition mirrors what is allowed for the data.

You also can use the ALTER TABLE statement to decrease a column's width. For example, suppose you want to use a single character to indicate the student's current year—1 for freshman, 2 for sophomore, and so on. However, the column Year is currently defined as varchar2(25). Listing 4.13 shows what happens when you try to do this.

INPUT/OUTPUT   **Listing 4.13. Attempting to decrease a column's width.**

```
SQL> alter table Student
  2  modify
  3  (Year varchar2(1));
(Year varchar2(1))
      *
ERROR at line 3:
ORA-01441: column to be modified must be empty to decrease column length
```

As you might have suspected, Oracle will not allow you to decrease a column's width if the column has values. Even if you update the Student table so that all the values for Year are no more than five characters, Oracle still will not allow you to reduce the width of the column, as you can see in Listing 4.14. You cannot reduce the width of the column until it is set to NULL.

INPUT/OUTPUT   **Listing 4.14. Another attempt to decrease a column's width.**

```
SQL> update Student
  2  set Year = substr(Year,1,5);

31 rows updated.

SQL> alter table Student modify
  2  (Year varchar2(5));
(Year varchar2(5))
   *
ERROR at line 2:
ORA-01441: column to be modified must be empty to decrease column length

SQL> update Student
  2  set Year = NULL;
```

```
31 rows updated.

SQL> alter table Student modify
  2  (Year varchar2(5));

Table altered.
```

Of course, once the column is set to NULL, all the values are lost. In reality, you'd make a copy of the table as it is so that you could reload the column values; you'll learn more about this on Day 6, "Using SQL to Modify Data."

Using a Primary Key

You should be sure to define a primary key for every table in your database for the following reasons:

☐ A primary key prevents duplicate rows from being inserted into a table. Depending on the circumstances, duplicate rows can be a nuisance or can cause an application to crash. For example, you wouldn't want two departments to have the same department ID; declaring the Department_ID as the primary key will prevent this from occurring.

☐ A table must have a primary key if it is going to be referenced by a foreign key in another table.

Defining a Primary Key During Table Creation

You can define a table's primary key in the CREATE TABLE statement with the following syntax:

```
CREATE TABLE table-name
(column-definition1,
...
column-definitionN,
[CONSTRAINT constraint-name] PRIMARY KEY (column1,...,columnN))
```

The variables are defined as follows:

table-name is a valid Oracle table name.

column-definition1 through column-definitionN are legal column declarations.

constraint-name is a constraint name that is assigned to the primary key constraint.

column1 through columnN are the columns that compose the primary key.

Listing 4.15 illustrates how the primary key prevents duplicate rows from being inserted into the table. The primary key is enforced, even though the first INSERT transaction hasn't been committed.

A *duplicate row* is defined as a row whose primary key columns have the same values as those of another row.

 Listing 4.15. Primary key is enforced.

```
SQL> insert into Department
  2  (Department_ID, Department_Name)
  3  values
  4  ('PSYCH', 'PSYCHOLOGY');

1 row created.

SQL> insert into Department
  2  (Department_ID, Department_Name)
  3  values
  4  ('PSYCH', 'PSYCHIATRY');
insert into Department
            *
ERROR at line 1:
ORA-00001: unique constraint (TYO.PK_DEPARTMENT) violated
```

You also have the option of defining the primary key after the table has been created.

> **TIP**
>
> In several situations, you need to know a constraint name. For example, when you want to drop a foreign key, you'll need to drop the constraint associated with the foreign key. Unless you've supplied the constraint name for the foreign key, you'll have to look up the constraint name. Therefore, providing Oracle with constraint names for primary and foreign keys is always a good idea.
>
> Consider naming primary key constraints as PK_tablename and foreign key constraints as FK_tablename_column, staying within the 30-character limit for Oracle object names. You also should specify names for check and unique constraints (for example, tablename_column_CK or tablename_column_UN).

Defining a Primary Key After Table Creation

You also have the option of defining a primary key constraint after a table has been created. Of course, the table may not have a primary key already defined. To define a primary key constraint for an existing table, use the ALTER TABLE statement, as shown in Listing 4.16.

4

INPUT/
OUTPUT
Listing 4.16. Adding a primary key.

```
SQL> create table Department
  2  (Department_ID     Varchar2(20),
  3   Department_Name   Varchar2(25)
  4   constraint NN_Department_Name NOT NULL);

Table created.

SQL> alter table Department add
  2  constraint PK_Department primary key (Department_ID);

Table altered.
```

The primary key constraint is enforced whether the primary key was defined when the table was first created or added after the table already exists.

The Foreign Key and Referential Integrity

Primary and foreign keys work together to enforce referential integrity. A foreign key in a table is a column, or set of columns, whose values are restricted to those of the primary key in another table. You should define foreign keys whenever possible. For client/server applications, the first line of defense for referential integrity is the client application software. The last line of defense for referential integrity is the primary and foreign keys that have been defined for the database.

As with a primary key, a foreign key can be declared when a table is first created.

Declaring a Foreign Key During Table Creation

To illustrate the definition of a foreign key, let's look at the Department and Instructor tables in the Flugle College sample database. Each department has a unique ID that is kept in the column Department_ID. Every instructor must belong to a single department. In a real application, you probably would want to allow for the possibility that an instructor could be interdisciplinary by belonging to more than one department.

Oracle enforces referential integrity by disallowing any operations that would permit a foreign key to have a value that doesn't exist in the table containing the referenced primary key. For example, Listing 4.17 demonstrates that you cannot insert a record that describes an instructor who belongs to a Department ID equal to 'PHYSICS' because that Department ID doesn't exist in the Department table.

4

INPUT/OUTPUT **Listing 4.17. Referential integrity is enforced.**

```
SQL> insert into Instructor
  2  (Instructor_ID, Department_ID, Last_Name)
  3  values
  4  ('S1000', 'PHYSICS', 'MICHELSON');
insert into Instructor
*
ERROR at line 1:
ORA-02291: integrity constraint (TYO.FK_INSTRUCTOR_INSTRUCTOR_ID)
violated - parent key not found
```

As an alternative, you can opt not to specify the datatype for a column that is a foreign key. For example, Listing 4.18 furnishes an example in which no datatype is specified in the declaration of Department_ID in the Course table. Instead, Oracle looks up the datatype and width for the Department_ID column in the Department table and uses those definitions when creating the Course table.

INPUT/OUTPUT **Listing 4.18. Datatype not specified for foreign key column.**

```
SQL> create table Course
  2  (Course_ID       Varchar2(5),
  3   Department_ID    constraint NN_Course_Department_ID NOT NULL,
  4   Title           Varchar2(60)
  5   constraint NN_Course_Title NOT NULL,
  6   Description     Varchar2(2000),
  7   Units           Number,
  8   Additional_Fees Number,
  9   Constraint PK_Course
 10   Primary key (Course_ID, Department_ID),
 11   Constraint FK_Course_Department_ID
 12   Foreign key (Department_ID) references Department (Department_ID));

Table created.

SQL> describe Course
 Name                            Null?     Type
 ------------------------------- --------- ----
 COURSE_ID                       NOT NULL  VARCHAR2(5)
 DEPARTMENT_ID                   NOT NULL  VARCHAR2(20)
 TITLE                           NOT NULL  VARCHAR2(60)
 DESCRIPTION                               VARCHAR2(2000)
 UNITS                                     NUMBER
 ADDITIONAL_FEES                           NUMBER
```

The advantage of not declaring a datatype for a foreign key column is that you are guaranteed that the foreign key column will have the same datatype definition as its primary key counterpart. The disadvantage is that you can't determine the foreign key column's datatype by examining the CREATE TABLE statement.

Declaring a Foreign Key After Table Creation

As an alternative to declaring a foreign key when you create a table, you have the option of declaring a foreign key on an existing table with the ALTER TABLE statement. Listing 4.19 provides an example of how a foreign key can be declared with the ALTER TABLE statement.

INPUT/OUTPUT **Listing 4.19. Adding a foreign key.**

```
SQL> create table Course
  2  (Course_ID       Varchar2(5),
  3   Department_ID   Varchar2(20)
  4   constraint NN_Course_Department_ID NOT NULL,
  5   Title           Varchar2(60)
  6   constraint NN_Course_Title NOT NULL,
  7   Description      Varchar2(2000),
  8   Units            Number,
  9   Additional_Fees Number,
 10   Constraint PK_Course
 11   Primary key (Course_ID, Department_ID));

Table created.

SQL> alter table Course add constraint FK_Course_Department_ID
  2  foreign key (Department_ID) references Department (Department_ID);

Table altered.
```

Primary and Foreign Key Columns

When you define a foreign key, Oracle verifies the following:

☐ A primary key has been defined for the table referenced by the foreign key.

☐ The number of columns composing the foreign key matches the number of primary key columns.

☐ The datatype and width of each foreign key column matches the datatype and width of each primary key column.

Listing 4.20 illustrates what happens if the primary key column datatype doesn't match the column intended to be a foreign key. For example, the Employee table contains employees that work for a company, and Employee_Dependent contains dependents of those employees. The primary key of the Employee table is Employee_ID. Of course, the Employee_Dependent table also contains Employee_ID. Observe that the Employee table's definition for Employee_ID is NUMBER(4), but the Employee_Dependent table's definition for Employee_ID is VARCHAR2(4). As a result, Oracle does not allow the foreign key to be defined for Employee_ID in Employee_Dependent, which references Employee_ID in Employee.

Listing 4.20. Foreign key cannot be created because of column datatype mismatch.

```
SQL> describe Employee
Name                             Null?    Type
-------------------------------- -------- ----
EMPLOYEE_ID                      NOT NULL NUMBER(4)
LAST_NAME                        NOT NULL VARCHAR2(30)
FIRST_NAME                       NOT NULL VARCHAR2(20)
MIDDLE_INITIAL                            CHAR(1)
HIRE_DATE                        NOT NULL DATE
TERMINATION_DATE                          DATE
DATE_OF_BIRTH                             DATE
MONTHLY_SALARY                            NUMBER(5)
MANAGER                          NOT NULL CHAR(1)
USERNAME                                  VARCHAR2(31)

SQL> describe Employee_Dependent
Name                             Null?    Type
-------------------------------- -------- ----
EMPLOYEE_ID                      NOT NULL VARCHAR2(4)
LAST_NAME                                 VARCHAR2(30)
FIRST_NAME                                VARCHAR2(20)
MIDDLE_INITIAL                            CHAR(1)
RELATIONSHIP                              VARCHAR2(30)

SQL> alter table Employee_Dependent add Constraint Employee_Dependent_FK1
  2            Foreign Key (Employee_ID) references Employee;
          Foreign Key (Employee_ID) references Employee
                      *
ERROR at line 2:
ORA-02256: number, type and size of referencing columns must match
referenced columns
```

Disabling and Enabling Key Constraints

As I mentioned previously, primary and foreign key constraints enforce two crucial aspects of the relational model: data and referential integrity. You may want to disable these constraints for at least two tasks: designing the database and migrating the organization's legacy data.

Dropping a Primary Key

During the database design process, you may need to drop a table's primary key.

To do so, use the ALTER TABLE statement with this syntax:

```
ALTER TABLE table-name DROP PRIMARY KEY;
```

The variable is defined as follows:

> table-name is the table associated with the primary key.

For the sake of illustration, suppose you create a table for the storage of accounts payable data and define the primary key to be the Vendor's invoice number, as shown in Listing 4.21. After inspecting some data and pondering this definition, you realize that two different vendors could easily supply the same invoice number. Therefore, you drop the primary key for the table.

INPUT/OUTPUT **Listing 4.21. Dropping a primary key.**

```
SQL> create table AP_Header (
  2  Bill_Number            NUMBER(4) NOT NULL,
  3  Vendor_Invoice_Number  VARCHAR2(10),
  4  Vendor_ID              VARCHAR2(6)  NOT NULL,
  5  Date_Received          DATE         NOT NULL,
  6  Bill_Status            VARCHAR2(5),
  7  primary key (Vendor_Invoice_Number));
Table created.

SQL> alter table AP_Header drop primary key;
Table altered.
```

What if you've already declared a foreign key in the AP_Detail table that references the primary key of AP_Header? If that is the case, Oracle does not allow you to drop AP_Header's primary key. Listing 4.22 illustrates this.

INPUT/OUTPUT **Listing 4.22. Unable to drop a primary key.**

```
SQL> create table AP_Detail (
  2  Bill_Number            NUMBER(4) NOT NULL,
  3  Vendor_Invoice_Number  VARCHAR2(10) NOT NULL,
  4  Item_Number            NUMBER(3) NOT NULL,
  5  Billed_Amount          NUMBER(8,2) NOT NULL,
  6  Approved_Amount        NUMBER(8,2),
  7  Paid_Amount            NUMBER(8,2),
  8  Constraint AP_Detail_FK Foreign Key (Vendor_Invoice_Number)
  9            References AP_Header);
Table created.

SQL> alter table AP_Header drop primary key;
alter table AP_Header drop primary key
*
ERROR at line 1:
ORA-02273: this unique/primary key is referenced by some foreign keys
```

There is an option to the DROP PRIMARY KEY clause; you can use the keyword CASCADE. Use this feature with caution! CASCADE drops the primary key as well as any foreign keys that reference it. Listing 4.23 shows how the primary key is successfully dropped with the CASCADE clause.

Listing 4.23. Dropping a primary key with the CASCADE clause.

```
SQL> alter table AP_Header drop primary key cascade;
Table altered.
```

Dropping a Foreign Key

During the database design process, you may find that you've mistakenly defined a column as a foreign key. Dropping a foreign key is a bit different than dropping a primary key.

Because a table can have more than one foreign key, the ALTER TABLE statement requires that you supply the constraint name associated with the foreign key, using this syntax:

```
ALTER TABLE table-name DROP CONSTRAINT constraint-name;
```

The variables are defined as follows:

  table-name is the table associated with the primary key.

  constraint-name is the constraint associated with the foreign key.

For instance, suppose that the AP_Header table has an additional column named Vendor_Status, which, coincidentally, has the same datatype and width as Vendor_ID. As Listing 4.24 shows, you mistakenly create a foreign key for Vendor_Status that references the primary key of the Vendor table. After you try to insert a value into the Vendor_Status column, you quickly realize your error and drop the foreign key assigned to the column.

Listing 4.24. Dropping a foreign key.

```
SQL> alter table AP_Header add constraint AP_Header_Vendor_Status_FK
  2                          foreign key (Vendor_Status) references Vendor;
Table altered.

SQL> alter table AP_Header drop constraint AP_Header_Vendor_Status_FK;
Table altered.
```

Declaring Unique Constraints

In addition to primary and foreign keys, Oracle enables you to indicate that a column must have unique values. A unique constraint is not a substitute for a primary key constraint. As an example, the Patient table contains a list of patients in a hospital. Each patient is assigned a Patient ID, which is used as the primary key. However, each patient also has a Social Security number that is unique. Listing 4.25 provides an example of how a unique Social Security number is enforced with a unique constraint.

INPUT/
OUTPUT **Listing 4.25. Creating a unique constraint.**

```
SQL> create table Patient (
  2  Patient_ID              varchar2(6) primary key,
  3  Last_Name               varchar2(30) not null,
  4  First_Name              varchar2(20) not null,
  5  Middle_Name             varchar2(20),
  6  Social_Security_Number  varchar2(9) unique,
  7  Insurance_Carrier_Code  varchar2(4));
Table created.

SQL> insert into Patient
  2  (Patient_ID, Last_Name, First_Name)
  3  values
  4  ('A901', 'NORTON', 'ED');
1 row created.

SQL> insert into Patient
  2  (Patient_ID, Last_Name, First_Name, Social_Security_Number)
  3  values
  4  ('A902', 'KRAMDEN', 'RALPH', '123456789');
1 row created.

SQL> insert into Patient
  2  (Patient_ID, Last_Name, First_Name, Social_Security_Number)
  3  values
  4  ('A903', 'NORTON', 'TRIXIE', '123456789');
insert into Patient
            *
ERROR at line 1:
ORA-00001: unique constraint (TYO.UQ_PATIENT_PATIENT_ID) violated
```

Differences Between Primary Key and Unique Constraints

Two differences between primary key and unique constraints are worth noting. First, a table can have only one primary key, but it can have many unique constraints. Second, when a primary key is defined, the columns that compose the primary key are automatically mandatory. When a unique constraint is declared, the columns that compose the unique constraint are not automatically defined to be mandatory; you must also specify that the column is NOT NULL.

Table Indexes

Any discussion of primary and foreign key constraints must also examine indexes—the topics are closely related. This section discusses what table indexes are and how they are used by both the application developer and Oracle.

4

NEW TERM A *table index* is an Oracle object that contains the values that exist in one or more columns in a table.

Oracle provides two types of table indexes: unique and nonunique. Unique indexes enforce primary key and unique constraints. Nonunique indexes can improve query performance. Both types of indexes are implemented internally via a B*-tree data structure. A B*-tree data structure is graphically depicted as a balanced, inverted tree in which each leaf represents an index value. Understanding the following concepts is critical when you design an application's database:

☐ An ORDER BY clause in a SELECT statement can reference any column in a table— whether or not the table has an existing index based on that column.

☐ An index cannot be composed of more than 16 columns.

☐ An index doesn't store NULL values.

☐ SQL does not have a statement that will enable you to inspect the contents of an index.

☐ An index can be created only for a table, not a view.

Do	**Don't**

DO create an index on columns that have a wide distribution of values, such as ZIP code.

DO create an index on columns so that the indexed columns contain 20 percent or less of the data in the table.

DON'T create a unique index instead of declaring a primary key.

DON'T overindex a table. You may improve data retrieval, but you could negatively affect the overall performance of the database.

DON'T create an index on a column that has a small distribution of values, such as gender (check with your DBA about the feasibility of using a bitmap index for such columns).

DON'T index small tables.

Creating an Index

Here is the basic syntax to use when creating an index:

```
CREATE [UNIQUE] INDEX index-name
ON table-name (column1, ... columnN);
```

The variables are defined as follows:

index-name is the name to be given to the index (subject to Oracle database object naming restrictions).

table-name is the table for which the index is created.

column1 through *columnN* are the columns to be used in creating the index.

Notice that the keyword UNIQUE is optional. If you don't include UNIQUE, the created index is nonunique. In other words, the nonunique index does not restrict the values of a set of columns in any way. If you include the keyword UNIQUE, the index prevents a duplicate set of column values from being stored in the table.

Listing 4.26 provides an example. The primary key of the Student table is Student_ID. However, you'll frequently query the Student table based on a student's last name. To improve the performance of those queries, you create a nonunique index.

INPUT/OUTPUT

Listing 4.26. Creating a nonunique index.

```
SQL> create index Student_Last_Name on
  2   Student (Last_Name);

Index created.
```

Why You Shouldn't Create Unique Indexes

Although CREATE UNIQUE INDEX is a legal Oracle statement, you shouldn't use it; instead, declare PRIMARY KEY and UNIQUE constraints. The two principal reasons for this advice are these:

☐ When you declare PRIMARY KEY and UNIQUE constraints, Oracle automatically creates the appropriate unique index to enforce the constraints.

☐ You won't be able to declare a FOREIGN KEY constraint unless you also declare a corresponding PRIMARY KEY constraint.

Viewing Constraints

When you declare a column as NOT NULL, Oracle treats the mandatory requirement as a constraint. In fact, this constraint is the only one that can be seen with the SQL*Plus DESCRIBE command. Listing 4.27 provides an example. If you describe the Instructor table in SQL*Plus, Oracle indicates that the Instructor table has three mandatory columns. This number is somewhat misleading because Instructor_ID was defined as the table's primary key—which is automatically NOT NULL.

Listing 4.27. Viewing NOT NULL constraints with SQL*Plus DESCRIBE.

```
SQL> describe Instructor
 Name                            Null?    Type
 ------------------------------- -------- ----
 INSTRUCTOR_ID                   NOT NULL VARCHAR2(20)
 DEPARTMENT_ID                   NOT NULL VARCHAR2(20)
 LAST_NAME                       NOT NULL VARCHAR2(25)
 FIRST_NAME                               VARCHAR2(25)
 MI                                       VARCHAR2(1)
 POSITION                                 VARCHAR2(25)
 TELEPHONE                                VARCHAR2(10)
 FAX                                      VARCHAR2(10)
 EMAIL                                    VARCHAR2(100)
```

You can use the Oracle data dictionary view named USER_CONSTRAINTS to see the constraints associated with a table. The columns returned by USER_CONSTRAINTS include

- ☐ CONSTRAINT_NAME
- ☐ CONSTRAINT_TYPE
- ☐ SEARCH_CONDITION

Listing 4.28 displays the results of a query of USER_CONSTRAINTS for all constraints associated with the Instructor table: two NOT NULL constraints, a CHECK constraint on the Position column, a primary key constraint that is indicated by a value of P for Constraint_Type, and a foreign key on Deparment ID.

NOTE

You'll notice that in the text I capitalize the first letter only of table and column names, but in the code I capitalize the whole name. For example, in Listing 4.28 on line 4, the word INSTRUCTOR must be all uppercase, or else nothing will be returned by the data dictionary. This is because the values in double quotes must be all uppercase.

Listing 4.28. Viewing constraints on the Instructor table.

```
SQL> select constraint_name, constraint_type, search_condition
  2  from user_constraints
  3  where
  4  table_name = 'INSTRUCTOR';
```

```
CONSTRAINT_NAME                    C SEARCH_CONDITION
- - - - - - - - - - - - - - - - - -  - - - - - - - - - - - - - - - - - - - - - -
NN_INSTRUCTOR_DEPT_ID              C DEPARTMENT_ID IS NOT NULL
NN_INSTRUCTOR_LAST_NAME            C LAST_NAME IS NOT NULL
CK_INSTRUCTOR_POSITION             C Position in ('ASSISTANT PROFES
                                     SOR', 'ASSOCIATE PROFESSOR',
                                                         'PROFESSOR
                                     ')

PK_INSTRUCTOR                      P
FK_INSTRUCTOR_DEPARTMENT_ID        R
```

Restricting Values with a Column CHECK Constraint

The CHECK constraint is a column-level constraint that serves at least two purposes.

- ☐ Some columns—often numeric—do not have a set of discrete values that can be referenced with a foreign key. However, you still need to constrain the value of such a column to a particular range.

- ☐ The legal range of a column is not constant; it must be calculated when the column value is inserted or updated.

The CHECK constraint is declared in a CREATE TABLE or ALTER_TABLE statement using this syntax:

column-name datatype [CONSTRAINT *constraint-name*] [CHECK (*condition*)]

The variables are defined as follows:

column-name is the column name.

datatype is the column's datatype, width, and scale.

constraint-name is the constraint name subject to Oracle database object-naming restrictions.

condition is a legal Oracle SQL condition that returns a Boolean value.

To illustrate this concept, Listing 4.29 shows how you can create a table that is used in a hospital database to store patient information. One of the columns in this table is the patient's body temperature in degrees Fahrenheit. You should restrict the possible values of this column by defining it as NUMBER(4,1). But this column still accepts numbers from 0.0 to 999.9—including some obviously nonsensical values for body temperature. You can use a CHECK constraint to restrict the range of the value to between 60.0 (for patients suffering from hypothermia) and 110.0.

**INPUT/
OUTPUT**   **Listing 4.29. Creating a CHECK constraint.**

```
SQL> create table Patient (
  2   Patient_ID      varchar2(6) primary key,
  3   Body_Temp_Deg_F  number(4,1) constraint Patient_Body_Temp
  4                    Check (Body_Temp_Deg_F >= 60.0 and
  5                           Body_Temp_Deg_F <= 110.0));
Table created.

SQL> insert into Patient
  2   (Patient_ID, Body_Temp_Deg_F)
  3   values
  4   ('A1001', 98.6);
1 row created.

SQL> insert into Patient
  2   (Patient_ID, Body_Temp_Deg_F)
  3   values
  4   ('Q7777', 111.2);
('Q7777', 111.2)
                *
ERROR at line 4:
ORA-02290: check constraint (TYO.CK_PATIENT_BODY_TEMP) violated
```

You can use Oracle built-in SQL functions in a CHECK constraint. As an example, Listing 4.30 displays the definition of a CHECK constraint which verifies that a patient's insurance status is either Y or N.

**INPUT/
OUTPUT**   **Listing 4.30. Using the IN operator in a CHECK constraint.**

```
SQL> create table Patient (
  2   Patient_ID      varchar2(6) primary key,
  3   Body_Temp_Deg_F  number(4,1) constraint Patient_Body_Temp
  4                    Check (Body_Temp_Deg_F >= 60.0 and
  5                           Body_Temp_Deg_F <= 110.0),
  6   Insurance_Status Char(1) constraint Patient_Insurance_Status
  7                    Check (Insurance_Status in ('Y','y','N','n')));
Table created.

SQL> insert into Patient
  2   (Patient_ID, Insurance_Status)
  3   values
  4   ('R4321','Y');
1 row created.

SQL> insert into Patient
  2   (Patient_ID, Insurance_Status)
  3   values
  4   ('U3030','U');
('U3030','U')
                *
ERROR at line 4:
ORA-02290: check constraint (TYO.CK_PATIENT_INSURANCE_STATUS) violated
```

ANALYSIS As you can see, the CHECK constraint is violated when you attempt to specify a value of U for Insurance_Status.

A Column Can Have More Than One CHECK Constraint

Oracle does not restrict the number of CHECK constraints that can be defined for a column or a table. Back to the Flugle College example, Listing 4.31 demonstrates how a single column—Amount_Approved—has two CHECK constraints defined.

INPUT/ OUTPUT
Listing 4.31. Single column with more than one CHECK constraint.

```
SQL> create table Loan_Application (
  2   Loan_Application_No        number(6) primary key,
  3   Borrower_Last_Name         varchar2(30) not null,
  4   Borrower_First_Name        varchar2(20) not null,
  5   Borrower_Middle_Name       varchar2(20),
  6   Amount_Requested           number(9,2) not null,
  7   Amount_Approved            number(9,2)
  8                              constraint Amount_Approved_Limit
  9                              check (Amount_Approved <= 1000000)
 10                              constraint Amount_Approved_Interval
 11                              check (mod(Amount_Approved,1000)=0)
 12  );
Table created.

SQL> insert into Loan_Application
  2   (Loan_Application_No, Borrower_Last_Name, Borrower_First_Name,
  3    Amount_Requested, Amount_Approved)
  4   values
  5   (2001, 'RUBRIK', 'STANLEY', 1000000, 999950);
insert into Loan_Application
                 *
ERROR at line 1:
ORA-02290: check constraint (TYO.CK_LOAN_APPLICATION1) violated

SQL> insert into Loan_Application
  2   (Loan_Application_No, Borrower_Last_Name, Borrower_First_Name,
  3    Amount_Requested, Amount_Approved)
  4   values
  5   (2001, 'RUBRIK', 'STANLEY', 1000000, 999000);
1 row created.

SQL> insert into Loan_Application
  2   (Loan_Application_No, Borrower_Last_Name, Borrower_First_Name,
  3    Amount_Requested, Amount_Approved)
  4   values
  5   (2001, 'RUBRIK', 'STANLEY', 1000000, 1001000);
insert into Loan_Application
                 *
ERROR at line 1:
ORA-02290: check constraint (TYO.CK_LOAN_APPLICATION2) violated
```

4

ANALYSIS   In the example in Listing 4.31, two constraints are defined for the Loan_Application table. The first constraint (lines 8 and 9) limit the approval amount to one million dollars, whereas the second constraint (lines 10 and 11) ensures that the approval amount is in thousand-dollar increments. You easily could combine both constraints into a single constraint. However, you should consider defining separate constraints if you think you might need to disable a single constraint while allowing other constraints to remain enabled.

Referencing Other Columns in a CHECK Constraint

One of the limitations of a column CHECK constraint is that it cannot reference other columns in the same table. Suppose you're responsible for defining a table for storing loan application information. In this table, Amount_Requested contains the loan amount requested by the borrower; Amount_Approved is the amount that was approved by the loan committee. The lender never approves an amount greater than that requested.

Listing 4.32 illustrates this rule. A column CHECK constraint cannot reference other columns. However, you can use a table constraint to reference any column in a table. By adding a comma after the definition of Amount_Approved, the column constraint becomes a table constraint.

INPUT/ OUTPUT
Listing 4.32. Using a table CHECK constraint instead of a column CHECK constraint.

```
SQL> create table Loan_Application (
  2   Loan_Application_No      number(6) primary key,
  3   Borrower_Last_Name       varchar2(30) not null,
  4   Borrower_First_Name      varchar2(20) not null,
  5   Borrower_Middle_Name     varchar2(20),
  6   Amount_Requested         number(9,2) not null,
  7   Amount_Approved          number(9,2)
  8                            constraint Amount_Approved_Limit
  9                            check (Amount_Approved <= Amount_Requested)
 10   );
)
*
ERROR at line 10:
ORA-02438: Column check constraint cannot reference other columns

SQL> create table Loan_Application (
  2           Loan_Application_No      number(6) primary key,
  3           Borrower_Last_Name       varchar2(30) not null,
  4           Borrower_First_Name      varchar2(20) not null,
  5           Borrower_Middle_Name     varchar2(20),
  6           Amount_Requested         number(9,2) not null,
  7           Amount_Approved          number(9,2),
  8               constraint Amount_Approved_Limit
  9               check (Amount_Approved <= Amount_Requested)
 10   );
Table created.
```

```
SQL> insert into Loan_Application
  2 (Loan_Application_No, Borrower_Last_Name, Borrower_First_Name,
  3  Amount_Requested, Amount_Approved)
  4 values
  5 (2001, 'CRANDALL', 'JULIE', 300000, 310000);
insert into Loan_Application
                *
ERROR at line 1:
ORA-02290: check constraint (TYO.AMOUNT_APPROVED_LIMIT_) violated

SQL> insert into Loan_Application
  2 (Loan_Application_No, Borrower_Last_Name, Borrower_First_Name,
  3  Amount_Requested, Amount_Approved)
  4 values
  5 (2001, 'CRANDALL', 'JULIE', 300000, 300000);
1 row created.
```

Using Pseudocolumns in a CHECK Constraint

A CHECK constraint cannot reference pseudocolumns such as SYSDATE, ROWNUM, and USER. If you need to define a business rule that refers to these pseudocolumns, rely on a database trigger to restrict column values. On Day 11, "More Programming Techniques with PL/SQL," I will pursue this topic in greater detail.

 A *pseudocolumn* is a built-in value (or function without arguments) that returns a specific piece of information by querying a table—usually DUAL. For instance, SYSDATE always returns the current date and time.

Common Restrictions on Modifying a Table

During the database-design phase, a developer typically experiments with an application's database structures to determine their accuracy and suitability. This task rarely can be done without populating tables with sample data. If a table requires a change—for example, an additional column—altering the table is much more convenient than dropping the table and recreating it with its new definition. However, sometimes the necessary change cannot be made without modifying the sample data.

Changing the Primary Key

Changing a table's primary key without disturbing the rest of a database design is often difficult. The reason is simple: Tables usually are related to one another through the declaration of foreign keys. A foreign key depends upon the existence of a primary key in another table. Therefore, if you change the primary key, the change can ripple throughout the entire database. In fact, Oracle prevents that from happening.

Changing a primary key is a two-step process: dropping the primary key and recreating it. This is illustrated in Listing 4.33. Suppose you had originally created the Course table with a primary key consisting only of the Course ID. After some thought, you realize that different departments will want to have courses with the same number. Therefore, you change the primary key to include both the Course ID and the Department ID.

INPUT/OUTPUT   **Listing 4.33. Changing a primary key.**

```
SQL> alter table Course add
  2   (primary key (Course_ID));

Table altered.

SQL> alter table Course drop primary key;

Table altered.

SQL> alter table Course add
  2   (primary key (Course_ID, Department_ID));

Table altered.
```

Script for Creating the Sample Database

Now that you have covered the basic techniques used to create tables, you're ready for a look at the script for creating our sample database which is shown in Listing 4.34.

The first portion of the script is used to drop all the tables. If you try to drop a table that is referenced by another table's foreign key, Oracle will return an error code.

The only exception to this is if you use the CASCADE clause in the DROP TABLE statement. Therefore, if you don't use the CASCADE clause, it is essential that the tables be dropped in an order such that the table being dropped is not referenced by a foreign key in any existing tables.

 NOTE

 Please note that this script can be found on the CD-ROM as \tyo\flugle.sql. To execute the script, you can use SQL*Plus or SQL Worksheet. If you're using SQL*Plus, enter @C:\TYO\flugle.sql (if you have installed the scripts from the CD-ROM onto your C drive in the TYO directory. If you're using SQL Worksheet, enter @C:\TYO\flugle.sql in the command buffer in the bottom window.

INPUT   **Listing 4.34. Creating the sample database tables.**

```
drop table Student_Schedule;

drop table Student;

drop table Class;

drop table Class_Location;

drop table Course;

drop table Schedule_Type_Details;

drop table Schedule_Type;

drop table Instructor;

drop table Department;

create table Department
(Department_ID      Varchar2(20),
Department_Name     Varchar2(25)
 constraint NN_Department_Name NOT NULL,
 constraint PK_Department
 primary key (Department_ID));

create table Student
(Student_ID      Varchar2(20),
 Last_Name       Varchar2(25)
 constraint NN_Student_Last_Name NOT NULL,
 First_Name      Varchar2(25)
 constraint NN_Student_First_Name NOT NULL,
 MI              Varchar2(1),
 Year            Varchar2(25),
 Street_Address  Varchar2(25),
 City            Varchar2(25),
 State           Varchar2(2),
 Zipcode         Varchar2(9),
 Telephone       Varchar2(10),
 Fax             Varchar2(10),
 Email           Varchar2(100),
 constraint PK_Student
 primary key (Student_ID));

create table Course
(Course_ID       Varchar2(5),
 Department_ID   Varchar2(20)
 constraint NN_Course_Department_ID NOT NULL,
 Title           Varchar2(60)
 constraint NN_Course_Title NOT NULL,
 Description     Varchar2(2000),
 Units           Number,
 Additional_Fees Number,
 Constraint PK_Course
```

4

continues

Listing 4.34. continued

```
Primary key (Course_ID, Department_ID),
Constraint FK_Course_Department_ID
Foreign key (Department_ID) references Department (Department_ID));

create table Instructor
(Instructor_ID      varchar2(20),
 Department_ID      varchar2(20)
 constraint NN_Instructor_Dept_ID NOT NULL,
 Last_Name          varchar2(25)
 constraint NN_Instructor_Last_Name NOT NULL,
 First_Name         varchar2(25),
 MI                 varchar2(1),
 Position           varchar2(25) constraint CK_Instructor_Position
 check (Position in ('ASSISTANT PROFESSOR', 'ASSOCIATE PROFESSOR',
                     'PROFESSOR')),
 Telephone          varchar2(10),
 Fax                varchar2(10),
 Email              varchar2(100),
 constraint PK_Instructor Primary Key (Instructor_ID),
 constraint FK_Instructor_Department_ID
 Foreign Key (Department_ID) references Department (Department_ID));

create table Schedule_Type
(Schedule_ID          varchar2(20),
 Schedule_Description varchar2(2000),
 constraint PK_Schedule_Type primary key (Schedule_ID));

create table Schedule_Type_Details
(Schedule_ID          varchar2(20),
 Day                  number
 constraint CK_Schedule_Det_Day check (Day between 1 and 7),
 Starting_Time        date,
 Duration             number,
 constraint PK_Schedule_Type_Details primary key (Schedule_ID, Day),
 constraint FK_Schedule_Det_ID
 foreign key (Schedule_ID) references Schedule_Type (Schedule_ID));

create table Class_Location
(Class_Building     varchar2(25),
 Class_Room         varchar2(25),
 Seating_Capacity   number,
 constraint PK_Class_Location primary key (Class_Building, Class_Room));

create table Class
(Class_ID           varchar2(20),
 Schedule_ID        varchar2(20),
 Class_Building     varchar2(25),
 Class_Room         varchar2(25),
 Course_ID          varchar2(5),
 Department_ID      varchar2(20),
 Instructor_ID      varchar2(20),
 Semester           varchar2(6),
 School_Year        date,
 constraint PK_Class primary key (Class_ID),
```

```
constraint FK_Class_Location
foreign key (Class_Building, Class_Room) references
  Class_Location (Class_Building, Class_Room),
constraint FK_Class_Schedule_ID
foreign key (Schedule_ID) references Schedule_Type (Schedule_ID),
constraint FK_Class_Course_ID
foreign key (Course_ID, Department_ID) references
   Course (Course_ID, Department_ID),
constraint FK_Class_Dept_ID
foreign key (Department_ID) references Department (Department_ID),
constraint FK_Class_Instructor_ID
foreign key (Instructor_ID) references Instructor (Instructor_ID));

create table Student_Schedule
(Student_ID          varchar2(20),
 Class_ID            varchar2(20),
 Grade               varchar2(2)
 constraint CK_Grade check (Grade in ('A', 'A+', 'A-', 'B', 'B+', 'B-',
                            'C', 'C+', 'C-', 'D', 'D+', 'D-',
                            'F', 'F+', 'F-')),
Date_Grade_Assigned date,
constraint PK_Student_Schedule
primary key (Student_ID, Class_ID),
constraint FK_Student_Schedule_Student_ID
foreign key (Student_ID) references Student (Student_ID),
constraint FK_Student_Schedule_Class
foreign key (Class_ID) references Class (Class_ID));
```

4

Summary

Keep the following ideas in mind when implementing your logical design:

☐ Use the CREATE TABLE statement via SQL*Plus or SQL Worksheet for greater control over the statement options or to process a script.

☐ Use the ALTER TABLE statement to modify an existing table.

☐ Define default values for columns where appropriate.

☐ Every table should have a primary key.

☐ Use foreign keys to enforce referential integrity.

☐ You can define a table's primary key by using the CREATE TABLE or ALTER TABLE statement.

☐ You can drop a table's primary key with the ALTER_TABLE statement.

☐ You can disable or enable a constraint by using the ALTER TABLE statement.

☐ You can drop a constraint with the ALTER TABLE statement.

☐ A table index can be defined for up to 16 columns.

☐ A table index may be unique or nonunique.

☐ Don't create unique indexes with the CREATE UNIQUE INDEX statement; instead, declare primary key and unique constraints and let Oracle create the indexes automatically.

☐ Use a CHECK constraint to restrict a column's value to a fixed or calculated range.

What Comes Next?

On Day 5, "Introduction to Structured Query Language (SQL)," you learn more about four very important SQL statements: SELECT, INSERT, UPDATE, and DELETE. These statements are used to retrieve and manipulate information in an Oracle database.

Q&A

Q What is the ideal number of indexes for a table?

A The answer is—it depends. At the very least, an index will be created automatically by the declaration of the primary key. Beyond that, you probably will want to add a nonunique index for each foreign key. You also may want to add a nonunique index for each column that is frequently part of a query condition and has a wide distribution of values. However, you should rarely create any additional indexes for tables with a small number of rows—for example, one hundred or less.

Q What is the advantage of declaring a column CHECK constraint? Can't the constraint be enforced in an application such as Oracle Forms or Visual Basic?

A Yes, it is possible and sometimes desirable to enforce a constraint also at the application level. However, you should consider the declarative constraints for a table and its columns to be the first "line of defense" for data integrity. Because a variety of tools are used in the client/server environment, you want to be certain that no one can assign invalid values to a column, regardless of the tool being used.

Q How do you drop or rename a column in a table?

A Oracle does not allow you to rename or drop a column directly. If you want to rename or drop a column, you have two choices: you can drop the table and recreate it, or you can create a new table based on a subset of the columns in the existing table. If you decide to use the latter approach, remember that the new table will not possess any constraints other than NOT NULL constraints.

Workshop

The purpose of the Workshop is to allow you to test your knowledge of the material discussed in the lesson. See if you can correctly answer the questions in the quiz and complete the exercise before you continue with tomorrow's lesson.

Quiz

1. What is wrong with this statement?

```
CREATE TABLE new_table (
first_col number,
second_col date
third_col number default sysdate);
```

2. Describe a SQL statement that might result in the following Oracle error message?

```
ORA-02266: unique/primary keys in table referenced by
➥enabled foreign keys
```

3. What is the difference between a column and table check constraint?

Exercise

The Instructor table has a column named Position. In the current design of this table, there is a CHECK constraint on the Position column that restricts the value to ASSISTANT PROFESSOR, ASSOCIATE PROFESSOR, and FULL PROFESSOR. Modify the database design so that an additional table, INSTRUCTOR_POSITION, is used to specify legal values for instructor position.

Day **5**

Introduction to Structured Query Language (SQL)

To develop an Oracle database application, it is essential that you develop a working knowledge of Structured Query Language (SQL). SQL is a powerful language that differs from traditional third-generation languages (3GLs), such as C and Pascal, in several significant ways:

- [ ] SQL is a nonprocedural language. You use SQL to tell Oracle *what* data to retrieve or modify without telling it *how* to do its job.

- [ ] SQL does not provide any flow-of-control programming constructs, function definitions, do-loops, or if-then-else statements. However, as you will see on Day 9, "Programming an Oracle Database with PL/SQL," Oracle provides procedural language extensions to SQL through a product called PL/SQL.

☐ SQL provides a fixed set of datatypes; you cannot define new datatypes. Unlike modern programming languages that enable you to define a datatype for a specific purpose, SQL forces you to choose from a set of predefined datatypes when you create or modify a column. In the future, though, you can expect Oracle to release an object-oriented database that will enable you to define datatypes specific to the application you're building.

One similarity between SQL and a traditional programming language is that both usually give you more than one way to accomplish the same goal—particularly when retrieving information. Various SQL statements may achieve the same results (but differ in efficiency or clarity).

Retrieving and Modifying Data

At the highest level, SQL statements can be broadly categorized as follows into three types:

☐ Data Manipulation Language (DML), which retrieves or modifies data

☐ Data Definition Language (DDL), which defines the structure of the data

☐ Data Control Language (DCL), which defines the privileges granted to database users

The category of DML contains four basic statements:

☐ SELECT, which retrieves rows from a table

☐ INSERT, which adds rows to a table

☐ UPDATE, which modifies existing rows in a table

☐ DELETE, which removes rows from a table

These statements are used most often by application developers. DDL and DCL statements are commonly used by a database designer and database administrator for establishing the database structures used by an application.

SQL Grammar

Here are some grammatical requirements to keep in mind when you're working with SQL.

☐ Every SQL statement is terminated by a semicolon.

☐ An SQL statement can be entered on one line or split across several lines for clarity. Most of the examples in this book split statements into readable portions.

☐ SQL isn't case sensitive; you can mix uppercase and lowercase when referencing SQL keywords (such as SELECT and INSERT), table names, and column names.

However, case does matter when referring to the contents of a column; if you ask for all customers whose last names begin with *a* and all customer names are stored in uppercase, you won't retrieve any rows at all.

NOTE Most of the examples in this chapter were produced with SQL*Plus. Of course, you can use whatever tool you prefer to enter SQL statements—for instance, SQL*Plus, SQL Worksheet, or Discoverer/2000. For the sake of brevity, I have removed the repeated column headings that SQL*Plus produces.

Syntax of the SELECT Statement

Of the four DML statements, the SELECT statement is the one that is executed most often in a real application because records are usually read more often than they are changed. A SELECT statement also can exist as a subquery in an UPDATE, INSERT, or DELETE statement, but that topic is discussed on Day 6, "Using SQL to Modify Data."

The SELECT statement is a tremendously powerful tool, and its syntax is complicated because of the many ways that tables, columns, functions, and operators can be combined into legal statements. Therefore, instead of looking at the full syntax of the SELECT statement, this section starts with some basic examples of the SELECT statement.

At a minimum, a SELECT statement contains the following two elements:

- ☐ The select list, a list of columns or expressions to be retrieved
- ☐ The FROM clause, the table from which to retrieve the rows

A Simple SELECT Statement

5

NOTE If you want to work through the examples in this lesson, follow the directions in this book's Introduction that describe the installation of the sample database.

A simple SELECT statement—a query that retrieves only the Student ID from the Student table—is shown in Listing 5.1.

INPUT/OUTPUT | **Listing 5.1. An initial SELECT statement.**

```
SQL> select Student_ID
  2  from Student;

STUDENT_ID
--------------------
10231300
10231301
10231302
10231305
10231306
10231308
10231309
10231322
10231314
10231315
10231317
10231319
10231320
10231325
10231326
10231328
10231329
10231327
10231330
10231316
10231303
10231310
10231318
10231324
10231304
10231312
10231321
10231313
10231311
10231323
10231307

31 rows selected.
```

If you want to retrieve both the Student ID and the student's last name, simply list the columns in the desired order, as shown in Listing 5.2.

Listing 5.2. Retrieving multiple columns.

```
SQL> select Student_ID, Last_Name
  2  from Student;

STUDENT_ID              LAST_NAME
--------------------    ------------------------
10231300                SMYTHE
10231301                HAN
10231302                GORDON
10231305                REYNOLDS
10231306                PARKER
10231308                TANAKA
10231309                COEN
10231322                NEWTON
10231314                PURCELL
10231315                JACKEL
10231317                ROSEN
10231319                MALLARD
10231320                GUSSEY
10231325                MICHAELS
10231326                DEURRE
10231328                WONG
10231329                ABBOT
10231327                POSEN
10231330                CLAUSEN
10231316                GOMEZ
10231303                MASSEY
10231310                FERGUSON
10231318                BING
10231324                ANASTATIA
10231304                CHIN
10231312                HOLMES
10231321                PLOWCHARD
10231313                JACKSON
10231311                FERNANDEZ
10231323                PINKWATER
10231307                MABEISI

31 rows selected.
```

If you want to retrieve all columns in a table, you can use an SQL shortcut (the *), as shown in Figure 5.1.

Figure 5.1.

*Selecting all the columns in a table with SQL*Plus.*

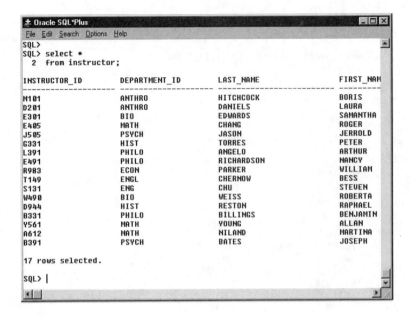

The Select List

If the select list contains multiple columns, the columns must be separated by commas. The select list also can contain valid expressions that may or may not contain columns. In addition, you can use a column more than once in a select list. The query in Listing 5.3 is completely valid.

INPUT/
OUTPUT

Listing 5.3. Retrieving a column more than once.

```
SQL> select Student_ID, Student_ID
  2  from Student;

STUDENT_ID           STUDENT_ID
-------------------  -------------------
10231300             10231300
10231301             10231301
10231302             10231302
10231305             10231305
10231306             10231306
10231308             10231308
10231309             10231309
10231322             10231322
10231314             10231314
10231315             10231315
10231317             10231317
10231319             10231319
10231320             10231320
```

5

```
10231325                10231325
10231326                10231326
10231328                10231328
10231329                10231329
10231327                10231327
10231330                10231330
10231316                10231316
10231303                10231303
10231310                10231310
10231318                10231318
10231324                10231324
10231304                10231304
10231312                10231312
10231321                10231321
10231313                10231313
10231311                10231311
10231323                10231323
10231307                10231307
```

31 rows selected.

TIP

> You can perform arithmetic computations by selecting the problem from a utility table named DUAL, as in
>
> `select 3.14159*20 from dual;`
>
> which returns
>
> `62.8318`

5

Results Returned by a SELECT

The results returned by every SELECT statement constitute a temporary table. Each retrieved record is a row in this temporary table, and each element of the select list is a column. If a query doesn't return any records, the temporary table can be thought of as empty. This behavior is a fundamental principle of the relational model.

Using Expressions in the Select List

In addition to specifying columns, you also can specify expressions in the select list. Expressions fall into the same datatypes as columns—character, numeric, and date. Through the use of operators, built-in functions, and constants, you can construct complex expressions to meet the needs of your application.

Keep in mind that Oracle considers each element in the select list to be a separate column, even if that expression references multiple columns.

Arithmetic and Logical Operators

The arithmetic and logical operators used in SQL are similar to those used in C:

Description	Operator
Addition	+
Subtraction	–
Multiplication	*
Division	/
Less than	<
Less than or equal to	<=
Greater than	>
Greater than or equal to	>=
Equal to	=
Not equal to	!=

As an example, the Course table contains the units for each course. If the current cost per unit is $250, the cost of the course is obtained with the SELECT statement in Listing 5.4.

Listing 5.4. Using an arithmetic operator in a SELECT statement.

```
SQL> select Title, Units*250
  2  from Course;

TITLE                                          UNITS*250
---------------------------------------------- ---------
INTRO TO ANTHROPOLOGY                                750
PRE-CALCULUS                                         750
GENERAL CALCULUS                                     750
NUMBER THEORY                                        750
ADVANCED ARITHMETIC                                  750
INTRO TO PSYCHOLOGY                                  750
ABNORMAL PSYCHOLOGY                                  750
EARLY AMERICAN HISTORY                               750
MODERN EUROPEAN HISTORY                              750
INTRO TO BIOLOGY                                     750
INTRO TO ECONOMICS                                   750
MONETARY POLICY                                      750
INTRO TO PHILOSOPHY                                  750
INTRO TO ENGLISH LIT                                 750
MODERN ENGLISH LIT                                   750
INTRO TO STRUCTURES                                  750
MODERN PHILOSOPHY                                    750
ANCIENT GREEK PHILOSOPHERS                           750
MAMMALIAN ANATOMY                                    750
INVERTEBRATE ANATOMY                                 750
WORKSHOP ON MARX                                     750
WORKSHOP ON JEFFERSON                                750
```

```
INTRO TO CIRCUIT THEORY                    750
INTRO TO DYNAMICS                          750
SEMINAR ON CHAOS                           500
SEMINAR ON NACIMERA                        500
PHYS ANTHRO FIELD TECHNIQUES               750
EVOLUTIONARY GRAMMAR                       500
SEMINAR ON THEME ANALYSIS                  500
WORKSHOP ON NEUROSES                       500
WORKSHOP ON NORMALITY                      500

31 rows selected.
```

TIP

Instead of trying to remember the precedence rules for arithmetic operators used in SQL statements, you should always use parentheses if you're uncertain about the correct way to evaluate an expression.

String Operators

One of the most important string operators in SQL is the concatenation operator, ¦¦. SQL syntax requires that string constants be enclosed in single quotes. This operator enables you to concatenate two or more strings, as shown in Listing 5.5.

INPUT/OUTPUT **Listing 5.5. Using a string operator.**

```
SQL> select Last_Name ¦¦ ': ' ¦¦ Position
  2  from Instructor;

LAST_NAME¦¦':'¦¦POSITION
--------------------------------------------------
HITCHCOCK: PROFESSOR
DANIELS: ASSOCIATE PROFESSOR
EDWARDS: PROFESSOR
CHANG: ASSISTANT PROFESSOR
JASON: ASSOCIATE PROFESSOR
TORRES: PROFESSOR
ANGELO: ASSOCIATE PROFESSOR
RICHARDSON: ASSISTANT PROFESSOR
PARKER: PROFESSOR
CHERNOW: ASSOCIATE PROFESSOR
CHU: PROFESSOR
WEISS: PROFESSOR
RESTON: ASSOCIATE PROFESSOR
BILLINGS: ASSISTANT PROFESSOR
YOUNG: ASSOCIATE PROFESSOR
NILAND: ASSOCIATE PROFESSOR
BATES: ASSISTANT PROFESSOR

17 rows selected.
```

5

The following are several reasons why you would want to concatenate strings:

☐ **To embed strings in the values returned by a query.** You want to address a form letter to your customers by combining a salutation, a blank, and the customer's last name:

```
select Salutation ¦¦ ' ' ¦¦ Last_Name
from Customer
order by Last_Name;
```

☐ **To combine strings.** Your application might be required to take a substring from one column and combine it with a substring from another column for display to the user.

☐ **To create new values that can be assigned to a column.** In the process of implementing your application, you might need to convert existing data from one format to another.

You can use the concatenation operator with more than two strings, as shown in Listing 5.6.

INPUT/OUTPUT **Listing 5.6. Multiple concatenations.**

```
SQL> select Last_Name ¦¦ ', ' ¦¦ Position ¦¦ ', can be contacted at ' ¦¦
  2  Email
  3  from Instructor;

LAST_NAME¦¦','¦¦POSITION¦¦',CANBECONTACTEDAT'¦¦EMAIL
----------------------------------------------------------------
HITCHCOCK, PROFESSOR, can be contacted at BHITCHCOCK@FLUGLE.EDU
DANIELS, ASSOCIATE PROFESSOR, can be contacted at LDANIELS@FLUGLE.EDU
EDWARDS, PROFESSOR, can be contacted at SEDWARDS@FLUGLE.EDU
CHANG, ASSISTANT PROFESSOR, can be contacted at RCHANG@FLUGLE.EDU
JASON, ASSOCIATE PROFESSOR, can be contacted at JJASON@FLUGLE.EDU
TORRES, PROFESSOR, can be contacted at PTORRES@FLUGLE.EDU
ANGELO, ASSOCIATE PROFESSOR, can be contacted at AANGELO@FLUGLE.EDU
RICHARDSON, ASSISTANT PROFESSOR, can be contacted at
➡NRICHARDSON@FLUGLE.EDU
PARKER, PROFESSOR, can be contacted at WPARKER@FLUGLE.EDU
CHERNOW, ASSOCIATE PROFESSOR, can be contacted at BCHERNOW@FLUGLE.EDU
CHU, PROFESSOR, can be contacted at SCHU@FLUGLE.EDU
WEISS, PROFESSOR, can be contacted at RWEISS@FLUGLE.EDU
RESTON, ASSOCIATE PROFESSOR, can be contacted at RRESTON@FLUGLE.EDU
BILLINGS, ASSISTANT PROFESSOR, can be contacted at BBILLINGS@FLUGLE.EDU
YOUNG, ASSOCIATE PROFESSOR, can be contacted at AYOUNG@FLUGLE.EDU
NILAND, ASSOCIATE PROFESSOR, can be contacted at MNILAND@FLUGLE.EDU
BATES, ASSISTANT PROFESSOR, can be contacted at JBATES@FLUGLE.EDU

17 rows selected.
```

5

Built-in Functions

Oracle provides a rich set of built-in functions that you can use to manipulate and convert different types of data. These functions can be categorized as

- ☐ Character functions
- ☐ Number functions
- ☐ Date functions
- ☐ Conversion functions
- ☐ Group functions
- ☐ Miscellaneous functions

You'll find explanations of many of these functions on Day 7, "Taking Advantage of SQL Built-In Functions."

Specifying Criteria in the WHERE Clause

You usually don't want to retrieve all the rows in a table, particularly if the table has many rows. SQL provides a WHERE clause in which you specify the criteria to be used for retrieving records.

A WHERE clause consists of one or more conditions that must be satisfied before a row is retrieved by the query. For example, if you want a list of freshmen attending Flugle College, you would specify Year = 'FRESHMAN' in the WHERE clause, as shown in Listing 5.7.

INPUT/OUTPUT **Listing 5.7. Specifying a criterion in a WHERE clause.**

```
SQL> select Last_Name, First_Name, Street_Address
  2  from Student
  3  where
  4  Year = 'FRESHMAN';

LAST_NAME                    FIRST_NAME                  STREET_ADDRESS
--------------------------   ------------------------    ------------------
SMYTHE                       JACKSON                     144 OLIVE AVE.
REYNOLDS                     PAULA                       7493 MAPLE ST.
TANAKA                       JEFFREY                     838 PECAN RD.
MALLARD                      HENRY                       123 WALNUT DR.
POSEN                        HUGO                        9100 MAPLE ST.
CLAUSEN                      THOMAS                      901 BIRCH RD.
GOMEZ                        LINDA                       9391 MAPLE ST.
MASSEY                       RICHARD                     431 PINE AVE.
ANASTATIA                    ANNA                        831 BIRCH RD.
HOLMES                       IVAN                        221 OLIVE AVE.

10 rows selected.
```

5

Combining Conditions with AND and OR

You can use the keywords AND and OR to combine multiple conditions that need to be satisfied in a query. For example, to see a list of sophomores whose street address contains the string ASH, you would use something like Listing 5.8 to specify both conditions in the WHERE clause.

INPUT/ OUTPUT **Listing 5.8. Using AND to combine query criteria.**

```
SQL> select Last_Name, First_Name, Street_Address
  2  from Student
  3  where
  4  Year = 'SOPHOMORE' and
  5  Street_Address like '%ASH%';


LAST_NAME                  FIRST_NAME                 STREET_ADDRESS
-----------------------    -----------------------    ----------------------
GORDON                     IVY                        544 ASH ST.
JACKEL                     LINDA                      493 ASH ST.
DEURRE                     PIERRE                     555 ASH ST.
PINKWATER                  PETER                      533 ASH ST.
```

Notice the word LIKE in the fourth line of the preceding example. This operator is one of SQL's most powerful tools.

SYNTAX

The basic syntax for using the LIKE operator is as follows:

column_name LIKE *'pattern'*

The variables are defined as follows:

> *column_name* is a valid column in the table referenced in the FROM clause.

> *pattern* is a string pattern for which you are searching.

The % serves as a wildcard in this context; it is the equivalent of zero or more characters. The _ (underscore) is used to signify a placeholder of any single character.

NOTE

> In the examples that follow, the keyword NULL is all uppercase. I've used uppercase to emphasize the word, but it isn't mandatory; you can use whatever case you choose with any of the Oracle SQL reserved words.

Sorting Data in the ORDER BY Clause

The ORDER BY clause designates which columns should be used to order the rows that are returned by the query. The ORDER BY clause is optional, but remember this: The order in which rows are returned by a query is *always* arbitrary (whether the table has been indexed or not). Therefore, you'll usually want to specify an ORDER BY clause in a SELECT statement.

For example, you might want a list of instructors at Flugle College sorted first by Department ID and then by instructor last and first names, as shown in Listing 5.9.

INPUT/OUTPUT **Listing 5.9. Ordering retrieved rows by multiple columns.**

```
SQL> select Department_ID, Last_Name, First_Name
  2  from Instructor
  3  order by Department_ID, Last_Name, First_Name;

DEPARTMENT_ID           LAST_NAME                 FIRST_NAME
-------------------     ---------------------     -------------------------
ANTHRO                  DANIELS                   LAURA
ANTHRO                  HITCHCOCK                 BORIS
BIO                     EDWARDS                   SAMANTHA
BIO                     WEISS                     ROBERTA
ECON                    PARKER                    WILLIAM
ENG                     CHU                       STEVEN
ENGL                    CHERNOW                   BESS
HIST                    RESTON                    RAPHAEL
HIST                    TORRES                    PETER
MATH                    CHANG                     ROGER
MATH                    NILAND                    MARTINA
MATH                    YOUNG                     ALLAN
PHILO                   ANGELO                    ARTHUR
PHILO                   BILLINGS                  BENJAMIN
PHILO                   RICHARDSON                NANCY
PSYCH                   BATES                     JOSEPH
PSYCH                   JASON                     JERROLD

17 rows selected.
```

NOTE

You can specify columns in an ORDER BY clause even if they aren't selected from the table, as shown in this example:

```
select Last_Name
from Instructor
order by Position
```

You also can specify columns in the ORDER BY clause regardless if the column is part of an index on the table or not.

By default, Oracle orders the rows in ascending order. To order the rows in descending order, you must add the keyword DESC (for descending) after the column name. You can specify ascending columns and descending columns in the same ORDER BY clause, as shown in Listing 5.10.

INPUT/ OUTPUT **Listing 5.10. Specifying descending order.**

```
SQL> select Department_ID, Last_Name, First_Name
  2  from Instructor
  3  order by Department_ID desc, Last_Name, First_Name;

DEPARTMENT_ID          LAST_NAME                        FIRST_NAME
-------------------    ------------------------         ------------------------
    PSYCH                  BATES                            JOSEPH
    PSYCH                  JASON                            JERROLD
    PHILO                  ANGELO                           ARTHUR
    PHILO                  BILLINGS                         BENJAMIN
    PHILO                  RICHARDSON                       NANCY
    MATH                   CHANG                            ROGER
    MATH                   NILAND                           MARTINA
    MATH                   YOUNG                            ALLAN
    HIST                   RESTON                           RAPHAEL
    HIST                   TORRES                           PETER
    ENGL                   CHERNOW                          BESS
    ENG                    CHU                              STEVEN
    ECON                   PARKER                           WILLIAM
    BIO                    EDWARDS                          SAMANTHA
    BIO                    WEISS                            ROBERTA
    ANTHRO                 DANIELS                          LAURA
    ANTHRO                 HITCHCOCK                        BORIS

17 rows selected.
```

Counting Rows in a Table

If you want to know how many rows in a table satisfy the specified criteria, but you really don't need to retrieve the rows themselves, you can use the COUNT function. COUNT returns a single row that reports the number of rows that satisfy the specified criteria. Listing 5.11 is an example.

INPUT/ OUTPUT **Listing 5.11. Counting rows in a table.**

```
SQL> select count(*)
  2  from Instructor
  3  where
  4  Position = 'ASSOCIATE PROFESSOR';
```

```
COUNT(*)
---------
        7
```

NOTE

> COUNT is a group function (which you will learn more about on Day 8, "More Sophisticated Queries with SQL"). The asterisk instructs Oracle to return all rows that satisfy the criteria. Instead of the asterisk, you can specify a column name, but if you do, Oracle returns only those rows where the specified column name has been assigned a value (in other words, rows where the column isn't null).

Finding Rows Where a Column Value Is NULL

One major difference between RDBMSs (Relational Database Management System) and older DBMS (Database Management System) technology is the concept of the null value. In non-relational database systems, a special value is used to indicate the absence of a value in a character or numeric field.

In a relational database, a NULL value for a column represents different things:

☐ A value for this column is not applicable for the row in question.

☐ The column has not yet been assigned a value. (For example, a student may not have a fax machine.)

If you want to retrieve records from a table where a specific column value isn't defined, you can specify the criteria in the WHERE clause. Listing 5.12 is a query that returns the names of students who do not have a fax number.

INPUT/OUTPUT   **Listing 5.12. Retrieving rows in which a column is NULL.**

```
SQL> select Last_Name, First_Name
  2  from Student
  3  where
  4  Fax is null;

LAST_NAME                  FIRST_NAME
-----------------------    -----------------------
SMYTHE                     JACKSON
HAN                        COREY
```

continues

Listing 5.12. continued

REYNOLDS	PAULA
PARKER	FREDERICK
TANAKA	JEFFREY
COEN	JOSEPH
NEWTON	ELEANOR
PURCELL	STEVEN
JACKEL	LINDA
ROSEN	ROSEMARY
MALLARD	HENRY
GUSSEY	LISA
MICHAELS	MARCUS
DEURRE	PIERRE
WONG	LE-MING
ABBOT	KENNETH
POSEN	HUGO
GOMEZ	LINDA
MASSEY	RICHARD
FERGUSON	RALPH
BING	RUDOLPH
ANASTATIA	ANNA
CHIN	MICHAEL
HOLMES	IVAN
PLOWCHARD	CATHERINE
FERNANDEZ	PAUL
PINKWATER	PETER
MABEISI	ANTON

28 rows selected.

You also can use the NOT operator to retrieve rows whose column values are not NULL. For example, you can count the number of students with fax numbers with the query in Listing 5.13.

**INPUT/
OUTPUT** **Listing 5.13. Retrieving rows in which a column is not NULL.**

```
SQL> select Last_Name, First_Name
  2  from Student
  3  where
  4  Fax is not null;
```

LAST_NAME	FIRST_NAME
GORDON	IVY
CLAUSEN	THOMAS
JACKSON	ROBERT

You should be aware of how NULL values are processed by arithmetic operations. To see how a NULL value differs from a value of zero, look at Listing 5.14. Suppose you have a table named Intelligence that has two columns—Last_Name and IQ.

5

INPUT/OUTPUT   **Listing 5.14. Retrieving all values of last name and IQ.**

```
SQL> select Last_Name, IQ
  2  from Intelligence;

LAST_NAME                          IQ
------------------------   ----------
SMITH                             100
GORDON                            125
JONES                             150
WILSON
RICHARDS
```

It so happens that IQ is NULL for Wilson and Richards. If you want to see the average IQ for the records in the Intelligence table, enter the query in Listing 5.15.

INPUT/OUTPUT   **Listing 5.15. Selecting the average IQ for non-NULL values of IQ.**

```
SQL> select avg(IQ) from Intelligence;

   AVG(IQ)
---------
       125
```

As you can see, the rows containing the NULL value for IQ were not used to compute the average IQ. Oracle computed the average IQ by calculating (100 + 125 + 150) / 3. If you change the NULL values to 0, the results are different, as shown in Listing 5.16.

NOTE   To change the column values in a table, you use the UPDATE statement. You will learn more about this on Day 6.

INPUT/OUTPUT   **Listing 5.16. Setting IQ to zero where it is currently NULL.**

```
SQL> update Intelligence
  2  set IQ = 0
  3  where
  4  IQ is NULL;

2 rows updated.

SQL> select Last_Name, IQ
```

continues

Listing 5.16. continued

```
  2  from Intelligence;

LAST_NAME                      IQ
------------------------- ----------
SMITH                         100
GORDON                        125
JONES                         150
WILSON                          0
RICHARDS                        0

SQL> select avg(IQ) from Intelligence;

  AVG(IQ)
---------
       75
```

Searching for Rows with the LIKE Operator

You have already seen an example of the use of the LIKE operator. Oracle users rely on the LIKE operator to search through a table when they're not sure of the exact spelling for the item they're interested in finding.

The benefactor of Flugle College, Reginald Flugle, established a scholarship fund for students whose last name contains the characters IN. As a result, the college registrar, Jean Smith, wants to notify all students whose last name contains this pattern that they may be eligible for this special scholarship. Listing 5.17 shows how she constructs a SELECT statement to find these students.

INPUT/
OUTPUT   **Listing 5.17. Using LIKE to search for a pattern.**

```
SQL> select Student_ID, Last_Name, First_Name
  2  from Student
  3  where
  4  Last_Name like '%IN%';

STUDENT_ID           LAST_NAME                FIRST_NAME
-------------------- ------------------------ ------------------------
10231318             BING                     RUDOLPH
10231304             CHIN                     MICHAEL
10231323             PINKWATER                PETER
```

Jean has been asked by the college president to prepare a list of courses whose description includes the word workshop. After pondering this problem for a while, Jean submits Listing 5.18 to Oracle.

**INPUT/
OUTPUT**

Listing 5.18. Retrieving courses in which the description contains the pattern workshop.

```
SQL> select Department_ID, Course_ID, Title
  2  from Course
  3  where
  4  Description like '%workshop%';
```

DEPARTMENT_ID	COURSE_ID	TITLE
ECON	189	MONETARY POLICY
PHILO	198	MODERN PHILOSOPHY
ECON	199	WORKSHOP ON MARX
HIST	199	WORKSHOP ON JEFFERSON
PSYCH	181	WORKSHOP ON NEUROSES

However, Jean realized that this query wouldn't include any course whose description started with the word Workshop because the first letter is a capital W. As a result, she modified the query as shown in Listing 5.19.

**INPUT/
OUTPUT**

Listing 5.19. Using the UPPER function for string comparison.

```
SQL> select Department_ID, Course_ID, Title
  2  from Course
  3  where
  4  upper(Description) like '%WORKSHOP%';
```

DEPARTMENT_ID	COURSE_ID	TITLE
ECON	189	MONETARY POLICY
PHILO	198	MODERN PHILOSOPHY
ECON	199	WORKSHOP ON MARX
HIST	199	WORKSHOP ON JEFFERSON
ENGL	193	SEMINAR ON THEME ANALYSIS
PSYCH	181	WORKSHOP ON NEUROSES

6 rows selected.

Jean was correct. Instead of returning only five records, the query now returns six records. By applying the UPPER function to the Description column, she was able to compare the contents of the column without worrying about whether the pattern was in uppercase or lowercase.

You can separate string patterns by the wildcard character, %, as shown in Listing 5.20.

5

INPUT/
OUTPUT **Listing 5.20. Using multiple wildcards.**

```
SQL> select Description
  2  from Course
  3  where
  4  upper(Description) like '%STUDY%BEHAVIOR%';

DESCRIPTION
-----------------------------------------------------------------
Discussion and field study of the strange behavior of the
➥Nacimera culture
```

Sometimes you really want to search for a string that contains the % character. Normally, the % character, contained in single quotes, is interpreted by the Oracle RDBMS as a wildcard. You place the escape character before the character that you want the Oracle RDBMS to interpret literally. As shown in Listing 5.21, you want to retrieve course descriptions that contain the character %; therefore, you place \% between wildcards.

INPUT/
OUTPUT **Listing 5.21. Using an escape character to refer to a literal character.**

```
SQL> select Description
  2  from Course
  3  where
  4  Description like '%\%%' escape '\';

DESCRIPTION
-----------------------------------------------------------------
Learn about advanced operations such as % and logarithms.
```

This query uses the backslash character (\) to tell Oracle that the % that follows the \ should be interpreted literally. You can use the same method when you want to search for an underscore (_), rather than have it represent any single character.

Here are some suggestions for using the LIKE operator in your searches:

☐ Apply the UPPER or LOWER function to the column you're searching so that all characters are in the same case.

☐ If you're looking for records where a string occurs at the beginning of a column, don't use the wildcard character at the beginning of the pattern:

```
select Department_ID, Title_ID, Description
from Course
where
upper(Description) like 'SEMINAR%';
```

☐ Likewise, if you're looking for records where a string occurs at the end of a column, don't use the wildcard character at the end of the pattern:

```
select Department_ID, Title_ID, Description
from Course
where
upper(Description) like '%TOPICS';
```

Searching for Rows with the BETWEEN Operator

Earlier in this lesson, I explained that a SELECT statement can be structured in more than one way to obtain the same result. The BETWEEN operator is a good example of this flexibility.

The BETWEEN operator is an inclusive operator and is quite flexible; it works with numeric, string, and date values. For example, suppose that the current cost of a unit at Flugle College is $250. Because the cost of a course is the sum of the unit cost and any additional fees, the list of courses whose cost is between $760 and $800 can be derived from the query in Listing 5.22.

INPUT/OUTPUT **Listing 5.22. Using the BETWEEN operator.**

```
SQL> select Title, Units*250 + Additional_Fees
  2  from Course
  3  where
  4  (Units*250 + Additional_Fees) between 760 and 800;

TITLE                                     UNITS*250+ADDITIONAL_FEES
---------------------------------------   -------------------------
ADVANCED ARITHMETIC                                             760
INTRO TO PSYCHOLOGY                                             775
ABNORMAL PSYCHOLOGY                                             770
INTRO TO ECONOMICS                                             775
INTRO TO CIRCUIT THEORY                                        795
INTRO TO DYNAMICS                                              785

6 rows selected.
```

The preceding query is really the same as that shown in Listing 5.23.

INPUT/OUTPUT **Listing 5.23. Alternative to using the BETWEEN operator.**

```
SQL> select Title, Units*250 + Additional_Fees
  2  from Course
  3  where
  4  (Units*250 + Additional_Fees) >= 760 and
```

continues

5

Listing 5.23. continued

```
   5  (Units*250 + Additional_Fees) <= 800;

TITLE                                      UNITS*250+ADDITIONAL_FEES
---------------------------------------    ------------------------
ADVANCED ARITHMETIC                                             760
INTRO TO PSYCHOLOGY                                             775
ABNORMAL PSYCHOLOGY                                             770
INTRO TO ECONOMICS                                             775
INTRO TO CIRCUIT THEORY                                        795
INTRO TO DYNAMICS                                              785

6 rows selected.
```

As you can see, the BETWEEN operator is the equivalent of two conditions that are ANDed together. When used appropriately, the BETWEEN operator simplifies a query.

The IN Operator

Another operator that compares the value of a column or expression with a list of possible values is the IN operator.

The syntax for the IN operator is

```
expression IN (expression1, expression2, ... expressionN)
```

The variables are defined as follows:

   expression is a valid SQL expression.

   expression1 through *expressionN* is a list of valid SQL expressions.

The IN operator returns a Boolean value that is either TRUE or FALSE:

   TRUE if the expression is equal to one of the values in the expression list

   FALSE if the expression is not equal to one of the values in the expression list

As an example of how to use the IN operator, suppose you want to retrieve only those instructors in the math, anthropology, or psychology departments. If you have a long list of possible values to check, the IN operator saves you some typing and saves Oracle's SQL statement parser some processing time. Listing 5.24 shows the code.

INPUT/ OUTPUT **Listing 5.24. Using the IN operator.**

```
SQL> select Last_Name, First_Name, Department_ID
  2  from Instructor
  3  where
  4  Department_ID in ('MATH','ANTHRO','PSYCH');
```

LAST_NAME	FIRST_NAME	DEPARTMENT_ID
HITCHCOCK	BORIS	ANTHRO
DANIELS	LAURA	ANTHRO
CHANG	ROGER	MATH
JASON	JERROLD	PSYCH
YOUNG	ALLAN	MATH
NILAND	MARTINA	MATH
BATES	JOSEPH	PSYCH

7 rows selected.

The alternative to the IN operator is shown in Listing 5.25.

INPUT/ OUTPUT **Listing 5.25. Alternative to using the IN operator.**

```
SQL> select Last_Name, First_Name, Department_ID
  2  from Instructor
  3  where
  4  Department_ID = 'MATH' or
  5  Department_ID = 'ANTHRO' or
  6  Department_ID = 'PSYCH';
```

LAST_NAME	FIRST_NAME	DEPARTMENT_ID
HITCHCOCK	BORIS	ANTHRO
DANIELS	LAURA	ANTHRO
CHANG	ROGER	MATH
JASON	JERROLD	PSYCH
YOUNG	ALLAN	MATH
NILAND	MARTINA	MATH
BATES	JOSEPH	PSYCH

7 rows selected.

5

You can combine the keyword NOT with the IN operator so that a condition is true if an expression is not equal to any of the expressions in the expression list. See Listing 5.26.

Listing 5.26. Using the NOT IN operator.

```
SQL> select Last_Name, First_Name, Department_ID
  2  from Instructor
  3  where
  4  Department_ID not in ('MATH','ANTHRO','PSYCH');

LAST_NAME                 FIRST_NAME                DEPARTMENT_ID
----------------------    ----------------------    --------------------
EDWARDS                   SAMANTHA                  BIO
TORRES                    PETER                     HIST
ANGELO                    ARTHUR                    PHILO
RICHARDSON                NANCY                     PHILO
PARKER                    WILLIAM                   ECON
CHERNOW                   BESS                      ENGL
CHU                       STEVEN                    ENG
WEISS                     ROBERTA                   BIO
RESTON                    RAPHAEL                   HIST
BILLINGS                  BENJAMIN                  PHILO

10 rows selected.
```

If you choose not to use the NOT IN operator, you must list each value that the expression or column should not equal, "tied" together with the and logical operator. Listing 5.27 shows an example.

Listing 5.27. Alternative to using the NOT IN operator.

```
SQL> select Last_Name, First_Name, Department_ID
  2  from Instructor
  3  where
  4  Department_ID != 'MATH' and
  5  Department_ID != 'ANTHRO' and
  6  Department_ID != 'PSYCH';

LAST_NAME                 FIRST_NAME                DEPARTMENT_ID
----------------------    ----------------------    --------------------
EDWARDS                   SAMANTHA                  BIO
TORRES                    PETER                     HIST
ANGELO                    ARTHUR                    PHILO
RICHARDSON                NANCY                     PHILO
PARKER                    WILLIAM                   ECON
CHERNOW                   BESS                      ENGL
CHU                       STEVEN                    ENG
WEISS                     ROBERTA                   BIO
RESTON                    RAPHAEL                   HIST
BILLINGS                  BENJAMIN                  PHILO

10 rows selected.
```

5

Referencing Columns with an Alias

When you specify a complex expression in a select list, you can document what the expression represents by assigning an alias to it.

The syntax for a select list is as follows:

```
expression_name1 [ [AS] alias_name1], ... , expression_nameN
➥[ [AS] alias_nameN]
```

The variables are defined as follows:

> *expression_name* is an expression that references zero or more column names.
>
> *alias_name* is an alias used to reference *expression_name* in other parts of the SELECT statement.

Please note that the keyword AS is optional.

You can use the example in Listing 5.23 to illustrate how you can use an alias. To reiterate, the current cost of a course at Flugle College is $250 per unit plus any additional fees, which is expressed with the query in Listing 5.28.

INPUT/OUTPUT **Listing 5.28. Specifying an alias in a SELECT statement.**

```
SQL> select Title, Units*250 + Additional_Fees as Course_Cost
  2  from Course
  3  where
  4  Department_ID = 'ECON';

TITLE                                        COURSE_COST
-------------------------------------------- -----------
INTRO TO ECONOMICS                                   775
MONETARY POLICY                                     1500
WORKSHOP ON MARX                                     750
```

By assigning the alias Course_Cost to the expression Units*250 + Additional_Fees, you gain two benefits:

☐ You now have a name that accurately describes the expression.

☐ You can reference an alias in the ORDER BY clause.

How to Use a Subquery

A subquery is defined as a SELECT statement that appears in some other DML statement—another SELECT statement, an UPDATE statement, a DELETE statement, or an INSERT statement.

In a SELECT statement, a subquery is part of a condition in the WHERE clause. The following query selects the title of each course whose additional fees are less than or equal to the average additional fees for all courses:

```
select Title
from Course
where
Additional_Fees <=
(select avg(Additional_Fees) from Course)
```

You should be aware of several things when you use subqueries:

- ☐ The subquery must be enclosed in parentheses.

- ☐ The number of *rows* returned by the subquery must match the number of values that the function or operator expects. In the preceding example the <= operator expects a single value to compare against, and the AVG function (which is a group function) returns a single value.

- ☐ The number of *columns* returned by the subquery must match the number of columns that the function or operator expects.

- ☐ The ORDER BY clause is not used within a subquery.

Creating a New Table with the SELECT Statement

Let's look at a form of the CREATE TABLE statement that uses a query to specify the structure of the table to be created. You may find this statement to be handy during application development and testing.

If you wanted to experiment with the contents of a table—add, delete, and update various rows—you would be well advised to create a copy of the table that you want to experiment with. Suppose that the existing table is a list of customers for the past 10 years and contains many records—say 100,000—but you want only a subset of those rows for your experiment. Specifically, you are interested only in those customers who live in California. You can create a table containing a subset of all customers by combining the CREATE TABLE statement with the SELECT statement, as shown in Listing 5.29.

Listing 5.29. Creating a table from a subset of rows in another table.

```
SQL> create table Customer_Subset
  2  as
  3  select *
  4  from Customer
  5  where
  6  State = 'CA';

Table created.
```

SYNTAX

Now, look closely at the syntax:

```
CREATE TABLE new_table_name
AS
select_stmt
```

The variables are defined as follows:

> *new_table_name* is the name of the table to be created.
>
> *select_stmt* is a valid SELECT statement.

In addition, you can use the CREATE TABLE statement and the SELECT statement together for another purpose. If you want to create another table that has the same structure as an existing table—with all the same column definitions but none of the data—you can use the following statement:

```
CREATE TABLE my_new_empty_table
AS
SELECT *
FROM existing_table
WHERE
1 = 2
```

Now, you're probably saying, "1 is never equal to 2." That's right. And that's why none of the rows in *existing_table* are copied into *my_new_empty_table*. The new table has the same set of column definitions as *existing_table* but no data. You could use any false statement to accomplish the same thing.

Summary

Today's lesson introduced some basic facts about SQL:

- ☐ Data Manipulation Language (DML) is a category of the SQL language that consists of the SELECT, INSERT, UPDATE, and DELETE statements

- ☐ Every SELECT statement contains a select list and a FROM clause that identifies the table from which the records will be retrieved.

- ☐ Typically, the SELECT statement also includes a WHERE clause that specifies criteria that the rows returned by the SELECT statement must satisfy. Also, the ORDER BY clause is used to specify the columns that should be used to determine the order in which the rows are returned by the query.

- ☐ The results returned by every SELECT statement can be thought of as a temporary table.

- ☐ Always explicitly specify the columns to be retrieved in the SELECT statement.

5

What Comes Next?

On Day 6, you learn how to use the other DML statements—INSERT, UPDATE, and DELETE—to change the contents of a table. You will see how a SELECT statement can be referenced in the UPDATE and DELETE statements to determine which rows to affect.

Q&A

Q Can the BETWEEN operator also be used for both numeric and character expressions?

A Yes. You have already seen an example of how the BETWEEN operator is used with numeric expression. Listing 5.31 is an example of how the BETWEEN operator can be used with a character expression to obtain a list of course titles that are between the character values S and W. Notice that the query in Listing 5.31 won't return any titles that begin with the phrase Workshop because that is "above" W.

INPUT/ OUTPUT **Listing 5.31. Using the BETWEEN operator with strings.**

```
SQL> select Title
  2  from Course
  3  where
  4  Title between 'S' and 'W';

TITLE
--------------------------------------
SEMINAR ON CHAOS
SEMINAR ON NACIMERA
SEMINAR ON THEME ANALYSIS
```

Q What is the internal value that Oracle uses to store a NULL value for a record?

A Generally, you won't be able to "see" that value. Furthermore, you really don't need to know what that value is because you will only be able to test a column for a NULL value using the IS NULL and IS NOT NULL comparisons. Alternatively, you could use a built-in function, NVL, that has two arguments: the first argument is the column or expression to be evaluated, and the second argument is the value to be returned if the first argument is equal to NULL.

Workshop

The purpose of the Workshop is to allow you to test your knowledge of the material discussed in the lesson. See if you can correctly answer the questions in the quiz and complete the exercise before you continue with tomorrow's lesson.

Quiz

1. True or false? You must include a column in the select list if you want to sort the rows returned by the SELECT statement by that column.

2. What is wrong with this statement:

```
select First_Name
from Student
order by Last_Name
where
Last_Name like '%IN%';
```

3. True or false? A column must be indexed before it can be specified in the ORDER BY clause.

Exercise

Using the Course table that was discussed in this lesson, construct a SELECT statement that will return the Department ID, Course ID, and Course Title, sorted by Department ID and Course ID, for any course whose description contains the phrase introduc, regardless of capitalization.

5

Day 6

Using SQL to Modify Data

Day 5, "Introduction to Structured Query Language (SQL)," briefly talked about the Data Manipulation Language (DML) facet of SQL and delved into the use of the SELECT statement. The SELECT statement can look at only the contents of tables; it does not have the capability to create or modify data. This lesson explores the use of the three remaining DML statements—INSERT, UPDATE, and DELETE.

In the course of developing an Oracle application, you probably will use a "front-end" tool, such as Oracle Forms, Visual Basic, or PowerBuilder, in which the application development environment internally generates many INSERT, UPDATE, and DELETE statements. However, almost every application requires the development of scripts containing SQL statements. Also, you may need to write PL/SQL procedures and functions that contain these statements.

Another reason for learning how to use SQL to modify data is to transform or migrate data from another database into an Oracle database. To migrate legacy data, you have to develop a set of scripts that contain SQL statements to "scrub" the legacy data—for example, correct invalid codes or values—before the data is added to your Oracle database.

SQL Data-Manipulation Language

On Day 3, "Logical Database Design," you learned about the three perspectives of a database: the user perspective, the conceptual perspective, and the physical perspective. The best way to fully comprehend how SQL modifies data is to focus on the conceptual perspective. Think of only tables, columns, and rows, and you'll master SQL and Oracle more quickly. Initially, don't worry about how Oracle executes SQL statements; instead, concentrate on the purpose of the SQL statement.

Here's another helpful hint for successful use of DML. When you think about the effect of an SQL statement (INSERT, UPDATE, or DELETE), visualize a set of rows, rather than individual rows, being affected.

The first things that many programmers and developers want to learn about Oracle are the internal operating system file formats and special codes. However, this approach is wrong! Keep in mind the following:

☐ The format of the Oracle database files is proprietary to Oracle Corporation.

☐ These formats and codes are subject to change with each new Oracle release.

☐ Your application is easier to maintain if you rely on an industry standard such as SQL rather than any knowledge you have about the Oracle file formats. Doing so also simplifies porting an SQL application from Oracle to another RDBMS.

Adding Rows with INSERT

The INSERT statement adds rows to a table. You supply literal values or expressions to be stored as rows in the table.

NOTE

> The term INSERT leads some new SQL users to think they can control *where* a row is inserted in a table. Remember that a large reason for the use of relational databases is the logical data independence they offer—in other words, a table has no implied ordering. A newly inserted row simply goes into a table at an arbitrary location.

INSERT Syntax

The INSERT statement takes two forms. The first form is

```
INSERT INTO table_name
[(column_name[,column_name]...[,column_name])]
VALUES
(column_value[,column_value]...[,column_value])
```

6

The variables are defined as follows:

> *table_name* is the table in which to insert the row.
>
> *column_name* is a column belonging to *table_name*.
>
> *column_value* is a literal value or an expression whose type matches the corresponding *column_name*.

For instance, suppose you want to add a new course to the Course table. Listing 6.1 contains the INSERT statement used to accomplish this.

INPUT/OUTPUT

Listing 6.1. Example of an INSERT statement.

```
SQL> insert into Course
  2  (Course_ID, Department_ID, Title, Description, Units, Additional_Fees)
  3  values
  4  ('501', 'PSYCH', 'PSYCH IN FILM',
  5  'Seminar on the portrayal of psychologists and psychiatrists in film',
  6  3, 25);

1 row created.
```

Notice that the number of columns in the list of column names must match the number of literal values or expressions that appear in parentheses after the keyword VALUES. Listing 6.2 contains an example of what occurs if six columns are specified but only five literal values are supplied. If you specify more column names than values, Oracle returns an error message. Of course, Oracle has no way of knowing which column value is missing.

INPUT/OUTPUT

Listing 6.2. More columns specified than values supplied in an INSERT statement.

```
SQL> insert into Course
  2  (Course_ID, Department_ID, Title, Description, Units, Additional_Fees)
  3  values
  4  ('501', 'PSYCH', 'PSYCH IN FILM',
  5  3, 25);
values
*
ERROR at line 3:
ORA-00947: not enough values
```

Conversely, Listing 6.3 illustrates what occurs if you specify fewer column names than values.

6

Listing 6.3. Fewer columns specified than values supplied in an INSERT statement.

```
SQL> insert into Course
  2  (Course_ID, Department_ID, Title, Description, Units)
  3  values
  4  ('501', 'PSYCH', 'PSYCH IN FILM',
  5  'Seminar on the portrayal of psychologists and psychiatrists in film',
  6  3, 25);
values
*
ERROR at line 3:
ORA-00913: too many values
```

If a column name referenced in an INSERT statement is misspelled, Oracle returns an error message. In Listing 6.4, the column Units is misspelled as Unit.

Listing 6.4. Column name misspelled in an INSERT statement.

```
SQL> insert into Course
  2  (Course_ID, Department_ID, Title, Description, Unit)
  3  values
  4  ('501', 'PSYCH', 'PSYCH IN FILM',
  5  'Seminar on the portrayal of psychologists and psychiatrists in film',
  6  3);
(Course_ID, Department_ID, Title, Description, Unit)
                                               *
ERROR at line 2:
ORA-00904: invalid column name
```

 TIP

> If you execute an INSERT with a long list of column names and Oracle returns ORA-00947 or ORA-00913, it's your responsibility to do the dirty work of matching the list of column names with the list of values or expressions. If you check and still can't find the problem, try reducing the number of columns and values to isolate the problem.

Specifying Values in the INSERT Statement

Each column value supplied in an INSERT statement must be one of the following:

☐ A NULL

☐ A literal value, such as 3.14159 or "Radish"

☐ An expression containing operators and functions, such as SUBSTR(Last_Name,1,4)

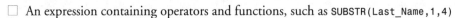

In an INSERT statement, you can mix literal values with expressions. Listing 6.5 demonstrates the use of an INSERT statement in which the additional fee for a course is specified as 10% of the number of units multiplied by $250 per unit.

**INPUT/
OUTPUT**

Listing 6.5. Using an expression in an INSERT statement.

```
SQL> insert into Course
  2 (Course_ID, Department_ID, Title, Description, Units, Additional_Fees)
  3 values
  4 ('501', 'PSYCH', 'PSYCH IN FILM',
  5 'Seminar on the portrayal of psychologists and psychiatrists in film',
  6 3, 0.10 * 3 * 250);

1 row created.

SQL> select Additional_Fees
  2 from Course
  3 where
  4 Course_ID = '501' and
  5 Department_ID = 'PSYCH';

ADDITIONAL_FEES
---------------
             75
```

Column and Value Datatype Must Match

With a few exceptions (which will be discussed), the datatypes for a column and its corresponding value must be identical. Inserting an alphanumeric string into a numeric column, for example, doesn't make any sense, as shown in Listing 6.6.

**INPUT/
OUTPUT**

Listing 6.6. Mismatch between column and value datatypes in an INSERT.

```
SQL> insert into Course
  2 (Course_ID, Department_ID, Title, Description, Units, Additional_Fees)
  3 values
  4 ('501', 'PSYCH', 'PSYCH IN FILM',
  5 'Seminar on the portrayal of psychologists and psychiatrists in film',
  6 3, 'Seventy-five dollars');
3, 'Seventy-five dollars')
   *
ERROR at line 6:
ORA-01722: invalid number
```

In the preceding example, Oracle returned an error code ORA-01722 because the string "Seventy-five dollars" cannot be stored in a column defined as a number. However, if the string is a valid number, the INSERT statement processes successfully, which is illustrated in Listing 6.7. This is an exception to the rule that a column and the value assigned to it must have the same datatype.

Listing 6.7. Conversion of a numeric value to a string in an INSERT.

INPUT/OUTPUT

```
SQL> insert into Course
  2  (Course_ID, Department_ID, Title, Description, Units, Additional_Fees)
  3  values
  4  ('501', 'PSYCH', 'PSYCH IN FILM',
  5  'Seminar on the portrayal of psychologists and psychiatrists in film',
  6  3, '75');

1 row created.
```

Another exception to this rule involves strings and dates. Refer to Listing 6.8 to see how a literal string that adheres to the Oracle default date format (*DD-MMM-YY*) can be inserted into a date column.

Listing 6.8. Inserting a date value with the default date format.

INPUT/OUTPUT

```
SQL> insert into Student_Schedule
  2  (Student_ID, Class_ID, Grade, Date_Grade_Assigned)
  3  values
  4  ('10231311', '104200', 'B', '02-JUN-97');

1 row created.
```

Although 02-JUN-97 is a string literal rather than a date literal, it can be assigned to Date_Grade_Assigned because it uses the default Oracle date format: *DD-MON-YY*.

Using Pseudocolumns as Values

Oracle provides a set of functions called *pseudocolumns*. Oracle named these functions "pseudocolumns" because to the uninitiated they appear to be columns. Two commonly used pseudocolumns are

USER	The Oracle user who is currently connected to the Oracle database
SYSDATE	The current date and time

You can use pseudocolumns in an INSERT statement to assign a value to a column. For instance, USER and SYSDATE can store the name of the Oracle user who created the row and the date and time when the row was inserted, as shown in Listing 6.9.

Listing 6.9. Using USER **and** SYSDATE **in an** INSERT.

```
SQL> insert into Student_Schedule
  2  (Student_ID, Class_ID, Grade, Date_Grade_Assigned,
  3  Created_Username, Created_Timestamp)
  4  values
  5  ('10231311', '104200', 'B', '02-JUN-97',
  6  USER, SYSDATE);

1 row created.
```

You can assign the pseudocolumn USER to a string column only. Similarly, you can assign the pseudocolumn SYSDATE to a date column only. You can manipulate these pseudocolumns by applying functions and operators. In Listing 6.10, a string literal is concatenated with the current user's name and stored in a string column—Created_Username.

Listing 6.10. Concatenating a pseudocolumn with a string literal.

```
SQL> insert into Student_Schedule
  2  (Student_ID, Class_ID, Grade, Date_Grade_Assigned,
  3  Created_Username, Created_Timestamp)
  4  values
  5  ('10231311', '104500', 'B-', '03-JUN-97',
  6  'User is: ' ¦¦ USER, SYSDATE);

1 row created.

SQL> select Student_ID, Grade, Created_Username, Created_Timestamp
  2  from Student_Schedule
  3  where
  4  Student_ID = '10231311' and
  5  Class_ID = '104500';

STUDENT_ID          GR CREATED_USERNAME              CREATED_T
------------------- -- ----------------------------- ---------
10231311            B- User is: TYO                  06-MAR-97
```

The INSERT statement specifies two pseudocolumns: USER and SYSDATE. The SELECT statement shows that USER and SYSDATE provided the expected values for the INSERT statement.

Why Columns Should Be Specified in an INSERT

If you look carefully at the syntax diagram for the INSERT statement in the online Oracle SQL Language Reference Manual, you'll notice that the column list is an optional element. Therefore, if you don't specify the column names to be assigned values, Oracle, by default, uses all the columns. In addition, the column order that Oracle uses is the order in which the columns were specified when the table was created; this order is the same order that you see when you apply the DESCRIBE command to a table in SQL*Plus.

As shown in Listing 6.11, if the column names are not specified in the INSERT statement, Oracle expects the first column to be the Class Building.

INPUT/OUTPUT

Listing 6.11. Danger of not specifying column names in an INSERT.

```
SQL> desc class_location
 Name                             Null?    Type
 ------------------------------   -------- ----
 CLASS_BUILDING                   NOT NULL VARCHAR2(25)
 CLASS_ROOM                       NOT NULL VARCHAR2(25)
 SEATING_CAPACITY                          NUMBER(38)

SQL> insert into Class_Location
  2  values
  3  ('250', 'MACLAREN COMPLEX', 500);

1 row created.

SQL> select Class_Building, Class_Room, Seating_Capacity
  2  from Class_Location
  3  where
  4  Class_Building = '250';

CLASS_BUILDING            CLASS_ROOM                 SEATING_CAPACITY
----------------------    ----------------------     ----------------
250                       MACLAREN COMPLEX           500
```

Because the column names were not specified in the INSERT statement, the value that was supposed to be stored in Class_Room, 250, looks fine—the row was successfully inserted into the table. However, the use of this syntax can be dangerous.

☐ The table definition might change; the number of columns might decrease or increase, and the INSERT fails as a result.

☐ The INSERT statement might be difficult to comprehend. The values might be indistinguishable from one another and, by accident, be transposed. Tracking down the problem without being able to visually match a column with its corresponding value is tricky.

☐ The INSERT statement might succeed, but the wrong data could be entered in the table. This situation can occur when two adjoining values with the same datatype are accidentally transposed. This scenario is the most serious of the potential dangers because Oracle might not return an error message to inform you that something is wrong.

6

Using a Subquery with INSERT

Up to this point, the examples have demonstrated how each execution of an INSERT statement can add a single row to a table. The following examples demonstrate how to perform an INSERT without specifying literal values.

INSERT Syntax with Subquery

The alternative form of the INSERT statement replaces the list of column values with a SELECT statement in the following way:

```
INSERT INTO table_name
[(column_name[,column_name]...[,column_name])]
select_statement
```

The variables are defined as follows:

> table_name is the table in which to insert the row.

> column_name is a column belonging to table_name.

> select_statement is a valid SELECT statement.

Assume that a table is used for storing information about instructors who no longer teach at Flugle College. As part of the centennial celebration at Flugle College, all previous instructors are being honored by being made active instructors.

NOTE

> Please note that the Inactive_Instructor table does not exist in the sample database. To add the inactive instructors to the Instructor table, use a subquery to select the rows from the Inactive_Instructor table and insert them into the Instructor table as demonstrated in Listing 6.12.

INPUT/ OUTPUT **Listing 6.12. Inserting rows with a subquery.**

```
SQL> insert into Instructor
  2  (Instructor_ID, Last_Name, First_Name, Department_ID)
  3  select Instructor_ID, Last_Name, First_Name, Department_ID
  4  from Inactive_Instructor;
5 rows created.
```

To use a subquery with an INSERT statement, the number of columns referenced in the INSERT statement must equal the number of items in the subquery's select list.

Generating Test Data

When you develop a database application, you need data to test the software. Developing a sizeable set of test data can be a tedious task. Fortunately, you can use the INSERT statement to duplicate and increase the size of the test data.

Listing 6.13 illustrates how you can use a subquery to copy the existing rows in a table to the same table. Suppose that the Instructor table initially contains 17 rows. If you perform an INSERT using a subquery that retrieves those 17 rows, your table grows to 34 rows. Of course, you can't successfully perform this insert unless you temporarily drop the primary key. If you perform the same INSERT once more, the Product table ends up with 68 rows. As you can see, the number of rows doubles each time you perform an INSERT.

Listing 6.13. Inserting rows into a table by copying the existing rows in the same table.

```
SQL> insert into Instructor
  2  (Instructor_ID, Department_ID, Last_Name)
  3  select Instructor_ID, Department_ID, Last_Name
  4  from Instructor;

17 rows created.
```

NOTE

If you use the copying technique to generate test data, the number of rows grows exponentially. If you start with 100 rows, the table will hold 12,800 rows after INSERT is performed seven times. If you don't perform a COMMIT after each INSERT, the rollback segments may not be able to store the uncommitted transaction and Oracle returns an error code of ORA-01653; the tablespace in which the rollback segments tried to allocate more space appears in the error message.

NEW TERM The COMMIT statement is used to permanently record all changes that the user has made to the database since the last COMMIT statement was issued or since the beginning of the database session, whichever is later.

NEW TERM The ROLLBACK statement is used to rescind all changes that the user has made to the database since the last COMMIT statement was issued or since the database session began, whichever is later.

Modifying Data with UPDATE

If you want to modify existing data in an Oracle database, you need use the UPDATE statement. With this statement, you can update zero or more rows in a table.

Basic Syntax of UPDATE

Like the INSERT statement, the syntax of the UPDATE statement is far simpler than that of the SELECT statement.

The UPDATE statement has the following syntax:

```
UPDATE table_name
SET column_name = expression [, column = expression] ...
                            [, column = expression]
[WHERE condition]
```

The variables are defined as follows:

> table_name is the table to be updated.
>
> column_name is a column in the table being updated.
>
> expression is a valid SQL expression.
>
> condition is a valid SQL condition.

As you can see, the UPDATE statement references a single table and assigns an expression to at least one column. The WHERE clause is optional; if an UPDATE statement doesn't contain a WHERE clause, the assignment of a value to a column will be applied to all rows in the table.

Changing the Value of More Than One Column

As the syntax for the UPDATE statement illustrates, an UPDATE statement can change the value for more than one column in a table. Listing 6.14 shows how an UPDATE statement assigns values to two columns: Position and Telephone.

INPUT/ OUTPUT

Listing 6.14. Changing the value of more than one column with an UPDATE.

```
SQL> update Instructor
  2  set
  3  Position = 'PROFESSOR',
  4  Telephone = '8055551212';

17 rows updated.
```

6

Think of Sets, Not Records

One way to demonstrate that SQL is set oriented is to look at an UPDATE statement that exchanges the values between two columns.

Listing 6.15 contains a query that selects the values for Instructor_ID, Telephone, and Fax that are currently in the Instructor table. You can swap the telephone and fax numbers in the Instructor table with a single UPDATE statement. You do not need to store the telephone and fax numbers in temporary variables as you would if you were using a programming language to swap these columns. The second query of the Instructor table shows that the swap of the two columns was successful.

INPUT/OUTPUT   **Listing 6.15. Illustration of the set-orientation of SQL.**

```
SQL> select Instructor_ID, Telephone, Fax
  2   from Instructor
  3   order by Instructor_ID;

INSTRUCTOR_ID         TELEPHONE   FAX
--------------------  ----------  ----------
A612
B331
B391
D201                  8055550131  8055559444
D944
E301
E405                  8055554455
E491
G331
J505
L391
M101                  8055550123  8055550321
R983
S131
T149
W490
Y561                  8055550123

17 rows selected.

SQL> update Instructor
  2   set
  3   Telephone = Fax,
  4   Fax = Telephone;

17 rows updated.

SQL> select Instructor_ID, Telephone, Fax
  2   from Instructor
  3   order by Instructor_ID;
```

```
INSTRUCTOR_ID          TELEPHONE  FAX
--------------------   ---------- ----------
A612
B331
B391
D201                   8055559444 8055550131
D944
E301
E405                              8055554455
E491
G331
J505
L391
M101                   8055550321 8055550123
R983
S131
T149
W490
Y561                              8055550123

17 rows selected.
```

Using a Subquery with an UPDATE

So far, this chapter has presented the use of conditions in the WHERE clause to restrict the rows that are affected by an UPDATE statement. Now look at how a subquery can be used with an UPDATE statement.

For example, suppose you want to reduce the additional fees for a course by $5 if the additional fees exceed the average additional fees. This can be done with a single UPDATE statement as shown in Listing 6.16. Notice that the subquery must be enclosed in parentheses.

**INPUT/
OUTPUT** **Listing 6.16. Using a subquery with an UPDATE.**

```
SQL> select Department_ID, Course_ID, Additional_Fees
  2  from Course
  3  order by Department_ID, Course_ID;

DEPART COURS ADDITIONAL_FEES
------ ----- ---------------
ANTHRO 101                 0
ANTHRO 174                55
ANTHRO 189               7.5
BIO    101                55
BIO    177                65
BIO    178                70
ECON   101                25
ECON   189               750
```

continues

Listing 6.16. continued

```
ECON   199                    0
ENG    101                   75
ENG    102                   45
ENG    103                   35
ENG    199                   45
ENGL   101                    0
ENGL   189                    0
ENGL   192                    0
ENGL   193                    0
HIST   115                    0
HIST   184                    0
HIST   199                    0
MATH   101                    0
MATH   189                    0
MATH   50                     0
MATH   51                    10
PHILO  101                    0
PHILO  174                    0
PHILO  198                    0
PSYCH  101                   25
PSYCH  181                   75
PSYCH  183                   45
PSYCH  185                   20
PSYCH  501                   75

32 rows selected.

SQL> update Course
  2  set Additional_Fees = Additional_Fees - 10
  3  where
  4  Additional_Fees >
  5  (select avg(Additional_Fees) from Course);

8 rows updated.

SQL> select Department_ID, Course_ID, Additional_Fees
  2  from Course
  3  order by Department_ID, Course_ID;

DEPART COURS ADDITIONAL_FEES
------ ----- ---------------
ANTHRO 101                 0
ANTHRO 174                45
ANTHRO 189               7.5
BIO    101                45
BIO    177                55
BIO    178                60
ECON   101                25
ECON   189               740
ECON   199                 0
ENG    101                65
ENG    102                45
ENG    103                35
ENG    199                45
```

```
ENGL    101                    0
ENGL    189                    0
ENGL    192                    0
ENGL    193                    0
HIST    115                    0
HIST    184                    0
HIST    199                    0
MATH    101                    0
MATH    189                    0
MATH    50                     0
MATH    51·                   10
PHILO   101                    0
PHILO   174                    0
PHILO   198                    0
PSYCH   101                   25
PSYCH   181                   65
PSYCH   183                   45
PSYCH   185                   20
PSYCH   501                   65

32 rows selected.
```

Throwing Out Data with the DELETE Statement

The DELETE statement removes rows from a table. You don't need to know the physical ordering of the rows in a table to perform a DELETE. Oracle uses the criteria in the WHERE clause to determine which rows to delete; the Oracle database engine determines the internal location of the rows.

DELETE Syntax

The DELETE statement has the simplest syntax of the four DML statements:

```
DELETE FROM table_name
[WHERE condition]
```

The variables are defined as follows:

   table_name is the table to be updated.

   condition is a valid SQL condition.

If you think that the SQL syntax is inconsistent, you're correct. For example, the syntax for the UPDATE statement (UPDATE *table_name*) differs from the syntax of the DELETE statement (DELETE FROM *table_name*). SQL has many other idiosyncrasies, and they aren't going to go away soon. If you want to take advantage of the power in SQL, concentrate on learning the syntax and working through a lot of examples. Listing 6.17 displays an example of a simple DELETE statement.

INPUT/ OUTPUT **Listing 6.17. Example of a DELETE statement.**

```
SQL> delete from Class
  2  where
  3  Department_ID = 'BIO';

1 row deleted.
```

NOTE

A DELETE statement will execute successfully, even if no rows are deleted from the table.

```
SQL> delete from Class
  2  where
  3  Department_ID = 'ANTHRO';

0 rows deleted.
```

Removing All Rows with the TRUNCATE TABLE Statement

In designing an application, you may need to delete all the rows in a table. If the table has many rows, using a DELETE to accomplish this task can be quite inefficient. As an alternative, you should consider using the TRUNCATE TABLE statement. The TRUNCATE TABLE statement deletes rows much faster than the DELETE statement does.

SYNTAX The TRUNCATE TABLE statement is typically used in the following way:

```
TRUNCATE TABLE table_name
```

The variable is defined as follows:

   table_name is the table to be truncated.

One caveat: the TRUNCATE TABLE statement is not a DML statement. Therefore, if you issue a TRUNCATE TABLE statement, you cannot change your mind and perform a rollback to recover the lost rows; the TRUNCATE TABLE statement is a one way trip.

Concurrency

An ideal information system provides concurrent access to multiple users. Of course, you also want to be sure that one user cannot step on another user's changes. For example, if one administrator in the anthropology department changes the description of a course, another administrator in the same department should not be able to change any information about the same course until the first administrator has committed her changes.

By the same token, the fact that an administrator in one department is changing information about a course offered by the department should not prevent anyone else from viewing the current information about that course or changing information about a different course.

Read Consistency and Read-Only Transactions

In a multiuser Oracle environment, Oracle provides what is termed "read consistency" at the SQL statement level. *Read consistency* means that a single SQL statement cannot return results that are contradictory or inconsistent. Listing 6.18 presents an example of this concept.

Suppose the chairperson of the biology department wants to know the number of units for each of the courses offered by the department.

INPUT/ OUTPUT **Listing 6.18. Example of read consistency.**

```
SQL> select Course_ID, Title, Units
  2  from Course
  3  where
  4  Department_ID = 'BIO'
  5  order by Course_ID;

COURSE_ID           TITLE                               UNITS
------------------- ------------------------------- ---------
101                 INTRO TO BIOLOGY                        3
177                 INVERTEBRATE ANATOMY                    3
178                 MAMMALIAN ANATOMY                       3
```

Just after the department head's query was submitted to the database, the college registrar updated all three-unit courses to four units. Statement-level consistency means that the query cannot return a row in which the number of units has been updated to four. Depending on when the college registrar commits her changes, the biology chairperson either sees the change or doesn't, but she will never see a partial change manifested in a single SQL statement.

However, even though Oracle provides consistency within a single SQL statement, its default behavior doesn't guarantee read consistency during more than one statement. If you query a table twice, you may obtain different results the second time if another Oracle user changes the table between your first and second queries.

You may encounter a situation in which you need more than single-statement read consistency. In fact, you may need to have read consistency across a particular transaction. For this purpose, you need to issue the following statement:

```
set transaction read only;
```

6

Setting a Column Value to NULL

The following are the various ways in which a column's value is set to NULL:

☐ The column is not assigned a value during an INSERT, and it has no default value.

☐ The column is explicitly assigned a NULL value during the INSERT.

☐ The column is explicitly set to NULL in an UPDATE.

Assigning a NULL During an INSERT

You can explicitly set a column to NULL in an INSERT statement as shown Listing 6.19.

INPUT/OUTPUT **Listing 6.19. Setting a column value to NULL in an INSERT.**

```
SQL> insert into Instructor
  2  (Instructor_ID, Department_ID, Last_Name, Telephone)
  3  values
  4  ('P331', 'ANTHRO', 'POULSON', NULL);

1 row created.
```

Setting a Column to NULL with an UPDATE

You can use the UPDATE statement to set a column's value to NULL. Listing 6.20 presents an example. After you have set the telephone number for Instructor ID Y561 to NULL, you can verify that Oracle has indeed made the change.

INPUT/OUTPUT **Listing 6.20. Setting a column value to NULL in an UPDATE.**

```
SQL> select Last_Name, Telephone
  2  from Instructor
  3  where
  4  Instructor_ID = 'Y561';

LAST_NAME                     TELEPHONE
------------------------      ----------
YOUNG                         8055550123

SQL> update Instructor
  2  set
  3  Telephone = NULL
  4  where
  5  Instructor_ID = 'Y561';

1 row updated.

SQL> select Last_Name, Telephone
  2  from Instructor
```

```
   3   where
   4   Instructor_ID = 'Y561';

LAST_NAME                    TELEPHONE
----------------------       ----------
YOUNG
```

One of the complaints about SQL is its inconsistent syntax. In the UPDATE statement, a NULL value is assigned to a column with the equal sign, (=). However, in the WHERE clause of a SELECT statement, use the word IS (or IS NOT) rather than an equal sign to test for a NULL value for a column. Therefore, you can wind up with UPDATE statements that look like what is shown in Listing 6.21.

INPUT/OUTPUT **Listing 6.21. Illustration of confusing SQL syntax.**

```
SQL> update Student
   2   set Fax = NULL
   3   where
   4   Fax is not null;

3 rows updated.
```

Default Values and NULL

When you create a table, specify a column as mandatory by adding NOT NULL after you name the column's datatype. A mandatory column must be assigned a value each time a row is inserted into a table. If you try to insert a row without specifying a value for a mandatory column, Oracle returns an error message. For instance, every course at Flugle College must have a Course ID, be associated with a particular department, and have a title. Listing 6.22 contains an INSERT statement that attempts to add a row to the Course table without specifying a value for the Title column, which is defined as NOT NULL.

INPUT/OUTPUT **Listing 6.22. Value not specified for a mandatory column in an INSERT.**

```
SQL> insert into Course
   2   (Course_ID, Department_ID)
   3   values
   4   ('901', 'ANTHRO');
insert into Course
            *
ERROR at line 1:
ORA-01400: mandatory (NOT NULL) column is missing or NULL during insert
```

6

Unfortunately, Oracle doesn't indicate the mandatory column (or columns) that need to be referenced in the INSERT statement. When you see an ORA-01400 error code, you have to compare the column list in the INSERT statement with the table definition.

A Transaction Is a Logical Unit of Work

Another powerful concept that you need to master is the transaction.

 A *transaction* is defined as a logical unit of work—a set of database changes to one or more tables that accomplishes a defined task.

A transaction begins after a COMMIT statement, a ROLLBACK statement, or an initial Oracle connection. A transaction ends when any of the following events occurs:

- ☐ A COMMIT statement is processed.
- ☐ A ROLLBACK statement is processed.
- ☐ The Oracle connection is terminated.

For example, suppose that Flugle College wants to increase the units for all courses by 50 percent. This can be accomplished with a single UPDATE statement that affects all the rows in the Course table.

Saving Work with COMMIT

You can think of a transaction as a change you make in a document using your favorite word processor. You may make several changes and either undo them or exit the program without saving the changes. When you instruct the word processor to save the file, you are permanently changing the file stored on disk.

Committing a transaction is similar to saving a file in Microsoft Word. The COMMIT statement commits a transaction. The COMMIT statement makes permanent all the database changes made since the execution of the previous COMMIT (or ROLLBACK). You can COMMIT only the database changes that you personally have made; the COMMIT statement that one user issues has no effect on another user's database changes.

Undoing Changes with ROLLBACK

Similarly, the ROLLBACK statement does the same thing that an Undo command does in a word processor, with one major exception: the ROLLBACK statement will undo all database changes made by the user since the last committed transaction or since the beginning of the session.

Look at the interplay between COMMIT and ROLLBACK. Listing 6.23 illustrates this concept. A simple query from table_1 returns four rows. If you delete the rows from table_1 and then query table_1 after you delete them, the query returns no rows. If you issue a ROLLBACK and query the table again, you see that the table is restored to the state in which it existed before you issued the DELETE statement.

Listing 6.23. Demonstration of COMMIT **and** ROLLBACK.

```
SQL> select * from table_1;
TABLE_1_COL
-----------
         99
         99
         99
         99

SQL> delete from table_1;
4 rows deleted.
SQL> select * from table_1;
no rows selected

SQL> rollback;
Rollback complete.
SQL> select * from table_1;
TABLE_1_COL
-----------
         99
         99
         99
         99
```

NOTE

Oracle performs an automatic commit for DDL statements such as CREATE TABLE. Also, any changes you make to the database are automatically committed after you enter a DDL statement. A ROLLBACK statement does not remove a table created via a CREATE TABLE statement. If you want to eliminate a table, you must use the DROP TABLE statement.

Savepoints

For transactions that involve the execution of multiple SQL statements, you might want to consider using *savepoints* as intermediate steps for the transaction. A savepoint is a label within a transaction that contains a subset of the changes made by the transaction. Listing 6.24 demonstrates how a savepoint is declared; you name a savepoint null_fax_numbers.

NEW TERM

You can think of a *savepoint* as a label within a transaction that references a subset of a transaction's changes.

Listing 6.24. Declaring a savepoint.

```
SQL> savepoint null_fax_numbers;
Savepoint created.
```

You use a savepoint along with a ROLLBACK statement; the savepoint gives you the option of rolling back a transaction to an intermediate point (a savepoint).

SYNTAX

The syntax for the ROLLBACK statement is

```
ROLLBACK [TO savepoint];
```

The variable is defined as follows:

savepoint is a previously named savepoint.

Consider the example shown in Listing 6.25. Imagine that your application has a transaction that updates three tables: table_1, table_2, and table_3. If Oracle returns an error on the update to table_2, you can roll back to the first savepoint, which is table_1_update.

INPUT/OUTPUT **Listing 6.25. Sample use of a savepoint.**

```
SQL> update table_1
  2   set table_1_col = 11;
4 rows updated.

SQL> savepoint table_1_update;
Savepoint created.

SQL> delete from table_2;
3 rows deleted.

SQL> rollback to table_1_update;
Rollback complete.

SQL> select * from table_2;
TABLE_2_COL
-----------
         99
         99
         99
```

You should use savepoints with care, however, because they add an additional layer of complexity to an application. Be sure that your transactions are well defined before you decide to implement savepoints.

Summary

Today's lesson discussed the use of these fundamental SQL statements:

- [ ] INSERT adds rows to a table.
- [ ] UPDATE modifies existing rows.
- [ ] DELETE removes rows from a table.

You can also use a subquery in conjunction with these statements.

The TRUNCATE statement irreversibly deletes all rows in a table.

A database transaction is a set of changes to one or more database tables, which constitutes a logical unit of work. You use the COMMIT statement to make the transaction permanent. Alternatively, you use the ROLLBACK statement to rescind the transaction.

What Comes Next?

On Day 7, "Taking Advantage of SQL Built-In Functions," you learn how to use a variety of functions in the four SQL statements—SELECT, INSERT, UPDATE, and DELETE.

Q&A

Q What is the syntax to indicate the beginning of a transaction?

A Typically, none. By default, a transaction begins with any change to any table since the last committed transaction or since the beginning of the database session— whichever is later. However, you must use the SET TRANSACTION READ ONLY to indicate the start of a read-only transaction.

Workshop

The purpose of the Workshop is to allow you to test your knowledge of the material discussed in the lesson. See if you can correctly answer the questions in the quiz and complete the exercise before you continue with tomorrow's lesson.

Quiz

1. Construct an SQL statement that adds a course with the following characteristics: Department ID = BIO, Course ID = 137, Title = INSECT BEHAVIOR, Description = In-depth study of insect societies and their behavior patterns, Units = 3, no additional fees.

2. Construct an SQL statement that charges $50 in additional fees for all courses in the philosophy department.

3. Construct an SQL statement that eliminates a scheduled class if it is offered by the English department or is going to be held in Flugle Hall.

6

Exercise

Several of the instructors at Flugle College have decided to create a new department called Integrated Studies. As a result, the English, History, and Philosophy departments will merge to become the Integrated Studies department. The department ID for this new department will be INTSTD. In the database, create the Integrated Studies department (without deleting the existing departments). Also, modify the contents of the Instructor table so that instructors in the English, History, and Philosophy department are now associated with the Integrated Studies department.

6

Day **7**

Taking Advantage of SQL Built-In Functions

This lesson examines the techniques that Oracle provides for manipulating strings, dates, and numbers. These techniques are useful in the following situations:

- ☐ Transforming strings from one form to another in a database application
- ☐ Generating reports
- ☐ Performing ad hoc queries
- ☐ Converting data from one database to another

Oracle provides an extensive set of built-in functions and operators for the conversion and manipulation of strings, dates, and numbers. The true power of these functions and operators is realized by nesting these functions within each other. This lesson presents several examples of this technique.

Manipulating Strings

Oracle provides several useful built-in functions that can be used to manipulate strings. You'll see a number of examples in the following pages.

Finding the Length of a String

You can use the LENGTH function to find the length of a string column. LENGTH returns a number equal to the number of characters in the argument, as shown in Listing 7.1.

INPUT/OUTPUT **Listing 7.1. Using the LENGTH function.**

```
SQL> select Last_Name, length(Last_Name)
  3   order by Last_Name;

LAST_NAME                      LENGTH(LAST_NAME)
------------------------       -----------------
ANGELO                                         6
BATES                                          5
BILLINGS                                       8
CHANG                                          5
CHERNOW                                        7
CHU                                            3
DANIELS                                        7
EDWARDS                                        7
HITCHCOCK                                      9
JASON                                          5
NILAND                                         6
PARKER                                         6
POULSON                                        7
RESTON                                         6
RICHARDSON                                    10
TORRES                                         6
WEISS                                          5
YOUNG                                          5

18 rows selected.
```

Extracting a Substring from a String

The SUBSTR function extracts a substring from a string.

The SUBSTR function is used in the following way:

SUBSTR (*string, starting character, number of characters*)

The variables are defined as follows:

string is a character column or string expression.

starting character is the starting position of the substring.

number of characters is the number of characters to return.

Listing 7.2 illustrates the use of the SUBSTR function to obtain the first four characters of the instructor's last name.

INPUT/OUTPUT

Listing 7.2. Using the SUBSTR function.

```
SQL> select Last_Name, substr(Last_Name,1,4)
  2  from Instructor
  3  order by Last_Name;

LAST_NAME                        SUBS
------------------------        ----
ANGELO                          ANGE
BATES                           BATE
BILLINGS                        BILL
CHANG                           CHAN
CHERNOW                         CHER
CHU                             CHU
DANIELS                         DANI
EDWARDS                         EDWA
HITCHCOCK                       HITC
JASON                           JASO
NILAND                          NILA
PARKER                          PARK
POULSON                         POUL
RESTON                          REST
RICHARDSON                      RICH
TORRES                          TORR
WEISS                           WEIS
YOUNG                           YOUN

18 rows selected.
```

In addition to using literal values in the SUBSTR function, you can use a function as an argument in the SUBSTR function. Listing 7.3 provides a good, although not very useful, example. Suppose you want to retrieve the last three characters of an instructor's last name. You would use the LENGTH function to find the last character position. To determine the correct starting character for the SUBSTR function, you subtract $n - 1$ from LENGTH, where n is the number of characters that you want to retrieve—in Listing 7.3, $3 - 1 = 2$.

INPUT/OUTPUT

Listing 7.3. Using the LENGTH function within the SUBSTR function.

```
SQL> select substr(Last_Name,length(Last_Name)-2,3)
  2  from Instructor
  3  order by Last_Name;

SUB
---
```

7

continues

Listing 7.3. continued

```
ELO
TES
NGS
ANG
NOW
CHU
ELS
RDS
OCK
SON
AND
KER
SON
TON
SON
RES
ISS
UNG

18 rows selected.
```

Finding Patterns in a String

You learned how to use the LIKE operator on Day 5, "Introduction to Structured Query Language (SQL)." As a quick review, you can use the LIKE operator to search for patterns in string expressions. In fact, you can perform very specific searches with carefully constructed patterns.

Listing 7.4 illustrates how to use the LIKE operator if you want to retrieve all rows in which a course description contains the pattern theory or theories.

| INPUT/
OUTPUT | **Listing 7.4. Using the LIKE operator.** |

```
SQL> column description format a40 word_wrapped
SQL> column title format a35
SQL> select Title, Description
  2  from Course
  3  where
  4  Description like '%theory%' or
  5  Description like '%theories%';

TITLE                                DESCRIPTION
-----------------------------        ----------------------------------------
NUMBER THEORY                        Introduction to number theory;
                                     characteristics of natural, rational,
                                     and irrational numbers; survey of lucky
                                     numbers
```

INTRO TO PSYCHOLOGY	A general introduction to the theory of human psychology. Topics include Freudian theory, theory of behavior, psychological development of the child, and other topics.
INTRO TO ECONOMICS	A general introduction to the "dismal" science of economics. Topics include supply and demand, the theory of money, theories of production, and other relevant topics.
INTRO TO STRUCTURES	A general introduction to the theory of mechanical structures including levers, gears, beams, and others.
MODERN PHILOSOPHY	A workshop on recent philosophical debates including bioethics, communication theory, social net theory, and philosophical relativism.
INTRO TO CIRCUIT THEORY	A general introduction to the theory of circuits, logical design, boolean theory, and other topics.
INTRO TO DYNAMICS	Introduction to the theory of dynamic systems, both linear and nonlinear.
SEMINAR ON CHAOS	Seminar will explore examples of chaos theory as applied to economic, biological, and physical systems. Class schedule TBD.
EVOLUTIONARY GRAMMAR	Seminar on current trends in English grammar. Topics include apostrophe theory and plurality.
WORKSHOP ON NEUROSES	Intense workshop on the development and perfection of various neuroses. Exploration of neuroses-psychoses transition theories.

10 rows selected.

Please note that the first two lines in Listing 7.4 are SQL*Plus commands. They were used to format the query output for this book.

Replacing a Portion of a String

A common data-manipulation task is transforming one pattern into another in a particular column. Suppose you wanted to change the course description in the Course table so that all descriptions that included the word seminar were replaced with the word discussion.

7

Fortunately, Oracle provides a function, REPLACE, that is used to manipulate a column by replacing one string with another string.

SYNTAX

The syntax for the REPLACE function is

REPLACE (*string*, *existing_string*, [*replacement_string*])

The variables are defined as follows:

> *string* is a string expression.
>
> *existing_string* is a string that might occur in *string*.
>
> *replacement_string* is an optional string with which to replace *existing_string*.

Listing 7.5 demonstrates how REPLACE can be used to change a course title in the Course table. First, a query displays the current course titles. An UPDATE statement is used with the REPLACE function to change occurrences of SEMINAR to DISCUSSION. Another query shows the effect of the UPDATE statement.

INPUT/OUTPUT **Listing 7.5. Using the REPLACE function.**

```
SQL> select Title
  2   from Course
  3   order by Title;

TITLE
----------------------------------
ABNORMAL PSYCHOLOGY
ADVANCED ARITHMETIC
ANCIENT GREEK PHILOSOPHERS
EARLY AMERICAN HISTORY
EVOLUTIONARY GRAMMAR
GENERAL CALCULUS
INTRO TO ANTHROPOLOGY
INTRO TO BIOLOGY
INTRO TO CIRCUIT THEORY
INTRO TO DYNAMICS
INTRO TO ECONOMICS
INTRO TO ENGLISH LIT
INTRO TO PHILOSOPHY
INTRO TO PSYCHOLOGY
INTRO TO STRUCTURES
INVERTEBRATE ANATOMY
MAMMALIAN ANATOMY
MODERN ENGLISH LIT
MODERN EUROPEAN HISTORY
MODERN PHILOSOPHY
MONETARY POLICY
NUMBER THEORY
PHYS ANTHRO FIELD TECHNIQUES
PRE-CALCULUS
PSYCH IN FILM
```

```
SEMINAR ON CHAOS
SEMINAR ON NACIMERA
SEMINAR ON THEME ANALYSIS
WORKSHOP ON JEFFERSON
WORKSHOP ON MARX
WORKSHOP ON NEUROSES
WORKSHOP ON NORMALITY

32 rows selected.

SQL> update Course
  2  set Title = replace(Title,'SEMINAR','DISCUSSION');

32 rows updated.

SQL> select Title
  2  from Course
  3  order by Title;

TITLE
----------------------------------
ABNORMAL PSYCHOLOGY
ADVANCED ARITHMETIC
ANCIENT GREEK PHILOSOPHERS
DISCUSSION ON CHAOS
DISCUSSION ON NACIMERA
DISCUSSION ON THEME ANALYSIS
EARLY AMERICAN HISTORY
EVOLUTIONARY GRAMMAR
GENERAL CALCULUS
INTRO TO ANTHROPOLOGY
INTRO TO BIOLOGY
INTRO TO CIRCUIT THEORY
INTRO TO DYNAMICS
INTRO TO ECONOMICS
INTRO TO ENGLISH LIT
INTRO TO PHILOSOPHY
INTRO TO PSYCHOLOGY
INTRO TO STRUCTURES
INVERTEBRATE ANATOMY
MAMMALIAN ANATOMY
MODERN ENGLISH LIT
MODERN EUROPEAN HISTORY
MODERN PHILOSOPHY
MONETARY POLICY
NUMBER THEORY
PHYS ANTHRO FIELD TECHNIQUES
PRE-CALCULUS
PSYCH IN FILM
WORKSHOP ON JEFFERSON
WORKSHOP ON MARX
WORKSHOP ON NEUROSES
WORKSHOP ON NORMALITY

32 rows selected.
```

7

NOTE

> If you don't specify a replacement string in the REPLACE function, the existing string will be removed from the column.

Trimming a String

If a character column contains leading or trailing spaces, a query based on a specified value for the column might return misleading results. To illustrate this point, take a look at Listing 7.6. First, an UPDATE statement is used to add a trailing space to First_Name. A query of the Instructor table for instructors whose first name is BORIS doesn't return any records, but a second query looking for a first name equal to 'BORIS ' returns the row that was modified.

INPUT/ OUTPUT **Listing 7.6. Dealing with trailing spaces.**

```
SQL> update Instructor
  2   set First_Name = First_Name || ' ';

18 rows updated.

SQL> select Instructor_ID, Last_Name, First_Name
  2   from Instructor
  3   where
  4   First_Name = 'BORIS';

no rows selected

SQL> select Instructor_ID, Last_Name, First_Name
  2   from Instructor
  3   where
  4   First_Name = 'BORIS ';

INSTRUCTOR_ID        LAST_NAME                        FIRST_NAME
-------------------  -------------------------------  ------------------------
M101                 HITCHCOCK                        BORIS
```

Of course, if you hadn't been aware of the trailing space, you would have been surprised by the fact that no rows were returned by the query.

TIP

> To avoid misleading query results, remove leading and trailing spaces before a row is added to a table or modified. Trailing spaces are far more common a problem than leading spaces because they aren't as obvious.

Oracle provides two functions for trimming spaces: LTRIM and RTRIM. LTRIM removes leading spaces in a string, and RTRIM trims a string's trailing spaces.

To trim leading and trailing spaces from a string, simply embed the RTRIM function inside the LTRIM function. If no leading or trailing spaces occur, LTRIM and RTRIM won't modify the existing string. Refer to Listing 7.7 to see how the RTRIM function is used.

INPUT/ OUTPUT **Listing 7.7. Using the RTRIM function to trim trailing spaces.**

```
SQL> update Instructor
  2   set First_Name = rtrim(First_Name)
  3   where
  4   First_Name like '% ';

18 rows updated.
```

Notice how the WHERE clause was used in Listing 7.7 to update only those rows in which First_Name contained a trailing space. RTRIM will trim trailing spaces without this WHERE clause. However, if you have a large table the performance of the UPDATE statement will be better if you use the WHERE clause to reduce the number of rows that RTRIM is applied against.

As you can see, LTRIM and RTRIM require a single argument: the string to be trimmed. You can also specify a second optional argument for both functions: an alternative set of characters to be trimmed from the string argument. As an example, please look at Listing 7.8. Suppose you have a table named Test_Trim with a single VARCHAR2 column named MY_COL. You know that some rows have leading characters that you want to trim off: x, y, and z. The LTRIM function is used in an UPDATE statement to remove the offending characters.

INPUT/ OUTPUT **Listing 7.8. Using the LTRIM function to remove leading characters.**

```
SQL> select my_col
  2   from test_trim;
MY_COL
----------------------------------------------------------
yzzxHello, world
zyxGoodbye, cruel world

SQL> update test_trim
  2   set my_col = ltrim(my_col,'xyz');
2 rows updated.
SQL> select my_col from test_trim;
MY_COL
----------------------------------------------------------
Hello, world
Goodbye, cruel world
```

7

You can eliminate other trailing characters by employing the same technique using RTRIM.

Padding a String

At some point, you may find yourself in a situation in which you need to pad a string with leading or trailing characters. Oracle provides two functions for this purpose: LPAD and RPAD.

LPAD

To left-pad a string, use the LPAD function.

The syntax is

```
LPAD (string, n, pad_string)
```

The variables are defined as follows:

string is the literal string or string column to be left padded.

n is the total length of the string returned by LPAD.

pad_string is the string to left-pad onto *string*.

Let's see how this works. Listing 7.9 shows how LPAD can pad a column with leading spaces.

INPUT/OUTPUT — Listing 7.9. Using LPAD to add leading spaces to a column.

```
SQL> select lpad(my_col,20) from test_trim;
LPAD(MY_COL,20)
--------------------
        Hello, world
Goodbye, cruel world
```

When *pad_string* is not supplied as an argument, LPAD uses a space to left-pad the string. You can specify a literal string that LPAD will use to left-pad the string. However, the number of characters that are padded on the string depends on the value of *n*. Listing 7.10 demonstrates how you can add a fixed value to the LENGTH function as an argument to LPAD. By increasing the number added to LENGTH, you can left-pad the *string* with *pad_string* more than once, as seen in the second query.

INPUT/OUTPUT — Listing 7.10. Using the LENGTH function as an argument to the LPAD function.

```
SQL> select lpad(my_col,length(my_col)+8,'You say ') from test_trim;
LPAD(MY_COL,LENGTH(MY_COL)+8,'YOUSAY')
----------------------------------------------------------------
You say Hello, world
You say Goodbye, cruel world

SQL> select lpad(my_col,length(my_col)+16,'You say ') from test_trim;
```

```
LPAD(MY_COL,LENGTH(MY_COL)+16,'YOUSAY')
--------------------------------------------------------------------
You say You say Hello, world
You say You say Goodbye, cruel world
```

You can also left-pad a string with the contents of another column. As you can see in the second query in Listing 7.11, MY_COL2 is left padded onto MY_COL. The number of times that this step is performed depends on the length of values in both columns. If MY_COL is equal to California and MY_COL2 is equal to Los Angeles, LPAD returns a string in which California (10 characters) is left padded with Los Angeles (11 characters) so that Los Angeles fills 40 characters.

INPUT/OUTPUT **Listing 7.11. Using LPAD to concatenate two columns.**

```
SQL> select * from test_trim;
MY_COL                          MY_COL2
----------------------------    ----------------------------
California                      Los Angeles
Michigan                        Jackson
Washington                      Seattle
Oregon                          Portland

SQL> select lpad(my_col,50,my_col2) from test_trim;
LPAD(MY_COL,50,MY_COL2)
--------------------------------------------------------
Los AngelesLos AngelesLos AngelesLos AngCalifornia
JacksonJacksonJacksonJacksonJacksonJacksonMichigan
SeattleSeattleSeattleSeattleSeattleSeattWashington
PortlandPortlandPortlandPortlandPortlandPortOregon
```

By combining these built-in functions, you can assemble elaborate expressions. Listing 7.12 uses the lengths of MY_COL and MY_COL2 as arguments to guarantee that left-padding occurs only once. Let's dissect the SELECT statement. LPAD's first argument is MY_COL2. For the second argument, you add the length of MY_COL2 to the length of MY_COL2 and add an additional 2 for the ', ' that will be placed between MY_COL and MY_COL2. Finally, for LPAD's third argument, you concatenate MY_COL2 with , .

INPUT/OUTPUT **Listing 7.12. Using LENGTH as an argument in LPAD.**

```
SQL> select lpad (my_col,
➥length(my_col)+length(my_col2)+2, my_col2 ¦¦ ', ')
  2 from test_trim;
LPAD(MY_COL,LENGTH(MY_COL)+LENGTH(MY_COL2)+2,MY_COL2¦¦', ')
--------------------------------------------------------------------
Los Angeles, California
Jackson, Michigan
Seattle, Washington
Portland, Oregon
```

7

RPAD

RPAD works just like LPAD.

SYNTAX

Use the following syntax:

RPAD (*string*, *n*, *pad_string*)

The variables are defined as follows:

string is the literal string or string column to be right-padded.

n is the number of times to right-pad *pad_string*.

pad_string is the string to right-pad onto *string*.

Changing the Case in a String

Oracle provides three functions that enable you to change the case of a string's characters:

☐ INITCAP converts the first character of each word to uppercase.

☐ LOWER converts all of the characters in a string to lowercase.

☐ UPPER converts all characters to uppercase.

All three functions have a single argument: the string expression to be manipulated. Listing 7.13 demonstrates the use of the UPPER and LOWER functions.

INPUT/ OUTPUT   **Listing 7.13. Using the UPPER and LOWER functions.**

```
SQL> select lower(Title), upper(Title)
  2  from Course
  3  order by Title;
```

LOWER(TITLE)	UPPER(TITLE)
abnormal psychology	ABNORMAL PSYCHOLOGY
advanced arithmetic	ADVANCED ARITHMETIC
ancient greek philosophers	ANCIENT GREEK PHILOSOPHERS
early american history	EARLY AMERICAN HISTORY
evolutionary grammar	EVOLUTIONARY GRAMMAR
general calculus	GENERAL CALCULUS
intro to anthropology	INTRO TO ANTHROPOLOGY
intro to biology	INTRO TO BIOLOGY
intro to circuit theory	INTRO TO CIRCUIT THEORY
intro to dynamics	INTRO TO DYNAMICS
intro to economics	INTRO TO ECONOMICS
intro to english lit	INTRO TO ENGLISH LIT
intro to philosophy	INTRO TO PHILOSOPHY
intro to psychology	INTRO TO PSYCHOLOGY
intro to structures	INTRO TO STRUCTURES
invertebrate anatomy	INVERTEBRATE ANATOMY
mammalian anatomy	MAMMALIAN ANATOMY
modern english lit	MODERN ENGLISH LIT
modern european history	MODERN EUROPEAN HISTORY

```
modern philosophy              MODERN PHILOSOPHY
monetary policy                MONETARY POLICY
number theory                  NUMBER THEORY
phys anthro field techniques   PHYS ANTHRO FIELD TECHNIQUES
pre-calculus                   PRE-CALCULUS
psych in film                  PSYCH IN FILM
seminar on chaos               SEMINAR ON CHAOS
seminar on nacimera            SEMINAR ON NACIMERA
seminar on theme analysis      SEMINAR ON THEME ANALYSIS
workshop on jefferson          WORKSHOP ON JEFFERSON
workshop on marx               WORKSHOP ON MARX
workshop on neuroses           WORKSHOP ON NEUROSES
workshop on normality          WORKSHOP ON NORMALITY

32 rows selected.
```

Listing 7.14 illustrates how the INITCAP function will convert all characters to lowercase and capitalize the first letter of each word.

INPUT/OUTPUT **Listing 7.14. Using the INITCAP function.**

```
SQL> select initcap(Title)
  2  from Course
  3  order by Title;

INITCAP(TITLE)
------------------------------------------------------------
Abnormal Psychology
Advanced Arithmetic
Ancient Greek Philosophers
Early American History
Evolutionary Grammar
General Calculus
Intro To Anthropology
Intro To Biology
Intro To Circuit Theory
Intro To Dynamics
Intro To Economics
Intro To English Lit
Intro To Philosophy
Intro To Psychology
Intro To Structures
Invertebrate Anatomy
Mammalian Anatomy
Modern English Lit
Modern European History
Modern Philosophy
Monetary Policy
Number Theory
Phys Anthro Field Techniques
Pre-Calculus
Psych In Film
```

7

continues

Listing 7.14. continued

```
Seminar On Chaos
Seminar On Nacimera
Seminar On Theme Analysis
Workshop On Jefferson
Workshop On Marx
Workshop On Neuroses
Workshop On Normality

32 rows selected.
```

Using the DECODE Function to Return a String

Many database applications reference columns that contain encoded information. Sometimes a database designer creates a table to store a code and its description, especially if the designer expects the codes to change. In other situations, the column containing the code stands alone without any additional description available in the database.

Day 3, "Logical Database Design," discussed the need for a table that would contain the details of a particular schedule—which days the class would meet and for how long. As a result, you created the Schedule_Type_Details table. One of the columns in this table, Day, stores the day of the week as an integer with Sunday represented as 1, Monday represented as 2, and so on.

Most users will find it inconvenient to decipher the contents of this table. Fortunately, the DECODE function can translate cryptic codes into something that users will have no difficulty in interpreting.

SYNTAX

Its syntax is

```
DECODE (expression, value1, returned_value1, ...
valueN, returned_valueN,
[default_returned_value])
```

The variables are defined as follows:

expression is a valid Oracle expression.

valueN is a possible value to which *expression* might be equal.

returned_valueN is the value returned by DECODE if *expression* is equal to *valueN*.

default_returned_value is an optional value returned by DECODE if *expression* is not equal to any of the values, *value1* through *valueN*.

Listing 7.15 shows how the DECODE function can translate the numeric Day into the day of the week.

INPUT/ OUTPUT **Listing 7.15. Using the DECODE function to translate a numeric value into a string value.**

```
SQL> select Schedule_ID, Day,
  2  decode (Day, 1, 'SUN', 2, 'MON', 3, 'TUE', 4, 'WED',
  3              5, 'THU', 6, 'FRI', 7, 'SAT')
  4  from Schedule_Type_Details
  5  order by Schedule_ID, Day;

SCHEDULE_ID               DAY DEC
-------------------- --------- ---
S180                        6 FRI
T10                         2 MON
T10                         4 WED
T10                         6 FRI
T13                         2 MON
T13                         4 WED
T13                         6 FRI
T15                         2 MON
T15                         4 WED
T15                         6 FRI
TT9                         3 TUE
TT9                         5 THU

12 rows selected.
```

Converting a Character to Its ASCII Numeric Value

At some point you may want to obtain the ASCII numeric equivalent of a character in a column. The ASCII function serves this purpose. It has a single string argument. ASCII returns the ASCII numeric equivalent of the first character of its argument. Listing 7.16 contains an example of the use of the ASCII function.

INPUT/ OUTPUT **Listing 7.16. Using the ASCII function.**

```
SQL> select Last_Name, ASCII(Last_Name)
  2  from Instructor
  3  order by Last_Name;

LAST_NAME                ASCII(LAST_NAME)
------------------------ ----------------
ANGELO                                 65
BATES                                  66
BILLINGS                               66
CHANG                                  67
CHERNOW                                67
CHU                                    67
DANIELS                                68
EDWARDS                                69
HITCHCOCK                              72
JASON                                  74
```

continues

Listing 7.16. continued

```
NILAND                           78
PARKER                           80
POULSON                          80
RESTON                           82
RICHARDSON                       82
TORRES                           84
WEISS                            87
YOUNG                            89

18 rows selected.
```

Manipulating Dates

You will find tremendous variation in the way that database systems treat dates and times. Fortunately, Oracle provides a special datatype—the `date`—for dealing with dates and times. This datatype has its own internal format with which you needn't be concerned, other than knowing that it provides for the storage of the century, year, month, day, hour, minute, and second. As this lesson points out, using this datatype where appropriate has many advantages.

The Oracle `date` Datatype

The Oracle `date` datatype is efficient because it requires only seven bytes of storage. In addition, when you define a column as a `date`, you can use all of Oracle's built-in functions that manipulate dates and times.

The Oracle `date` datatype is also extremely convenient for the application developer. One can argue about whether or not the algorithms used by Oracle are optimal; you may feel that other methods are more efficient for storing date and time values. But without question, using the Oracle `date` datatype can save you a significant amount of time and effort in application development. In fact, because the advantages of this datatype are so clear, you really should use the Oracle `date` datatype whenever you need to store date or time information.

Using the `date` Datatype to Store Time Information

The Oracle `date` datatype also stores time information: hour, minute, and second. You can use a column defined as a `date` to store only date information, only time information, or both.

If you choose not to use the `date` datatype for storing date and time information, you will be forced to use other algorithms for manipulating the formats you have defined. You won't be able to use any of Oracle's built-in functions for manipulating dates and times. A task that could have been accomplished in a single SELECT statement will require additional processing in a programming language or development environment. The following scenario shows the consequences of *not* using the Oracle `date` datatype when its use is appropriate.

Suppose that you need to store the hire date for each instructor and a possible termination date. If you made an incorrect decision and decided to store the instructor's hire date as a numeric value in the format YYMMDD, the hire date for an employee hired on May 9, 1957, would be stored as 570509. Listing 7.17 contains a description of the Instructor table if it included a column for storing the hire date.

Listing 7.17. Instructor table with hire date stored as a number.

```
SQL> desc Instructor
 Name                            Null?    Type
 ------------------------------- -------- ----
 INSTRUCTOR_ID                            VARCHAR2(20)
 DEPARTMENT_ID                   NOT NULL VARCHAR2(20)
 LAST_NAME                       NOT NULL VARCHAR2(25)
 FIRST_NAME                               VARCHAR2(25)
 MI                                       VARCHAR2(1)
 POSITION                                 VARCHAR2(25)
 TELEPHONE                                VARCHAR2(10)
 FAX                                      VARCHAR2(10)
 EMAIL                                    VARCHAR2(100)
 HIRE_DATE                                NUMBER(6)
```

Cleverly (or so you thought), you decided to use a format of YYMMDD so that the hire date could be ordered either in ascending or descending order. You could use a SELECT statement to retrieve rows from the Instructor table ordered by hire date. But this approach has a few problems, namely:

☐ **An erroneous assumption.** When an instructor is hired after 1999, the preceding SELECT statement will not return the correct result. An instructor hired in 2000 and beyond will show up at the beginning of the list because the format stores only the last two digits of the year in which an instructor was hired.

☐ **More work and lower reliability.** Because you can't rely on Oracle date validation, the burden of developing an algorithm for validating a hire date is on your shoulders.

☐ **Limited functionality.** If you need to query a table based on date arithmetic, what could have been accomplished with a single SELECT statement incorporating built-in functions will instead require additional processing. You can't write a SELECT statement that will retrieve all employees whose hire date is less than the mean hire date.

Using the Oracle date datatype instead helps to ensure that any application you develop will be portable to other platforms.

7

Date formats are supported on every platform on which Oracle runs. If you are planning to run an application on a variety of operating systems, you'll find that using the Oracle date datatype is easier than trying to support a variety of date and time formats for each operating system.

The Current Date and Time: SYSDATE

Oracle has a number of values called pseudocolumns that can be referenced in SQL statements. One of these values is SYSDATE. Despite its name, SYSDATE also contains time information. Like the date datatype, SYSDATE is accurate to the nearest second. SYSDATE is an extremely useful construct for time-stamping rows during an insert or update operation. Many of the examples in this lesson use SYSDATE.

The Oracle Date Format Model

Because the date datatype stores the values for century, year, day, month, hour, minute, and second, each of these values can be extracted and formatted independently. Also, the date and time elements can be abbreviated or fully spelled out according to the format that you specify.

NOTE

Because the Oracle date datatype includes century, you should not have any problems related to year 2000 if you use the Oracle date datatype for columns that contain date information.

You also have the option of repeating a date or time element in different formats. As you recall, the Schedule_Type_Details table contains the starting time for each day of a particular Schedule ID. For example, one schedule might describe a Monday/Wednesday/Friday schedule that begins at 10:00 a.m. and has a duration of 50 minutes. The Starting Time column contains only information about the starting hour and minute. Therefore, you must use the to_char function, along with a date/time format, to translate the internal date value to an external character value. Listing 7.18 shows how you can display the contents of the Schedule_Type_Details table.

INPUT/OUTPUT **Listing 7.18. Converting a date and time value to a string.**

```
SQL> select Schedule_ID, Day, Starting_Time, to_char(Starting_Time,'HH:MI PM')
  2  from Schedule_Type_Details
  3  order by Schedule_ID, Day;

SCHED   DAY STARTING_ TO_CHAR(STARTING_TIME,'HH:MIPM')
-----   --- --------- ------------------------------------------------
S180      6 01-MAR-97 09:00 AM
T10       2 01-MAR-97 10:00 AM
T10       4 01-MAR-97 10:00 AM
```

```
T10      6 01-MAR-97 10:00 AM
T13      2 01-MAR-97 01:00 PM
T13      4 01-MAR-97 01:00 PM
T13      6 01-MAR-97 01:00 PM
T15      2 01-MAR-97 03:00 PM
T15      4 01-MAR-97 03:00 PM
T15      6 01-MAR-97 03:00 PM
TT9      3 01-MAR-97 09:00 AM
TT9      5 01-MAR-97 09:00 AM

12 rows selected.
```

NOTE

You can use SYSDATE and the DUAL table to experiment with various date and time formats. You can select SYSDATE from the DUAL table, but don't insert any rows into the DUAL table—it must have only one row for some Oracle tools to work correctly.

Table 7.1 contains a list of the valid elements that can be used in the date format.

Table 7.1. List of date format elements.

Format Element	Description	Range
SS	Second	0–59
SSSSS	Seconds past midnight	0–86399
MI	Minute	0–59
HH	Hour	0–12
HH24	Military hour	0–23
DD	Day of the month	1–31 (depends on month)
DAY	Day of the week, spelled out	SUNDAY–SATURDAY
D	Day of the week	1–7
DDD	Day of the year	1–366 (depends on year)
MM	Month number	1–12
MON	Abbreviated month	JAN–DEC
MONTH	Month, spelled out	JANUARY–DECEMBER
YY	Last two digits of year	For example, 96
YYYY	Full year value	For example, 1996

continues

7

Table 7.1. continued

Format Element	Description	Range
YEAR	Year, spelled out	For example, NINETEEN NINETY-SEVEN
CC	Century	For example, 19
Q	Quarter	1–4
J	Julian day	For example, 2448000
W	Week of the month	1–5
WW	Week of the year	1–52

The Oracle Default Date Format

The default date format is DD-MON-YY. For instance, 01-JAN-98 is a date in accordance with Oracle's default date format. You can specify dates with this format model without using any other functions or datatype conversion. But if you need to display or specify dates in a different format, then you'll need to use a built-in function to specify the format model you want to use.

If you try to assign a string that doesn't adhere to this default format to a date column, Oracle will probably return an error. For example, if the first two digits are greater than 31, Oracle will always return the error code ORA-01847. If the abbreviation for the month is not JAN, FEB, MAR, APR, MAY, JUN, JUL, AUG, SEP, OCT, NOV, or DEC, Oracle will return error code ORA-01843. If the day of the month is not within the valid range for that particular month, Oracle will return error code ORA-01839. Table 7.2 contains a list of Oracle error codes related to the manipulation of date values.

Table 7.2. Oracle error codes related to dates.

Oracle Error Code	Description
ORA-01847	Day of month must be between 1 and last day of month
ORA-01813	Hour may be specified once
ORA-01839	Date not valid for month specified

NOTE

We are rapidly approaching a new millennium. Because the beginning years of the 21st century will be in the same range as the days in a month, there no doubt will be some confusion between the year and the day of the month. For example, if you want to assign the date

January 2, 2003, you could very easily switch the digits and enter 03-JAN-02 instead of 02-JAN-03. In either case, Oracle would accept the date as valid according to the date format.

Converting Dates to Strings

You need to remember that a date column value remains a date until you convert it to some other datatype. If, for example, you want to extract the first character of a date column value, you'll need to convert the value to a string using a built-in function named TO_CHAR.

SYNTAX

The format for this function is

TO_CHAR(date_value,date_format)

The variables are defined as follows:

> date_value is a literal date value, a date value from a column, or a date value returned by a built-in function.

> date_format is a valid Oracle date format.

Listing 7.19 shows how a query can use the TO_CHAR function to return the employee hire date using the format MONTH DD, YYYY.

INPUT/OUTPUT

Listing 7.19. Converting a date value to a string.

```
SQL> select Last_Name, First_Name,
  2  to_char(Hire_Date,'MONTH DD, YYYY') H_DATE
  3  from Employee
  4  order by Hire_Date;
LAST_NAME                      FIRST_NAME              H_DATE
------------------------------ ----------------------- --------------------
SMITH                          JEAN                    APRIL     10, 1982
HERNANDEZ                      RANDY                   NOVEMBER  18, 1983
GLEASON                        PAUL                    APRIL     05, 1984
BARRETT                        SARAH                   JANUARY   16, 1989
HIGGINS                        BEN                     FEBRUARY  11, 1989
YEN                            CINDY                   JUNE      09, 1991
GILROY                         MAX                     SEPTEMBER 22, 1992
CARSON                         BETH                    DECEMBER  12, 1992
SWANSON                        HARRY                   MAY       18, 1993
9 rows selected.
```

Once a date value has been converted to a string with the TO_CHAR function, you can use it as an argument in other string functions. For example, you can use the function SUBSTR to extract a substring from a string. Listing 7.20 demonstrates how to use the SUBSTR function to extract the first letter of the employee's month of hire.

7

Listing 7.20. Embedding the TO_CHAR function within the SUBSTR function.

```
SQL> select Last_Name, First_Name,
  2   substr(to_char(Hire_Date,'MON'),1,1) the_first_letter_of_the_month
  3   from Employee
  4   order by the_first_letter_of_the_month;
LAST_NAME                        FIRST_NAME                T
-------------------------------- ------------------------- -
SMITH                            JEAN                      A
GLEASON                          PAUL                      A
CARSON                           BETH                      D
HIGGINS                          BEN                       F
BARRETT                          SARAH                     J
YEN                              CINDY                     J
SWANSON                          HARRY                     M
HERNANDEZ                        RANDY                     N
GILROY                           MAX                       S
9 rows selected.
```

The next section looks at some of the many ways in which dates and times can be displayed. You have a tremendous amount of flexibility in how to display and specify these values.

Converting Strings to Dates

Not surprisingly, the conversion of string values to dates is similar to the conversion of dates to strings. Instead of using the TO_CHAR built-in function, you use the TO_DATE built-in function because the goal is to specify a date value using a legal date format.

The arguments of the TO_DATE function are the reverse of the arguments of the TO_CHAR function.

TO_DATE (*string_value*, *date_format*)

The variables are defined as follows:

string_value is a literal string value, a string value from a column, or a string value returned by a built-in function.

date_format is a valid Oracle date format.

For example, if you want to convert a string that doesn't use the Oracle default date format (DD-MON-YY), you would use the TO_DATE function. Listing 7.21 shows how a query can be used to determine the number of days that have elapsed since the American bicentennial.

INPUT/OUTPUT **Listing 7.21. An example of date arithmetic.**

```
SQL> select SYSDATE - TO_DATE('07-04-1976','MM-DD-YYYY')
  2  from dual;
SYSDATE-TO_DATE('07-04-1976','MM-DD-YYYY')
------------------------------------------
                                6878.9465
```

Dates and Time

Remember that every column defined using the date datatype contains both a date and a time value. If you are interested in storing only a time value in this column, the date value will be set to a default value. Listing 7.21 illustrates the use of a common format for displaying time—HH:MI:SS.

INPUT/OUTPUT **Listing 7.21. Using a time format in the TO_CHAR function.**

```
SQL> select Employee_ID,
➥to_char(Time_Clocked_In,'HH:MI:SS') Time_Clocked_In
  2  from Time_Clock
  3  order by Employee_ID;
EMPLOYEE_ID TIME_CLOCKED_IN
----------- ---------------------------------------------------------
       1002 09:02:03
       1003 08:51:12
       1004 08:59:33
       1005 09:22:12
```

Remember that the Oracle date datatype is capable of storing time to the nearest second.

SYNTAX

If you want to use a 24-hour time format, the time format should be specified in the following way:

```
SELECT TO_CHAR(arrival_time,'HH24:MI:SS') FROM DUAL;
```

NOTE

It's very easy to confuse months and minutes in date and time formats. For example, Oracle will accept the following INSERT statement, even though it really isn't what you intended (MM instead of MI):

```
INSERT INTO EMPLOYEE
(EMPLOYEE_ID, START_TIME)
VALUES
(1033,TO_CHAR('08:05','HH24:MM');
```

7

> Oracle will interpret this statement as follows: The start time for employee number 1033 is set to 8:00 a.m. and the month of May. Because MM is always between 1 and 12, Oracle always accepts the supplied value, even though it isn't what you intended.

Oracle also has a time format model that enables you to express a time as seconds past midnight. In the following example, assume that the current time is 2:00 a.m.:

```
SELECT TO_CHAR(SYSDATE,'SSSSS') FROM DUAL;
7200     which is the equivalent of two hours
```

By using the time format model SSSSS, Oracle returns the date expressed in seconds past midnight. The time 2:00 a.m. represents two hours past midnight, which is equal to 7,200 seconds.

Calculating the Difference Between Two Dates

Another advantage of using the Oracle date datatype is that it supports date arithmetic. You can add or subtract days from an existing date, for example:

```
select sysdate + 7 from dual;
```

By adding 7 to SYSDATE, you can obtain the date a week from the current date. Similarly, you can subtract days from a date value to calculate an earlier date.

Specifying a Numeric Column

As you've already seen, a column's datatype is specified in the CREATE TABLE and ALTER TABLE statements.

The general syntax for specifying a numeric datatype is

```
NUMBER ([precision [, scale]])
```

The variables are defined as follows:

> precision is an optional argument that specifies the number of digits of precision that Oracle should store for column values.

> scale is an optional argument indicating the number of digits to the right of the decimal point that Oracle should store for column values.

If you don't specify precision or scale, Oracle accepts a number of up to 38 digits of precision—the maximum precision that Oracle offers. When you specify a column, consider limiting the width of numeric values by using an appropriate precision. For example, if a column stores a patient's body temperature in degrees Fahrenheit, you would specify the column as

```
Body_Temp_F Number(4,1)
```

A precision of 4 and a scale of 1 allow Body_Temp_F to store a total of four digits, including one digit to the right of the decimal point. Listing 7.22 demonstrates how temperatures that are within the specified precision and scale are accepted by the Oracle database.

INPUT/ OUTPUT ### Listing 7.22. Oracle accepts numbers within specified precision and scale.

```
SQL> update Patient
  2   set Body_Temp_F = 99.2
  3   where
  4   Patient_ID = 'A2002';
1 row updated.
SQL> update Patient
  2   set Body_Temp_F = 103.8
  3   where
  4   Patient_ID = 'E3893';
1 row updated.
```

Listing 7.23 illustrates how the Oracle database doesn't allow a value that violates the precision and scale to be stored.

INPUT/ OUTPUT ### Listing 7.23. Oracle database rejects values outside specified precision and scale.

```
SQL> update Patient
  2   set Body_Temp_F = 1003.8
  3   where
  4   Patient_ID = 'N3393';
set Body_Temp_F = 1003.8
    *
ERROR at line 2:
ORA-01438: value larger than specified precision allows for this column
```

Of course, this definition for Body_Temp_F allows values up to 999.9 degrees Fahrenheit—an impossible value for humans. In addition to specifying the precision and scale, you also need to specify a CHECK constraint for this column to restrict its values to a range.

If you specify a value for *precision* but not for *scale*, Oracle truncates the fractional value of a real number before storing the value in the column. This concept is shown in Listing 7.24.

7

Listing 7.24. Fractional value is truncated.

```
SQL> create table Number_Demo (
  2  Int_Value     number(3),
  3  Real_Value    number(3,1),
  4  Num_Value     number);
Table created.

SQL> insert into Number_Demo
  2  (Int_Value)
  3  values
  4  (12.2);
1 row created.

SQL> select Int_Value
  2  from Number_Demo;
INT_VALUE
---------
       12
```

If values for *precision* and *scale* have been furnished and you store a numeric value whose scale exceeds the column's scale, Oracle truncates the fractional value to the column's scale, as shown in Listing 7.25.

Listing 7.25. Fractional value is truncated to scale defined for column.

```
SQL> insert into Number_Demo
  2  (Real_Value)
  3  values
  4  (3.144);
1 row created.

SQL> select Real_Value
  2  from Number_Demo;
REAL_VALUE
----------
       3.1
```

In addition to the NUMBER datatype, Oracle accepts the following keywords that describe a numeric column:

☐ NUMERIC, DECIMAL, and DEC

☐ INTEGER, INT, and SMALLINT

☐ FLOAT, DOUBLE PRECISION, and REAL

Oracle supports these other datatypes to provide compatibility with ANSI SQL and other relational database systems such as IBM SQL/DS and DB2. The NUMERIC, DECIMAL, and DEC datatypes are identical to the NUMBER datatype. INTEGER, INT, and SMALLINT are translated to NUMBER(38). FLOAT, DOUBLE PRECISION, and REAL are all translated to NUMBER. Unless you are converting a database schema from some non-Oracle database, you should generally use the NUMBER datatype when specifying columns.

How Oracle Stores Numbers

Oracle doesn't store numbers in the manner used by programming languages such as C and FORTRAN. For example, in C a floating-point variable requires the same amount of storage regardless of its value, whereas in Oracle the number of bytes used to store a number depends on the number's precision. To illustrate this fact, you can use an Oracle built-in function called VSIZE, which returns the number of bytes used by its argument.

Listing 7.26 contains a query of a table that contains a number column named Num_Value. To the right of the column value is VSIZE(Num_Value)—which returns the number of bytes used to store Num_Value. Oracle can store two digits of precision in one byte. Another byte is used for storing the sign and exponent.

**INPUT/
OUTPUT**

Listing 7.26. Determining the storage required by a number.

```
SQL> select Num_Value, vsize(Num_Value)
  2  from Number_Demo;
NUM_VALUE VSIZE(NUM_VALUE)
--------- ----------------
      123                3
     1234                3
    12345                4
   123456                4
  1234567                5
 12345678                5
123456789                6
12345.679                6
```

Converting a Number to a String

You will typically want to convert a numeric value to a string value for two reasons.

☐ To change the display format of a number in a form or report

☐ To concatenate a numeric expression with a string for use in a form or report

Automatic Conversion of a Number to a String

In some situations SQL automatically converts a number to a string. Listing 7.27 demonstrates how Oracle converts a specified number to a character value if it is being stored in a VARCHAR2 column.

7

INPUT/
OUTPUT
Listing 7.27. Automatic conversion of a number to a string.

```
SQL> insert into Course
  2 (Course_ID, Department_ID, Title, Additional_Fees)
  3 values
  4 (782, 'BIO', 'INVERTEBRATE CLONING LAB', 275);

1 row created.

SQL> select Course_ID, Department_ID, Title
  2 from Course
  3 where
  4 Course_ID = '782';

COURS DEPARTMENT_ID         TITLE
----- -------------------   --------------------------------------------
782   BIO                   INVERTEBRATE CLONING LAB
```

If you look at the row that was inserted in Listing 7.27, you can see that the number 782, which was used to specify a value for Course_ID, has been converted to a VARCHAR2 value of 782, which is stored in the Course_ID column.

Using TO_CHAR to Convert a Number to a String

The TO_CHAR function is used to *explicitly* convert a number to a string.

Its syntax is

```
TO_CHAR (number [,format])
```

The variables are defined as follows:

>   number is the numeric expression to be converted.

>   format is the optional format model to be used by TO_CHAR.

Listing 7.28 provides an example of the use of TO_CHAR without a format. Notice that the first column—Real_Value—is right-justified by SQL*Plus, whereas the second column—to_char(Real_Value)—is left-justified by SQL*Plus because it is a character column.

INPUT/
OUTPUT
Listing 7.28. Using the TO_CHAR function without a format to convert a number to a string.

```
SQL> select Real_Value, to_char(Real_Value)
  2 from Number_Demo;
REAL_VALUE TO_CHAR(REAL_VALUE)
---------- ----------------------------------------
       3.1 3.1
```

This is an appropriate point to discuss the Oracle number format model. The code segments contained in Listings 7.29 through 7.32 show the most important format model elements— the ones that you'll rely on most often.

To specify the number of digits to display, use 9 for each digit. You also can add a comma and decimal point to the specified format. Please refer to Listing 7.29 for an example.

Listing 7.29. Using a numeric format mask.

```
SQL> select Course_ID, Title, to_char(Additional_Fees, '9,999.99')
  2  from Course
  3  where
  4  Department_ID = 'BIO'
  5  order by Course_ID;

COURS TITLE                                              TO_CHAR(A
----- -------------------------------------------------- ---------
101   INTRO TO BIOLOGY                                       55.00
177   INVERTEBRATE ANATOMY                                   65.00
178   MAMMALIAN ANATOMY                                      70.00
```

To display a number with leading zeros, use 0 at the beginning of the format, as shown in Listing 7.30.

Listing 7.30. Using a leading zero in a numeric format mask.

```
SQL> select Course_ID, Title, to_char(Additional_Fees, '099.99')
  2  from Course
  3  where
  4  Department_ID = 'ECON'
  5  order by Course_ID;

COURS TITLE                                              TO_CHAR
----- -------------------------------------------------- -------
101   INTRO TO ECONOMICS                                  025.00
189   MONETARY POLICY                                     750.00
199   WORKSHOP ON MARX                                    000.00
```

To display a leading dollar sign, begin the format with a $ (see Listing 7.31).

7

Listing 7.31. Specifying a dollar sign in a numeric format mask.

```
SQL> select Course_ID, Title, to_char(Additional_Fees, '$999.99')
  2  from Course
  3  where
  4  Department_ID = 'ECON'
  5  order by Course_ID;

COURS TITLE                                              TO_CHAR(
----- ---------------------------------------------      --------
101   INTRO TO ECONOMICS                                  $25.00
189   MONETARY POLICY                                    $750.00
199   WORKSHOP ON MARX                                     $.00
```

If you want a number to appear in scientific notation, follow the specified precision with EEEE (see Listing 7.32).

Listing 7.32. Specifying scientific notation in a format mask.

```
SQL> select Num_Value, to_char(Num_Value,'9.9999EEEE')
  2  from Number_Demo
  3  order by Num_Value;
NUM_VALUE TO_CHAR(NUM_
--------- ------------
      123  1.2300E+02
     1234  1.2340E+03
    12345  1.2345E+04
12345.679  1.2346E+04
```

Converting a String to a Number

The TO_NUMBER function is the converse of TO_CHAR: It converts a character expression to a number by specifying a format.

The syntax for TO_NUMBER is

```
TO_NUMBER (string [,format])
```

The variables are defined as follows:

  string is the character expression to be converted.

  format is the optional format model to be used by TO_NUMBER.

TO_NUMBER uses the same format model as TO_CHAR. Listing 7.33 shows how you would convert a string value, representing earnings per share, to a number.

Listing 7.33. Using the TO_NUMBER function.

```
SQL> update Security_Price
  2  set Last_Qtr_EPS = to_number('$2.81','$999.99')
  3  where
  4  Symbol = 'ZGEGE';
1 row updated.

SQL> select Symbol, Last_Qtr_EPS
  2  from Security_Price
  3  where
  4  Symbol = 'ZGEGE';
SYMBO LAST_QTR_EPS
----- ------------
ZGEGE         2.81
```

Using Statistical Built-In Functions

Oracle furnishes the following statistical functions that are actually group functions:

☐ AVG(*value*), which computes the average, or mean, of its argument from the set of rows to which it is applied

☐ STDDEV(*value*), which returns the standard deviation of its argument from the set of rows it operates upon

☐ VARIANCE(*value*), which returns the variance of its argument from the set against which it is exercised

Because these group functions are more complex, their use is described in detail on Day 8, "More Sophisticated Queries with SQL."

Rounding and Truncating Numbers

Oracle provides four built-in functions related to rounding and truncating fractional numbers.

```
ROUND(value,[scale])
TRUNC(value,[scale])
FLOOR(value)
CEIL(value)
```

In these functions *value* is a numeric expression, and *scale* is an optional argument indicating the number of digits that the function should use for rounding or truncating. (The default is 0.)

The following examples show how you can use each function.

ROUND

The ROUND function has two arguments: the numeric expression and an optional number of digits to be used for rounding. If the second argument isn't supplied, ROUND returns the value of its numeric argument rounded to the nearest integer. If the second argument is supplied,

ROUND returns the value of its numeric argument rounded to the nearest fractional number with the specified number of digits to the right of the decimal point. ROUND can be used with literal values, as shown in Listing 7.34.

INPUT/OUTPUT **Listing 7.34. Using the ROUND function.**

```
SQL> select round(123.2) from dual;
ROUND(123.2)
------------
         123

SQL> select round(123.27,1) from dual;
ROUND(123.27,1)
---------------
         123.3

SQL> select round(101.8) from dual;
ROUND(101.8)
------------
         102
```

TRUNC

The TRUNC function is similar to the ROUND function. However, instead of rounding to the nearest integer, TRUNC removes the fractional portion of its numeric argument. You can supply a literal number to TRUNC as seen in Listing 7.35.

INPUT/OUTPUT **Listing 7.35. Truncating a number.**

```
SQL> select trunc(123.33), trunc(123.567,2)
  2  from dual;
TRUNC(123.33) TRUNC(123.567,2)
------------- ----------------
          123           123.56
```

FLOOR

The FLOOR function is almost identical to the TRUNC function except that FLOOR cannot truncate to a fractional number. The FLOOR function returns the integer that is less than or equal to its numeric argument as you can see in Listing 7.36.

INPUT/OUTPUT **Listing 7.36. Using the FLOOR function.**

```
SQL> select floor(128.3), floor(129.8)
  2  from dual;
FLOOR(128.3) FLOOR(129.8)
------------ ------------
         128          129
```

CEIL

The CEIL function returns a *ceiling* integer for its numeric argument—the smallest integer that is greater than or equal to its argument. CEIL can accept constants. See the example in Listing 7.37.

**INPUT/
OUTPUT** **Listing 7.37. Using the CEIL function.**

```
SQL> select ceil(128.3), ceil(129.8)
  2  from dual;
CEIL(128.3) CEIL(129.8)
----------- -----------
        129         130
```

Finding the Largest or Smallest Value

You can use the MAX and MIN functions to retrieve the largest and smallest values for a particular column in a table. Technically, MAX and MIN are group functions. However, you aren't required to specify the SELECT statement's GROUP BY clause to use these functions. As an example, Listing 7.38 demonstrates how you would retrieve the largest and smallest estimates for Additional_Fees from the Course table.

**INPUT/
OUTPUT** **Listing 7.38. Using MIN and MAX.**

```
SQL> select min(Additional_Fees), max(Additional_Fees)
  2  from Course;

MIN(ADDITIONAL_FEES) MAX(ADDITIONAL_FEES)
-------------------- --------------------
                   0                  750
```

Determining If a Value Is Null

When developing an Oracle application, you are bound to encounter situations in which a screen or report will return information about a column that can be null. If you want to return a specific value in place of a null value, you can use Oracle's NVL function to make the replacement.

Here is the syntax:

NVL (*column-value*, *substitute-value*)

The variables are defined as follows:

column-value is the column value to evaluate.

substitute-value is the value that the NVL function will return if *column-value* is null.

Listing 7.39 provides an example. Let's imagine we modify the Course table so that Additional_Fees is set to null if it is zero. Next, you query the Course table and see that many of the rows don't have a value for Additional_Fees. Next, you query the Course table using the NVL function to return a zero if Additional_Fees is null.

INPUT/OUTPUT **Listing 7.39. Using the NVL function.**

```
SQL> update course
  2   set additional_fees = null
  3   where additional_fees = 0;

15 rows updated.

SQL> select Department_ID, Course_ID, Additional_Fees
  2   from Course
  3   order by Department_ID, Course_ID;
```

DEPART	COURS	ADDITIONAL_FEES
ANTHRO	101	
ANTHRO	174	55
ANTHRO	189	7.5
BIO	101	55
BIO	177	65
BIO	178	70
ECON	101	25
ECON	189	750
ECON	199	
ENG	101	75
ENG	102	45
ENG	103	35
ENG	199	45
ENGL	101	
ENGL	189	
ENGL	192	
ENGL	193	
HIST	115	
HIST	184	
HIST	199	
MATH	101	
MATH	189	
MATH	50	
MATH	51	10
PHILO	101	
PHILO	174	
PHILO	198	
PSYCH	101	25
PSYCH	181	75
PSYCH	183	45
PSYCH	185	20
PSYCH	501	75

```
32 rows selected.
```

```
SQL> select Department_ID, Course_ID, nvl(Additional_Fees,0)
  2  from Course
  3  order by Department_ID, Course_ID;

DEPART COURS NVL(ADDITIONAL_FEES,0)
------ ----- ---------------------
ANTHRO 101                       0
ANTHRO 174                      55
ANTHRO 189                     7.5
BIO    101                      55
BIO    177                      65
BIO    178                      70
ECON   101                      25
ECON   189                     750
ECON   199                       0
ENG    101                      75
ENG    102                      45
ENG    103                      35
ENG    199                      45
ENGL   101                       0
ENGL   189                       0
ENGL   192                       0
ENGL   193                       0
HIST   115                       0
HIST   184                       0
HIST   199                       0
MATH   101                       0
MATH   189                       0
MATH   50                        0
MATH   51                       10
PHILO  101                       0
PHILO  174                       0
PHILO  198                       0
PSYCH  101                      25
PSYCH  181                      75
PSYCH  183                      45
PSYCH  185                      20
PSYCH  501                      75

32 rows selected.
```

Summary

This lesson demonstrated a variety of operators and built-in functions that can be used with string, numeric, and date/time values. Some of the string built-in functions included:

- [ ] SUBSTR returns a specified portion of a string.
- [ ] LENGTH returns the length of a string expression.
- [ ] LPAD and RPAD apply left padding and right padding to strings.
- [ ] LTRIM and RTRIM perform left trimming and right trimming on spaces and other characters.

- [ ] REPLACE substitutes one string for another string.
- [ ] LOWER, UPPER, and INITCAP control the use of uppercase and lowercase in a string.
- [ ] DECODE translates column values.
- [ ] ASCII returns the ASCII numeric equivalent of a character.
- [ ] INSTR provides the character position in which a pattern is found in a string.

In addition, this lesson included the following information about date and time values:

- [ ] The Oracle date datatype stores date and time information to a resolution of a second.
- [ ] The Oracle date datatype should be used whenever possible, even when storing only date or only time information.
- [ ] SYSDATE is a pseudocolumn that always returns the current date and time down to the second.
- [ ] The default Oracle date format is DD-MON-YY—for example, 01-JAN-98 for January 1, 1998.
- [ ] The TO_CHAR function converts date values to strings.
- [ ] The TO_DATE function converts strings to date values.

Keep the following concepts in mind when you are constructing SQL statements for your application:

- [ ] Specify numeric columns with the NUMBER datatype.
- [ ] You can convert a numeric expression to a string with the TO_CHAR function.
- [ ] You can convert a character expression to a number by using the TO_NUMBER function.
- [ ] MAX and MIN are group functions that will return the maximum and minimum values for a particular column or expression from a set of rows.
- [ ] The NVL function returns a different value—such as 0 or N/A—in place of the null value.

What Comes Next?

On Day 8, you learn how to use more advanced features of SQL such as the use of group functions, joining two or more tables, and other topics.

Q&A

Q Can Oracle built-in functions be used only with SQL*Plus or SQL Worksheet?

A No, you can use the built-in function with any tool that enables you to specify an SQL statement—for example, Oracle Forms or Powerbuilder.

Workshop

The purpose of the Workshop is to allow you to test your knowledge of the material discussed in the lesson. See if you can correctly answer the questions in the quiz and complete the exercise before you continue with tomorrow's lesson.

Quiz

1. Construct an SQL statement that will retrieve each row from the Instructor table as shown in this example:

   ```
   Professor Parker
   ```

2. Construct an SQL statement that will retrieve the instructor whose last name appears first in an alphabetic order.

Exercise

Create a table, named NEW_CLASS, using a CREATE TABLE <xyz> AS ... statement based on a join of the Class, Schedule_Type, and Schedule_Type_Details tables that contains the following columns:

- ☐ Class ID
- ☐ Department_ID
- ☐ Course_ID
- ☐ Day of the week spelled out
- ☐ Time spelled out (for example, 11:00 a.m.)

7

In Review

It's been a productive week. On Day 1, you learned about the origin of the relational database and the development of the client/server computing architecture. Hopefully, Day 2 will help you remember the key issues in developing an Oracle database application. On Day 3, you learned about the basic concepts of relational database theory; you also saw how these concepts were applied to a sample database. On Day 4, you learned how to create the objects in an Oracle database, such as tables and indexes. The material on Day 5 focused on the use of SQL to retrieve data from an Oracle database. Day 6 discussed the use of SQL to modify the contents of a table. Finally, on Day 7, you learned about the use of SQL built-in functions.

1

2

3

4

5

6

7

WEEK

2

8

9

10

11

12

13

14

At A Glance

During Week 2, you'll learn more about SQL, including the use of built-in functions. The use of PL/SQL, Oracle's procedural language extension to SQL, is discussed during this week as well. Finally, the last three lessons of the week address Oracle Forms, one of the components of Developer/2000. Here's a day-by-day summary of Week 2.

☐ **Day 8, "More Sophisticated Queries with SQL"**
In this lesson, you'll learn about retrieving information from two or more related tables, grouping rows by column, and other set operations supported by SQL.

☐ **Day 9, "Programming an Oracle Database with PL/SQL"**
This is the first of three lessons that focus on the use of PL/SQL, Oracle's programmatic extension to SQL. You'll learn about the basic elements of a PL/SQL subprogram and some of the flow-of-control statements that are commonly used in PL/SQL.

☐ **Day 10, "Program Development in PL/SQL"**

Continuing from the previous day, this lesson discusses additional PL/SQL datatypes, such as %TYPE and %ROWTYPE. You'll also learn how to create a PL/SQL package.

☐ **Day 11, "More Programming Techniques with PL/SQL"**

Many important topics are addressed in this lesson, including the use of cursors in retrieving rows, using PL/SQL in database triggers, and exception handling.

☐ **Day 12, "Developer/2000: Introduction to Oracle Forms"**

This is the first of five lessons that discuss the components of Developer/2000. Three of these lessons—Days 12, 13, and 14—focus on Oracle Forms.

☐ **Day 13, "Devloper/2000: Developing a User Interface with Oracle Forms"**

In another lesson on Oracle Forms, you'll learn how to build a master-detail form, change the appearance of a form, and set the properties for form objects.

☐ **Day 14, "Developer/2000: Application Development with Oracle Forms"**

This is the last lesson on Oracle Forms. This lesson covers the use of Oracle Forms triggers to validate user input, the use of menus in a forms application, and other topics.

Day 8

More Sophisticated Queries with SQL

You already have seen how the SELECT statement can retrieve records from a single table, but retrieving records is only one of the many features of this versatile statement. This lesson examines the more advanced features of the SELECT statement: the GROUP BY clause, the HAVING clause, and the join operation. You'll see how powerful the SELECT statement truly is.

The syntax of the SELECT statement is fairly difficult to decipher, and you can't really understand the use of its clauses just by studying the syntax diagrams shown in the Oracle documentation. Therefore, you should look at the many examples in this lesson. I'll show you what works and what doesn't.

Built-In Group Functions

The first subject for discussion is the Oracle built-in functions that operate on groups of rows. Be warned: This topic is a good example of SQL's quirky characteristics. Even though these functions are group functions, they do *not* require the use of a GROUP BY clause.

☐ COUNT counts the number of rows that Oracle retrieves based on the supplied criteria.

☐ MAX and MIN return the minimum and maximum values for the specified column.

☐ AVG and SUM compute a column's average and total value.

☐ STDDEV and VARIANCE compute a column's standard deviation and variance.

Each of these functions returns a single value. A few detailed examples follow.

The COUNT Function

The COUNT function comes in two flavors: COUNT(*), which counts all the rows in a table that satisfy any specified criteria, and COUNT(*column-name*), which counts all the rows in a table that have a non-null value for *column-name* and satisfy any specified criteria.

To demonstrate the use of COUNT(*), Listing 8.1 illustrates how you would count the number of courses offered by the Biology department.

INPUT/OUTPUT **Listing 8.1. A SELECT statement with a WHERE clause.**

```
SQL> select count(*)
  2  from Course
  3  where
  4  Department_ID = 'BIO';

COUNT(*)
---------
        3
```

If you want to count the number of students who have fax numbers, supply Fax as an argument to the COUNT function as shown in Listing 8.2.

INPUT/OUTPUT **Listing 8.2. Using the COUNT function to determine the number of rows in a table.**

```
SQL> select count(*)
  2  from Student;

COUNT(*)
---------
       31
```

8

```
SQL> select count(Fax)
  2  from Student;

COUNT(FAX)
----------
         3
```

You should be aware that the COUNT function returns a single row, even if the count is zero.

Obtaining Maximum and Minimum Values

You can combine the MAX and MIN functions in a single SELECT statement. Listing 8.3 demonstrates the use of these functions. The first query applies the functions to a numeric column—Additional_Fees. The second query applies the MAX and MIN functions to a character column—Instructor_ID.

Listing 8.3. The MAX and MIN functions used with different column datatypes.

```
SQL> select max(Additional_Fees), min(Additional_Fees)
  2  from Course;

MAX(ADDITIONAL_FEES) MIN(ADDITIONAL_FEES)
-------------------- --------------------
                 750                    0

SQL> select max(Instructor_ID), min(Instructor_ID)
  2  from Instructor;

MAX(INSTRUCTOR_ID)   MIN(INSTRUCTOR_ID)
-------------------- --------------------
Y561                 A612
```

Using AVG and SUM

AVG and SUM work in the same way as MIN and MAX. Listing 8.4 provides an example. A query of the Course table retrieves the average and total of the additional fees charged for a course.

Listing 8.4. Using the AVG and SUM functions.

```
SQL> select avg(Additional_Fees), sum(Additional_Fees)
  2  from Course;

AVG(ADDITIONAL_FEES) SUM(ADDITIONAL_FEES)
-------------------- --------------------
           46.171875               1477.5
```

Note that the AVG function does not use null values in its calculation.

Combining Group Functions with Other Columns

You cannot combine group functions and columns in the select list of a SELECT statement without using a GROUP BY clause. Listing 8.5 provides an example of a query in which two items compose the select list—Department_ID and sum(Additional_Fees). However, Oracle returns an error. To understand why, it helps to think in these terms: A group function returns a single row, but Department_ID returns as many rows as exist in the table. It simply doesn't make sense to return both these values at the same time; instead, Oracle returns an error message. However, by using a GROUP BY clause, you can combine group functions and columns in the select list. The next few sections look further at the use of the GROUP BY clause.

 Listing 8.5. Incorrect syntax in a SELECT statement.

```
SQL> select Department_ID, sum(Additional_Fees)
  2  from Course;
select Department_ID, sum(Additional_Fees)
       *
ERROR at line 1:
ORA-00937: not a single-group group function
```

Looking for Distinct Rows

The SELECT statement has an optional keyword that we haven't discussed yet: DISTINCT. This keyword follows SELECT and instructs Oracle to return only rows that have distinct values for the specified columns. As an example, Listing 8.6 uses a query to obtain a list of the cities in which students live.

 Listing 8.6. Using a query to retrieve a set of distinct values.

```
SQL> select distinct City
  2  from Student;

CITY
------------------------
DOVER
SPRINGFIELD
```

The DISTINCT option is very useful for finding a column's set of values. It offers a method that you can use for quickly determining how values are clustered in a table. If you don't specify the DISTINCT option, Oracle retrieves all rows that satisfy the criteria in the WHERE clause. By default, Oracle uses the ALL option to retrieve all rows. Specifically, the following SELECT statements are equivalent:

```
select City from Student;
```

and

```
select all City from Student;
```

Grouping Rows

The GROUP BY clause is another section of the SELECT statement. This optional clause tells Oracle to group rows based on the distinct values that exist for the specified columns. In addition, the HAVING clause can be used in conjunction with the GROUP BY clause to further restrict the retrieved rows.

Even though this topic is best explained by example, here's a quick look at the syntax first.

SYNTAX

```
SELECT select-list
FROM table-list
[WHERE
condition [AND ¦ OR]
...
condition]
[GROUP BY column1, column2, ..., columnN]
[HAVING condition]
[ORDER BY column1, column2, ...]
```

The variables are defined as follows:

select-list is a set of columns and expressions from the tables listed in table-list.

table-list is the tables from which rows are retrieved.

condition is a valid Oracle SQL condition.

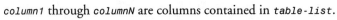 column1 through columnN are columns contained in table-list.

TIP It is easy to mix these elements—columns, expressions, tables, and conditions—into a SELECT statement that Oracle rejects. In addition, you can construct statements that Oracle processes without errors but whose results are difficult to interpret. When these things happen, the best solution is to go back to basics. Study your SELECT statement. If it no longer makes sense, use SQL*Plus or a similar tool to break it down, element by element, until it does. Analyze your use of group functions, the GROUP BY and HAVING clauses, and any join conditions.

Listing 8.7 gives an example of a query that retrieves a list of the Department_IDs that exist
in the Course table.

INPUT/ OUTPUT **Listing 8.7. Example of the GROUP BY clause.**

```
SQL> select Department_ID
  2   from Course
  3   group by Department_ID;

DEPARTMENT_ID
--------------------
ANTHRO
BIO
ECON
ENG
ENGL
HIST
MATH
PHILO
PSYCH

9 rows selected.
```

Listing 8.8 illustrates how to count the number of courses that are associated with each
Department_ID.

INPUT/ OUTPUT **Listing 8.8. Using the COUNT function with the GROUP BY clause.**

```
SQL> select Department_ID, count(*)
  2   from Course
  3   group by Department_ID;

DEPARTMENT_ID          COUNT(*)
--------------------   ---------
ANTHRO                        3
BIO                           3
ECON                          3
ENG                           4
ENGL                          4
HIST                          3
MATH                          4
PHILO                         3
PSYCH                         5

9 rows selected.
```

Now consider the use of both the GROUP BY and HAVING clauses. You can use the HAVING clause
to retrieve those departments that have exactly two courses, as displayed in Listing 8.9.

**INPUT/
OUTPUT** **Listing 8.9. Using the GROUP BY and HAVING clauses.**

```
SQL> select Department_ID, count(*)
  2  from Course
  3  group by Department_ID
  4  having count(*) = 4;
```

DEPARTMENT_ID	COUNT(*)
ENG	4
ENGL	4
MATH	4

Group functions cannot be combined with columns in the select list unless you use the GROUP BY clause. For instance, you can obtain the average value for additional fees per department as shown in Listing 8.10.

**INPUT/
OUTPUT** **Listing 8.10. Combining the AVG function with the GROUP BY clause.**

```
SQL> select Department_ID, avg(Additional_Fees)
  2  from Course
  3  group by Department_ID;
```

DEPARTMENT_ID	AVG(ADDITIONAL_FEES)
ANTHRO	20.833333
BIO	63.333333
ECON	258.33333
ENG	50
ENGL	0
HIST	0
MATH	2.5
PHILO	0
PSYCH	48

```
9 rows selected.
```

In the next example, you'll look at a different use for a database: a patient information system for a hospital. Another use of the HAVING and GROUP BY clauses is in the identification of duplicate rows. For example, you might not be able to add a primary key to a table because the primary key column contains duplicate values, as illustrated in Listing 8.11. A query that uses the GROUP BY and HAVING clauses identifies which Patient_IDs have more than one value. A second query determines which row should be deleted. After it is deleted, the primary key is successfully added to the table.

Listing 8.11. Identifying duplicate rows.

```
SQL> alter table Patient add
  2   constraint Patient_PK
  3   primary key (Patient_ID);
alter table Patient add
*
ERROR at line 1:
ORA-02299: cannot add or enable constraint (TYO.PATIENT_PK)-
duplicate keys found

SQL> select Patient_ID
  2   from Patient
  3   having count(*) > 1
  4   group by Patient_ID;
PATIEN
------
GG9999

SQL> select *
  2   from Patient
  3   where
  4   Patient_ID = 'GG9999';
PATIEN BODY_TEMP_DEG_F FEVER_CLASS
------ --------------- -------------------
GG9999          107.6 LETHAL FEVER
GG9999            107

SQL> delete from Patient
  2   where Patient_ID = 'GG9999' and Body_Temp_Deg_F = 107;
1 row deleted.

SQL> alter table Patient add
  2   constraint Patient_PK
  3   primary key (Patient_ID);
Table altered.
```

Dealing with Hierarchical Information

I've included the topic of hierarchical information in this lesson, rather than in one of the earlier lessons on SQL, to avoid confusion. An example of hierarchical data is a manufacturing bill of materials (BOM) that describes all the parts, subassemblies, and assemblies that compose a finished product; an aircraft manufacturer might have a BOM that consists of thousands of levels and millions of parts.

NEW TERM   *Hierarchical data* is information contained in a table that has, at a minimum, a column that specifies the *parent* or *higher-level* key and another column that specifies the primary key of the current row.

8

Can relational databases in general and SQL in particular support this type of hierarchy? The answer is mixed. The good news is that SQL does provide some support for hierarchical data via the CONNECT BY clause. The bad news is that the support is quite limited, and the syntax is not intuitive. Nevertheless, I'll show you an example of how to use SQL to navigate through hierarchical data.

A three-column table illustrates the use of the CONNECT BY clause.

Product_ID	The product of interest
Assembly_ID	The assembly or subassembly to which the Product_ID belongs
Description	The product description

This table design is based upon the concept that every product belongs to the finished product or an assembly—except for the finished product itself. The rows in the Product_Assembly table demonstrate this concept. A camera, the X1000, is composed of several parts and one subassembly, B200. Listing 8.12 displays the contents of the Product_Assembly table.

**INPUT/
OUTPUT** **Listing 8.12. Contents of the Product_Assembly table.**

```
SQL> select Assembly_ID, Product_ID, Description
  2  from Product_Assembly
  3  order by Assembly_ID, Product_ID;
ASSEMBLY_ID  PRODUCT_ID  DESCRIPTION
-----------  ----------  ------------------------------------------------
B200         I101        Titanium alloy, teflon-coated iris
B200         S42         Variable-speed shutter, standard
B200         W123        Manual film advance, winder
X1000        B200        Black body, stainless steel frame camera body
X1000        F100        Blue filter - standard
X1000        F55         Xenon flash unit
X1000        L100        100mm lens - standard
X1000        S04         4 foot camera strap, leather
             X1000       Complete camera
9 rows selected.
```

Given the small quantity of data presented, you can easily visualize the organization of the parts. However, the purpose of this example is to demonstrate how you can retrieve the organization of a hierarchy.

Listing 8.13 provides an example of how to retrieve hierarchical data with the SELECT statement. The SELECT statement contains two new clauses: START WITH and CONNECT BY. The START WITH clause identifies the top-level row for which Oracle should retrieve subordinate rows—in this example, you want to find the subordinate rows of the X1000. The CONNECT BY clause tells Oracle how to present the rows, and the PRIOR operator tells Oracle to present the rows so that each child row's Assembly_ID is equal to its parent row's Product_ID.

Listing 8.13. Retrieving hierarchical information from a table.

```
SQL> select lpad(' ',2*(level-1)) ¦¦ Assembly_ID Assembly_ID,
  2    Product_ID, Description
  3    from Product_Assembly
  4    start with Product_ID = 'X1000'
  5    connect by prior Product_ID = Assembly_ID;
ASSEMBLY_ID   PRODUCT_ID   DESCRIPTION
-----------   ----------   -----------------------------------------
              X1000        Complete camera
    X1000     L100         100mm lens - standard
    X1000     B200         Black body, stainless steel frame camera body
      B200    S42          Variable-speed shutter, standard
      B200    I101         Titanium alloy, teflon-coated iris
      B200    W123         Manual film advance, winder
    X1000     S04          4 foot camera strap, leather
    X1000     F100         Blue filter - standard
    X1000     F55          Xenon flash unit
9 rows selected.
```

 To indent each row to indicate its hierarchical level, I embedded LEVEL inside the LPAD function so that the number of blanks returned by LPAD corresponds to the hierarchical level. (LEVEL is a pseudocolumn that returns the hierarchical level for each row—from 1 for the highest level to N for the most detailed level.) LPAD is concatenated with Assembly_ID.

> Be cautious in how you construct your data model. Be absolutely certain that you have to support hierarchical information before you employ CONNECT BY and START WITH. There are restrictions on hierarchical queries. For example, a hierarchical query cannot perform a join.

WARNING

To look at a particular subassembly, specify the Assembly_ID in the START WITH clause. The SELECT statement contained in Listing 8.14 illustrates this procedure; it also shows the value of LEVEL for each row.

Listing 8.14. Using LEVEL to indent the output of a hierarchical query.

```
SQL> select lpad(' ',2*(level-1)) ¦¦ Assembly_ID Assembly_ID,
  2    Product_ID, Level, Description
  3    from Product_Assembly
  4    start with Product_ID = 'B200'
  5    connect by prior Product_ID = Assembly_ID;
```

```
ASSEMBLY_ID   PRODUCT_ID LEVEL DESCRIPTION
-----------   ---------- ----- --------------------------------------------
X1000         B200           1 Black body, stainless steel frame camera body
B200          S42            2 Variable-speed shutter, standard
B200          I101           2 Titanium alloy, teflon-coated iris
B200          W123           2 Manual film advance, winder
```

You should be aware of a couple of issues when using a hierarchical SELECT statement. First, a hierarchical SELECT statement cannot also be used to join two or more tables (covered later in this lesson). Second, if you specify an ORDER BY clause, you destroy the hierarchical ordering of the rows returned by the query.

Do	Don't

DO use a hierarchical structure for a table if it represents multilevel hierarchical information. The structure should include a parent key column.

DON'T use a hierarchical structure unless the information that you're modeling has multiple hierarchy levels.

Using the EXISTS Operator

In addition to the other SQL operators, you should be familiar with the EXISTS operator. This operator operates on a subquery and returns a Boolean value:

- ☐ TRUE if the subquery returns at least one row
- ☐ FALSE if no rows are returned by the subquery

Consider the example shown in Listing 8.15, which is based on the Class and Instructor tables. Imagine that you want to determine which instructors, by name, are scheduled to teach a course. Using the EXISTS operator, you submit a query.

INPUT/ OUTPUT | **Listing 8.15. Using the EXISTS operator.**

```
SQL> select Last_Name, First_Name, Position
  2  from Instructor I
  3  where
  4  exists
  5  (select * from Class C
  6   where
  7   I.Instructor_ID = C.Instructor_ID);
```

continues

Listing 8.15. continued

```
LAST_NAME                   FIRST_NAME                POSITION
- - - - - - - - - - - - - - - - -    - - - - - - - - - - - - - - - - -   - - - - - - - - - - - - -
CHANG                       ROGER                     ASSISTANT PROFESSOR
JASON                       JERROLD                   ASSOCIATE PROFESSOR
TORRES                      PETER                     PROFESSOR
RICHARDSON                  NANCY                     ASSISTANT PROFESSOR
PARKER                      WILLIAM                   PROFESSOR
CHERNOW                     BESS                      ASSOCIATE PROFESSOR
CHU                         STEVEN                    PROFESSOR
WEISS                       ROBERTA                   PROFESSOR
RESTON                      RAPHAEL                   ASSOCIATE PROFESSOR

9 rows selected.
```

The EXISTS operator is useful in situations in which you're not interested in the column values returned by the subquery. Notice how table aliases—C for Class and I for Instructor—were used to reduce the amount of typing and improve the readability of the query. You can also preface the EXISTS operator with the logical operator NOT. For instance, Listing 8.16 illustrates how you can retrieve a list of instructors who are *not* scheduled to teach a class.

NEW TERM An *alias* is an alternative name for a table, column, or expression used in a query. An alias exists only during the query. You use an alias to simplify or clarify a query.

INPUT/ OUTPUT ## Listing 8.16. Another example of using the EXISTS operator.

```
SQL> select Last_Name, First_Name, Position
  2  from Instructor I
  3  where
  4  not exists
  5  (select * from Class C
  6  where
  7  I.Instructor_ID = C.Instructor_ID);

LAST_NAME                   FIRST_NAME                POSITION
- - - - - - - - - - - - - - - - -    - - - - - - - - - - - - - - - - -   - - - - - - - - - - - - -
HITCHCOCK                   BORIS                     PROFESSOR
DANIELS                     LAURA                     ASSOCIATE PROFESSOR
EDWARDS                     SAMANTHA                  PROFESSOR
ANGELO                      ARTHUR                    ASSOCIATE PROFESSOR
BILLINGS                    BENJAMIN                  ASSISTANT PROFESSOR
YOUNG                       ALLAN                     ASSOCIATE PROFESSOR
NILAND                      MARTINA                   ASSOCIATE PROFESSOR
BATES                       JOSEPH                    ASSISTANT PROFESSOR
POULSON                     RANIER                    PROFESSOR

9 rows selected.
```

ANALYSIS   As you can see in line 5, a subquery retrieves the columns from the Class table for each class that the instructor identified by Instructor_ID is teaching. The NOT EXISTS operator will prevent the query from returning Last_Name, First_Name, and Position if the subquery returns any rows.

The Join Operation

Now that you have a working knowledge of SQL, you are ready to delve into the world of joins. A *join* can retrieve rows from two or more tables that share a common set of values. A relational database would be of little value if it weren't for the join operation.

NEW TERM   A *join* is a query that retrieves rows from two or more tables. An *equi-join* is a join that retrieves rows from two or more tables in which one or more columns in one table are equal to one or more columns in the second table.

The *join operation* is the mechanism that allows tables to be related to one another. A join operation retrieves columns from two or more tables. To join two tables, for example, the retrieval criteria will typically specify the condition that a column in the first table—which is defined as a foreign key—is equal to a column in the second table—which is the primary key referenced by the foreign key. A join's WHERE clause may contain additional conditions. This type of join operation is referred to as an *equi-join*. For example, in the sample database, you will want to join the Instructor and Department tables so that you can retrieve related information from both tables with a single SQL statement.

The general syntax for the SELECT statement enables you to join more than two tables.

```
SELECT select-list
FROM table1, table2, ... , tableN
WHERE table1.column1 = table2.column2 and
...
table2.column3 = tableN.columnN
...
additional-conditions
```

The variables are defined as follows:

select-list is the set of columns and expressions from *table1* through *tableN*.

table1 through *tableN* are the tables from which column values are retrieved.

column1 through *columnN* are the columns in *table1* through *tableN* that are related.

    additional-conditions are optional query criteria.

Please note that you are not required to reference *column1* through *columnN* in the *select-list*.

A Simple Two-Table Join

A simple two-table join can illustrate the use of this syntax. The Class table identifies the instructor for a class by Instructor_ID. The Instructor table contains detailed information about each instructor. By joining the Class table with the Instructor table based on the Instructor_ID column, you can retrieve additional customer data.

INPUT/OUTPUT **Listing 8.17. A simple two-table join.**

```
SQL> select Class_ID, Course_ID, Last_Name, First_Name, Position
  2  from Class C, Instructor I
  3  where
  4  C.Instructor_ID = I.Instructor_ID
  5  order by Class_ID;

CLASS_ID   COURS LAST_NAME        FIRST_NAME       POSITION
---------- ----- ---------------- ---------------- ----------------------
103400     183   JASON            JERROLD          ASSOCIATE PROFESSOR
103600     50    CHANG            ROGER            ASSISTANT PROFESSOR
104200     198   RICHARDSON       NANCY            ASSISTANT PROFESSOR
104500     184   RESTON           RAPHAEL          ASSOCIATE PROFESSOR
108300     101   CHERNOW          BESS             ASSOCIATE PROFESSOR
108400     115   TORRES           PETER            PROFESSOR
108600     183   JASON            JERROLD          ASSOCIATE PROFESSOR
109100     101   WEISS            ROBERTA          PROFESSOR
110300     199   CHU              STEVEN           PROFESSOR
120200     199   PARKER           WILLIAM          PROFESSOR

10 rows selected.
```

Look at each element of the SELECT statement. The select list consists of five columns: Class_ID, Course_ID, Last_Name, First_Name, and Position. The tables in the FROM clause are Class and Instructor. The WHERE clause instructs the Oracle RDBMS to return only rows in which Instructor_ID in the Class table can be matched with a row in the Instructor table that has the same value for Instructor_ID.

There is no restriction on the order of the columns in the *select-list*. Also, there is no requirement that one or more columns even be selected from each table in the join. For example, Listing 8.18 shows a valid join in which the select list contains no columns from the Class table.

INPUT/OUTPUT **Listing 8.18. Join select list containing columns from only one table.**

```
SQL> select Last_Name, First_Name, Position
  2  from Class C, Instructor I
  3  where
```

```
  4  C.Instructor_ID = I.Instructor_ID
  5  order by Class_ID;

LAST_NAME         FIRST_NAME        POSITION
-------------     -------------     -------------------------
JASON             JERROLD           ASSOCIATE PROFESSOR
CHANG             ROGER             ASSISTANT PROFESSOR
RICHARDSON        NANCY             ASSISTANT PROFESSOR
RESTON            RAPHAEL           ASSOCIATE PROFESSOR
CHERNOW           BESS              ASSOCIATE PROFESSOR
TORRES            PETER             PROFESSOR
JASON             JERROLD           ASSOCIATE PROFESSOR
WEISS             ROBERTA           PROFESSOR
CHU               STEVEN            PROFESSOR
PARKER            WILLIAM           PROFESSOR

10 rows selected.
```

Ambiguous Columns

Each reference to a column in a join must be unambiguous. In this context, *unambiguous* means that if the column exists in more than one of the tables referenced in the join, the column name is qualified by the table name. Oracle returns an error message if you reference a column ambiguously. Listing 8.19 demonstrates a join that contains an ambiguous column—Instructor_ID.

INPUT/OUTPUT **Listing 8.19. Ambiguous column in a join.**

```
SQL> select Instructor_ID, Position
  2  from Class C, Instructor I
  3  where
  4  C.Instructor_ID = I.Instructor_ID
  5  order by Class_ID;
select Instructor_ID, Position
       *
ERROR at line 1:
ORA-00918: column ambiguously defined
```

Oracle returns the error message because Instructor_ID, which is part of the select list, appears in both the Class and Instructor tables. To correct this problem, you must qualify the Instructor_ID column with the table name or alias. Listing 8.20 demonstrates how an ambiguous column can be qualified in the select list.

Listing 8.20. Qualifying an ambiguous column in the select list.

```
SQL> select I.Instructor_ID, Position
  2  from Class C, Instructor I
  3  where
  4  C.Instructor_ID = I.Instructor_ID
  5  order by Class_ID;

INSTRUCTOR_ID          POSITION
-------------------    -------------------------
J505                   ASSOCIATE PROFESSOR
E405                   ASSISTANT PROFESSOR
E491                   ASSISTANT PROFESSOR
D944                   ASSOCIATE PROFESSOR
T149                   ASSOCIATE PROFESSOR
G331                   PROFESSOR
J505                   ASSOCIATE PROFESSOR
W490                   PROFESSOR
S131                   PROFESSOR
R983                   PROFESSOR

10 rows selected.
```

Beware of the Cartesian Product

When you're first learning to join multiple tables, a common error is to forget to provide a join condition in the WHERE clause. If you forget a join condition, you notice two things: the query takes considerably longer to execute, and the number of retrieved records is much larger than you expect.

 The technical term for a join that does not have a join condition is a *Cartesian product.*

Consider the example shown in Listing 8.21. Two tables, Class and Instructor, are listed in the FROM clause without a join condition. The Class table has 10 rows and the Class Location table has 13 rows. The query does not have a join condition instructing Oracle to retrieve the columns from each table based on Class_Building and Class_Room. As a result, Oracle returns all possible combinations of the two tables, which is 10 times 13, or 130 rows.

Listing 8.21. Cartesian product produced by a join that is missing a join condition.

```
SQL> select Class_ID, Seating_Capacity
  2  from Class, Class_Location
  3  order by Class_ID;
```

```
CLASS_ID   SEATING_CAPACITY
---------- ----------------
103400                  200
103400                  120
103400                   80
103400                   45
103400                   35
103400                   45
103400                   45
103400                   90
103400                   50
...
108600                  200
108600                   80
108600                   90
108600                   50
109100                   45
109100                   40
110300                   50
110300                   45
110300                   40
110300                   45
110300                   40
110300                   35
120200                   80

130 rows selected.
```

Multiple Table Joins

As you see, the syntax for the SELECT statement doesn't limit the number of tables that can be joined. As an example, refer to Listing 8.22, which joins three tables—Class, Course, and Instructor—to retrieve detailed information about each class.

**INPUT/
OUTPUT**   **Listing 8.22. A three-table join.**

```
SQL> select Class_ID, CL.Course_ID, CL.Department_ID, Title, Last_Name
  2  from Class CL, Course CO, Instructor I
  3  where
  4  CL.Course_ID = CO.Course_ID and
  5  CL.Department_ID = CO.Department_ID and
  6  CL.Instructor_ID = I.Instructor_ID
  7  order by Class_ID;

CLASS_ID   COURS DEPARTME TITLE                                      LAST_NAME
---------- ----- -------- ------------------------------------------ ------------
103400     183   PSYCH    WORKSHOP ON NORMALITY                       JASON
103600     50    MATH     PRE-CALCULUS                               CHANG
104200     198   PHILO    MODERN PHILOSOPHY                          RICHARDSON
104500     184   HIST     MODERN EUROPEAN HISTORY                    RESTON
108300     101   ENGL     INTRO TO ENGLISH LIT                       CHERNOW
108400     115   HIST     EARLY AMERICAN HISTORY                     TORRES
```

continues

Listing 8.22. continued

```
108600    183    PSYCH    WORKSHOP ON NORMALITY        JASON
109100    101    BIO      INTRO TO BIOLOGY             WEISS
110300    199    ENG      SEMINAR ON CHAOS             CHU
120200    199    ECON     WORKSHOP ON MARX             PARKER

10 rows selected.
```

Notice that an alias has been specified for each of the three tables:

- ☐ CL for Class
- ☐ CO for Course
- ☐ I for Instructor

Although table aliases are optional, you should use them in multiple-table joins because they reduce the size of the SELECT statement and simplify its appearance.

Examine each of the join conditions found in Listing 8.22. The first two join conditions are used to join the Class and Course tables based on Course_ID and Department_ID. These tables have two join conditions because the primary key of the Course table is Course_ID *and* Department_ID. The third join condition is used to join the Class and Instructor tables based on Instructor_ID.

Self-Join

Another form of a two-table join is the *self-join*. This type of join is used when a table has a foreign key that references its own primary key. A good example of this type is the Product_Assembly table discussed earlier in this lesson. The primary key of the Product Assembly table is Product_ID. Every product—except a complete product—belongs to an assembly. Therefore, Assembly_ID is a foreign key that references Product_ID (see Figure 8.1).

Figure 8.1.

Example of a table's primary key referenced by its foreign key.

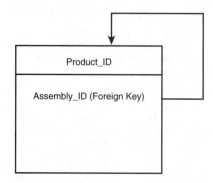

As an example of a self-join, suppose that you want to retrieve the description of each product and the description of the assembly to which it belongs. As Listing 8.23 illustrates, the join statement must define an alias for both copies of the table. The join condition—P1.Assembly_ID = P2.Product_ID—causes Oracle to retrieve product information from P1 and assembly information from P2.

INPUT/OUTPUT **Listing 8.23. Example of a self-join.**

```
SQL> select P1.Description || ' is part of ' || P2.Description
                                        "Assembly Breakdown"
  2  from Product_Assembly P1, Product_Assembly P2
  3  where
  4  P1.Assembly_ID = P2.Product_ID
  5  order by P1.Assembly_ID, P1.Product_ID;
Assembly Breakdown
--------------------------------------------------------------
Titanium alloy, teflon-coated iris is part of Black body, stainless ste
Variable-speed shutter, standard is part of Black body, stainless steel
Manual film advance, winder is part of Black body, stainless steel fram
Black body, stainless steel frame camera body is part of Complete camer
Blue filter - standard is part of Complete camera
Xenon flash unit is part of Complete camera
100mm lens - standard is part of Complete camera
4 foot camera strap, leather is part of Complete camera
8 rows selected.
```

Outer Joins

In this section, you'll see how another type of join is used—the outer join. To understand the difference between a regular join (that is, an equi-join) and an outer join, let's take another look at a regular join. A multiple-table join returns columns from each table where the join conditions are met. Consider the example shown in Listing 8.24. The instructors at Flugle College may or may not be scheduled to teach a class during a particular semester. In addition to teaching, the staff members at Flugle College are also expected to be engaged in original research in their fields. Listing 8.24 contains a join of the Instructor and Class tables. Notice that the query only retrieves instructors who are scheduled to teach a class.

INPUT/OUTPUT **Listing 8.24. Equi-join of the Instructor and Class tables.**

```
SQL> select I.Department_ID, Last_Name, First_Name, Class_ID
  2  from Instructor I, Class C
  3  where
  4  I.Instructor_ID = C.Instructor_ID
  5  order by I.Department_ID, Last_Name;
```

continues

Listing 8.24. continued

```
DEPARTME LAST_NAME        FIRST_NAME       CLASS_ID
-------- ---------------- ---------------- ----------
BIO      WEISS            ROBERTA          109100
ECON     PARKER           WILLIAM          120200
ENG      CHU              STEVEN           110300
ENGL     CHERNOW          BESS             108300
HIST     RESTON           RAPHAEL          104500
HIST     TORRES           PETER            108400
MATH     CHANG            ROGER            103600
PHILO    RICHARDSON       NANCY            104200
PSYCH    JASON            JERROLD          108600
PSYCH    JASON            JERROLD          103400

10 rows selected.
```

If you want to retrieve instructor information whether or not an instructor is teaching a class, you must use the outer join operator by appending (+) (a plus sign within parentheses) to the optional column in the join condition. Listing 8.25 illustrates the use of the outer join operator.

INPUT/OUTPUT **Listing 8.25. An outer join.**

```
SQL> select I.Department_ID, Last_Name, First_Name, Class_ID
  2  from Instructor I, Class C
  3  where
  4  I.Instructor_ID = C.Instructor_ID (+)
  5  order by I.Department_ID, Last_Name;

DEPARTMENT_ID         LAST_NAME        FIRST_NAME CLASS_ID
--------------------- ---------------- ---------- --------------------
ANTHRO                DANIELS          LAURA
ANTHRO                HITCHCOCK        BORIS
ANTHRO                POULSON          RANIER
BIO                   EDWARDS          SAMANTHA
BIO                   WEISS            ROBERTA    109100
ECON                  PARKER           WILLIAM    120200
ENG                   CHU              STEVEN     110300
ENGL                  CHERNOW          BESS       108300
HIST                  RESTON           RAPHAEL    104500
HIST                  TORRES           PETER      108400
MATH                  CHANG            ROGER      103600
MATH                  NILAND           MARTINA
MATH                  YOUNG            ALLAN
PHILO                 ANGELO           ARTHUR
PHILO                 BILLINGS         BENJAMIN
PHILO                 RICHARDSON       NANCY      104200
PSYCH                 BATES            JOSEPH
PSYCH                 JASON            JERROLD    108600
PSYCH                 JASON            JERROLD    103400

19 rows selected.
```

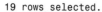

If an instructor is not teaching a class, Oracle returns a null for the Class_ID—or any other column that you select from the Class table. Listing 8.26 demonstrates how you can obtain a list of instructors who are not teaching a class by adding another condition to the WHERE clause—Class_ID is null.

INPUT/OUTPUT **Listing 8.26. Another outer join.**

```
SQL> select I.Department_ID, Last_Name, First_Name
  2  from Instructor I, Class C
  3  where
  4  I.Instructor_ID = C.Instructor_ID (+) and
  5  Class_ID is null
  6  order by I.Department_ID, Last_Name;

DEPARTMENT_ID        LAST_NAME         FIRST_NAME
------------------   ---------------   ----------
ANTHRO               DANIELS           LAURA
ANTHRO               HITCHCOCK         BORIS
ANTHRO               POULSON           RANIER
BIO                  EDWARDS           SAMANTHA
MATH                 NILAND            MARTINA
MATH                 YOUNG             ALLAN
PHILO                ANGELO            ARTHUR
PHILO                BILLINGS          BENJAMIN
PSYCH                BATES             JOSEPH

9 rows selected.
```

Using Set Operators in the SELECT Statement

The SQL language is a partial implementation of the relational model as envisioned by Codd, the father of relational theory. As part of that implementation, Oracle's version of SQL provides three set operators: INTERSECT, UNION, and MINUS.

The INTERSECT Operator

The INTERSECT operator returns the rows that are common between two sets of rows.

The syntax for using the INTERSECT operator is

SYNTAX

```
select-stmt1
INTERSECT
select-stmt2
[order-by-clause]
```

The variables are defined as follows:

select-stmt1 and *select-stmt2* are valid SELECT statements.

order-by-clause is an ORDER BY clause that references the columns by number rather than by name.

Here are some requirements and considerations for using the INTERSECT operator:

☐ The two SELECT statements may not contain an ORDER BY clause; however, you can order the results of the entire INTERSECT operation.

☐ The number of columns retrieved by *select-stmt1* must be equal to the number of columns retrieved by *select-stmt2*.

☐ The datatypes of the columns retrieved by *select-stmt1* must match the datatypes of the columns retrieved by *select-stmt2*.

☐ The optional *order-by-clause* differs from the usual ORDER BY clause in a SELECT statement because the columns used for ordering *must* be referenced by number rather than by name. The reason that the columns in the *order-by-clause* must be referenced by number rather than by name is that SQL does not require that the column names retrieved by *select-stmt1* be identical to the column names retrieved by *select-stmt2*. Therefore, you must indicate the columns to be used in ordering results by their position in the select list.

Consider the following typical scenario for using the INTERSECT operator. As the dean of Flugle College, you suspect that some of Flugle's instructors are also teaching at Hoover College, Flugle's archrival. A list of instructors at Hoover College, archrival of Flugle College, has come into your possession as shown in Listing 8.27. The first query retrieves the instructors at Flugle College. The second query retrieves the instructors at Hoover College. The third query uses the INTERSECT operator to find the common instructors between the two tables.

Listing 8.27. Contents of Instructor table for Flugle and Hoover Colleges.

```
SQL> select Last_Name, First_Name, MI, Position
  2  from Instructor;

LAST_NAME       FIRST_NAME M POSITION
--------------- ----------- - ------------------------
HITCHCOCK       BORIS         PROFESSOR
DANIELS         LAURA         ASSOCIATE PROFESSOR
EDWARDS         SAMANTHA      PROFESSOR
CHANG           ROGER         ASSISTANT PROFESSOR
JASON           JERROLD       ASSOCIATE PROFESSOR
TORRES          PETER         PROFESSOR
```

8

```
ANGELO          ARTHUR       ASSOCIATE PROFESSOR
RICHARDSON      NANCY        ASSISTANT PROFESSOR
PARKER          WILLIAM      PROFESSOR
CHERNOW         BESS         ASSOCIATE PROFESSOR
CHU             STEVEN       PROFESSOR
WEISS           ROBERTA      PROFESSOR
RESTON          RAPHAEL      ASSOCIATE PROFESSOR
BILLINGS        BENJAMIN     ASSISTANT PROFESSOR
YOUNG           ALLAN        ASSOCIATE PROFESSOR
NILAND          MARTINA      ASSOCIATE PROFESSOR
BATES           JOSEPH       ASSISTANT PROFESSOR
POULSON         RANIER       PROFESSOR

18 rows selected.

SQL> select Last_Name, First_Name, MI, Position
  2  from Hoover_Instructor;

LAST_NAME                FIRST_NAME         M POSITION
-----------------------  -----------------  - --------------------
CHANG                    ROGER                ASSISTANT PROFESSOR
JASON                    JERROLD              ASSOCIATE PROFESSOR
TORRES                   PETER                PROFESSOR
CHERNOW                  BESS                 ASSOCIATE PROFESSOR
CHU                      STEVEN               PROFESSOR
RESTON                   RAPHAEL              ASSOCIATE PROFESSOR
YOUNG                    ALLAN                ASSOCIATE PROFESSOR
NILAND                   MARTINA              ASSOCIATE PROFESSOR
BATES                    JOSEPH               ASSISTANT PROFESSOR
HUSTON                   MYRON              T PROFESSOR
RABINOWITZ               KERMIT             A LECTURER
CHRISTIANSON             PAUL               V PROFESSOR

12 rows selected.

SQL> select Last_Name, First_Name, MI, Position
  2  from Instructor
  3  intersect
  4  select Last_Name, First_Name, MI, Position
  5  from Hoover_Instructor;

LAST_NAME                FIRST_NAME         M POSITION
-----------------------  -----------------  - --------------------
BATES                    JOSEPH               ASSISTANT PROFESSOR
CHANG                    ROGER                ASSISTANT PROFESSOR
CHERNOW                  BESS                 ASSOCIATE PROFESSOR
CHU                      STEVEN               PROFESSOR
JASON                    JERROLD              ASSOCIATE PROFESSOR
NILAND                   MARTINA              ASSOCIATE PROFESSOR
RESTON                   RAPHAEL              ASSOCIATE PROFESSOR
TORRES                   PETER                PROFESSOR
YOUNG                    ALLAN                ASSOCIATE PROFESSOR

9 rows selected.
```

If you visually inspect the rows that exist in each table, you can confirm that the two tables do indeed have the nine rows in common.

The UNION **Operator**

Sooner or later, you'll find yourself in a situation in which you need to combine the rows from similar tables to produce a report or to create a table for analysis. Even though the tables represent similar information, they may differ considerably. To accomplish this task, you should consider using the UNION operator.

The syntax for this set operator is pretty simple:

```
select-stmt1
UNION
select-stmt2
[order-by-clause]
```

The variables are defined as follows:

select-stmt1 and select-stmt2 are valid SELECT statements.

order-by-clause is an optional ORDER BY clause that references the columns by number rather than by name.

The UNION operator combines the rows returned by the first SELECT statement with the rows returned by the second SELECT statement. Keep the following things in mind when you use the UNION operator:

☐ The two SELECT statements may not contain an ORDER BY clause; however, you can order the results of the entire UNION operation.

☐ The number of columns retrieved by select-stmt1 must be equal to the number of columns retrieved by select-stmt2.

☐ The datatypes of the columns retrieved by select-stmt1 must match the datatypes of the columns retrieved by select-stmt2.

☐ The optional order-by-clause differs from the usual ORDER BY clause in a SELECT statement because the columns used for ordering must be referenced by number rather than by name. The reason that the columns must be referenced by number is that SQL does not require that the column names retrieved by select-stmt1 be identical to the column names retrieved by select-stmt2.

To illustrate the use of UNION, imagine that you have been given the task of consolidating information from two seismology labs. The first table is from the Department of Geophysics at the University of Northern South Dakota; the other table is from a private research institution, RIND. Listing 8.28 describes the structure of the two tables.

**INPUT/
OUTPUT**   **Listing 8.28. Description of two tables for seismic events.**

```
SQL> desc UNSD_Event
 Name                              Null?     Type
 -------------------------------- --------   ----
 EVENT_NO                                    NUMBER
 EPICENTER_LATITUDE                          NUMBER
 EPICENTER_LONGITUDE                         NUMBER
 EVENT_MAGNITUDE                             NUMBER
 EVENT_TIME                                  DATE
 EVENT_WAVE                                  CHAR(1)
 INSTRUMENT_NAME                             VARCHAR2(30)

SQL> desc RIND_Event
 Name                              Null?     Type
 -------------------------------- --------   ----
 LOCATION_LAT                                NUMBER
 LOCATION_LON                                NUMBER
 RICHTER_NUMBER                              NUMBER
 DATE_TIME                                   VARCHAR2(30)
 WAVE_TYPE                                   CHAR(1)
```

ANALYSIS   Stop for a moment to examine the similarities and differences between UNSD_Event and RIND_Event. First of all, both tables store information about seismic events. However, UNSD_Event has two extra columns: Event_No and Instrument_Name. Both tables store the epicenter latitude and longitude, the magnitude, and the wave type (P or S). However, UNSD_Event defines Event_Time as a DATE, whereas RIND_Event uses VARCHAR2 for storing the event date and time in Date_Time. Listing 8.29 illustrates what happens if you try to perform a UNION without converting Event_Time in UNSD_Event and Date_Time in RIND_Event to a common datatype.

**INPUT/
OUTPUT**   **Listing 8.29. UNION operator used with columns with different datatypes.**

```
SQL> select Epicenter_Latitude, Epicenter_Longitude, Event_Magnitude,
            Event_Time, Event_Wave
  2  from UNSD_Event
  3  UNION
  4  select Location_Lat, Location_Lon, Richter_Number, Date_Time, Wave_Type
  5  from RIND_Event;
select Epicenter_Latitude, Epicenter_Longitude, Event_Magnitude,
            Event_Time, Event_Wave
            *
ERROR at line 1:
ORA-01790: expression must have same datatype as corresponding expression
```

You can force both columns to have the same datatype by converting Date_Time in the
RIND_Event table to a date value by using the TO_DATE function, as shown in Listing 8.30.

**INPUT/
OUTPUT**

Listing 8.30. Using a function to force both columns to have the same datatype.

```
SQL> select Epicenter_Latitude, Epicenter_Longitude, Event_Magnitude,
            Event_Time, Event_Wave
  2  from UNSD_Event
  3  UNION
  4  select Location_Lat, Location_Lon, Richter_Number,
            TO_DATE(Date_Time,'MM-DD-YY HH:MI:SS'), Wave_Type
  5  from RIND_Event;
EPICENTER_LATITUDE EPICENTER_LONGITUDE EVENT_MAGNITUDE EVENT_TIM E
------------------ ------------------- --------------- --------- -
             12.83              189.85             5.8 25-APR-95 P
             22.33              233.31             5.9 03-FEB-95 P
             23.33              179.11             5.3 10-JAN-95 P
             29.84              238.41             6.2 22-MAR-95 S
             31.17              208.33             6.6 19-APR-95 S
             31.84              241.21             6.1 12-MAR-95 S
             37.81              211.84             6.4 11-JAN-95 S
7 rows selected.
```

If you want to order the results by Event_Time, you can use the ORDER BY clause. However,
instead of referring to the column by name, you must reference it by its order in the select
list. Listing 8.31 shows how all the rows retrieved by the UNION are ordered by Event_Time,
which is the fourth item in the select list.

**INPUT/
OUTPUT**

Listing 8.31. Ordering the rows retrieved by a UNION.

```
SQL> select Epicenter_Latitude, Epicenter_Longitude, Event_Magnitude,
            Event_Time, Event_Wave
  2  from UNSD_Event
  3  UNION
  4  select Location_Lat, Location_Lon, Richter_Number,
            TO_DATE(Date_Time,'MM-DD-YY HH:MI:SS'), Wave_Type
  5  from RIND_Event
  6  order by 4;
EPICENTER_LATITUDE EPICENTER_LONGITUDE EVENT_MAGNITUDE EVENT_TIM E
------------------ ------------------- --------------- --------- -
             23.33              179.11             5.3 10-JAN-95 P
             37.81              211.84             6.4 11-JAN-95 S
             22.33              233.31             5.9 03-FEB-95 P
             31.84              241.21             6.1 12-MAR-95 S
             29.84              238.41             6.2 22-MAR-95 S
             31.17              208.33             6.6 19-APR-95 S
             12.83              189.85             5.8 25-APR-95 P
7 rows selected.
```

The MINUS Operator

In addition to the INTERSECT and UNION operators, Oracle also provides the MINUS operator for comparing one set of rows to another set.

SYNTAX

The syntax for using the MINUS operator resembles the syntax for the UNION operator:

```
select-stmt1
MINUS
select-stmt2
[order-by-clause]
```

The variables are defined as follows:

    select-stmt1 and *select-stmt2* are valid SELECT statements.

    order-by-clause is an ORDER BY clause that references the columns by number rather than by name.

The requirements and considerations for using the MINUS operator are essentially the same as those for the INTERSECT and UNION operators. To illustrate the use of the MINUS operator, consider again the Instructor and Hoover_Instructor tables. You want to determine which instructors at Flugle College are not also teaching at Hoover College. Listing 8.32 shows an example of how the MINUS operator can be used to accomplish this. The query returns nine rows, which represent the instructors at Flugle College who do not teach at Hoover College.

**INPUT/
OUTPUT**

Listing 8.32. Using the MINUS operator.

```
SQL> select Last_Name, First_Name, MI, Position
  2  from Instructor
  3  minus
  4  select Last_Name, First_Name, MI, Position
  5  from Hoover_Instructor;

LAST_NAME        FIRST_NAME M POSITION
---------------  ---------- - ------------------------
ANGELO           ARTHUR       ASSOCIATE PROFESSOR
BILLINGS         BENJAMIN     ASSISTANT PROFESSOR
DANIELS          LAURA        ASSOCIATE PROFESSOR
EDWARDS          SAMANTHA     PROFESSOR
HITCHCOCK        BORIS        PROFESSOR
PARKER           WILLIAM      PROFESSOR
POULSON          RANIER       PROFESSOR
RICHARDSON       NANCY        ASSISTANT PROFESSOR
WEISS            ROBERTA      PROFESSOR

9 rows selected.
```

However, the query in Listing 8.32 doesn't tell anything about the instructors at Hoover College who don't teach at Flugle College. To view this information, the two SELECT statements must be reversed, as shown in Listing 8.33.

Listing 8.33. Reversing the SELECT statements associated with the MINUS operator.

```
SQL> select Last_Name, First_Name, MI, Position
  2  from Hoover_Instructor
  3  minus
  4  select Last_Name, First_Name, MI, Position
  5  from Instructor;

LAST_NAME        FIRST_NAME M POSITION
---------------- ---------- - ------------------------
CHRISTIANSON     PAUL       V PROFESSOR
HUSTON           MYRON      T PROFESSOR
RABINOWITZ       KERMIT     A LECTURER
```

This example demonstrates that MINUS doesn't tell you all the differences between the two tables—it returns only those rows in the first set that can't be found in the second set. Also, you can specify a WHERE clause in the SELECT statements used by the MINUS operator.

Creating a Table by Selecting from Another Table

When you develop a new database application, you usually go through a phase of experimenting with various table designs. Whether you use legacy data or artificial data, it's nice to have some simple methods for experimentation. One DDL statement that you might want to use is CREATE TABLE—with a subquery.

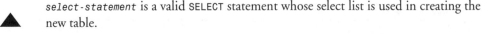

The syntax is

```
CREATE TABLE table-name
[(column-definition1, ... , column-definitionN)]
AS
select-statement
```

The variables are defined as follows:

table-name is the name of the new Oracle table.

column-definition1 through *column-definitionN* are optional column definitions that are used to specify different column names to be associated with the values returned by the subquery.

select-statement is a valid SELECT statement whose select list is used in creating the new table.

For example, Listing 8.34 contains a statement to create a new table whose rows are a subset of a subset of an existing table.

Listing 8.34. Creating a table based on a subquery.

```
SQL> create table Anthro_Instructors
  2  as
  3  select * from Instructor
  4  where
  5  Department_ID = 'ANTHRO';

Table created.

SQL> select Department_ID, Last_Name, First_Name
  2  from Anthro_Instructors;

DEPARTMENT_ID        LAST_NAME         FIRST_NAME
-------------------- ----------------- ----------
ANTHRO               HITCHCOCK         BORIS
ANTHRO               DANIELS           LAURA
ANTHRO               POULSON           RANIER
```

Notice that Oracle doesn't tell you how many rows are inserted into the new table. In fact, you can create a new table that is empty by specifying an impossible condition, as demonstrated in Listing 8.35.

 Listing 8.35. Creating an empty table.

```
SQL> create table Empty_Instructor
  2  as
  3  select * from Instructor
  4  where
  5  1=2;

Table created.

SQL> select count(*) from Empty_Instructor;

COUNT(*)
--------
       0
```

 TIP

Oracle rejects the CREATE TABLE statement if the subquery references a LONG or LONG RAW column. If you need to copy rows from a LONG column in one table to another, use the SQL*Plus COPY command. It does support the copying of LONG column values.

NOTE

> When used with a subquery, the CREATE TABLE statement copies only one kind of table or column constraint: the NOT NULL constraint. If you want the new table to have all the existing constraints, you have to specify them with an ALTER TABLE statement.

Using Views

A *view* is a query of one or more tables that provides another way of presenting information. A view does not actually contain or store its own data; in fact, you can think of a view as a virtual table. The only storage that a view actually requires is the SELECT statement that defines it.

NEW TERM A *view* is a stored query based on a query of one or more tables.

You can use a view to perform the following tasks:

☐ Maintain finer control over security

☐ Hide complexity from a developer or user

☐ Rename columns

View Syntax

The syntax for creating a view is really quite simple.

To define a view, use this syntax:

```
CREATE VIEW view-name
(column1,...,columnN)
AS
select-statement
```

The variables are defined as follows:

> *view-name* is the name of the view (subject to the same requirements as other Oracle object names).
>
> *column1* through *columnN* are the column names of the view that correspond to the columns referenced in *select-statement*.

> *select-statement* is a valid Oracle SELECT statement.

The following simple view is based on a single table. Suppose several administrators at Flugle College have requested a very simple way to retrieve the current cost for each course. The current cost for a course is the number of units multiplied by $250 per unit plus any additional fees. Even though you've shown the administrators how to construct a simple query, they want you to streamline the process.

Listing 8.36 illustrates the view that you define to meet their needs. Here is a description of each line in the SQL statement that creates the view. The first line specifies the name of the view: Course_Cost. The second line lists the five columns that compose the view: Course_ID, Department_ID, Title, Description, and Cost. The third line indicates that the view is to be created from a query. The fourth line specifies the first four columns to be returned by the view: Course_ID, Department_ID, Title, and Description. The fifth line indicates that the fifth column in the view—Cost—is calculated by multiplying Units by $250 per unit and adding Additional_Fees.

**INPUT/
OUTPUT** **Listing 8.36. Creating a simple view.**

```
SQL> create view Course_Cost
  2  (Course_ID, Department_ID, Title, Description, Cost)
  3  as
  4  select Course_ID, Department_ID, Title, Description,
  5  Units*250 + Additional_Fees
  6  from Course;

View created.

SQL> select Department_ID, Course_ID, Title, Cost
  2  from Course_Cost
  3  order by Department_ID, Course_ID;
```

DEPARTMENT	COURS	TITLE	COST
ANTHRO	101	INTRO TO ANTHROPOLOGY	750
ANTHRO	174	PHYS ANTHRO FIELD TECHNIQUES	805
ANTHRO	189	SEMINAR ON NACIMERA	507.5
BIO	101	INTRO TO BIOLOGY	805
BIO	177	INVERTEBRATE ANATOMY	815
BIO	178	MAMMALIAN ANATOMY	820
ECON	101	INTRO TO ECONOMICS	775
ECON	189	MONETARY POLICY	1500
ECON	199	WORKSHOP ON MARX	750
ENG	101	INTRO TO STRUCTURES	825
ENG	102	INTRO TO CIRCUIT THEORY	795
ENG	103	INTRO TO DYNAMICS	785
ENG	199	SEMINAR ON CHAOS	545
ENGL	101	INTRO TO ENGLISH LIT	750
ENGL	189	EVOLUTIONARY GRAMMAR	500
ENGL	192	MODERN ENGLISH LIT	750
ENGL	193	SEMINAR ON THEME ANALYSIS	500
HIST	115	EARLY AMERICAN HISTORY	750
HIST	184	MODERN EUROPEAN HISTORY	750
HIST	199	WORKSHOP ON JEFFERSON	750
MATH	101	GENERAL CALCULUS	750

continues

Listing 8.36. continued

```
MATH       189    NUMBER THEORY                  750
MATH       50     PRE-CALCULUS                   750
MATH       51     ADVANCED ARITHMETIC            760
PHILO      101    INTRO TO PHILOSOPHY            750
PHILO      174    ANCIENT GREEK PHILOSOPHERS     750
PHILO      198    MODERN PHILOSOPHY              750
PSYCH      101    INTRO TO PSYCHOLOGY            775
PSYCH      181    WORKSHOP ON NEUROSES           575
PSYCH      183    WORKSHOP ON NORMALITY          545
PSYCH      185    ABNORMAL PSYCHOLOGY            770
PSYCH      501    PSYCH IN FILM                  825

32 rows selected.
```

Restricting Data Access with a View

Oracle provides several mechanisms for restricting data access: views, database triggers, and table and column privileges. Specific privileges on these objects can be granted to database roles and individual users. You need to assess the security requirements of your application to determine which method is most appropriate.

If you use a view to restrict data access, several methods are available to you. Each method offers a different level of control over data access, from coarse to very fine. A coarse control enables you to define a view that is a subset of its base table. For example, the Student table includes address information, which you may not want to share with all users who need access to the table. Listing 8.37 shows how to create a view of the Student table that doesn't include the personal information. A very fine level of control can be achieved with a database trigger; an example is presented on Day 12, "Developer/2000: Introduction to Oracle Forms."

| INPUT/ OUTPUT | ### Listing 8.37. Creating a view based on a subset of a table's columns. |

```
SQL> create view Student_No_Personal
  2  as
  3  select Student_ID, Last_Name, First_Name, MI, Year, Email
  4  from Student;

View created.

SQL> describe Student_No_Personal
 Name                              Null?    Type
 -------------------------------   -------- ----
 STUDENT_ID                        NOT NULL VARCHAR2(20)
 LAST_NAME                         NOT NULL VARCHAR2(25)
 FIRST_NAME                        NOT NULL VARCHAR2(25)
 MI                                         VARCHAR2(1)
 YEAR                                       VARCHAR2(25)
 EMAIL                                      VARCHAR2(100)
```

As you see in Listing 8.37, the SQL*Plus DESCRIBE command doesn't indicate whether the object description belongs to a table or view. Even if the user knows that the student's address is stored in the Student table, the view can't return the column because it isn't contained in the view definition.

Hiding Complexity with a View

During application development, you must often deal with developers and users who have differing organizational perspectives and a broad range of technical sophistication. As a result, you should use the mechanisms that Oracle offers to customize the environment for developers and users.

I include developers in this category because, like users, their knowledge of SQL in general and Oracle in particular does vary. For example, many forms and reports require the joining of several tables. The use of views can simplify this process because, as the application architect, *you* can define the views with which developers need to be concerned.

Views are also an excellent way to customize the database environment for end users. This is especially true for large organizations that access the same information for different purposes. Typically, each group has its own name for referring to the same piece of information. Because of the widespread use of third-party ad hoc query tools such as Business Objects, IQ Objects, and Oracle Discoverer/2000, a column name should accurately describe the information it contains to help an end user determine which columns to query. By creating a view, you can customize the column names that a group of users sees.

A view can hide the complexity that exists in a multiple-table join. By defining a view, users are freed from learning the idiosyncrasies of the SELECT statement. For instance, if you want to provide a consolidated view of a scheduled class at Flugle College, you might join information from the Class, Course, and Instructor tables. Listing 8.38 contains the CREATE VIEW statement used to construct the view based on the three-table join.

INPUT/OUTPUT **Listing 8.38. A view based on a multiple-table join.**

```
SQL> create view Class_Summary as
  2  select Class_ID, Class_Building, Class_Room,
  3         CL.Department_ID, CL.Course_ID, CO.Title,
  4         Last_Name, First_Name
  5  from Class CL, Course CO, Instructor I
  6  where
  7  CL.Department_ID = CO.Department_ID and
  8  CL.Course_ID     = CO.Course_ID and
  9  CL.Instructor_ID = I.Instructor_ID;

View created.
```

Using the Class_Summary view, the user can simply select the desired columns without specifying any join conditions. Listing 8.39 illustrates how a user can select those classes whose titles include the phrase INTRO.

INPUT/ OUTPUT **Listing 8.39. Selecting from a view.**

```
SQL> select Class_ID, Class_Building, Class_Room,
  2         Department_ID, Course_ID, Title, Last_Name
  3  from Class_Summary
  4  where
  5  Title like '%INTRO%';

CLASS_  CLASS_BUILDING CLAS DEPART COURS TITLE                LAST_NAME
------  -------------- ---- ------ ----- -------------------- ---------
109100 FLUGLE HALL     180 BIO    101   INTRO TO BIOLOGY     WEISS
108300 FLUGLE HALL     150 ENGL   101   INTRO TO ENGLISH LIT CHERNOW
```

Summary

This lesson focused on these features of SQL:

☐ Oracle provides group functions such as MAX and MIN that return a single value for an entire set of rows.

☐ The SELECT statement has two optional clauses—GROUP BY and HAVING—that return rows grouped by a common value for specified columns.

☐ Hierarchical data can be organized through the CONNECT BY clause. You must indicate a starting condition with the START WITH clause.

☐ A join operation is a SELECT statement whose FROM clause has two or more tables and one or more join conditions that typically equate primary and foreign keys.

☐ The INTERSECT operator returns the set of common rows that are found in two sets of rows.

☐ The UNION operator returns the distinct rows that exist in two sets of rows.

☐ The MINUS operator returns the rows in one set that are not found in a second set.

What Comes Next?

On Day 9, "Programming an Oracle Database with PL/SQL," you learn about the basic elements of PL/SQL such as flow-of-control statements, variable declaration, and procedure and function declarations.

Q&A

Q Can two tables, A and B, be joined by columns if the first column's datatype in table A is not the same as the second column's datatype in table B?

A Yes, it's possible. For example, you can use a conversion function, such as TO_CHAR, TO_DATE, or TO_NUMBER, to convert the first column so that the datatype returned by the function is the same as the second column's datatype.

Workshop

The purpose of the Workshop is to allow you to test your knowledge of the material discussed in the lesson. See whether you can correctly answer the questions in the quiz and complete the exercise before you continue with tomorrow's lesson.

Quiz

1. Construct an SQL statement that retrieves the last name of an instructor who is teaching a course with additional fees greater than $50.

2. Construct an SQL statement that retrieves a list of cities in which students reside and the number of students that reside in each city.

3. Create a view that lists each class—its Class_ID, Department_ID, and Course_ID—for those classes that meet on Mondays.

Exercise

The number of instructors is 18. The number of classes being offered is 10. However, the number of distinct Instructor_IDs in the Class table is nine. Using these tables and SQL, provide a complete explanation.

Day **9**

Programming an Oracle Database with PL/SQL

Up to this point, I've presented SQL as a language without procedural capabilities. However, Oracle offers procedural language extensions to SQL through the PL/SQL language. PL/SQL is the basis for the following application logic elements:

☐ **SQL*Plus script:** An SQL*Plus script can incorporate PL/SQL block subprograms.

☐ **Stored procedure or function:** A stored procedure or function is a PL/SQL subprogram that can be invoked by a client application, a database trigger, or an Oracle tool application trigger.

☐ **Database trigger:** A database trigger is a PL/SQL subprogram that performs some action based on the execution of a DML statement—such as INSERT, UPDATE, or DELETE—against a database table.

☐ **Package:** A set of PL/SQL procedures, functions, cursors, and other PL/SQL variables are bundled together into a package.

☐ **Application trigger:** Oracle application development tools such as Oracle Forms and Oracle Reports are equipped with a PL/SQL engine so that developers can construct application triggers using PL/SQL.

The purpose of today's lesson is to introduce the fundamental elements of PL/SQL. You should feel comfortable with the syntax and use of PL/SQL before you attempt to design stored procedures on Day 10, "Program Development in PL/SQL," and Day 11, "More Programming Techniques with PL/SQL." This lesson addresses the features contained in PL/SQL through version 2.3.

 TIP
Don't use SQL*Plus to type in each line of a PL/SQL script. If you make a typo, SQL*Plus won't provide any feedback until it reads the / that terminates the PL/SQL block—SQL*Plus passes the entire block to the PL/SQL engine only when the block is complete. The PL/SQL engine is a component of the Oracle RDBMS. Instead, use a text editor, such as Notepad, for developing your PL/SQL scripts. You can paste the script directly into SQL*Plus or invoke it with the START or @ command. On Day 16, you'll learn about Procedure Builder, which is far superior to SQL*Plus for PL/SQL program development. There are other third-party products that provide similar capabilities; for instance, you may also want to evaluate Platinum's SQL Station Coder (www.platinum.com) or DBCorp's WEB*PL browser-based PL/SQL development tool (www.dbcorp.ab.ca).

PL/SQL Is a Block-Structured Language

PL/SQL is a block-structured language with a syntax similar to the C programming language. In addition to supporting embedded SQL statements, PL/SQL offers standard programming constructs such as procedure and function declarations, control statements such as IF-THEN-ELSE and LOOP, and declared variables. A PL/SQL program consists of procedures, functions, or anonymous blocks. An *anonymous block* is an unnamed PL/SQL block that has no arguments and returns no value. Anonymous blocks are common in scripts that are executed in an SQL*Plus session.

From a top-level perspective, Figure 9.1 illustrates the structure of a PL/SQL block, which includes an optional declaration section, an executable section, and an optional section for handling PL/SQL and SQL exceptions and errors.

Figure 9.1.

Top-level structure of a PL/SQL block.

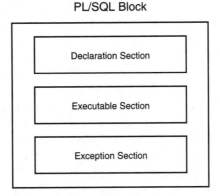

PL/SQL Block

Declaration Section

Executable Section

Exception Section

Let's look at a simple anonymous PL/SQL block that generates some test data. Listing 9.1 contains an anonymous block which is executed from an SQL*Plus script and inserts 100 rows into TEST_TABLE.

Listing 9.1. Execution of an anonymous PL/SQL block in SQL*Plus.

INPUT/
OUTPUT

```
SQL> @c:\tyo\day10_1
SQL> drop table test_table;
Table dropped.
SQL>
SQL> create table test_table (
  2  record_number      int,
  3  current_date       date);
Table created.
SQL>
SQL> DECLARE
  2
  2  max_records CONSTANT int := 100;
  3  i             int := 1;
  4
  4  BEGIN
  5
  5  FOR i IN 1..max_records LOOP
  6
  6    INSERT INTO test_table
  7          (record_number, current_date)
  8    VALUES
  9          (i, SYSDATE);
 10
 10  END LOOP;
 11
 11  COMMIT;
 12  END;
/
PL/SQL procedure successfully completed.
```

ANALYSIS Take a look at some of the elements in the previous PL/SQL script. This script is an anonymous PL/SQL block because it has no name—it isn't declared as a procedure, function, or package. All the lines in this script are contained in a single SQL*Plus script. The first two SQL commands drop the TEST_TABLE and then create it. The PL/SQL block actually starts with the word DECLARE. The declaration section declares a constant, max_records (in line 2), and a variable, i (in line 3), which serves as a counter. The beginning of the executable portion of the block is designated by BEGIN (in line 4). The block contains a single FOR LOOP (in line 5) that inserts a row into TEST_TABLE while i is less than or equal to max_records. When the FOR LOOP completes, the transaction is committed (in line 11). The last line of the script is a /, which causes SQL*Plus to submit the PL/SQL block to the PL/SQL engine. Unless a PL/SQL compilation error occurs, the only feedback that SQL*Plus provides is a message: PL/SQL procedure successfully completed. In the next lesson, you'll see how to produce diagnostics from PL/SQL, which enables you to see the progress of a PL/SQL subprogram's execution.

The Declaration Section

The declaration section of a PL/SQL block is optional. However, you must declare all variables and constants that are referenced in the PL/SQL statements. To include a declaration section in a PL/SQL block, begin the PL/SQL block with the word DECLARE. Each variable or constant declaration consists of its name, datatype, and an optional default value. As with all PL/SQL statements, each variable and constant declaration is terminated with a semicolon. Listing 9.2 contains some examples of declared variables and constants.

INPUT **Listing 9.2. Examples of declared variables and constants.**

```
Fax_Number              VARCHAR2(10);
Current_Used_Value      NUMBER(6,2) := 100.00;
Max_Current_Used_Value       REAL := 9999.99;
State                   VARCHAR2(2) := 'CA';
```

The Executable Section

The executable section of a PL/SQL block follows the keyword BEGIN. Each PL/SQL statement is terminated by a semicolon. These statements can be categorized as follows:

☐ Assignment statements

☐ Flow-of-control statements

☐ SQL statements

☐ Cursor statements

The Exception Section

An exception is an error condition that occurs during the execution of a PL/SQL program. An exception might be predefined—for instance, an INSERT statement attempts to add a duplicate row to a table, resulting in the DUP_VAL_ON_INDEX exception being raised. You can also define your own exceptions that are specific to your application. The exception section defines the exception handlers invoked for both predefined and user-defined exceptions. Each exception handler consists of one or more PL/SQL statements.

Declaring Variables with PL/SQL

Another capability provided by PL/SQL—but not SQL—is additional datatypes. In addition to the normal Oracle SQL datatypes, PL/SQL enables you to declare variables with these datatypes:

BOOLEAN	A Boolean variable can be assigned the predefined constants TRUE, FALSE, or NULL.
BINARY_INTEGER	This type is used for manipulating signed integers in the range of −2,147,483,647 to 2,147,483,647.
NATURAL	A subset of BINARY_INTEGER, this datatype is the set of integers from 0 to 2,147,483,647.
POSITIVE	Another subset of BINARY_INTEGER, this datatype is the set of integers from 1 to 2,147,483,647.
%TYPE	This designation enables you to declare a variable's datatype as being equivalent to the specified column's datatype, resulting in PL/SQL code that is easier to maintain.
%ROWTYPE	With this datatype you can declare a composite variable that is equivalent to a row in the specified table. The composite variable is composed of the column names and datatypes in the referenced table.

In addition, PL/SQL provides two composite datatypes: TABLE and RECORD. You'll learn more about them on Day 10.

Using %TYPE to Declare a Variable

The syntax for declaring a variable with %TYPE is

```
variable-name    table-name.column-name%TYPE;
```

The variables are defined as follows:

variable-name is the variable that you are declaring.

table-name is the table that contains a column whose type the variable will assume.

column-name is a column defined in *table-name*.

For example, you declare a variable to store a repair depot technician's name in this way:

```
Tech_Name    Depot_Estimate.Technician%TYPE;
```

The benefit of using %TYPE in a variable declaration is that the PL/SQL code is dependent on the definition of the Technician column in the Depot_Estimate table.

Using %ROWTYPE to Declare a Variable

The syntax for declaring a variable with %ROWTYPE is

```
variable-name    table-name%ROWTYPE;
```

The variables are defined as follows:

   variable-name is the composite variable that you are declaring.

   table-name is the table whose structure the composite variable will assume.

For instance, a composite variable that stores a row from the Depot_Estimate table is declared like this:

```
Depot_Est_Row    Depot_Estimate%ROWTYPE;
```

An element of Depot_Est_Row can be accessed in this manner:

```
Depot_Est_Row.Technician := 'RICHARDSON';
```

Some Familiar Control Structures

Several PL/SQL statements control the flow of execution of a PL/SQL subprogram.

- [ ] IF-THEN-ELSIF
- [ ] LOOP
- [ ] EXIT
- [ ] WHILE LOOP
- [ ] FOR LOOP
- [ ] GOTO
- [ ] NULL

Before you can build stored procedures and triggers, you should be familiar with the basics of PL/SQL programming. The next part of this lesson explores the detailed use of these statements.

The IF Statement

The syntax of PL/SQL's IF-THEN-ELSIF statement differs somewhat from that of the comparable statement in the C programming language.

The PL/SQL syntax is

```
IF condition THEN
   statement; ...  statement;
[ELSIF condition THEN
statement; ...  statement;]
...
[ELSIF condition THEN
statement; ...  statement;]
[ELSE
statement; ...  statement;]
END IF;
```

The variables are defined as follows:

> condition is a valid PL/SQL condition.
>
> statement is a valid PL/SQL statement.

Regarding the IF-THEN-ELSIF statement, be aware of these facts:

☐ The ELSIF and ELSE clauses are optional.

☐ An IF statement can have multiple ELSIF clauses but only one ELSE clause.

☐ Note the spelling: ELSIF, not ELSEIF.

Listing 9.3 demonstrates a simple example of the IF-THEN-ELSIF statement.

INPUT **Listing 9.3. Using the IF-THEN-ELSIF statement.**

```
if MOD(i,5) = 0 then
  rec_number := 5;
elsif MOD(i,7) = 0 then
  rec_number := 7;
else
  rec_number := i;
end if;
```

The Simple LOOP Statement

SYNTAX

The most basic type of loop is the LOOP statement without any additional qualifiers.

```
LOOP
   statement; ... statement;
END LOOP;
```

The variable is defined as follows:

▲

    statement is any valid PL/SQL statement, including another LOOP.

Obviously, this loop is an infinite loop. To exit this loop when a required condition is satisfied, use the EXIT statement.

The EXIT Statement

The EXIT statement has two forms:

☐ EXIT without any other clauses—an unconditional exit

☐ EXIT [*label-name*] WHEN *condition*

The first form of EXIT causes control to exit the loop that encloses the EXIT statement.

The second form of EXIT causes control to exit the enclosing loop when the specified condition is met, as shown in Listing 9.4.

| INPUT/ OUTPUT | **Listing 9.4. Using the EXIT statement.** |

```
SQL> declare
  2
  2   i  positive := 1;
  3   max_loops constant positive := 100;
  4
  4   begin
  5
  5   loop
  6
  6     i := i + 1;
  7     exit when i > max_loops;
  8
  8   end loop;
  9
  9   end;
 10   /
PL/SQL procedure successfully completed.
```

The WHILE-LOOP **Statement**

The WHILE-LOOP statement adds a condition to a loop.

```
WHILE condition LOOP
    statement; ... statement;
END LOOP;
```

The variables are defined as follows:

condition is a valid PL/SQL condition.

statement is a valid PL/SQL statement.

Listing 9.5 demonstrates the use of the WHILE-LOOP statement.

INPUT   **Listing 9.5. Using the WHILE-LOOP statement.**

```
WHILE I < 100 LOOP
    I := I + 1;
    insert into temp_table (rec_number) values (I);
END LOOP;
```

The FOR-LOOP **Statement**

The FOR-LOOP is quite similar to the WHILE-LOOP.

Here's the syntax:

```
FOR loop-variable IN [REVERSE] lower-bound..upper-bound LOOP
    statement; ... statement;
END LOOP;
```

The variables are defined as follows:

loop-variable is an integer variable that serves as a counter.

lower-bound is the lower bound of the increment range.

upper-bound is the upper bound of the increment range.

REVERSE is an optional keyword that, if used, causes the loop to decrement from upper-bound to lower-bound.

Listing 9.6 demonstrates the use of a FOR-LOOP statement.

INPUT   **Listing 9.6. Using a FOR-LOOP statement.**

```
for i in 1..max_loops loop
    j := j + j;
    dbms_output.put_line('j: ' || to_char(j));
end loop;
```

The GOTO Statement

Yes, PL/SQL allows you to use the potentially dangerous GOTO statement. Of course, to use GOTO, you must provide a label to which control is transferred. In PL/SQL, a statement label is defined in this way:

```
<<my_label>>
```

Listing 9.7 provides an example of how a GOTO statement and a label can be used as an alternative to the EXIT statement.

**INPUT/
OUTPUT**   **Listing 9.7. Using the GOTO statement.**

```
SQL> declare
  2
  2   i  positive := 1;
  3   max_loops constant positive := 100;
  4
  4   begin
  5
  5   i := 1;
  6
  6   loop
  7
  7     i := i + 1;
  8     if i > max_loops then
  9        goto more_processing;
 10     end if;
 11
 11   end loop;
 12
 12   <<more_processing>>
 13   i := 1;
 14
 14   end;
 15   /
PL/SQL procedure successfully completed.
```

The NULL Statement

For certain situations, you should indicate to PL/SQL that no action is to be taken. For instance, in an exception handler, you might not want to do anything when a particular exception occurs. For the sake of clarity, use the NULL statement in an IF-THEN-ELSIF to indicate that no action is to be taken for a particular ELSIF clause.

Unfortunately, Oracle chose to name this statement NULL, even though it has nothing to do with the null value. Listing 9.8 demonstrates how the NULL statement can be used.

INPUT   **Listing 9.8. Using the NULL statement.**

```
if (mod(i,10) = 0) then
  i := i + 1;
else
    NULL;
end if;
```

The Assignment Statement

As you've already seen, PL/SQL uses := to assign a value to a PL/SQL variable. You can define a constant's value or a variable's default value in the declaration section. One point is worth noting: You can't assign a NULL to a variable that was declared using the %TYPE notation when the referenced column is defined as NOT NULL.

Including Comments in a PL/SQL Subprogram

PL/SQL gives you two ways to document your code. First, you can add a comment on any line by placing a -- followed by the comment, as shown:

```
Depot_Est_Row.Technician := Last_Tech_Name;
-- Assign the name of the last technician involved
```

You can also add comments in the *C style*—by enclosing them within /* and */. This method is best suited for including multiline comments, as shown in Listing 9.9.

INPUT   **Listing 9.9. Commenting PL/SQL code.**

```
j := j + 1;
/* The next section inserts a row into the Utility_Audit table
   to record the name of the current Oracle user and the
   current date and time (SYSDATE).
*/
insert into Utility_Audit
...
```

Using SQL Statements in a PL/SQL Program

You can use SQL statements in an anonymous block, procedure, or function as they are used in SQL*Plus, with a few differences. As with other PL/SQL statements, each SQL statement must be terminated by a semicolon. However, PL/SQL enables you to reference declared variables in an SQL statement. Listing 9.10 provides an example of how declared variables are referenced in an SQL statement.

INPUT **Listing 9.10. Referencing variables in an SQL statement.**

```
DECLARE
max_records CONSTANT int := 100;
i           int := 1;
BEGIN
FOR i IN 1..max_records LOOP
  if (mod(i,10) = 0) then
    INSERT INTO test_table
           (record_number, current_date)
    VALUES
           (i, SYSDATE);
  else
    NULL;
  end if;
END LOOP;
COMMIT;
END;
/
```

In this example the INSERT statement uses the numeric variable i and the pseudocolumn SYSDATE to place values in the Record_Number and Current_Date columns.

PL/SQL and the SELECT Statement

In a PL/SQL subprogram, the SELECT statement employs another clause—INTO—to identify the PL/SQL variables that should receive column values. Place the INTO clause between the select list and the FROM clause. Listing 9.11 contains an example of an anonymous PL/SQL block that contains a SELECT statement.

INPUT/OUTPUT **Listing 9.11. Using a SELECT statement in a PL/SQL block.**

```
SQL> set serveroutput on
SQL>
SQL> declare
  2
  2  Average_Body_Temp      Patient.Body_Temp_Deg_F%type;
  3
  3  begin
  4
  4  dbms_output.enable;
  5
  5  select avg(Body_Temp_Deg_F)
  6    into Average_Body_Temp
  7    from Patient;
  8
  8  dbms_output.put_line('Average body temp in Deg. F: ' ||
     to_char(Average_Body_Temp,'999.99'));
  9
  9  end;
 10  /
Average body temp in Deg. F:    99.80
PL/SQL procedure successfully completed.
```

PL/SQL Subprograms

PL/SQL also supports the use of subprograms—named procedures and functions. A PL/SQL procedure performs some action and can accept optional parameters. A PL/SQL function returns a value of some specified datatype and can also accept optional parameters.

Using Sub-Blocks

PL/SQL enables you to include sub-blocks within a block. For instance, Listing 9.12 displays an anonymous block that contains another anonymous sub-block that has its own declaration section.

INPUT/ OUTPUT   **Listing 9.12. Example of a sub-block.**

```
SQL> declare
  2
  2  max_i       constant int := 100;
  3  i           int := 1;
  4  rec_number  int;
  5
  5  begin
  6
  6  for i in 1..max_i loop
  7
  7    if mod(i,5) = 0 then
  8      rec_number := 5;
  9    elsif mod(i,7) = 0 then
 10      rec_number := 7;
 11    else
 12      rec_number := i;
 13    end if;
 14
 14    insert into test_table
 15      (record_number, current_date)
 16      values
 17      (rec_number, sysdate);
 18
 18  -- Here is a sub-block:
 19
 19    declare
 20    max_j constant int := 20;
 21    j int := 1;
 22
 22    begin
 23
 23      for j in 1..max_j loop
 24
 24        rec_number := rec_number * j;
 25
 25        insert into test_table
```

continues

Listing 9.12. continued

```
26          (record_number, current_date)
27          values
28          (rec_number, sysdate);
29
29      end loop;
30
30    end;
31
31    commit;
32  end loop;
33
33  end;
34  /
PL/SQL procedure successfully completed.
SQL> select count(*) from test_table;
 COUNT(*)
---------
    2100
```

 ANALYSIS The first line of Listing 9.12 begins the declaration section of the anonymous block. On line 5, the execution section of the main block begins. The declaration section of the sub-block begins at line 19; line 22 marks the beginning of the execution section of the sub-block.

> **TIP** Although PL/SQL supports the capability to embed blocks within one another, this practice is not desirable for two reasons. First, it reduces the readability—and the resulting maintainability—of your code. Second, embedded blocks can't be used by other PL/SQL subprograms. You should strive to design procedures and functions for improved code reuse and maintainability.

Declaring a Procedure

In addition to anonymous blocks, you can also declare PL/SQL procedures and functions.

SYNTAX

The syntax for declaring a procedure is

```
PROCEDURE procedure-name [(argument1 ... [, argumentN) ] IS
[local-variable-declarations]
BEGIN
executable-section
[exception-section]
END [procedure-name];
```

The variables are defined as follows:

procedure-name is the procedure name and subject to Oracle database object-naming restrictions.

argument1 through *argumentN* are optional argument declarations that consist of:

argument-name [IN ¦ OUT] *datatype* [{:= ¦ DEFAULT} *value*]

local-variable-declarations are optional declarations of variables, constants, and other procedures and functions local to *procedure-name*.

executable-section is the PL/SQL statements that compose the procedure.

exception-section is the optional exception-handling section of the procedure.

NOTE

The distinction between stored procedures and procedures that are declared and used in anonymous blocks is important. The procedures that are declared and called in anonymous blocks are *temporal*; when the anonymous block has completed execution, they no longer exist as far as Oracle is concerned. A stored procedure that is created with a CREATE PROCEDURE statement or contained in a package is *permanent* in the sense that it can be invoked by an SQL*Plus script, a PL/SQL subprogram, or a database trigger.

To illustrate this syntax, Listing 9.13 contains an example of an anonymous block that declares a procedure named Record_Patient_Temp_Deg_C. This procedure has two arguments: the patient ID and the patient's body temperature as measured in degrees Centigrade (see line 4). On line 3, the variable High_Fever is initialized to 42. On line 17, the procedure is invoked with two arguments: New_Patient_ID (which is GG9999) and High_Fever. The SELECT statement that follows the anonymous block demonstrates that the procedure did what it was supposed to—it converted 42 degrees Centigrade to 107.6 degrees Fahrenheit.

 Listing 9.13. Example of a procedure.

```
SQL> declare
  2
  2  New_Patient_ID   Patient.Patient_ID%type;
  3  High_Fever       constant real := 42.0;
  4
  4  procedure Record_Patient_Temp_Deg_C (Patient_ID varchar2,
  5                                        Body_Temp_Deg_C real) is
  6
```

continues

Listing 9.13. continued

```
  6  Temp_Deg_F real;
  7
  7  begin
  8
  8    Temp_Deg_F := (9.0/5.0)*Body_Temp_Deg_C + 32.0;
  9
  9    insert into Patient
 10    (Patient_ID, Body_Temp_Deg_F)
 11    values
 12    (Patient_ID, Temp_Deg_F);
 13
 13    commit;
 14  end;
 15
 15  begin
 16
 16  New_Patient_ID := 'GG9999';
 17
 17  Record_Patient_Temp_Deg_C (New_Patient_ID, High_Fever);
 18
 18  end;
 19  /
PL/SQL procedure successfully completed.

SQL> select Patient_ID, Body_Temp_Deg_F
  2  from Patient
  3  where
  4  Patient_ID = 'GG9999';
PATIEN BODY_TEMP_DEG_F
------ ---------------
GG9999          107.6
```

Listing 9.14 demonstrates that the variables declared within a procedure are not accessible outside of the procedure.

INPUT/OUTPUT   ## Listing 9.14. Example of variable scope in PL/SQL.

```
SQL> declare
  2
  2  procedure Delete_Patients is
  3
  3  Temp_Deg_F real;
  4
  4  begin
  5
  5    delete from Patient
  6    where
  7    Patient_ID = 'GG3333';
```

```
 8
 8     commit;
 9
 9   end;
10
10   begin
11
11   Temp_Deg_F := 100.0;
12
12   end;
13   /
Temp_Deg_F := 100.0;
*
ERROR at line 11:
ORA-06550: line 11, column 1:
PLS-00201: identifier 'TEMP_DEG_F' must be declared
ORA-06550: line 11, column 1:
PL/SQL: Statement ignored
```

ANALYSIS   Listing 9.14 begins with the declaration section of an anonymous block. At line 2, a procedure, Delete_Patients, is declared; within the procedure, the variable Temp_Deg_F is declared as a REAL. However, at line 11, the anonymous block references Temp_Deg_F, which results in the PL/SQL error message PLS-00201. This listing illustrates that the scope of a local variable in a procedure or function doesn't extend to another subprogram that invokes that procedure or function.

For further information on the use of stored procedures, see the lesson on Day 11.

Declaring a Function

A PL/SQL function declaration is similar to a procedure declaration—except that the function returns a value of a predefined datatype.

SYNTAX

The syntax for declaring a function is

```
FUNCTION function-name [(argument1 ... [, argumentN) ]
RETURN function-datatype IS
[local-variable-declarations]
BEGIN
executable-section
[exception-section]
END [function-name];
```

The variables are defined as follows:

   function-name is the function name and subject to Oracle database object-naming restrictions.

argument1 through *argumentN* are optional argument declarations that consist of

> *argument-name* [IN ¦ OUT] *datatype* [{:= ¦ DEFAULT} *value*]

function-datatype is the datatype returned by *function-name*.

local-variable-declarations are optional declarations of variables, constants, and other procedures and functions local to *function-name*.

executable-section is the PL/SQL statements that compose the function.

exception-section is the optional exception-handling section of the function.

For instance, Listing 9.15 provides an example of the declaration and use of a function. The function, Max_Additional_Fees, has a single argument, Dept_ID (see line 3). The function returns the Course_ID that has the highest additional fees of all courses in the specified department (the SELECT statement begins on line 9). The anonymous block calls the function with Dept_ID equal to ECON (see line 24) and the function returns Course_ID 189. The query at the end of Listing 9.15 shows that 189 does indeed have the highest additional fees.

INPUT/OUTPUT ## Listing 9.15. Example of a function.

```
SQL> declare
  2
  2  Course_ID  Course.Course_ID%type;
  3
  3  function Max_Additional_Fees (Dept_ID IN varchar2)
  4          return varchar2 is
  5
  5  Additional_Fees Course.Additional_Fees%type;
  6  Units           Course.Units%type;
  7  Course_ID       Course.Course_ID%type;
  8
  8  begin
  9
  9  select Course_ID
 10  into   Course_ID
 11  from Course
 12  where
 13  Department_ID = Dept_ID and
 14  Additional_Fees =
 15  (select max(Additional_Fees)
 16   from Course
 17   where
 18   Department_ID = Dept_ID);
 19
 19  return Course_ID;
 20
 20  end;
 21
 21  --  Beginning of executable section of anonymous block.
 22
 22  begin
```

```
23
23  dbms_output.enable;
24
24  Course_ID := Max_Additional_Fees ('ECON');
25
25  dbms_output.put_line('Course_ID: ' || Course_ID);
26
26  end;
27  /
Course_ID: 189

PL/SQL procedure successfully completed.

SQL> select Course_ID, Additional_Fees
  2  from Course
  3  where
  4  Department_ID = 'ECON'
  5  order by Course_ID;

COURS ADDITIONAL_FEES
----- ---------------
101                25
189               750
199                 0
```

Procedure and Function Arguments

Each procedure and function argument can optionally be defined as one of the following:

IN   The value of the argument is passed to the procedure or function, but no value is returned to the calling PL/SQL subprogram. Within a procedure or function, you can't assign a value to an argument declared as IN; you can only reference the value of this type of argument.

OUT   The procedure or function doesn't use the passed value but does return a value to the calling PL/SQL subprogram. Within a procedure or function, you can't reference the value of an argument declared as OUT; you can only assign a value to this type of argument.

IN OUT   The value of the argument is passed to the procedure or function and is also returned to the calling PL/SQL subprogram. An argument declared as IN OUT can be referenced and assigned a value within its procedure or function.

Listing 9.16 presents an example of how all three types of arguments are used.

INPUT/
OUTPUT

Listing 9.16. Use of different argument types—IN, OUT, and IN OUT.

```
SQL> declare
  2
  2   This_Arg1 number;
  3   This_Arg2 number;
  4   This_Arg3 number;
  5
  5   procedure Different_Arguments
  6            (arg1 IN      number,
  7             arg2 OUT     number,
  8             arg3 IN OUT  number) is
  9
  9   begin
 10
 10   arg2 := arg1;
 11   arg3 := arg3 + 1;
 12
 12   end;
 13
 13   --   Beginning of executable section of anonymous block.
 14
 14   begin
 15
 15   This_Arg1 := 3.14159;
 16
 16   Different_Arguments (This_Arg1, This_Arg2, This_Arg3);
 17
 17   end;
 18   /
PL/SQL procedure successfully completed.
```

Summary

This lesson discussed these basic features of PL/SQL:

☐ PL/SQL is a block-structured language in which a block consists of an optional declaration section, an executable section, and an optional exception-handling section.

☐ Some additional datatypes are available in PL/SQL's SQL-extensions: BINARY_INTEGER, NATURAL, POSITIVE, %TYPE, %ROWTYPE, TABLE, and RECORD.

☐ Executable PL/SQL statements include IF-THEN-ELSIF, LOOP, EXIT, the WHILE-LOOP, the FOR-LOOP, and GOTO.

☐ A PL/SQL subprogram can include SQL statements that reference PL/SQL variables.

☐ A PL/SQL subprogram can declare its own procedures and functions.

Do	Don't

DO use PL/SQL for enforcing business rules in the Oracle database.

DO use PL/SQL to construct packages that can be invoked by applications written in Oracle Forms, Reports, and Graphics.

DON'T construct PL/SQL subprograms to handle user input directly; instead, use an application development tool that provides the end-user with a graphical user interface (GUI).

What Comes Next?

On Day 10, you learn much more about the declaration and use of procedures, functions, and packages.

Q&A

Q Can a function call other procedures and functions and can a procedure call other procedures and functions?

A Yes, this is supported by PL/SQL. In fact, PL/SQL also supports recursion.

Workshop

The purpose of the Workshop is to allow you to test your knowledge of the material discussed in the lesson. See if you can correctly answer the questions in the quiz and complete the exercise before you continue with tomorrow's lesson.

Quiz

1. Name the three sections of a PL/SQL subprogram.
2. True or false? A PL/SQL variable that stores a column value must have the same name as the column.
3. Why is it a good practice to use %TYPE when declaring variables?

Exercise

Construct an anonymous block that declares a procedure that will set the additional fees for a course to $50 if there are no current additional fees. The procedure should have only one argument—Department_ID—and should perform this action only for the value of Department_ID supplied to the procedure.

Day 10

Program Development with PL/SQL

During our last lesson, you learned about some of the programming constructs used in PL/SQL. In this lesson, you learn how to construct PL/SQL modules—procedures, functions, and packages—that are stored in an Oracle database. You'll also learn about the use of PL/SQL datatypes that aren't available in SQL.

A stored procedure or function is a PL/SQL program stored in an Oracle database and invoked by a user, either directly or indirectly. The benefits of using stored procedures and functions are:

☐ **Efficiency:** In a client/server architecture, a client application issues SQL requests to a database server. As the number of users increases, so does the number of SQL requests, and the network can quickly become the performance bottleneck. The use of stored procedures offers a significant performance improvement because a single call to a stored procedure can invoke multiple SQL statements that are executed on the server, thereby reducing network traffic.

☐ **Reusability:** A PL/SQL program is written once and can be used in a variety of situations—in SQL scripts, in database triggers, and in client application logic.

☐ **Portability:** You can use a stored procedure in any Oracle8 database, regardless of platform. Consequently, you don't have to deal with compatibility issues such as the operating system and compiler releases. If Oracle8 is supported by the platform, the stored procedure can be ported to it without any additional changes. Of course, if the stored procedure contains references to file and directory names, you might need to make additional changes.

☐ **Maintainability:** A stored procedure is designed to perform a specific task. Such a task might be required by a database trigger, an SQL*Plus script, an application program, or another stored procedure. By calling the same stored procedure from all of these sources, you reduce the cost of software maintenance.

NOTE

You can use different tools to create and maintain stored procedures, functions, and packages. In this lesson, you learn how to use SQL*Plus or SQL Worksheet to do this. However, there are several advantages to a tool such as Oracle Procedure Builder, a component of Developer/2000. First, Procedure Builder has a PL/SQL stored program editor that makes it easy to modify your PL/SQL code. Second, you can compile your stored program by simply pressing a button in the editor. Third, any compilation errors are conveniently displayed in a separate window. There are third-party PL/SQL editors that you also may want to evaluate before you plunge into a serious PL/SQL project.

Creating a Stored Procedure or Function

Using a text processor, such as Notepad or WordPad, to construct a stored procedure is a good idea. A better idea is to use one of the components in Oracle Developer/2000—Procedure Builder—which is discussed during the lesson on Day 16, "Developer/2000: Using Oracle Graphics and Procedure Builder." With Notepad or WordPad open, you can copy the stored procedure and paste it into SQL*Plus or SQL Worksheet for development and testing.

SYNTAX

The syntax for creating a stored procedure is as follows:

```
CREATE [OR REPLACE] PROCEDURE procedure-name
[(argument1 ... [, argumentN) ] IS
[local-variable-declarations]
BEGIN
executable-section
```

```
[exception-section]
END [procedure-name];
```

The variables are defined as follows:

procedure-name is the procedure name subject to Oracle database object-naming restrictions.

argument1 through argumentN are optional argument declarations that consist of

```
argument-name [IN ¦ OUT] datatype [ {:= ¦ DEFAULT} value]
```

local-variable-declarations are optional declarations of variables, constants, and other procedures and functions local to procedure-name.

executable-section are the PL/SQL statements that compose the procedure.

exception-section is the optional exception handling section of the procedure.

For example, Listing 10.1 contains a stored procedure that has a single argument used by the DELETE statement to determine which classes to remove from the Course table.

10

Listing 10.1. Creating a stored procedure with a single argument.

INPUT/
OUTPUT

```
SQL> create or replace procedure Delete_Specified_Course
  2          (Description_Phrase varchar2) is
  3
  3  begin
  4
  4  delete from Course
  5  where
  6  upper(Description) like Description_Phrase;
  7
  7  end;
  8  /
Procedure created.
```

SYNTAX

The syntax for creating a stored function is very similar to the syntax for creating a stored procedure. Of course, a stored function also must return a value.

```
CREATE [OR REPLACE] FUNCTION function-name
[(argument1 ... [, argumentN) ]
RETURN function-datatype IS
[local-variable-declarations]
BEGIN
executable-section
[exception-section]
RETURN function-value
END [function-name];
```

The variables are defined as follows:

function-name is the function name subject to Oracle database object-naming restrictions.

argument1 through *argumentN* are optional argument declarations that consist of

    argument-name [IN ¦ OUT] *datatype* [{:= ¦ DEFAULT} *value*]

function-datatype is the datatype of the value returned by the function.

local-variable-declarations are optional declarations of variables, constants, and other procedures and functions local to *function-name*.

executable-section are the PL/SQL statements that compose the function.

exception-section is the optional exception-handling section of the function.

function-value is the value that the function returns to the caller.

NOTE

The difference between a stored procedure and a stored function is that a stored procedure does not return a value whereas a stored function does return a value. As a result, a stored function can be called in an SQL statement in the same manner as a built-in function; a stored procedure cannot. However, stored procedures and functions can both return a modified argument value if the argument was declared as OUT or IN OUT.

Listing 10.2 illustrates how to create a stored function that obtains the grade point average of a student.

Listing 10.2. Creating a stored function with a single argument.

INPUT

```
create or replace function student_GPA (arg_student_ID IN varchar2)
   return number is

GPA number;

begin

select avg(decode(grade, 'A+', 4.25, 'A', 4, 'A-', 3.75,
                         'B+', 3.25, 'B', 3, 'B-', 2.75,
                         'C+', 2.25, 'C', 2, 'C-', 1.75,
                         'D+', 1.25, 'D', 1, 'D-', 0.75, 'F', 0))
into GPA
from student_schedule
where
```

```
student_id = arg_student_id;

return GPA;

end;
```

NOTE

Many of the examples in this lesson call a package named *dbms_output*. This package provides a set of procedures and functions that are useful for displaying values from within a PL/SQL block. To use the package with SQL*Plus, enter the following statement before any procedure or function calls are made to dbms_output:

```
set serveroutput on
```

Obtaining Error Messages When Creating Stored Procedures

If Oracle detects errors when you create a stored PL/SQL program, it issues a nondescript message indicating that errors occurred—without providing any additional details. For example, Listing 10.3 demonstrates what happens if you try to create a stored procedure with a syntax error. To view the errors resulting from the attempted compilation of the PL/SQL code, you can use the SQL*Plus command show errors, which displays the specific PL/SQL compilation errors.

INPUT/ OUTPUT

Listing 10.3. An error message returned by Oracle during compilation of a stored procedure.

```
SQL> create or replace procedure show_inserts IS
  2
  2  max_records constant int := 100;
  3  i           int := 1;
  4
  4  begin
  5
  5  dbms_output.enable;
  6
  6  for i in 1..max_records loop
  7
  7    if (mod(i,10) = 0) then
  8      insert into test_table
  9            (record_number, current_date)
 10      values
 11            (i, SYSDATE)
 12      dbms_output.put_line('The value of i is ' || to_char(i));
```

continues

Listing 10.3. continued

```
13
13    else
14      null;
15
15    end if;
16
16  end loop;
17
17  end;
18  /
Warning: Procedure created with compilation errors.
SQL> show errors
Errors for PROCEDURE SHOW_INSERTS:
LINE/COL ERROR
-------- -------------------------------------------------------------
12/5     PLS-00103: Encountered the symbol "DBMS_OUTPUT" when expecting
         one of the following:
         ;
         ; was inserted before "DBMS_OUTPUT" to continue.
```

ANALYSIS In an attempt to create or replace the procedure show_inserts, Oracle returned a warning, just after line 18, indicating that there were compilation errors. To see the specific error, you issue the command show errors. As you can see on line 11, the INSERT statement isn't terminated with a semicolon.

Retrieving a Stored Procedure

After a stored procedure has been created, you might want to look at the source code of a PL/SQL program. However, even if the SQL script that was used to create the stored procedure isn't available, you can still retrieve the source code of a stored procedure by querying an Oracle data dictionary view.

The Oracle data dictionary is a group of tables that contain information about the Oracle database itself. Because these data dictionary tables are somewhat cryptic in structure, Oracle defines a set of views that provide a more coherent perspective of the data dictionary (please refer to Day 8, "More Sophisticated Queries with SQL," for more information about views). One of these views is named USER_SOURCE, which provides four columns:

NAME Contains the name of the procedure, function, package, or package body

TYPE Indicates whether the source code belongs to a procedure, function, package, or package body

TEXT Contains a line of the source code

LINE Contains the line number of the source code contained in TEXT

As an example, suppose that you created a stored procedure named DROP_CLASS. If you want to see the source code of DROP_CLASS, query the USER_SOURCE data dictionary view, as illustrated in Listing 10.4.

INPUT/OUTPUT

Listing 10.4. Retrieving the source code for a stored procedure.

```
SQL> select line, text
  2  from user_source
  3  where
  4  name = 'DROP_CLASS'
  5  order by line;

LINE TEXT
---- ----------------------------------------------------------------
   1 procedure drop_class (arg_student_ID IN varchar2,
   2                       arg_class_ID   IN varchar2,
   3                       status       OUT number) is
   4
   5 counter   number;
   6
   7 begin
   8
   9 status := 0;
  10
  11 -- Verify that this class really is part of the student's schedule.
  12
  13 select count(*) into counter
  14 from student_schedule
  15 where
  16 student_id = arg_student_id and
  17 class_id   = arg_class_id;
  18
  19 if counter = 1 then
  20   delete from student_schedule
  21   where
  22   student_id = arg_student_id and
  23   class_id   = arg_class_id;
  24   status := -1;
  25 end if;
  26
  27 end;

27 rows selected.
```

Obtaining a List of Procedures, Functions, Packages, and Package Bodies

You can query USER_OBJECTS to obtain a list of stored procedures, functions, packages, and package bodies owned by the Oracle account to which you are currently connected. If you wanted to see all of the these objects, regardless of ownership, you would query DBA_OBJECTS rather than USER_OBJECTS. The OBJECT_TYPE column in DBA_OBJECTS indicates the type of the object: table, view, procedure, and so on.

To obtain a list of the types of database objects owned by a user, use the query shown in Listing 10.5.

Listing 10.5. Determining the object types owned by the current user.

```
SQL> select distinct object_type
  2  from user_objects;

OBJECT_TYPE
------------
FUNCTION
INDEX
PACKAGE
PACKAGE BODY
PROCEDURE
TABLE
VIEW

7 rows selected.
```

Forward Declaration of Procedures and Functions

PL/SQL requires that you declare any identifier—constant, variable, cursor, procedure, or function—using it elsewhere in a PL/SQL subprogram. This requirement can cause a problem when two subprograms reference each other, as shown in Listing 10.6.

Listing 10.6. Function referenced before declaration.

```
SQL> set serveroutput on
SQL>
SQL> declare
  2
  2  function Medicare_Patient (Patient_ID IN varchar2)
  3          return number is
  4
  4  status    number;
  5  Pat_ID    varchar2(6);
  6
  6  begin
```

10

```
 7
 7   if Insurable_Patient (Pat_ID) = 2 then
 8      status := 1;
 9   end if;
10
10   return status;
11
11   end Medicare_Patient;
12
12
12   function Insurable_Patient (Patient_ID IN varchar2)
13            return number is
14
14   status    number;
15   Pat_ID    varchar2(6);
16
16   begin
17
17   if Medicare_Patient (Pat_ID) = 2 then
18      status := 1;
19   end if;
20
20   return status;
21
21   end Insurable_Patient;
22
22   --   Executable portion of anonymous block.
23
23   begin
24
24   dbms_output.enable;
25
25   end;
26   /
declare
 *
ERROR at line 1:
ORA-06550: line 7, column 4:
PLS-00313: 'INSURABLE_PATIENT' not declared in this scope
ORA-06550: line 7, column 1:
PL/SQL: Statement ignored
```

ANALYSIS As you can see in Listing 10.6, PL/SQL doesn't recognize the reference to Insurable_Patient in the function Medicare_Patient (line 7) because the declaration of Insurable_Patient occurs after the declaration of Medicare_Patient (line 2). To circumvent this dilemma, you include a forward declaration of the subprogram in the declare section. The *forward declaration* is a declaration of the subprogram, its arguments, and return type. Listing 10.7 demonstrates how to specify a forward declaration for Insurable_Patient (line 2) for the preceding example.

10

Listing 10.7. Providing a forward declaration for a function.

```
SQL> set serveroutput on
SQL>
SQL> declare
  2
  2  function Insurable_Patient (Patient_ID IN varchar2) return number;
  3
  3  function Medicare_Patient (Patient_ID IN varchar2)
  4          return number is
  5
  5  status   number;
  6  Pat_ID   varchar2(6);
  7
  7  begin
  8
  8  if Insurable_Patient (Pat_ID) = 2 then
  9     status := 1;
 10  end if;
 11
 11  return status;
 12
 12  end Medicare_Patient;
 13
 13
 13  function Insurable_Patient (Patient_ID IN varchar2)
 14          return number is
 15
 15  status   number;
 16  Pat_ID   varchar2(6);
 17
 17  begin
 18
 18  if Medicare_Patient (Pat_ID) = 2 then
 19     status := 1;
 20  end if;
 21
 21  return status;
 22
 22  end Insurable_Patient;
 23
 23  --  Executable portion of anonymous block.
 24
 24  begin
 25
 25  dbms_output.enable;
 26
 26  end;
 27  /
PL/SQL procedure successfully completed.
```

Using Stored Functions in a SQL Statement

With release 7.1 of the Oracle RDBMS, it became possible to reference a stored function within a SQL statement. This feature is enormously powerful because it extends the functionality of a single SQL statement to include the logic contained in a stored function. Let's look at an elementary example of how this functionality is achieved.

Because Oracle doesn't offer a built-in function for converting temperature from Fahrenheit to centigrade, you create a stored function to perform the conversion, as demonstrated in Listing 10.8. After the stored function has been successfully created, you can use it in a SELECT statement.

INPUT/ OUTPUT **Listing 10.8. Using a stored function in a SELECT statement.**

```
SQL> create or replace function DegF_to_DegC (Deg_F IN number)
  2         return number is
  3
  3  Deg_C  number;
  4
  4  begin
  5
  5  Deg_C := (5.0/9.0)*(Deg_F - 32);
  6
  6  return Deg_C;
  7
  7  end DegF_to_DegC;
  8  /
Function created.

SQL> select body_temp, degf_to_degc(body_temp)
  2  from patient;
BODY_TEMP DEGF_TO_DEGC(BODY_TEMP)
--------- -----------------------
    99.2               37.333333
   100.2               37.888889
   103.8               39.888889
```

Once you create a stored function, it is always available for use.

Storing Results to a Table

Although PL/SQL doesn't have any built-in support for communicating with the user, you can still use PL/SQL to provide results to a user or another program by

☐ Writing information to an intermediate table that a user or program can query.

☐ Using the procedures and functions available in the Oracle-supplied package
    `DBMS_OUTPUT`.

You've already seen an example of how PL/SQL can write to an intermediate table. When
compiling PL/SQL stored procedures and functions, the PL/SQL engine itself writes error
messages to a data dictionary table that can be queried by the developer. If you want to provide
output via SQL*Plus, using `DBMS_OUTPUT` is a good strategy. If you need to pass many values
to a user or a program, writing the results to a table makes more sense.

Invoking a Stored Procedure or Function

The method for invoking a stored procedure or function depends on the context.

For SQL*Plus, use the `execute` command (this syntax is for a stored procedure that doesn't
have any arguments) in the following way:

```
execute show_inserts;
```

From a PL/SQL subprogram, simply reference the stored procedure or function with any
required arguments. During Day 14, "Developer/2000: Application Development with
Oracle Forms," you learn how to invoke a stored procedure or function from within an
Oracle Forms application.

Packages

A package is a group of related PL/SQL procedures and functions. Like the Ada programming
language, a PL/SQL package consists of a package specification and a package body. You can
construct packages that are application specific—for instance, a package named *patient_data*
would contain procedures and functions related to the manipulation and retrieval of hospital
patient information. Furthermore, a package could contain procedures and functions that
provide a common service, such as the conversion of location information from one
coordinate system to another.

NEW TERM   A *package* is a collection of related PL/SQL procedures and functions that is stored
            in an Oracle database. To create a package, you must create a package specification
            and a package body.

Declaring a Package

The general syntax for creating a package specification is as follows:

```
CREATE [OR REPLACE] PACKAGE package-name IS
declaration-section
END package-name;
```

10

The variables are defined as follows:

package-name is the name of the package to be created and is subject to Oracle database object-naming restrictions.

declaration-section consists of type, variable, cursor, procedure, and function declarations.

As an example, Listing 10.9 contains the package specification for the Flugle College Information System.

INPUT **Listing 10.9. Declaring a package specification.**

```
create or replace package Flugle is

function register_for_class (arg_student_ID IN varchar2,
                             arg_class_ID   IN varchar2)
  return number;

function schedule_conflict (arg_student_ID IN varchar2,
                            arg_class_ID   IN varchar2)
  return number;

procedure drop_class (arg_student_ID IN varchar2,
                      arg_class_ID   IN varchar2,
                      status     OUT number);

procedure assign_instructor (arg_class_ID      IN varchar2,
                             arg_instructor_ID IN varchar2,
                             status          OUT number);

procedure assign_grade (arg_student_ID IN varchar2,
                        arg_class_ID   IN varchar2,
                        arg_grade      IN varchar2,
                        status     OUT number);

function student_GPA (arg_student_ID IN varchar2)
   return number;

END;
```

ANALYSIS The Flugle package contains seven items: three procedures and three functions:

- [ ] Procedure `drop_class`
- [ ] Procedure `assign_instructor`
- [ ] Procedure `assign_grade`
- [ ] Function `register_for_class`
- [ ] Function `schedule_conflict`
- [ ] Function `student_GPA`

TIP

When creating package specifications or package bodies in a script, use the OR REPLACE clause. Oracle also offers the DROP PACKAGE and DROP PACKAGE BODY statements, but the OR_REPLACE clause saves you the trouble of having to remember whether or not you've dropped a package before you attempt to create it.

Declaring a Package Body

A package body contains the public and private elements of a package. It hides the details of how cursors, procedures, and functions are actually implemented—details that should be hidden from developers.

SYNTAX

A package body is declared using the following syntax:

```
CREATE PACKAGE BODY package-name IS
declaration-section
procedure-bodies;
function-bodies;
initialization-section
END package-name;
```

The package variables are defined as follows:

package-name is the name of the package to be created and is subject to Oracle database object-naming restrictions.

declaration-section consists of type, variable, and cursor declarations.

procedure-bodies consists of the executable sections of each procedure that was declared in the package specification.

function-bodies consists of the executable sections of each function that was declared in the package specification.

initialization-section is an optional section that is executed once when the package is first referenced.

Listing 10.10 lists the contents of the Flugle package body, which contains the details of each procedure and function that is part of the package.

INPUT **Listing 10.10. Declaring a package body.**

```
create or replace package flugle is

-- Declare some exceptions.

schedule_conflict_exists exception;
already_registered       exception;
```

```
not_registered              exception;

-- Declare values for status.

conflicting_classes number := -2;
unsuccessful         number := -1;
normal               number := 0;

-- *********************************************************
-- Function register_for_class
--
function register_for_class (arg_student_ID IN varchar2,
                             arg_class_ID   IN varchar2)
   return number is

status number;
counter number;

begin

-- Determine if the student isn't already registered for this class.

select count(*) into counter
from student_schedule
where
student_id = arg_student_id and
class_id   = arg_class_id;

if counter > 0 then
--
-- The student is already registered for this class.
--
   raise already_registered;
else
--
-- The student isn't registered for this class.
-- Determine if there is a schedule conflict.
--
  if schedule_conflict(arg_student_id, arg_class_id) = 0 then
    insert into student_schedule
    (student_id, class_id)
    values
    (arg_student_id, arg_class_id);
  else
    raise schedule_conflict_exists;
  end if;
end if;

status := normal;

return status;

exception
  when schedule_conflict_exists then
    raise_application_error (-20001, 'Schedule conflict exists');
  when already_registered then
```

continues

Listing 10.10. continued

```
      raise_application_error (-20002,
➥'Student is already registered for class');
    when others then
      null;
end;

-- ********************************************************
-- Function schedule_conflict
--
function schedule_conflict (arg_student_ID IN varchar2,
                            arg_class_ID   IN varchar2)
   return number is

-- Declare a cursor to look for other classes with the same schedule
-- as this one.

cursor get_other_classes is
      select SS.Class_ID
      from Student_Schedule SS, Class C
      where
      SS.Class_ID = C.Class_ID and
      (C.Semester, C.School_Year, C.Schedule_ID) =
      (select Semester, School_Year, Schedule_ID
       from Class
       where
       Class_ID = arg_class_ID);

Conflicting_Class_ID  Class.Class_ID%type;
status  number;

begin

-- Need to look at the other classes in the student's schedule
-- for the same semester and school year.

for get_other_classes_Rec in get_other_classes loop

  fetch get_other_classes into Conflicting_Class_ID;
  exit when get_other_classes%notfound;

end loop;

close get_other_classes;

if get_other_classes%rowcount > 0 then
  status := conflicting_classes;
else
  status := normal;
end if;

return status;

end;

-- ********************************************************
```

```
-- Procedure drop_class
--
procedure drop_class (arg_student_ID IN varchar2,
                      arg_class_ID   IN varchar2,
                      status      OUT number) is

counter  number;

begin

-- Verify that this class really is part of the student's schedule.

select count(*) into counter
from student_schedule
where
student_id = arg_student_id and
class_id   = arg_class_id;

if counter = 1 then
delete from student_schedule
where
student_id = arg_student_id and
class_id   = arg_class_id;
end if;

end;

-- ********************************************************
-- Procedure assign_instructor
--
procedure assign_instructor (arg_class_ID     IN varchar2,
                             arg_instructor_ID IN varchar2,
                             status        OUT number) is

counter              number;

begin

-- Determine if this instructor is associated with the department
-- that offers this class.

select count(*)
into counter
from Instructor I, Class C
where
C.Class_ID = arg_class_ID and
I.Instructor_ID = arg_instructor_ID and
C.Department_ID = I.Department_ID;

if counter = 0 then
  status := unsuccessful;
else
--
-- Assign this instructor to this class.
--
  update class
```

continues

Listing 10.10. continued

```
    set
    Instructor_ID = arg_instructor_ID
    where
    Class_ID = arg_class_ID;

    status := normal;

end if;

end;

-- ********************************************************
-- Procedure assign_grade
--
procedure assign_grade (arg_student_ID IN  varchar2,
                        arg_class_ID   IN  varchar2,
                        arg_grade      IN  varchar2,
                        status         OUT number) is
counter number;

begin

--   Determine if the student is registered for this class.

select count(*) into counter
from student_schedule
where
student_id = arg_student_id and
class_id   = arg_class_id;

if counter = 0 then
--
-- The student is not taking this class.
--
   raise not_registered;
else
--
--   Assign the grade for this class.
--
   update student_schedule
   set
   grade = arg_grade
   where
   student_id = arg_student_id and
   class_id   = arg_class_id;
end if;

exception
   when not_registered then
     raise_application_error (-21003,
➥'Student not registered for class');
   when others then
     null;
```

10

```
end;

--  **********************************************************
--  Function student_GPA
--
function student_GPA (arg_student_ID IN varchar2)
   return number is

GPA number;

begin

--
-- Calculate the average grade point for this student based on all
-- classes for which a grade has been assigned.

select avg(decode(grade, 'A+', 4.25, 'A', 4, 'A-', 3.75,
                         'B+', 3.25, 'B', 3, 'B-', 2.75,
                         'C+', 2.25, 'C', 2, 'C-', 1.75,
                         'D+', 1.25, 'D', 1, 'D-', 0.75, 'F', 0))
into GPA
from student_schedule
where
student_id = arg_student_id;

return GPA;

end;

end;
```

Once the Flugle package body has been created, you can invoke a function in the package. Take a look at Listing 10.11. The UPDATE statement is used to set the instructor for Class 104200 to null. The SELECT statement that follows it proves that there is no instructor assigned for the class. Next, an anonymous block is used to call Assign_Instructor to assign Instructor E491 to class 104200. The status is 0, which indicates that the procedure was successful. Lastly, the final SELECT statement indicates that the instructor has indeed been assigned to the class.

INPUT/OUTPUT

Listing 10.11. Referencing a procedure in a package from an anonymous PL/SQL block.

```
SQL> set serveroutput on
SQL>
SQL> update class
  2  set
  3  Instructor_ID = null
  4  where
  5  class_ID = '104200';
```

continues

Listing 10.11. continued

```
1 row updated.

SQL> select Instructor_ID
  2  from Class
  3  where
  4  Class_ID = '104200';

INSTRUCTOR_ID
--------------------

SQL> declare
  2
  2  status           number;
  3
  3  begin
  4
  4  dbms_output.enable;
  5
  5
  5  Flugle.Assign_Instructor ('104200', 'E491', status);
  6
  6  dbms_output.put_line('Status: ' ¦¦ to_char(status));
  7
  7  end;
  8  /
Status: 0

PL/SQL procedure successfully completed.

SQL> select Instructor_ID
  2  from Class
  3  where
  4  Class_ID = '104200';

INSTRUCTOR_ID
--------------------
E491
```

Designing a Package for Use by Database Triggers

The procedures and functions contained in a package can be referenced from SQL*Plus scripts, PL/SQL subprograms, client application scripts (such as Oracle Forms or PowerBuilder)—as well as database triggers. However, a database trigger can't call any stored procedure, function, or packaged subprogram that contains a COMMIT, ROLLBACK, or SAVEPOINT statement. Therefore, if you want the flexibility of calling a package's subprograms from a database trigger, be sure that none of the procedures and functions in the package commit or roll back transactions. See Day 11, "More Programming Techniques with PL/SQL," for more information about database triggers.

10

Additional PL/SQL Datatypes

On Day 9, "Programming an Oracle Database with PL/SQL," I presented some of the essentials of PL/SQL programming. As you've seen, PL/SQL supports all the datatypes that are available in SQL. However, PL/SQL also provides the following additional datatypes that aren't available for use in ordinary SQL statements:

- [ ] BOOLEAN
- [ ] BINARY_INTEGER, NATURAL, and POSITIVE
- [ ] %TYPE
- [ ] %ROWTYPE
- [ ] The PL/SQL table (or array)
- [ ] The user-defined record

The BOOLEAN Datatype

One of the additional datatypes that PL/SQL supports is BOOLEAN. Listing 10.12 illustrates how you declare a BOOLEAN variable. You also can initialize a BOOLEAN variable to either TRUE or FALSE.

INPUT/OUTPUT

Listing 10.12. Declaring a BOOLEAN variable and initializing it.

```
SQL> set serveroutput on
SQL>
SQL> declare
  2  Payment_Is_Late  boolean := TRUE;
  3
  3  begin
  4
  4  dbms_output.enable;
  5
  5  if Payment_Is_Late then
  6     dbms_output.put_line('The payment is late!');
  7  end if;
  8
  8  end;
  9  /
The payment is late!
PL/SQL procedure successfully completed.
```

ANALYSIS In line 2, the BOOLEAN variable, Payment_Is_Late, is initialized to TRUE. In line 5, Payment_Is_Late is evaluated; because line 5 is equal to TRUE, line 6 is executed.

Until you assign a value to it, a BOOLEAN variable has the null value. In Listing 10.13, the BOOLEAN expression Day_of_Month > 5 is assigned to the BOOLEAN variable Payment_Is_Late.

Listing 10.13. Assigning BOOLEAN expressions to a BOOLEAN variable.

```
SQL> set serveroutput on
SQL>
SQL> declare
  2    Payment_Is_Late   boolean;
  3    Day_of_Month      integer;
  4
  4  begin
  5
  5  dbms_output.enable;
  6
  6  select to_number(to_char(sysdate,'DD'))
  7    into Day_of_Month
  8  from dual;
  9
  9  Payment_Is_Late := Day_of_Month > 3;
 10
 10  if Payment_Is_Late then
 11      dbms_output.put_line('The payment is late!');
 12  end if;
 13
 13  end;
 14  /
The payment is late!
PL/SQL procedure successfully completed.
```

The BINARY_INTEGER Datatype

The BINARY_INTEGER datatype stores signed integers in the range of –2,147,483,647 to 2,147,483,647. PL/SQL also provides two other datatypes that are subtypes of BINARY_INTEGER.

☐ NATURAL can store integers in the range of 0 to 2,147,483,647.

☐ POSITIVE can store integers in the range of 1 to 2,147,483,647.

You might want to declare variables that would never have a fractional part, such as a loop counter, with the NATURAL or POSITIVE datatype.

When you assign a real number to a variable that has been declared as BINARY_INTEGER, NATURAL, or POSITIVE, the number is truncated. Listing 10.14 provides an example of this.

Listing 10.14. A real number is truncated when assigned to a PL/SQL integer datatype.

```
SQL> declare
  2    Counter            natural;
  3
  3  begin
  4
```

```
4   dbms_output.enable;
5
5   Counter := 103.2;
6
6   dbms_output.put_line('Counter: ' || to_char(Counter,'999.999'));
7
7   end;
8   /
Counter:  103.000
```

Using %TYPE

PL/SQL offers two notations for referencing Oracle table and column datatypes.

☐ Use %TYPE to declare a variable with the same datatype as a specified column (or previously declared variable).

☐ Use %ROWTYPE to declare a composite variable whose structure mirrors that of a specified table or cursor.

These two datatypes help integrate PL/SQL code with the table and column definitions that exist in the Oracle data dictionary.

To define a variable as having the same datatype as a column, use the %TYPE designation with the following syntax:

```
variable-name table-name.column-name%TYPE;
```

The variables are defined as follows:

   variable-name is the PL/SQL variable being declared.

   table-name.column-name specifies the column whose datatype should be used for *variable-name*.

The beauty of using %TYPE is that it generally reduces the amount of work needed to maintain PL/SQL code. For example, you can increase or decrease the width of a column without having to change the declaration of any PL/SQL variables based on that column.

Using %ROWTYPE

You use the %ROWTYPE designation to declare a variable—a record, really—whose structure is identical to the structure of a specified table.

%ROWTYPE is used with the following syntax:

```
variable-name table-name%ROWTYPE;
```

The variables are defined as follows:

   variable-name is the PL/SQL variable being declared.

   table-name specifies the table to which *variable-name* corresponds.

For example, a record named Instructor_Rec is declared as Instructor%ROWTYPE. As a result, Instructor_Rec's fields have the same names and datatypes as the columns of the Instructor table.

INPUT/OUTPUT **Listing 10.15. Using %ROWTYPE in a SELECT statement.**

```
SQLWKS> declare
     2>
     3> Instructor_Rec      Instructor%ROWTYPE;
     4>
     5> begin
     6>
     7> dbms_output.enable;
     8>
     9> select *
    10> into Instructor_Rec
    11> from Instructor
    12> where
    13> Instructor_ID = 'P331';
    14>
    15> dbms_output.put_line('Instructor ID: ' ||
➥Instructor_Rec.Instructor_ID);
    16> dbms_output.put_line('Last Name: ' || Instructor_Rec.Last_Name);
    17> dbms_output.put_line('First Name: ' ||
➥Instructor_Rec.First_Name);
    18>
    19> end;
    20> /
Statement processed.
Instructor ID: P331
Last Name: POULSON
First Name: RANIER
```

As you can see (line 15 through 17), the fields of a %ROWTYPE record are referenced by

variable-name.field-name

variable-name is the name of the declared %ROWTYPE variable.

field-name is the name of a column in the table specified in *variable-name*'s declaration.

WARNING

Although you can reference a record declared using %ROWTYPE in a SELECT statement, you cannot reference the entire record with the INSERT statement. For instance, PL/SQL rejects the following INSERT statement:

```
SQL> declare
   2  Patient_Rec  Patient%rowtype;
   3
```

10

```
 3  begin
 4
 4  Patient_Rec.Patient_ID        := 'HHH111';
 5  Patient_Rec.Body_Temp_Deg_F   := 102.7;
 6
 6  insert into Patient
 7  (Patient_ID, Body_Temp_Deg_F)
 8  values
 9  Patient_Rec;
10
10  end;
11  /
Patient_Rec;
*
ERROR at line 9:
ORA-06550: line 9, column 1:
PLS-00103: Encountered the symbol "PATIENT_REC"
           when expecting one of the follow
an aggregate
Resuming parse at line 9, column 12.
```

Instead, you must specify each component of the Patient_Rec record that corresponds to the columns specified in the INSERT statement.

You also can assign one variable to another variable if they are both declared using the %ROWTYPE designation for the same table. Listing 10.16 illustrates this concept by assigning New_Patient to ER_Patient.

Listing 10.16. Assigning PL/SQL variables based on %ROWTYPE.

INPUT/
OUTPUT

```
SQL> declare
  2
  2  New_Patient    Patient%ROWTYPE;
  3  ER_Patient     Patient%ROWTYPE;
  4
  4  begin
  5
  5  dbms_output.enable;
  6
  6  select *
  7  into New_Patient
  8  from Patient
  9  where
 10  Patient_ID = 'ZZ0123';
 11
 11  ER_Patient := New_Patient;
 12
 12  dbms_output.put_line('ER_Patient.Body_Temp_Deg_F: ' ||
```

continues

Listing 10.16. continued

```
13                              to_char(ER_Patient.Body_Temp_Deg_F));
14
14  end;
15  /
ER_Patient.Body_Temp_Deg_F: 98.6
```

However, you cannot assign one %ROWTYPE variable to another %ROWTYPE variable if the two variables don't point to the same database table, even if the two tables are identical.

INPUT/
OUTPUT

Listing 10.17. %ROWTYPE **variables based on different tables cannot be assigned to one another.**

```
SQL> create table Identical_Patient as
  2  select * from Patient;
Table created.
SQL> set serveroutput on
SQL>
SQL> declare
  2
  2  New_Patient    Patient%ROWTYPE;
  3  ER_Patient     Identical_Patient%ROWTYPE;
  4
  4  begin
  5
  5  dbms_output.enable;
  6
  6  select *
  7  into New_Patient
  8  from Patient
  9  where
 10  Patient_ID = 'ZZ0123';
 11
 11  ER_Patient := New_Patient;
 12
 12  dbms_output.put_line('ER_Patient.Body_Temp_Deg_F: ' ||
 13                       to_char(ER_Patient.Body_Temp_Deg_F));
 14
 14  end;
 15  /
declare
 *
ERROR at line 1:
ORA-06550: line 11, column 15:
PLS-00382: expression is of wrong type
ORA-06550: line 11, column 1:
PL/SQL: Statement ignored
```

More Complex Datatypes: Tables and Records

PL/SQL supports two additional composite datatypes: *tables* and *records*. Each of these objects is first declared as a datatype, and then the actual PL/SQL table or record is declared based upon the specified datatype.

You can think of a PL/SQL table as an array: it consists of a single field. Also, you don't declare an upper limit on the number of elements that a PL/SQL table can contain; its size is dynamic.

 NEW TERM A *PL/SQL table* is a collection of elements of the same type, ordered by an index number.

 NOTE

It is unfortunate that Oracle chose to apply the label *table* to a structure that is more appropriately described as an array. A PL/SQL table, unlike a database table, is composed of a single column. As with an array, the values of a PL/SQL table are accessed by an index. Just remember that a PL/SQL table and a database table are two distinct objects with very specific characteristics and uses.

10

A user-defined record offers more flexibility than the %ROWTYPE designation. You should consider using a user-defined record when both of the following conditions are true:

☐ You need only a subset of the table's columns.

☐ You also want to store associated or *derived* information in the record.

The following section delves into the use of PL/SQL tables.

 TIP

If you declare a user-defined record type that is associated with a database table, use the %TYPE designation for each field that mirrors a column in the database table. It reduces the effort needed to maintain PL/SQL code in response to those inevitable database changes.

Declaring PL/SQL Tables

SYNTAX

A type for a PL/SQL table is declared using the following syntax:

```
TYPE type-name IS TABLE OF
table-name.column-name%TYPE
INDEX BY BINARY_INTEGER;
```

The variables are defined as follows:

type-name is the name of the declared type.

table-name.column-name specifies the column whose datatype is the base type for
type-name.

After you've declared a PL/SQL table type, you can then declare variables based on that type.
For example, in Listing 10.18, which contains an anonymous PL/SQL block, Class_ID_Tab
is declared as a table of the column Class_ID in the Class table. A cursor FOR LOOP selects each
Class_ID from the Class table and assigns it to an element in Class_ID_Tab. The example
shown in Listing 10.18 was performed using SQL Worksheet.

**INPUT/
OUTPUT** **Listing 10.18. Using a PL/SQL table.**

```
SQLWKS> set serveroutput on
Server Output              ON
SQLWKS> declare
    2>
    3> type Class_ID_Type is table of Class.Class_ID%TYPE
    4> index by binary_integer;
    5>
    6> Class_ID_Tab        Class_ID_Type;
    7> i                   binary_integer := 0;
    8> final_count         binary_integer;
    9>
   10> begin
   11>
   12> dbms_output.enable;
   13>
   14> for Class_ID_Rec in (select Class_ID from Class) loop
   15>
   16>   i := i + 1;
   17>   Class_ID_Tab(i) := Class_ID_Rec.Class_ID;
   18>
   19> end loop;
   20>
   21> final_count := i;
   22>
   23> for i in 1..final_count loop
   24>
   25>   dbms_output.put_line('Class_ID_Tab(' || to_char(i) || ') = ' ||
   26>                         Class_ID_Tab(i));
   27> end loop;
   28>
   29> end;
   30> /
Statement processed.
Class_ID_Tab(1) = 104200
Class_ID_Tab(2) = 104500
Class_ID_Tab(3) = 109100
Class_ID_Tab(4) = 120200
```

```
Class_ID_Tab(5)  = 110300
Class_ID_Tab(6)  = 108300
Class_ID_Tab(7)  = 108400
Class_ID_Tab(8)  = 108600
Class_ID_Tab(9)  = 103400
Class_ID_Tab(10) = 103600
```

You can pass a PL/SQL table as an argument to a procedure or function. Along with the PL/SQL table, you'll also want to pass a BINARY_INTEGER variable that indicates the number of elements in the PL/SQL table. Listing 10.19 illustrates an example of a procedure that returns a PL/SQL table containing Course_IDs for which the additional fees exceed $50.

INPUT/ OUTPUT **Listing 10.19. Returning a PL/SQL table.**

```
SQLWKS> declare
    2>
    3> type Course_ID_Type is table of Course.Course_ID%TYPE
    4>    index by binary_integer;
    5> Course_ID_Tab    Course_ID_Type;
    6>
    7> i                     binary_integer := 0;
    8> Total_Number          binary_integer;
    9>
   10> procedure Get_Course_IDs (Num_Rows out binary_integer,
   11>                           Course_ID_Table out Course_ID_Type) is
   12>
   13> i    binary_integer := 0;
   14>
   15> begin
   16>
   17> for Course_ID_Rec in (select Course_ID from Course
   18>        where Additional_Fees > 50) loop
   19>
   20>   i := i + 1;
   21>   Course_ID_Table(i) := Course_ID_Rec.Course_ID;
   22>
   23> end loop;
   24>
   25> Num_Rows := i;
   26>
   27> end Get_Course_IDs;
   28>
   29> --  Main block.
   30>
   31> begin
   32>
   33> dbms_output.enable;
   34>
   35> Get_Course_IDs (Total_Number, Course_ID_Tab);
   36>
   37> for i in 1..Total_Number loop
   38>   exit when Course_ID_Tab(i) = NULL;
```

continues

Listing 10.19. continued

```
39>    dbms_output.put_line('Course_ID_Tab(' || to_char(i) ||
40>                         ') = ' || Course_ID_Tab(i));
41> end loop;
42>
43> end;
44> /

Statement processed.
Course_ID_Tab(1) = 101
Course_ID_Tab(2) = 189
Course_ID_Tab(3) = 101
Course_ID_Tab(4) = 178
Course_ID_Tab(5) = 177
Course_ID_Tab(6) = 174
Course_ID_Tab(7) = 181
Course_ID_Tab(8) = 501
```

ANALYSIS   In Listing 10.19, the first line begins with the declaration section of an anonymous block. The type `Course_ID_Type` is declared in line 3. A procedure, `Get_Course_IDs`, is declared beginning on line 10. In line 13, the index for the PL/SQL table `Course_ID_Table` is initialized to 0. The execution section of the anonymous block begins on line 31. The procedure `Get_Course_IDs` is invoked on line 35 in the execution section of the anonymous block.

NOTE

> PL/SQL doesn't restrict the range of the PL/SQL table index; you could start at –100, 0, 1, or any other number that is appropriate.

Declaring User-Defined Records

The process for using a user-defined record is much like that of a PL/SQL table: you define a datatype for the record and then declare variables based on the new type.

The following is the syntax for declaring a record type:

```
TYPE type-name IS RECORD
(field-name field-datatype [NOT NULL] [initial-value],
...
 field-name field-datatype [NOT NULL] [initial-value]);
```

The variables for declaring a record type are defined as follows:

> *type-name* is the name of the declared record type.

> *field-name* is the name of the field and subject to PL/SQL variable-name restrictions.

field-datatype is the datatype of the field, which can be a specific PL/SQL datatype (such as NUMBER or BOOLEAN) or can reference a column's datatype using the %TYPE designation.

initial-value is an initial value that must be assigned to *field-name* if it's declared as NOT NULL.

TIP

> One advantage of the user-defined record is that you can declare fields for storing derived data in a record that isn't stored in the associated database table.

Listing 10.20 illustrates the declaration of a user-defined record type. In this case, we're declaring a record type named Patient_Rec_Type that is composed of three fields: Patient_ID, Body_Temp, and Bed_Number. The first two fields exist in the Patient table; however, Body_Temp has a different name—Body_Temp_Deg_F—in the table. The third field, Bed_Number, doesn't exist in the Patient table.

**INPUT/
OUTPUT**   **Listing 10.20. Using a user-defined record type.**

```
SQL> declare
  2
  2   type Patient_Rec_Type is record
  3   (Patient_ID    Patient.Patient_ID%TYPE,
  4    Body_Temp     Patient.Body_Temp_Deg_F%TYPE,
  5    Bed_Number    varchar2(4));
  6
  6   Patient_Rec   Patient_Rec_Type;
  7
  7   begin
  8
  8   dbms_output.enable;
  9
  9   Patient_Rec.Patient_ID := 'ZZ0123';
 10   Patient_Rec.Body_Temp  := 98.6;
 11   Patient_Rec.Bed_Number := 'A123';
 12
 12   dbms_output.put_line('Patient ID: ' || Patient_Rec.Patient_ID);
 13   dbms_output.put_line('Body_Temp: ' || to_char(Patient_Rec.Body_Temp));
 14   dbms_output.put_line('Bed Number: ' || Patient_Rec.Bed_Number);
 15
 15   insert into Patient
 16   (Patient_ID, Body_Temp_Deg_F)
 17   values
 18   (Patient_Rec.Patient_ID, Patient_Rec.Body_Temp);
 19
 19   end;
 20   /
```

continues

Listing 10.20. continued

```
Patient ID: ZZ0123
Body_Temp: 98.6
Bed Number: A123
```

Specifying Default Values for Variables

By default, all variables are initialized to NULL whenever you enter a procedure, function, or anonymous block. You can initialize a variable in the PL/SQL declare section in two ways:

```
variable-name    data-type  := initial-value;
```

or

```
variable-name    data-type  DEFAULT initial-value;
```

Here is an anonymous block that illustrates both methods of initializing a PL/SQL variable:

```
SQL> declare
  2
  2  i               natural := 33;
  3  my_string       varchar2(30) default 'JACKSON';
  4
  4  begin
  5
  5  dbms_output.enable;
  6
  6  end;
  7  /
PL/SQL procedure successfully completed.
```

One reason to specify a default value for a variable is that the resulting code is often easier to understand and maintain. By specifying a default value, you are making fewer assumptions about how the code will behave.

Summary

This lesson focused on the following concepts:

- [ ] You can use the Oracle DDL statements CREATE PROCEDURE and CREATE FUNCTION to create stored procedures and functions, respectively.

- [ ] A stored procedure or function is composed of PL/SQL declarations and executable statements that are compiled and stored in the database.

- [ ] You can define arguments for a stored procedure or function that input only, output only, or input and output.

□ Oracle supplies a pre-defined package, DBMS_OUTPUT, that contains routines for displaying information from within a PL/SQL subprogram.

□ A stored function can be referenced in an Oracle SQL statement. The datatype of each value passed to the function must match its corresponding argument.

□ A package is a group of related procedures and functions. A package has a specification and a body.

□ A package specification is created via the CREATE PACKAGE statement. A package body is created with the CREATE PACKAGE BODY statement.

□ PL/SQL supports several datatypes that aren't available for use in Oracle SQL statements: BOOLEAN, BINARY_INTEGER, NATURAL, and POSITIVE.

□ A BOOLEAN variable can have a value of TRUE, FALSE, or NULL.

□ By using %TYPE, you can declare a variable to have the same datatype as a particular column in a table.

□ Use the designation %ROWTYPE to declare a record whose structure is equivalent to a specified table. You also can use %ROWTYPE to declare a record with the same structure as a cursor.

□ A PL/SQL table is a user-declared datatype that you can think of as an unbounded array composed of one field. To declare a PL/SQL table, you must first declare a table datatype.

□ A user-defined record consists of one or more fields. Each field's datatype may be explicitly declared using an Oracle SQL or PL/SQL datatype, or it uses the %TYPE designation to point to the datatype of a database column. A field may be declared as NOT NULL and initialized in its declaration.

What Comes Next?

On Day 11, you learn about several important aspects of PL/SQL—how to handle errors, how to retrieve multiple rows with a cursor, and how to write a trigger on a table.

Q&A

Q Is it better to create a package that contains procedures and functions rather than individual procedures and functions?

A From a software development perspective, it's better to create a package. By creating a package specification, the interface—the names of each procedure and function and its arguments—is separate from the PL/SQL code that implements the interface.

Workshop

The purpose of the Workshop is to allow you to test your knowledge of the material discussed in the lesson. See if you can correctly answer the questions in the quiz and complete the exercises before you continue with tomorrow's lesson.

Quiz

1. True or false: A stored procedure can call a stored function, but a stored function cannot call a stored procedure.

2. Name three reasons for using stored procedures, functions, and packages in an application.

3. What tools can be used to develop PL/SQL subprograms?

4. If `"x > 32"` is assigned to a PL/SQL variable, what is the datatype of the variable?

Exercises

1. Create an anonymous PL/SQL block that will call the `Assign_Grade` procedure in the Flugle package and assign a B to Anna Anastatia for Biology 101.

2. A student, Jackson Smythe, has created a stored function named `Change_My_Grade` with two arguments: `Student ID` and `Class ID`. The function changes the grade for any specified student and class to an A+. Write out the statements that will create this function.

10

Day 11

More Programming Techniques with PL/SQL

Today's lesson is the final discussion of SQL and PL/SQL before you venture into the use of Developer/2000 and Power Objects in building applications. The material in this lesson falls into three categories:

☐ How to handle errors in a PL/SQL subprogram. You'll learn how to define an exception handler for Oracle errors and user-defined exceptions. Also, you'll see some examples of pre-defined exceptions.

☐ Declaring and using cursors in a PL/SQL subprogram to retrieve multiple rows from the database.

☐ Using PL/SQL to construct a database trigger. You'll learn how to use a trigger to validate data, enforce security, or record changes made to a table.

Handling Errors in PL/SQL

The Oracle Error Messages and Codes manual lists all error codes and messages, not including operating-specific errors. At some point, your application will probably encounter some of these errors. In PL/SQL, Oracle errors are referred to as *exceptions*. Some of the exceptions have pre-defined names that can be referenced in PL/SQL subprograms. In addition to these pre-defined Oracle exceptions, you can define application-specific exceptions in a PL/SQL subprogram.

 An *exception* is a pre-defined or user-defined application error that is raised automatically by the Oracle RDBMS or raised intentionally in a PL/SQL subprogram.

One method for handling errors in a PL/SQL subprogram is to check for any Oracle error code after each SQL statement. The problem with that approach is that the resulting subprogram can be difficult to follow. As an alternative, PL/SQL enables you to specify what processing should take place for a particular exception. This section of the PL/SQL subprogram is called the *exception section* of a PL/SQL subprogram. A pre-defined exception is said to be "raised" when an Oracle error occurs during the execution of a PL/SQL subprogram. You raise a user-defined exception by invoking the RAISE statement at an appropriate location in the PL/SQL code.

For example, suppose you have written a PL/SQL subprogram that loads information from a *flat file* into a table in the database. If the flat file contains an invalid number—for example, 3.1A instead of 3.14—a pre-defined exception will be raised when the PL/SQL subprogram tries to insert a row with the invalid number.

The Exception Section

The exception section is an optional section of a PL/SQL subprogram that tells PL/SQL how to handle particular exceptions.

The syntax for the exception section is as follows:

```
EXCEPTION
  WHEN exception-name1 THEN
    PL/SQL-statements;
  ...
  WHEN exception-nameN THEN
    PL/SQL-statements;
  ...
  [WHEN OTHERS THEN
    PL/SQL-statements;]
END;
```

The variables are defined as follows:

exception-name1 through *exception-nameN* are the names of pre-defined and user-defined exceptions.

PL/SQL-statements is one or more PL/SQL statements that are executed when the exception is raised.

To illustrate, Listing 11.1 contains a PL/SQL block with an exception section. Note that the exception section contains two exception handlers: one for a pre-defined exception—the TOO_MANY_ROWS exception (in line 11)—and one for all other exceptions—signified by the word OTHERS (in line 13).

INPUT/OUTPUT

Listing 11.1. Handling the TOO_MANY_ROWS exception.

```
SQL> declare
  2
  2  Course_Rec    Course%ROWTYPE;
  3
  3  begin
  4
  4  dbms_output.enable;
  5
  5  select *
  6  into Course_Rec
  7  from Course
  8  where
  9  Department_ID = 'BIO';
 10
 10  exception
 11    when TOO_MANY_ROWS then
 12      dbms_output.put_line('TOO_MANY_ROWS raised - use a cursor');
 13    when OTHERS then
 14      NULL;
 15  end;
 16  /
TOO_MANY_ROWS raised - use a cursor
```

If you remove the exception handler for OTHERS and cause an exception to be raised that doesn't have an exception handler, PL/SQL returns an error message. Listing 11.2 shows an example—a string of 18 characters is assigned to a variable that can store up to five characters, resulting in an Oracle error.

Listing 11.2. Exception section doesn't handle OTHERS exceptions.

```
SQL> declare
  2
  2  xyz    varchar2(5);
  3
  3  begin
  4
  4  dbms_output.enable;
  5
  5  xyz := 'This will not fit!';
  6
  6  exception
  7
  7    when TOO_MANY_ROWS then
  8      dbms_output.put_line('TOO_MANY_ROWS Exception Raised');
  9      dbms_output.put_line('Occurred in anonymous block');
 10
 10  end;
 11  /
declare
*
ERROR at line 1:
ORA-06502: PL/SQL: numeric or value error
ORA-06512: at line 5
```

Pre-Defined Exceptions

All exceptions can be categorized as either pre-defined or user defined. Pre-defined exceptions are automatically raised; for example, an SQL statement that references a table that doesn't exist results in an Oracle error. As an example, your PL/SQL subprogram may contain a SELECT statement that, in some circumstances, returns no rows; this will cause the NO_DATA_FOUND exception to be raised. Pre-defined exceptions have meaningful names. Here are some pre-defined exceptions that you might encounter when developing an Oracle application:

- [ ] DUP_VAL_ON_INDEX
- [ ] INVALID_NUMBER
- [ ] NO_DATA_FOUND
- [ ] TOO_MANY_ROWS
- [ ] VALUE_ERROR

The following sections look at which condition can trigger each of these pre-defined exceptions.

The DUP_VAL_ON_INDEX **Exception**

The DUP_VAL_ON_INDEX is raised when an SQL statement attempts to create a duplicate value in a column on which a unique index exists. To illustrate, Listing 11.3 contains an anonymous PL/SQL block that tries to update the Course table so that all rows have the same value for Course_ID, thereby raising the DUP_VAL_ON_INDEX exception.

INPUT/
OUTPUT

Listing 11.3. Handling the DUP_VAL_ON_INDEX **exception.**

```
SQL> declare
  2
  2  begin
  3
  3  dbms_output.enable;
  4
  4  update Course
  5  set
  6  Department_ID = 'BIO',
  7  Course_ID = '101';
  8
  8  exception
  9    when DUP_VAL_ON_INDEX then
 10      dbms_output.put_line('DUP_VAL_ON_INDEX exception raised');
 11  end;
 12  /
DUP_VAL_ON_INDEX exception raised

PL/SQL procedure successfully completed.
```

The INVALID_NUMBER **Exception**

The INVALID_NUMBER exception is raised when an SQL statement specifies an invalid number. For instance, Listing 11.4 provides an example of an anonymous PL/SQL block that attempts to update the Additional Fees column in the Course table. The exception is raised because the To_Number function attempts to convert a string variable, Bogus_Value, to a number.

INPUT/
OUTPUT

Listing 11.4. Handling the INVALID_NUMBER **exception.**

```
SQL> declare
  2
  2  Bogus_Value    varchar2(30) := 'NOT A NUMBER';
  3
  3  begin
  4
  4  dbms_output.enable;
  5
  5  update Course
  6  set
```

continues

Listing 11.4. continued

```
7   Additional_Fees = to_number(Bogus_Value);
8
8   exception
9     when INVALID_NUMBER then
10        dbms_output.put_line('INVALID_NUMBER exception raised');
11  end;
12  /
INVALID_NUMBER exception raised

PL/SQL procedure successfully completed.
```

The NO_DATA_FOUND Exception

The NO_DATA_FOUND exception is raised when a SELECT statement doesn't return any rows, as shown in Listing 11.5.

Listing 11.5. The NO_DATA_FOUND exception is raised without an exception handler.

```
SQL> declare
  2
  2   Course_Rec   Course%ROWTYPE;
  3
  3   begin
  4
  4   dbms_output.enable;
  5
  5   select *
  6   into Course_Rec
  7   from Course
  8   where
  9   Course_ID = '777';
 10
 10   end;
 11  /
declare
*
ERROR at line 1:
ORA-01403: no data found
ORA-06512: at line 5
```

After you add an exception handler for NO_DATA_FOUND (in line 11), PL/SQL no longer returns the error—no data returned—to the calling environment, as shown in Listing 11.6.

Listing 11.6. Handling the NO_DATA_FOUND **exception.**

```
SQL> declare
  2
  2    Course_Rec Course%ROWTYPE;
  3
  3    begin
  4
  4    dbms_output.enable;
  5
  5    select *
  6    into Course_Rec
  7    from Course
  8    where
  9    Course_ID = '777';
 10
 10    exception
 11      when NO_DATA_FOUND then
 12        dbms_output.put_line('No data returned');
 13      when OTHERS then
 14        NULL;
 15    end;
 16    /
No data returned

PL/SQL procedure successfully completed.
```

The TOO_MANY_ROWS Exception

In the PL/SQL environment, a SELECT statement cannot retrieve more than one row without raising the TOO_MANY_ROWS exception. To retrieve an arbitrary number of rows from a query, you can use a cursor, which you can think of as a window on the results returned by a query. Listing 11.7 provides an example of how an exception handler is used for the TOO_MANY_ROWS exception.

Listing 11.7. Handling the TOO_MANY_ROWS **exception.**

```
SQL> declare
  2
  2    Course_Rec    Course%ROWTYPE;
  3
  3    begin
  4
  4    dbms_output.enable;
  5
  5    select *
  6    into Course_Rec
  7    from Course
  8    where
```

continues

Listing 11.7. continued

```
 9  Department_ID = 'BIO';
10
10  exception
11    when TOO_MANY_ROWS then
12      dbms_output.put_line('TOO_MANY_ROWS raised - use a cursor');
13    when OTHERS then
14      NULL;
15  end;
16  /
TOO_MANY_ROWS raised - use a cursor

PL/SQL procedure successfully completed.
```

The VALUE_ERROR Exception

The VALUE_ERROR exception is raised in a number of situations related to truncation and conversion errors. For example, Listing 11.8 illustrates a PL/SQL block (beginning with the first line) that tries to assign the string More than 5 characters to a variable that has been declared as VARCHAR2(5).

INPUT/
OUTPUT   **Listing 11.8. Handling the VALUE_ERROR exception.**

```
SQL> declare
  2
  2  xyz  varchar2(5);
  3
  3  begin
  4
  4  dbms_output.enable;
  5
  5  xyz := 'More than 5 characters';
  6
  6  exception
  7
  7    when VALUE_ERROR then
  8      dbms_output.put_line('VALUE_ERROR raised');
  9
  9    when OTHERS then
 10      NULL;
 11
 11  end;
 12  /
VALUE_ERROR raised
```

11

Declaring an Exception

In addition to dealing with the pre-defined exceptions, you also can define application-specific exceptions and declare them in the following way:

exception-name EXCEPTION;

The variable *exception-name* is the declared exception and subject to PL/SQL object-naming restrictions.

Listing 11.9 provides an example that declares an exception named Life_Threatening_Fever that is raised if a patient's body temperature exceeds 106 degrees Fahrenheit.

**INPUT/
OUTPUT** **Listing 11.9. Declaring an application exception.**

```
SQL> declare
   2
   2  Life_Threatening_Fever  exception;
   3  Patient_ID    Patient.Patient_ID%TYPE;
   4
   4  begin
   5
   5  dbms_output.enable;
   6
   6  for Patient_Rec in
   7    (select Patient_ID, Body_Temp_Deg_F from Patient) loop
   8
   8    if Patient_Rec.Body_Temp_Deg_F > 106.0 then
   9
   9      Patient_ID := Patient_Rec.Patient_ID;
  10      raise Life_Threatening_Fever;
  11
  11    end if;
  12  end loop;
  13
  13  exception
  14
  14    when Life_Threatening_Fever then
  15      dbms_output.put_line(Patient_ID ¦¦ ' has a life ' ¦¦
  16                          'threatening fever!');
  17
  17  end;
  18  /
GG9999 has a life threatening fever!
```

Success or Failure: Inspecting SQLCODE and SQLERRM

SQLCODE is a pre-defined symbol that contains the Oracle error status of the previously executed PL/SQL statement. If an SQL statement executes without errors, SQLCODE is equal to 0.

SQLERRM is a PL/SQL symbol that contains the error message associated with SQLCODE. If an SQL statement executes successfully, SQLCODE is equal to 0 and SQLERRM contains the string ORA-0000: normal, successful completion, as shown in Listing 11.10.

INPUT/OUTPUT **Listing 11.10. Referencing SQLCODE and SQLERRM.**

```
SQL> declare
  2
  2  begin
  3
  3  dbms_output.enable;
  4
  4  dbms_output.put_line('SQLCODE: ' || to_char(SQLCODE));
  5  dbms_output.put_line('SQLERRM: ' || SQLERRM);
  6
  6  end;
  7  /
SQLCODE: 0
SQLERRM: ORA-0000: normal, successful completion
```

If an error actually occurs, SQLCODE and SQLERRM contain the applicable code and message, respectively—as shown in the output of Listing 11.11.

INPUT/OUTPUT **Listing 11.11. Referencing SQLCODE and SQLERRM in the exception section.**

```
SQL> declare
  2  Class_Rec    Class%ROWTYPE;
  3
  3  begin
  4
  4  dbms_output.enable;
  5
  5  select *
  6  into Class_Rec
  7  from Class;
  8
  8  exception
  9    when OTHERS then
 10      dbms_output.put_line('SQLCODE: ' || to_char(SQLCODE));
```

```
11      dbms_output.put_line(SQLERRM);
12  end;
13  /
SQLCODE: -1422
ORA-01422: exact fetch returns more than requested number of rows

PL/SQL procedure successfully completed.
```

Returning Errors with
RAISE_APPLICATION_ERROR

Oracle provides a procedure named RAISE_APPLICATION_ERROR in the DBMS_STANDARD package. You can use this procedure to return application-specific error messages to a caller—such as SQL*Plus, a PL/SQL subprogram, or a client application. Oracle reserves error codes in the range of -20000 to -20999 for these user-defined errors. For instance, Listing 11.12 illustrates a PL/SQL block that declares an exception named Fever_Out_of_Range. A cursor FOR LOOP (in line 6) reads through each row in the Patient table. If a patient's temperature exceeds 115 degrees Fahrenheit, the Fever_Out_of_Range exception is raised (in line 8). In the exception section, the exception handler for Fever_Out_of_Range calls RAISE_APPLICATION_ERROR and passes it an error code of -20000 and a relevant error message (in line 14).

**INPUT/
OUTPUT** **Listing 11.12. Raising an application-specific exception.**

```
SQL> declare
  2
  2   Fever_Out_of_Range exception;
  3   Patient_ID          Patient.Patient_ID%TYPE;
  4
  4   begin
  5
  5   dbms_output.enable;
  6
  6   for Patient_Rec in
  7     (select Patient_ID, Body_Temp_Deg_F from Patient) loop
  8
  8     if Patient_Rec.Body_Temp_Deg_F > 115.0 then
  9
  9       raise Fever_Out_of_Range;
 10
 10     end if;
 11
 11   end loop;
 12
 12   exception
 13
```

continues

Listing 11.12. continued

```
13    when Fever_Out_of_Range then
14      raise_application_error (-20000,
            'Fever is out of the range 65 Deg. F to 115 Deg. F');
15
15  end;
16  /
declare
*
ERROR at line 1:
ORA-20000: Fever is out of the range 65 Deg. F to 115 Deg. F
ORA-06512: at line 14
```

Retrieving Data with a Cursor

When you're using SQL*Plus or SQL Worksheet, you can submit a query without being concerned with the number of rows that are returned. It doesn't matter whether the query retrieves zero, one, or a thousand rows. However, this situation isn't true for PL/SQL subprograms. You cannot use an ordinary SELECT statement to retrieve more than one row. If a SELECT statement in a PL/SQL subprogram—whether it's an anonymous block, a stored procedure, or a trigger—retrieves more than one row, Oracle returns an error message. Obviously, the capability to retrieve more than one row is essential, and some mechanism to do so must be available. The resource that Oracle provides to accomplish this job is the cursor. Cursors are automatically created and used by Oracle utilities such as SQL*Plus.

NEW TERM   A *cursor* is a mechanism for programmatically retrieving an arbitrary number of rows with a SELECT statement.

Listing 11.13 illustrates how Oracle returns an error because the SELECT statement returns more than one instructor.

INPUT/ OUTPUT   **Listing 11.13. Oracle error resulting from SELECT statement that returns more than one row.**

```
SQL> declare
  2
  2    Instructor_ID    Instructor.Instructor_ID%type;
  3    Last_Name        Instructor.Last_Name%type;
  4    First_Name       Instructor.First_Name%type;
  5
  5  begin
  6
  6  select Instructor_ID, Last_Name, First_Name
  7  into   Instructor_ID, Last_Name, First_Name
  8  from Instructor
  9  order by Instructor_ID;
```

```
10
10  end;
11  /
declare
*
ERROR at line 1:
ORA-01422: exact fetch returns more than requested number of rows
ORA-06512: at line 6
```

You can think of a cursor as a window into the result set of a query. (See Figure 11.1.) You will generally perform four steps when you use a cursor:

1. **Declare the cursor.** The cursor is assigned a name and associated with a SELECT statement, which is parsed.

2. **Open the cursor.** The Oracle RDBMS executes the query associated with the cursor and determines the qualified rows (active set).

3. **Fetch rows from the cursor.** The values for each row are returned to the PL/SQL subprogram environment. Rows are returned one at a time.

4. **Close the cursor.** All resources consumed by Oracle related to the cursor are released.

Figure 11.1.

An illustration of a cursor.

Active Set

Instructor ID	Last Name	First Name
A612	NILAND	MARTINA
B331	BILLINGS	BENJAMIN
B391	BATES	JOSEPH
D201	DANIELS	LAURA
D944	**RESTON**	**RAPHAEL**
E301	EDWARDS	SAMANTHA
E405	CHANG	ROGER
E491	RICHARDSON	NANCY
G331	TORRES	PETER
J505	JASON	JERROLD

Cursor

NOTE

In PL/SQL, a SELECT statement that returns more than one row raises the pre-defined exception TOO_MANY_ROWS.

Here is a stored function that determines if a specified class conflicts with a student's schedule. The function—Schedule_Conflict—has two arguments: Student_ID and Class_ID. It

determines if there is a conflict by looking for any other classes that are part of the student's
current schedule that have the same schedule as the proposed class. A cursor is used to perform
this query. Listing 11.14 contains the full text of the function.

INPUT/
OUTPUT **Listing 11.14. Using a cursor in a stored function.**

```
SQL> create or replace function schedule_conflict (arg_student_ID IN varchar2,
  2                              arg_class_ID   IN varchar2)
  3    return number is
  4
  4  conflicting_classes  number := -1;
  5  normal               number := 0;
  6
  6  cursor get_other_classes is
  7          select SS.Class_ID
  8          from Student_Schedule SS, Class C
  9          where
 10          SS.Class_ID = C.Class_ID and
 11          (C.Semester, C.School_Year, C.Schedule_ID) =
 12          (select Semester, School_Year, Schedule_ID
 13           from Class
 14           where
 15           Class_ID = arg_class_ID);
 16
 16  Conflicting_Class_ID  Class.Class_ID%type;
 17  status  number;
 18
 18  begin
 19
 19  -- Need to look at the other classes in the student's schedule
 20  -- for the same semester and school year.
 21
 21  open get_other_classes;
 22
 22  loop
 23
 23    fetch get_other_classes into Conflicting_Class_ID;
 24    exit when get_other_classes%notfound;
 25
 25  end loop;
 26
 26  if get_other_classes%rowcount > 0 then
 27    status := conflicting_classes;
 28  else
 29    status := normal;
 30  end if;
 31
 31  close get_other_classes;
 32
 32  return status;
 33
 33  end;
 34  /
```

```
Function created.

SQL> select Student_ID, Class_ID
  2  from Student_Schedule
  3  where
  4  Student_ID = '10231311';

STUDENT_ID          CLASS_ID
------------------- -------------------
10231311            104200
10231311            104500

SQL> select schedule_conflict('10231311','104200') from dual;

SCHEDULE_CONFLICT('10231311','104200')
--------------------------------------
                                    -1
```

ANALYSIS Here's a look at each step of this cursor in detail. First, beginning at line 6, the cursor—Get_Other_Classes—is declared as a join between two tables—Student_Schedule and Class. Second, the cursor is opened within the executable section of the stored function (in line 21). Third, a loop statement fetches rows from the cursor until no more rows are retrieved (in line 23).

As you can see at the end of Listing 11.14, a query of the Student_Schedule table shows that Student ID 10231311 is registered for two classes: 104200 and 104500. The function is invoked in the final SELECT statement; it checks to see if class 104200 for student 10231311 will result in a conflict. Of course it will, because the student is already enrolled in the class. The function returns –1, which indicates that the status is conflicting classes.

Declaring a Cursor

Every cursor must be declared before it can be used. Declaring a cursor means giving it a name and specifying the SELECT statement with which the cursor is associated.

SYNTAX

The basic syntax used in PL/SQL to declare a cursor is as follows:

```
CURSOR cursor-name
[(parameter1 parameter1-datatype [:= default1],
...
 parameterN parameterN-datatype [:= defaultN])]
IS select-stmt;
```

The variables are defined in this way:

cursor-name is the name of the cursor and subject to Oracle object-naming requirements.

parameter1 is the name of the first parameter to be supplied to the cursor.

parameter1-datatype is the datatype for parameter1.

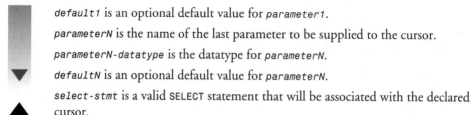

default1 is an optional default value for *parameter1*.

parameterN is the name of the last parameter to be supplied to the cursor.

parameterN-datatype is the datatype for *parameterN*.

defaultN is an optional default value for *parameterN*.

select-stmt is a valid SELECT statement that will be associated with the declared cursor.

Listing 11.15 illustrates two different cursors—the first cursor has three parameters without default values and the second cursor has three parameters with specified default values.

Listing 11.15. Cursors with and without default values for parameters.

INPUT

```
cursor patients_with_hypertension
        (patient_age number,
         normal_dyastolic,
         normal_systolic) is
         select patient_id, age, dyastolic, systolic
         from patient
         where
         dyastolic > normal_dyastolic * (age+200)/200 and
         systolic > normal_systolic * (age+200)/200;

cursor patients_with_hypertension
         (patient_age number default 55,
          normal_dyastolic number default 70,
          normal_systolic  number default 130) is
          select patient_id, age, dyastolic, systolic
          from patient
          where
          dyastolic > normal_dyastolic * (age+200)/200 and
          systolic > normal_systolic * (age+200)/200;
```

NOTE

If you use any of the Oracle precompilers—for example, Pro*C— you'll need to use a cursor to retrieve more than one row via a SELECT statement.

Opening a Cursor

Before you can fetch rows from a cursor, you must open the cursor. When the cursor is opened, its SELECT statement is executed and Oracle constructs a list of the qualified rows.

These rows are referred to as the *active set*. If the cursor was declared without any parameters, the syntax is very simple:

```
open my_cursor;
```

If the cursor was declared with parameters, you must supply a PL/SQL variable or a literal value for each parameter when you open the cursor, as shown in Listing 11.16.

**INPUT/
OUTPUT**   ## Listing 11.16. Declaring a cursor with parameters.

```
SQL> declare
  2
  2  cursor patients_with_hypertension
  3         (patient_age number,
  4          normal_dyastolic number) is
  5          select patient_id
  6          from patient
  7          where
  8          dyastolic > normal_dyastolic * (age+200)/200 and
  9          systolic > 180;
 10
 10  Patient_ID Patient.Patient_ID%type;
 11
 11  begin
 12
 12  open patients_with_hypertension (45, 80);
 13
 13  end;
 14  /
PL/SQL procedure successfully completed.
```

If the cursor was declared with parameters—and default values were specified for those parameters—you aren't required to furnish a PL/SQL variable or a literal value for each parameter, as illustrated in Listing 11.17.

**INPUT/
OUTPUT**   ## Listing 11.17. Default values for cursor parameters used.

```
SQL> declare
  2
  2  cursor patients_with_hypertension
  3         (patient_age number default 55,
  4          normal_dyastolic number default 70,
  5          normal_systolic  number default 130) is
  6          select patient_id
  7          from patient
  8          where
  9          dyastolic > normal_dyastolic * (age+200)/200 and
 10          systolic > normal_systolic * (age+200)/200;
 11
```

continues

Listing 11.17. continued

```
11   Patient_ID Patient.Patient_ID%type;
12
12   begin
13
13   dbms_output.enable;
14
14   open patients_with_hypertension;
15
15   loop
16
16      fetch patients_with_hypertension
17            into Patient_ID;
18      exit when patients_with_hypertension%notfound;
19
19      dbms_output.put_line(patient_record.patient_id);
20
20   end loop;
21
21   end;
22   /
```

```
N3393
PL/SQL procedure successfully completed.
```

If the cursor was declared with parameters—but no default values were specified for those parameters—you must supply a PL/SQL variable or a literal value for each parameter. Listing 11.18 illustrates how Oracle will reject the open cursor statement if the required arguments are not supplied.

INPUT/ OUTPUT

Listing 11.18. Oracle returns an error when arguments are not supplied for the cursor.

```
SQL> declare
  2
  2   cursor patients_with_hypertension
  3         (patient_age number,
  4          normal_dyastolic number,
  5          normal_systolic number) is
  6          select patient_id
  7          from patient
  8          where
  9          dyastolic > normal_dyastolic * (age+200)/200 and
 10          systolic > 180;
 11
 11   Patient_ID Patient.Patient_ID%type;
 12
 12   begin
 13
 13   open patients_with_hypertension;
```

11

```
14
14  end;
15  /
declare
*
ERROR at line 1:
ORA-06550: line 13, column 1:
PLS-00306: wrong number or types of arguments
           in call to 'PATIENTS_WITH_HYPERTENSION'
ORA-06550: line 13, column 1:
PL/SQL: SQL Statement ignored
```

Fetching Rows from a Cursor

Once the cursor has been opened, the query has been executed and the qualified rows have been identified. To retrieve the rows, you must execute the FETCH statement, which retrieves the value of each column specified in the cursor's SELECT statement and places it in a PL/SQL variable. In general, you'll want to fetch rows within a loop. To illustrate, Listing 11.19 contains an anonymous PL/SQL block (starting with the first line) that fetches rows from the Instructor table.

**INPUT/
OUTPUT**   **Listing 11.19. Fetching rows from a cursor.**

```
SQL> declare
  2
  2   Instructor_ID    Instructor.Instructor_ID%type;
  3   Last_Name        Instructor.Last_Name%type;
  4   First_Name       Instructor.First_Name%type;
  5
  5   cursor get_instructors is
  6     select Instructor_ID, Last_Name, First_Name
  7     from Instructor
  8     order by Instructor_ID;
  9
  9   begin
 10
 10   dbms_output.enable;
 11
 11   open get_instructors;
 12
 12   loop
 13
 13     fetch get_instructors into
 14       Instructor_ID, Last_Name, First_Name;
 15     exit when get_instructors%notfound;
 16
 16     dbms_output.put_line(Instructor_ID);
 17
 17   end loop;
```

continues

Listing 11.19. continued

```
18
18   end;
19   /

A612
B331
B391
D201
D944
E301
E405
E491
G331
J505
L391
M101
P331
R983
S131
T149
W490
Y561

PL/SQL procedure successfully completed.
```

You should use the EXIT statement to exit the loop when all rows have been fetched from the cursor.

SYNTAX

The syntax to use is as follows:

```
EXIT [label] [WHEN condition]
```

The variables are defined as follows:

label is an optional label name that specifies which loop should be exited.

condition is a PL/SQL condition that returns a Boolean value.

Four specific attributes are associated with declared cursors: %ROWCOUNT, %FOUND, %NOTFOUND, and %ISOPEN. These attributes are referenced by placing them after a cursor's name. To terminate a loop with the EXIT statement, reference a cursor's %NOTFOUND attribute in the following way:

```
exit when get_instructors%notfound;
```

Closing a Cursor

You must close a cursor for two reasons:

☐ To reopen it with a different set of parameter values

☐ To release the resources consumed by the cursor

If a PL/SQL program doesn't close a cursor, Oracle closes the cursor when the subprogram disconnects from the Oracle database, either by terminating or by performing a DISCONNECT. Closing a cursor is straightforward:

```
close get_instructors;
```

Listing 11.20 shows you how to supply a different set of parameter values to a cursor by closing the cursor, changing the parameter values, and reopening the cursor. It uses the patients_with_hypertension cursor to illustrate this process. First, the cursor is opened with age set to 50 and normal_dyastolic set to 80 (line 14). The rows are fetched in a loop (line 16), and the cursor is closed. Next, the cursor is reopened with age equal to 40 and normal_dyastolic set at 70 (line 22). The rows are fetched in a loop with different results.

Listing 11.20. Changing a cursor's arguments by closing and reopening the cursor.

INPUT/
OUTPUT

```
SQL> declare
  2
  2  Patient_ID    Patient.Patient_ID%type;
  3  Age           Patient.Age%type;
  4  Dyastolic     Patient.Dyastolic%type;
  5
  5  cursor patients_with_hypertension
  6         (patient_age number,
  7          normal_dyastolic number) is
  8          select patient_id, age, dyastolic
  9          from patient
 10          where
 11          dyastolic > normal_dyastolic * (age+200)/200;
 12
 12  begin
 13
 13  dbms_output.enable;
 14
 14  open patients_with_hypertension (50, 80);
 15
 15  loop
 16
 16     fetch patients_with_hypertension
 17          into Patient_ID, Age, Dyastolic;
 18     exit when patients_with_hypertension%notfound;
 19
 19     dbms_output.put_line('With age=50, dyas=80: ' || Patient_ID);
 20
 20  end loop;
 21
 21  close patients_with_hypertension;
 22
 22  open patients_with_hypertension (40, 70);
 23
 23  loop
```

continues

Listing 11.20. continued

```
24
24        fetch patients_with_hypertension
25              into Patient_ID, Age, Dyastolic;
26        exit when patients_with_hypertension%notfound;
27
27        dbms_output.put_line('With age=40, dyas=70: ' || Patient_ID);
28
28   end loop;
29
29   close patients_with_hypertension;
30
30   end;
31   /

With age=50, dyas=80: N3393
With age=40, dyas=70: A2002
With age=40, dyas=70: N3393
With age=40, dyas=70: E3893
PL/SQL procedure successfully completed.
```

Working with Cursor FOR Loops

As an alternative to opening, fetching, and closing a cursor, Oracle furnishes another approach—the cursor FOR loop. With the cursor FOR loop, Oracle implicitly declares a variable—the loop index—that is of the same record type as the cursor's *record*, as shown in Listing 11.21.

INPUT/ OUTPUT   Listing 11.21. Using a cursor FOR loop.

```
SQL> declare
  2
  2    Instructor_ID    Instructor.Instructor_ID%type;
  3    Last_Name        Instructor.Last_Name%type;
  4    First_Name       Instructor.First_Name%type;
  5
  5    cursor Get_Associate_Profs is
  6      select Instructor_ID, Last_Name, First_Name
  7      from Instructor
  8      where Position = 'ASSOCIATE PROFESSOR'
  9      order by Instructor_ID;
 10
 10   begin
 11
 11   dbms_output.enable;
 12
 12   for Get_Associate_Profs_Rec in Get_Associate_Profs loop
 13
 13     dbms_output.put_line('Last name: ' ||
         ➥Get_Associate_Profs_Rec.Last_Name);
```

```
14
14   end loop;
15
15   end;
16   /

Last name: NILAND
Last name: DANIELS
Last name: RESTON
Last name: JASON
Last name: ANGELO
Last name: CHERNOW
Last name: YOUNG

PL/SQL procedure successfully completed.
```

The name that follows FOR is the loop index that is implicitly declared. However, Listing 11.22 demonstrates that you can't reference the loop index—Get_Associate_Profs_Rec—outside of the loop statement.

Listing 11.22. Oracle returns an error when the cursor loop index is referenced outside of loop.

INPUT/OUTPUT

```
SQL> declare
2
2    Instructor_ID     Instructor.Instructor_ID%type;
3    Last_Name         Instructor.Last_Name%type;
4    First_Name        Instructor.First_Name%type;
5
5    cursor Get_Associate_Profs is
6      select Instructor_ID, Last_Name, First_Name
7      from Instructor
8      where Position = 'ASSOCIATE PROFESSOR'
9      order by Instructor_ID;
10
10   begin
11
11   dbms_output.enable;
12
12   for Get_Associate_Profs_Rec in Get_Associate_Profs loop
13
13     dbms_output.put_line('Last name: ' ||
     ➥Get_Associate_Profs_Rec.Last_Name);
14
14   end loop;
15
15   Last_Name := Get_Associate_Profs_Rec.Last_Name;
16
16   end;
17   /
```

continues

Listing 11.22. continued

```
declare
 *
ERROR at line 1:
ORA-06550: line 15, column 14:
PLS-00201: identifier 'GET_ASSOCIATE_PROFS_REC.LAST_NAME' must be declared
ORA-06550: line 15, column 1:
PL/SQL: Statement ignored
```

Was It %FOUND or %NOTFOUND

The previous examples used the %NOTFOUND attribute to determine whether a FETCH statement retrieved a row. When all of the rows in the active set have been fetched and the last FETCH statement fails to retrieve a row, %NOTFOUND evaluates to TRUE.

 NOTE

> Before the FETCH statement is invoked, %NOTFOUND returns a NULL. If your PL/SQL program has a loop in which the FETCH statement might not be called, you should consider testing for the condition of %NOTFOUND evaluating to NULL.

Getting the Number of Rows with %ROWCOUNT

You don't need a counter to keep track of the number of rows that are fetched from a cursor. Instead, reference the cursor's %ROWCOUNT attribute. As you can see in line 13 in Listing 11.23, %ROWCOUNT returns the *running* count of the rows that have been fetched.

 INPUT/ OUTPUT **Listing 11.23. Using %ROWCOUNT to determine the number of rows fetched from a cursor.**

```
SQL> declare
  2
  2    Instructor_ID    Instructor.Instructor_ID%type;
  3    Last_Name        Instructor.Last_Name%type;
  4    First_Name       Instructor.First_Name%type;
  5
  5    cursor Get_Associate_Profs is
  6    select Instructor_ID, Last_Name, First_Name
  7    from Instructor
```

```
 8  where Position = 'ASSOCIATE PROFESSOR'
 9  order by Instructor_ID;
10
10  begin
11
11  dbms_output.enable;
12
12  for Get_Associate_Profs_Rec in Get_Associate_Profs loop
13
13    dbms_output.put_line ('Rowcount: ' ||
      ➥Get_Associate_Profs%rowcount);
14
14  end loop;
15
15  end;
16  /

Rowcount: 1
Rowcount: 2
Rowcount: 3
Rowcount: 4
Rowcount: 5
Rowcount: 6
Rowcount: 7

PL/SQL procedure successfully completed.
```

Instead of exiting a loop when there are no more rows in the cursor, Listing 11.24 demonstrates how you can specify an exit condition when a specified %ROWCOUNT is achieved (see line 13).

Listing 11.24. Exiting a cursor loop after a specified number of rows are fetched.

INPUT/
OUTPUT

```
SQL> declare
 2
 2  Instructor_ID    Instructor.Instructor_ID%type;
 3  Last_Name        Instructor.Last_Name%type;
 4  First_Name       Instructor.First_Name%type;
 5
 5  cursor Get_Associate_Profs is
 6  select Instructor_ID, Last_Name, First_Name
 7  from Instructor
 8  where Position = 'ASSOCIATE PROFESSOR'
 9  order by Instructor_ID;
10
10  begin
11
11  dbms_output.enable;
12
12  for Get_Associate_Profs_Rec in Get_Associate_Profs loop
13
```

continues

Listing 11.24. continued

```
13    exit when Get_Associate_Profs%rowcount >= 5;
14    dbms_output.put_line ('Rowcount: ' || Get_Associate_Profs%rowcount);
15
15  end loop;
16
16  end;
17  /

Rowcount: 1
Rowcount: 2
Rowcount: 3
Rowcount: 4

PL/SQL procedure successfully completed.
```

As you can see in Listings 11.23 and 11.24, you can use %ROWCOUNT to keep track of the number of rows that have been fetched from a cursor.

Enforcing Business Rules with Database Triggers

Using everything that you've learned about SQL and PL/SQL, it's time to explore the world of database triggers. In an information system that uses a non-relational database as its foundation, the business rules of the organization served by the system are implemented in application software. For instance, one business rule might be that if the inventory on hand for a part falls below the stocking level for that part, an order for the required quantity is entered into the system. You would commonly enforce this rule by writing a routine in COBOL or some other programming language that is invoked at an appropriate point in the application. However, this method presents several problems:

☐ The rule is enforced only if an application program or tool invokes the routine. If some other tool is used to modify records in the database, the rule isn't enforced.

☐ Obtaining a list of the algorithms that are used to enforce business rules is difficult. You have to rely on documentation (which might not be entirely accurate) or face the drudgery of reviewing application software.

Oracle, along with other modern RDBMSs, provides a mechanism—the database trigger—that eases the task of implementing an organization's business rules. A *database trigger* is a group of PL/SQL statements that is executed when an SQL statement—a DELETE, UPDATE, or INSERT statement—is applied to a table. You can use a database trigger to perform the following tasks:

☐ Enforce a sophisticated security policy

☐ Change a column value based on the value of other columns in the same table or a different table

☐ Perform complex validation of column values—for instance, you might need to compare a column value to some aggregate column value from a different table

☐ Document changes to a record by writing modified values to another table

NEW TERM A *database trigger* is a group of PL/SQL statements that are executed when the contents of a table are modified in some way—either through an INSERT, UPDATE, or DELETE statement.

This lesson examines the details of creating triggers for various purposes.

Creating a Trigger

You'll want to use a text editor to write your triggers. The Oracle statement CREATE TRIGGER creates (or replaces) a trigger that's fired when a specified event occurs on a table.

SYNTAX

The syntax for the CREATE TRIGGER statement is as follows:

```
CREATE [OR REPLACE] TRIGGER trigger-name {BEFORE ¦ AFTER}
triggering-event ON table-name
[FOR EACH ROW]
[WHEN (condition)]
PL/SQL-block
```

The variables are defined as follows:

trigger-name is the name of the trigger to create and is subject to Oracle object-naming restrictions.

triggering-event is either INSERT, UPDATE, or DELETE corresponding to the three DML statements.

table-name is the name of the table with which the trigger is associated.

FOR EACH ROW is an optional clause that, when used, causes the trigger to fire for each affected row.

condition is an optional Oracle Boolean condition that, when TRUE, enables the trigger to fire.

PL/SQL-block is the PL/SQL block that is executed when the trigger fires—referred to as the *trigger body*.

The following sections discuss the use of these CREATE TRIGGER statement elements.

Statement-Level and Row-Level Triggers

A database trigger fits in one of the following two classifications:

- *Statement-level* triggers don't include the clause FOR EACH ROW in the CREATE TRIGGER statement.
- *Row-level* triggers do include the clause FOR EACH ROW in the CREATE TRIGGER statement.

A statement-level trigger fires only once for the triggering event and doesn't have access to the column values of each row that is affected by the trigger. A row-level trigger fires for each row that is affected by the trigger and can access the original and new column values processed by the SQL statement.

You generally use a statement-level trigger to process information about the SQL statement that caused the trigger to fire—for instance, who executed it and when. You typically use a row-level trigger when you need to know the column values of a row to implement a business rule.

Referencing Column Values in the Trigger Body

Within the trigger body, a row-level trigger can reference the column values of the row that existed when the trigger was fired. These values depend on which SQL statement caused the trigger to fire.

- For an INSERT statement, the values that will be inserted are contained in :new.column-name, where column-name is a column in the table.
- For an UPDATE statement, the original value for a column is contained in :old.column-name; the new value for a column is contained in :new.column-name.
- For a DELETE statement, the column values of the row being deleted are contained in :old.column-name.

Triggering Events

When you create a trigger, you specify what event will cause the trigger to fire. The three possible events are

- The insertion of a new row in the table through an INSERT statement
- The modification of a set of rows (or no rows) via an UPDATE statement
- The deletion of a set of rows (or no rows) with a DELETE statement

In addition, you can combine these triggering events so that a trigger fires whenever a DELETE or INSERT or UPDATE statement is executed, as shown in Listing 11.25.

Listing 11.25. Declaring a trigger that fires on any triggering event.

```
SQL> create or replace trigger Block_Trade_After_All After
  2  insert or update or delete on Tab1
  3  for each row
  4
  4  declare
  5
  5  begin
  6
  6  insert into Tab11
  7  (col11)
  8  values
  9  (11);
 10
 10  end;
 11  /
Trigger created.
```

BEFORE and AFTER Triggers

A BEFORE row-level trigger is fired before the triggering event is executed. As a result, you can use a BEFORE row-level trigger to modify a row's column values. An AFTER row-level trigger fires after the triggering event has occurred. You can't modify column values with an AFTER trigger.

Possible Triggers for a Table

Based on all of the permutations you can use in the CREATE TRIGGER statement, a single table can have up to 12 types of triggers:

☐ Six row-level triggers for BEFORE DELETE, BEFORE INSERT, BEFORE UPDATE, AFTER DELETE, AFTER INSERT, and AFTER UPDATE

☐ Six statement-level triggers for BEFORE DELETE, BEFORE INSERT, BEFORE UPDATE, AFTER DELETE, AFTER INSERT, and AFTER UPDATE

TIP

If you're considering the use of an entity-relationship modeling tool for database design—which you should—you'll find that most of them will automatically generate database triggers based on the primary and foreign key relationships you define. Some tools, such as ERwin from LogicWorks, either create the triggers directly via an Oracle connection or store the triggers in a script file. If you choose the latter method, you can modify the trigger creation script by adding application-specific business rules to any triggers that have been generated.

Just because you can create all 12 types of triggers for a table doesn't mean that you must! In fact, you should be judicious when creating triggers for your tables.

NOTE

Oracle Version 7.1 or higher supports multiple triggers of the same type on the same table. In contrast, Oracle 7.0 installations that used snapshots couldn't create AFTER ROW triggers for the master table because the snapshot logs used AFTER ROW triggers on the same table. However, unless you're planning to use an AFTER ROW trigger for a table referenced by a snapshot, you should avoid defining multiple triggers of the same type for a given table—the potential for design error and confusion is too great.

The next part of this lesson explores some uses for database triggers.

Validating Column Values with a Trigger

As the DBA for a credit card company, you are responsible for implementing credit policy via database triggers. Company research has shown that the probability of credit card fraud is greater than 80 percent when more than $1,000 in credit charges have accumulated on a single account within three days. The director of operations wants to record any account that meets this criteria in a separate table where it can be investigated in detail.

To accomplish this task, you create a trigger on the Credit_Charge_Log table that fires before a row is inserted. The trigger looks at the total amount of charges for the specified card number for the past three days, and if the total exceeds $1,000, it performs an INSERT in the Credit_Charge_Attempt_Log table where the record will be investigated by credit agents. Listing 11.26 illustrates how to create this trigger.

 INPUT/ OUTPUT **Listing 11.26. Creating a before insert trigger.**

```
SQL> create or replace trigger Credit_Charge_Log_Ins_Before before
  2   insert on Credit_Charge_Log
  3   for each row
  4
  4   declare
  5
  5   total_for_past_3_days   number;
  6
  6   begin
  7
  7   --   Check the credit charges for the past 3 days.
  8   --   If they total more than $1000.00, log this entry
```

11

```
 9  --  in the Credit_Charge_Attempt_Log for further handling.
10
10  select sum(amount)
11  into total_for_past_3_days
12  from Credit_Charge_Log
13  where
14  Card_Number = :new.Card_Number and
15  Transaction_Date >= sysdate-3;
16
16  if total_for_past_3_days > 1000.00 then
17
17     insert into Credit_Charge_Attempt_Log
18        (Card_Number, Amount, Vendor_ID, Transaction_Date)
19        values
20        (:new.Card_Number, :new.Amount,
            :new.Vendor_ID, :new.Transaction_Date);
21
21  end if;
22
22  end;
23  /
Trigger created.
```

To set up the trigger so that it will fire, initialize the contents of the Credit_Charge_Log table with several rows, as shown in Listing 11.27.

Listing 11.27. Contents of the Credit_Charge_Log table before the next row is inserted.

```
SQL> select * from credit_charge_log;
CARD_NUMBER          AMOUNT VENDOR_I TRANSACTI
----------------- -------- -------- ---------
8343124443239383     128.33 12345678 19-JUN-95
9453128834232243      83.12 98765432 18-JUN-95
4644732212887321      431.1 18181818 19-JUN-95
0944583312453477     211.94 09090909 18-JUN-95
0944583312453477     413.81 08080808 18-JUN-95
0944583312453477     455.31 91919191 19-JUN-95
0944583312453477        225 12341234 20-JUN-95
0944583312453477     512.22 12341234 20-JUN-95
8 rows selected.
```

Before a row is inserted into the table for card number 0944583312453477, the trigger is fired. It queries the table to see if the charges for that card number for the past three days exceed $1,000. If they do, a row is added to the Credit_Charge_Attempt_Log table, as you can see in Listing 11.28 (see line 1). Because more than $1,000 in charges have been made on card number 0944583312453477 in the past three days, the trigger inserts a row into Credit_Charge_Attempt_Log.

Listing 11.28. Trigger fires when row is inserted into Credit_Charge_Log table.

```
SQL> insert into Credit_Charge_Log
  2  (Card_Number, Amount, Vendor_ID, Transaction_Date)
  3  values
  4  ('0944583312453477', 128.28, '43214321', '20-JUN-95');
1 row created.

SQL> select * from Credit_Charge_Attempt_Log;
CARD_NUMBER             AMOUNT VENDOR_I TRANSACTI
-----------------     -------- -------- ---------
0944583312453477       128.28 43214321 20-JUN-95
```

Enforcing Security with a Trigger

Here's an example of how you can use a database trigger to enforce a security policy. Acme Corporation's database is designed so that a row must be inserted into the Shipment table for an actual shipment to be made. The Shipment table has a column, Manual_Check, that indicates whether a shipping clerk should verify by phone the accuracy of the shipping request. To reduce the likelihood of fraud, corporate policy is that a shipping clerk should check any shipping request that has been entered after normal working hours—5:00 P.M.

As the DBA, you are responsible for implementing this policy. As shown in Listing 11.29, you create a trigger, Shipment_Ins_Before, that will fire before the execution of an INSERT statement on the Shipment table. The trigger body consists of a single PL/SQL statement—the assignment of Y to the column Manual_Check. In addition, you decide to use a WHEN clause so that the trigger only fires after 5:00 P.M.(or 17:00 using a 24-hour clock).

Listing 11.29. Creating a trigger that must satisfy a condition before firing.

```
SQL> create or replace trigger Shipment_Ins_Before before
  2  insert on Shipment
  3  for each row
  4  when (to_number(to_char(sysdate,'HH24')) > 17)
  5
  5  declare
  6
  6  begin
  7
  7  :new.Manual_Check := 'Y';
  8
  8  end;
  9  /
Trigger created.
```

11

Now that the trigger has been created, you can test it. As you can see in Listing 11.30, the current time is later than 5:00 p.m.—it is actually 7:00 p.m. When a row is inserted into the Shipment table, the Manual_Check column is set to Y as intended.

INPUT/OUTPUT | **Listing 11.30. Trigger checks time and fires.**

```
SQL> select to_char(sysdate,'HH24') from dual;
TO_CHAR(SYSDATE,'HH24')
----------------------------------------------------------------
19

SQL> insert into Shipment
  2  (Shipment_ID, Product_Code, Quantity, Customer_ID)
  3  values
  4  ('SHIP1001', 'PROD123', 100, 'CUST999');
1 row created.

SQL> select * from Shipment;
SHIPMENT_ID   PRODUCT_CODE   QUANTITY CUSTOMER_ID  M ENTERED_BY
-----------   ------------   -------- ------------ - --------------------
SHIP1001      PROD123            100 CUST999       Y
```

Setting Column Values with a Trigger

Another use for a trigger is to set a column to a particular value before an SQL statement takes effect. The following scenario demonstrates this process. Suppose a table named Block_Trade_Log is used to record block trading on the NASDAQ. The table contains the following: the stock symbol, the trading price, the number of blocks that were traded, when the trade occurred, whether the blocks were bought or sold, and the three-day running average for the stock. When a row is inserted into the table, a trigger is used to set the value for Running_Avg_3_Days. Listing 11.31 illustrates how the trigger is created.

INPUT | **Listing 11.31. Setting a column value in a trigger.**

```
create or replace trigger Block_Trade_Log_BI before
insert on Block_Trade_Log
for each row

declare
Running_Avg number;

begin

select avg(price)
into Running_Avg
from Block_Trade_Log
```

continues

Listing 11.31. continued

```
where
Stock_Symbol = :new.Stock_Symbol and
Timestamp >= SYSDATE-3;

:new.Running_Avg_3_Days := Running_Avg;

end;
/
```

Notice that the value of Running_Avg_3_Days is set by assigning the value to
:new.Running_Avg_3_Days. Remember: If the triggering event is an INSERT, the column values
that are actually stored in the table are referenced with :new.

Listing 11.32 displays the contents of the Block_Trade_Log table. Notice the two rows for
stock symbol QQQQQ: one at $102.125 and the other at $103.5. When another row for
stock symbol QQQQQ is inserted into Block_Trade_Log, the trigger fires and computes the
three-day running average for that security—102.8125—and assigns it to the column
Running_Avg_3_Days.

INPUT/ OUTPUT   ## Listing 11.32. Firing the trigger with an INSERT statement.

```
SQL> select * from block_trade_log;
STOCK_     PRICE BLOCKS_TRADED B RUNNING_AVG_3_DAYS TIMESTAMP
------ ---------- ------------- - ------------------ ---------
QQQQQ    102.125           100 B                     19-JUN-95
QQQQQ     103.5            100 S                     19-JUN-95
VVVVV     55.75           3000 S                     19-JUN-95
VVVVV     55.5            1000 B                     20-JUN-95

SQL> insert into block_trade_log
  2  (Stock_Symbol, Price, Blocks_Traded, Bought_Sold, Timestamp)
  3  values
  4  ('&stock',&price,&numblocks,'&BS','&date')
  5  ;

Enter value for stock: QQQQQ
Enter value for price: 104.25
Enter value for numblocks: 300
Enter value for bs: B
Enter value for date: 20-JUN-95
old   4: ('&stock',&price,&numblocks,'&BS','&date')
new   4: ('QQQQQ',104.25,300,'B','20-JUN-95')
1 row created.

SQL> select * from block_trade_log;
```

```
STOCK_    PRICE BLOCKS_TRADED B RUNNING_AVG_3_DAYS TIMESTAMP
------  -------- ------------- - ------------------ ---------
QQQQQ   102.125           100 B                     19-JUN-95
QQQQQ     103.5           100 S                     19-JUN-95
VVVVV     55.75          3000 S                     19-JUN-95
VVVVV      55.5          1000 B                     20-JUN-95
QQQQQ    104.25           300 B           102.8125  20-JUN-95
```

Cascading Triggers

The interaction of triggers can be quite complex. For example, you can create a trigger that, when fired, causes another trigger to fire. Triggers that behave in this way are called *cascading triggers*. To illustrate the concept of cascading triggers, look at three simple tables in Listing 11.33—tab1, tab2, and tab3. Initially, each table has a single row.

INPUT/ OUTPUT **Listing 11.33. Firing the trigger with an INSERT statement.**

```
create table tab1
(col1    number);
create table tab2
(col2    number);
create table tab3
(col3    number);

SQL> select * from tab1;
     COL1
---------
        7

SQL> select * from tab2;
     COL2
---------
       10

SQL> select * from tab3;
     COL3
---------
       13
```

For table tab1, create a row-level BEFORE UPDATE trigger that will insert the old value of the col1 column from tab1 into tab2, as shown in Listing 11.34. For table tab2, create a row-level BEFORE INSERT trigger that updates table tab3 and sets the value of col3 to the new value of col2. Finally, for table tab3, create a statement-level AFTER UPDATE trigger that inserts a row into tab3 with the value of col3 equal to 27.

Listing 11.34. Creating a trigger that will cause another trigger to fire.

```
SQL> create or replace trigger tab1_Update_Before before
  2  update on tab1
  3  for each row
  4
  4  declare
  5
  5  begin
  6
  6  insert into tab2
  7  (col2)
  8  values
  9  (:old.col1);
 10
 10  end;
 11  /
Trigger created.

SQL> create or replace trigger tab2_Insert_Before before
  2  insert on tab2
  3  for each row
  4
  4  declare
  5
  5  begin
  6
  6  update tab3
  7  set
  8  col3 = :new.col2;
  9
  9  end;
 10  /
Trigger created.

SQL> create or replace trigger tab3_Update_After after
  2  update on tab3
  3
  3  declare
  4
  4  begin
  5
  5  insert into tab3
  6  (col3)
  7  values
  8  (27);
  9
  9  end;
 10  /
Trigger created.
```

NOTE

A table is *mutating* when its contents are being changed by an INSERT, UPDATE, or DELETE statement that hasn't yet committed. A row-level trigger cannot read or modify the contents of a mutating table because a mutating table is in a state of flux. The only exception to this rule is that a BEFORE INSERT row-level trigger for a table with a foreign key may modify columns in the table containing the primary key. For more information about mutating tables, please refer to Chapter 8 of the *Oracle7 Server Application Developer's Guide*, available online. If you have loaded the Oracle documentation on your Windows 95 PC, you'll find this document in C:\Orawin95\Doc\A32536_1.PDF; it is a PDF (Adobe Portable Document Format) file that can be read using the Adobe Acrobat Reader.

Now, what will happen when a row in tab1 is updated? As you can see in Listing 11.35, the following changes have taken place:

☐ In tab1, the value of col1 was updated to 8.

☐ In tab2, trigger Tab1_Update_Before inserted a new row with the old value of col1: 7.

☐ In tab3, trigger Tab2_Insert_Before fired as a result of the new row in tab2 and set the value of col3 to be the same as the value that was inserted into tab2: 7. When tab3 was updated, trigger Tab3_Update_Before inserted another row into tab3 with the value 27.

INPUT/ OUTPUT   **Listing 11.35. Testing the cascading triggers.**

```
SQL> update tab1
  2  set col1 = 8;
1 row updated.
SQL> select * from tab1;
     COL1
    --------
          8
SQL> select * from tab2;
     COL2
    --------
         10
          7
SQL> select * from tab3;
     COL3
    --------
          7
         27
```

TIP

By default, the number of cascaded triggers that can fire is limited to 32. However, keep this in mind—your ability to understand the ramifications of an INSERT, UPDATE, or DELETE statement is inversely proportional to the number of cascading triggers associated with that SQL statement. In other words, keep it straightforward.

COMMIT and ROLLBACK Cannot Be Used in Triggers

You cannot execute a COMMIT or ROLLBACK statement in a database trigger.

NEW TERM *Rollback* is the process of rescinding or undoing all database changes made by a user since the last COMMIT was issued or since the beginning of the database session.

Also, a trigger may not call a stored procedure, function, or package subprogram that performs a COMMIT or ROLLBACK. Oracle maintains this restriction for a good reason. If a trigger encounters an error, all database changes that have been propagated by the trigger should be rolled back. But if the trigger committed some portion of those database changes, Oracle would not be able to roll back the entire transaction.

Calling Stored Procedures from a Trigger

You can call a stored procedure or function, whether standalone or part of a package, from the PL/SQL body of a database trigger. As an example, here is a version of the trigger Block_Trade_Log_BI, originally shown in Listing 11.31, that calls the stored function Get_3_Day_Running_Avg. The trigger is based on the Block_Trade_Log table previously discussed in this lesson. Listing 11.36 contains the stored function that the trigger will reference.

INPUT/ OUTPUT

Listing 11.36. Creating the stored function to be called by a trigger.

```
SQL> create or replace function Get_3_Day_Running_Avg
  2                      (Stock_Symb in varchar2)
  3                      return number is
  4
  4  Running_Avg    number;
  5
  5  begin
  6
```

11

```
 6  select avg(price)
 7  into Running_Avg
 8  from Block_Trade_Log
 9  where
10  Stock_Symbol = Stock_Symb and
11  Timestamp >= SYSDATE-3;
12
12  return Running_Avg;
13
13  end;
14  /
Function created.
```

Listing 11.37 contains a modified version of Block_Trade_Log_BI that calls the stored function Get_3_Day_Running_Avg.

INPUT/OUTPUT

Listing 11.37. Modifying the stored function to be called by a trigger.

```
SQL> create or replace trigger Block_Trade_Log_BI before
  2  insert on Block_Trade_Log
  3  for each row
  4
  4  declare
  5
  5  Running_Avg   number;
  6
  6  begin
  7
  7  :new.Running_Avg_3_Days :=
     ➥Get_3_Day_Running_Avg (:new.Stock_Symbol);
  8
  8  end;
  9  /
Trigger created.
```

Dropping, Enabling, and Disabling Triggers

If you've decided that you absolutely don't want a particular trigger, you can drop it with the following statement:

```
DROP TRIGGER trigger-name;
```

The variable trigger-name is the name of the trigger to be dropped.

For example, to drop the DELETE AFTER trigger on the Repair Header table, issue the following statement via SQL*Plus:

```
SQL> drop trigger Repair_Header_Delete_After;
Trigger dropped.
```

Sometimes, dropping a trigger is too drastic. Instead, you might want to deactivate a trigger temporarily. You can disable a trigger until enabling it again makes sense. To disable a trigger temporarily, use the ALTER TRIGGER statement

```
ALTER TRIGGER trigger-name DISABLE;
```

The variable `trigger-name` is the trigger to disable.

The following example disables the trigger Repair_Header_Delete_After:

```
SQL> alter trigger Repair_Header_Delete_After disable;
Trigger altered.
```

To enable a disabled trigger, use the statement

```
ALTER TRIGGER trigger-name ENABLE;
```

The variable `trigger-name` is the trigger to enable.

For instance, you can enable Repair_Header_Delete_After by issuing the following command:

```
SQL> alter trigger Repair_Header_Delete_After enable;
Trigger altered.
```

Summary

Congratulations! You've covered a lot of material in this lesson. The most important concepts in this lesson were as follows:

- ☐ In PL/SQL an error or warning is called an exception.
- ☐ A number of pre-defined exceptions are associated with Oracle SQL errors.
- ☐ An exception handler is a series of PL/SQL statements that are executed in response to a raised exception.
- ☐ You may declare application-specific exceptions and specify exception handlers for them.
- ☐ A PL/SQL block may have an exception section that contains one or more exception handlers.
- ☐ You use the RAISE statement to raise a user-defined exception.
- ☐ Oracle provides a procedure named RAISE_APPLICATION_ERROR to return an application-specific error to the caller of a PL/SQL subprogram.
- ☐ You must use a cursor if a query might return more than one row.

☐ A cursor is a window into the set of rows retrieved by a query.

☐ You must declare every explicit cursor in the declaration section of a PL/SQL subprogram.

☐ You can declare a cursor with parameters that have optional default values. The value of each parameter may be specified when the cursor is opened.

☐ The query associated with a cursor is executed when the cursor is opened.

☐ You obtain the results of a query by fetching rows from a cursor.

☐ Every cursor has four attributes: %NOTFOUND, %FOUND, %ISOPEN, and %ROWCOUNT.

☐ A PL/SQL subprogram can have multiple cursors open simultaneously.

☐ A database trigger is a PL/SQL block that executes when a triggering event—INSERT, UPDATE, or DELETE—occurs.

☐ You define a trigger with the CREATE TRIGGER statement, which can be issued from SQL*Plus.

☐ You can use a trigger for a variety of purposes that include enforcing a security policy, performing complex validation of column values, and calculating the default column values.

☐ A row-level trigger fires for each row that is affected by a trigger. You can inspect or modify a row's column values with a row-level trigger.

☐ A statement-level trigger is fired only once by the triggering event. You cannot use a statement-level trigger to access the column values of any row.

☐ A BEFORE trigger fires before its triggering event. An AFTER trigger fires after its triggering event.

☐ A trigger may have an optional clause that specifies a condition that must be true for the trigger to fire.

☐ You can drop a trigger with the DROP TRIGGER statement.

☐ You can enable or disable a trigger by using the ALTER TRIGGER statement.

☐ A trigger body cannot contain a COMMIT or ROLLBACK statement.

☐ You can invoke a stored procedure or function from within the trigger body.

What Comes Next?

Now that you're familiar with SQL and PL/SQL, it's time to move on to something completely different. On Day 12, "Developer/2000: Introduction to Oracle Forms," you are introduced to the tool that you'll use to build a client/server application.

Q&A

Q **Is it possible to create a trigger that will fire if a row is read during a query?**

A No, a trigger will only fire for an INSERT, UPDATE, or DELETE. You can use the auditing capability in the Oracle RDBMS to record each query submitted by a user.

Q **What is the advantage to using a trigger to check for a condition that is already enforced by referential integrity?**

A Some entity-relationship design tools generate triggers that seem superfluous. That is, the generated triggers check for violations of referential integrity and return specific error messages. Without such a trigger, the Oracle RDBMS would return an error message indicating that referential integrity was violated but would not specifically identify the offending columns or relationships. These generated triggers make it easy for both developer and user to determine why the operation was disallowed.

Q **Is it always necessary to close a cursor?**

A It is if you want to change a value of a variable that is used by the cursor and reopen it. In general, it's good practice to close a cursor when it's no longer needed.

Workshop

The purpose of the Workshop is to allow you to test your knowledge of the material discussed in the lesson. See if you can correctly answer the questions in the quiz and complete the exercises before you continue with tomorrow's lesson.

Quiz

1. How are SQLCODE and SQLERRM used in PL/SQL subprograms?
2. True or false? A PL/SQL subprogram may have multiple cursors open at the same time.
3. What are the benefits of using database triggers?
4. What kind of database trigger would you use if you wanted to modify the value to be stored in a column when a new row is added to a table?

Exercises

1. Create a stored function, Teaching_Load, that has a single argument—a Department ID. Teaching_Load should return the average number of courses that instructors in the specified department are currently teaching.

2. Create a stored procedure, Suitable_Locations, that has a single argument—seating capacity. Suitable_Locations should print out the first three buildings and rooms whose seating capacity exceeds the specified seating capacity.

3. Write a before-delete trigger on the Instructor table that will raise an exception if an instructor is scheduled to teach a class.

11

Day 12

Developer/2000: Introduction to Oracle Forms

Up to this point, you've learned a considerable amount about using SQL to create an Oracle database, query a table, and modify the contents of a table. You've also learned how to use PL/SQL to develop application logic in the form of stored procedures, functions, and packages—and how to create database triggers for different purposes.

Now it's time to delve into the development of an Oracle application with Developer/2000. In this lesson, and Days 14 through 17, you'll learn the role that each component of Developer/2000—Oracle Forms, Oracle Reports, Oracle Graphics, and Procedure Builder—plays in the development of a client-server application.

What Is Developer/2000?

Developer/2000 is a family of products that are used to design and build client-server applications. These applications can be deployed to the Windows, Mac, and UNIX Motif environments. In addition, you also can deploy character-mode versions of your applications. There are four principal components of Developer/2000:

☐ **Oracle Forms:** Used for designing and generating a forms-based application. These forms can include data entry forms, query forms, and browse forms.

☐ **Oracle Reports:** Used for designing a wide range of reports from very simple to very complex. A report can be previewed on a screen before printing or can automatically be sent to a printer.

☐ **Oracle Graphics:** Enables you to define queries that, when executed, generate business graphs at run-time.

☐ **Procedure Builder:** Used to design and manage PL/SQL code in the database server—stored procedures, functions, and packages.

This lesson focuses on the use of Oracle Forms.

Building a Simple Form with Forms Designer

Let's dive right into using Oracle Forms. This section guides you through the building of a form that will enable you to view and modify student information.

1. To invoke the Forms Designer, from the Start button, press Programs | Oracle Developer/2000 for Win95 | Forms Designer.

2. The Forms Designer program then displays the Object Navigator (see Figure 12.1).

Before going any further, you should connect to the Oracle database.

Connecting to an Oracle Database

To connect Forms Designer to an Oracle database, select File | Connect from the menu. A dialog box is displayed, prompting you for the username, password, and database to use for establishing an Oracle database connection. If you are using Personal Oracle for development, enter the following:

Username	`flugle`
Password	`flugle`
Database	Leave blank

12

Figure 12.1.

Forms Designer first displays Object Navigator.

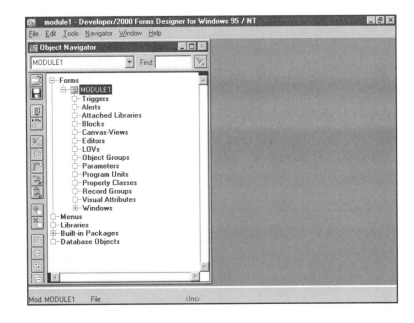

If you're using an Oracle Server for development, enter, as shown in Figure 12.2, the following items:

Username   `flugle`

Password   `flugle`

Database   `flugle` (assuming that you already have used SQL*Net Easy Configuration to create a database alias named `flugle` that points to the Oracle database where you have loaded the sample tables)

For both cases, click the Connect button. If there are no error messages, you can assume that you have successfully connected to the database.

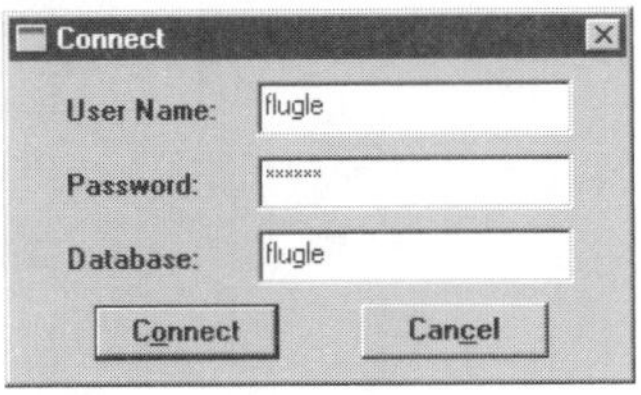

Figure 12.2.

Connecting to an Oracle database from Forms Designer.

12

Creating a New Block

By default, Forms Designer opens a new form, named Module1, when it's first invoked. There are three elements that appear in almost all forms:

- ☐ One or more blocks
- ☐ A Canvas-View
- ☐ A window

Continue building your simple form by creating a block. Oracle Forms uses a block to map fields in a form to columns in an Oracle table. From the menu, select Tools | New Block. A dialog window, entitled New Block Options, is displayed. There are four tabs on this window: General, Items, Layout, and Master/Detail. When the window is invoked, the General tab is displayed. Notice that the Base Table field contains <NONE> (see Figure 12.3).

Figure 12.3.

The New Block Options window is first displayed.

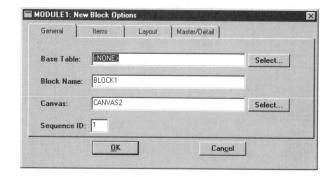

To identify the Student table, press the Select button to the right of the Base Table field. The Forms Designer displays another window, which contains five checkboxes, to determine which database objects you should be able to choose from. By default, two checkboxes are selected—Current User and Tables (see Figure 12.4). Using these default values, click OK.

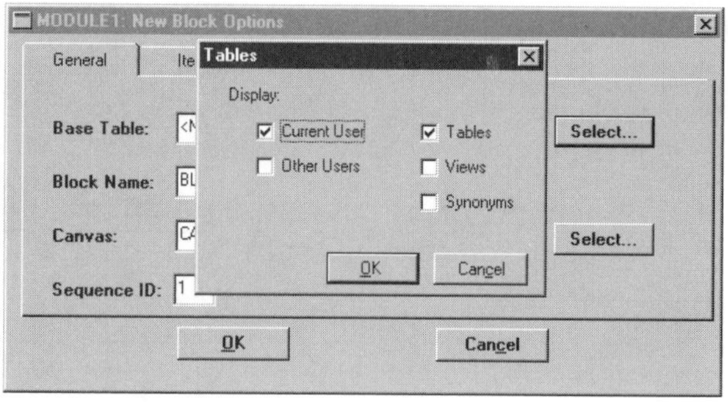

Figure 12.4.

Forms Designer provides choices for database objects to be displayed.

The Forms Designer now displays a window which contains a list of the tables owned by flugle. Scroll down the list until you see the Student table. Select the table with the mouse and click OK (see Figure 12.5).

Figure 12.5.

Selecting the Student table for the new block.

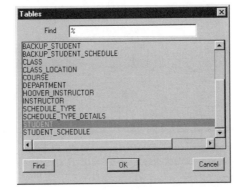

The Forms Designer now returns to the New Block Options window. However, now the Base Table field contains the table that you selected—Student (see Figure 12.6).

Figure 12.6.

The base table for the new block is now Student.

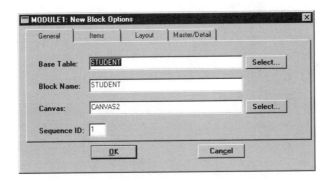

Now look at two of the other tabs on the New Block Options window. Select the Items tab. At this point, the list box beneath the Select Columns button is empty. Click the Select Columns button. By default, all the columns in the selected table are included in the form (see Figure 12.7).

There are a few other things worth noting about the Items tab folder. If a column has a leading +, it will be included in the form; if it has a leading -, it won't be included. The label for each item is based on the column's name. An underscore in a column name is transformed into a space for that column's label. The initial character of each word in a column's label is capitalized. Each item also has a type. By default, each selected item is a Text Item.

Figure 12.7.

Specifying the items to be included in the new block.

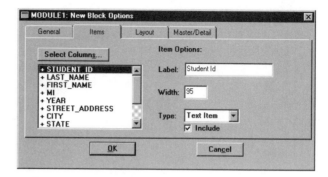

Now take a look at the layout of the new block. Select the Layout tab. There are two layout styles that can be specified from the list in the Style field, Tabular and Form; select Form. The Form style is used to display one record at a time. There also are two possible orientations for the new block; select Horizontal.

There are three checkboxes shown under Options. If checked, the Integrity Constraints checkbox generates the necessary triggers to enforce the table and column constraints that exist for this table. Select the Integrity Constraints checkbox. If checked, the Button Palette checkbox generates a group of buttons that can be used to navigate through the records in the form or modify the records displayed in the form. Select the Button Palette checkbox. Don't check the Scrollbar checkbox; because this block displays only one record at a time, there's no need for a scrollbar. Figure 12.8 shows what you should see in the Layout tab folder after you've made these selections.

Figure 12.8.

Specifying the layout for the new block.

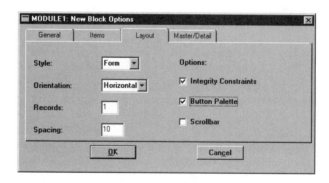

For the time being, you can ignore the Master/Detail tab folder; you'll be using it in the next lesson. To create the new block, click OK. The Forms Designer returns you to the Object Navigator. However, you should now see two blocks displayed in the Object Navigator—Student and Button_Palette (see Figure 12.9). You also should notice that there's a + to the left of the Canvas-Views item; if you scroll down, you will also see a + to the left of the Window item. The +'s indicate that a Canvas-View and a window were automatically generated when you created the Student block.

Figure 12.9.

Looking at the new items in the Object Navigator.

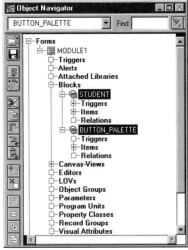

Testing the New Form

The form is now ready to test. From the menu, select File | Run or click the green signal light on the toolbar. A window, entitled Developer/2000 Forms Runtime for Windows 95/NT [WINDOW0], is displayed with the new form contained within it. Maximize both windows (see Figure 12.10). You'll notice that a default menu is displayed at the top of the window.

Now take a look at the standard behavior of a form. To execute a query, select Query | Execute from the menu. The form queries the Student table. You will see the first record that was retrieved from the Student table. In the lower-left corner of the window, you should see a label, Count: 1, which indicates the order of the record that was retrieved from the table. The line in which this is displayed is called the *status line*.

 The *status line* is the area at the bottom of a form (at runtime) that displays pertinent information, such as the number of the currently displayed record.

 The *message line* appears above the status line and provides feedback and error messages to the user.

The line above the status line is referred to as the *message line*. For example, if you want to know how many records are retrieved by querying the block's table, select Query | Count hits from the menu. For the Student table, the message line displays FRM-40355: Query will retrieve 31 records.

Figure 12.10.

Testing the new form.

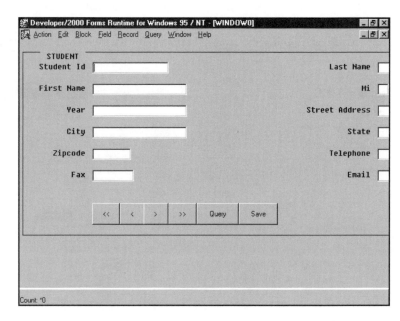

To navigate to the next field in a block, press the Tab key. For instance, to move from the Student ID field to the Last Name field, press Tab. The window moves to the right and the field is highlighted as shown in Figure 12.11. To return to the previous field, press Shift+Tab.

NOTE

Because you didn't specify the order in which rows should be retrieved from the Student table, the rows are retrieved in an arbitrary order—which could be by ascending Student ID. You'll learn how to specify the order that a block uses to retrieve rows.

Navigating Through a Form

There are two ways you can navigate to the next record in the form: You can select Record | Next from the menu, or you can click on > on the Button Palette. Either way, the next record will be displayed in the form. Also, the count shown in the lower-left corner will increment—in this case, it will be 2. You also can use the up and down arrow keys to navigate through the records in a form. The down arrow displays the next record, and the up arrow displays the previous record. If you try to navigate before the first record, the message line displays FRM-40100: At first record. If you try to navigate past the last record, the message line displays FRM-40352: Last record of query retrieved.

Figure 12.11.
Navigating through the fields of the new form.

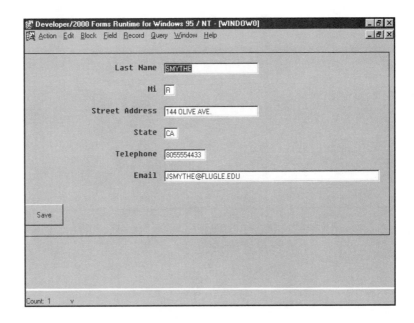

The status line also displays a few other characters. If there are more records before the current record, the status line displays a ^. If there are more records after the current record, the status line displays a v. For example, suppose a query returns 10 records. If the form is positioned at record 1—the first record—you see only a v in the status line. If you press the down arrow key to navigate to the next row, the status line displays ^ and v, indicating that there are records both before and after the current record. If you navigate to the last record, the status line only displays a ^.

Query Behavior of Oracle Forms

Oracle Forms provides some basic query capabilities that don't require any special programming on the part of the developer. A form can process a query in two steps. The first step requires that the form be placed in ENTER-QUERY mode. While in ENTER-QUERY mode, the user can enter query criteria into one or more fields on the form. The next step is for the form to execute the query. When the query is executed, the query criteria is used to process the query. Take a look at a few examples with the Student form.

You can switch to ENTER-QUERY mode by selecting Query | Enter from the menu, by pressing F7, or by clicking the Query button on the Button Palette. You can tell that the form is in ENTER-QUERY mode—the message line displays Enter a query; press F8 to execute, Ctrl+q to cancel, and the status line displays Count: *0 ENTER QUERY.

Tab to the Year field and enter **FRESHMAN** (see Figure 12.12). To execute the query, select Query | Execute from the menu, press F8, or click the Query button again.

Figure 12.12.

Entering a query criterion in Enter Query mode.

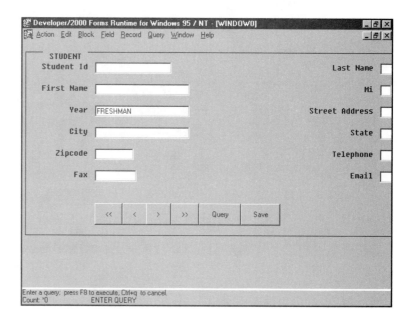

Take a look at an example in which query criteria are entered in more than one field. Enter query mode by selecting Query | Enter from the menu, pressing F7, or clicking the Query button. In the Year field, enter SENIOR. In the City field, enter SPRINGFIELD. Figure 12.13 displays what you should see when you execute the query. If you look at the status line, you'll notice that there is an asterisk before the record count. This indicates that only one student meets both criteria.

While in ENTER-QUERY mode, you also can use % to signify a wildcard within a field. For example, enter query mode. In the Last Name field, enter L%M% and execute the query. This criterion will return those students whose last name begins with L and also contains an M. This query happens to return two students, with last names MALLARD and MICHAELS.

Another powerful feature of Oracle Forms is the ability to use the logical operators >, >=, <, <=, and !=. For example, if you wanted to find all freshmen who do not live in DOVER and whose first names start with the letter G or greater, you would enter > G in the First Name field, FRESHMAN in the Year field, and != 'DOVER' in the City field. When you execute the query, you should retrieve five records—freshmen with first names Paula, Henry, Linda, Richard, and Ivan, who all live in Springfield.

If you're in ENTER-QUERY mode and don't want to proceed with the query, you can exit query mode by either selecting Query | Cancel from the menu or by pressing Control+q. If you're only interested in knowing the number of records that will be returned by a query without seeing the records themselves, you can use the Count Hits command to obtain that number.

12

For example, if you want to know how many sophomores there are, place the form in ENTER-QUERY mode and enter **SOPHOMORE** in the Year field. You can count the number of records by selecting Query | Count Hits from the menu or by pressing Shift+F2. The number of records that satisfy the query criteria is displayed on the message line.

Figure 12.13.

A single record returned from query in which query criteria were entered in two fields.

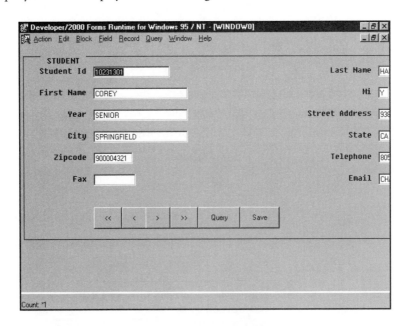

Modifying a Record with Oracle Forms

At any given time, a form is either in NORMAL mode or in ENTER-QUERY mode. You cannot modify any records while the form is in ENTER-QUERY mode; it must be in NORMAL mode to modify or delete an existing record or create a new record. If you want to change an existing record, navigate to the record and field that you want to modify. For example, if you want to change Peter Pinkwater's first name from Peter to Pierre, query the table to retrieve his record and tab to the First Name field and enter the new first name.

To create a new record, select Record | Insert from the menu or press F6. As an example, use the form you have created to add another student to the Student table. After you select Record | Insert from the menu or press F6, the cursor will be positioned at the first field in the record—Student ID. Enter the following values for the fields:

Student ID	**99991234**
Last Name	**THOMAS**
First Name	**KAREN**

MI   G

Year   FRESHMAN

Street Address 133 SEQUOIA DR.

City   SPRINGFIELD

State   CA

Zipcode   900004321

Telephone   8055551291

Fax   <NULL>

Email   KTHOMAS@FLUGLE.EDU

To save the record that you just created, you have several choices:

☐ You can select Action | Save from the menu.

☐ You can press F10.

☐ You can wait until you perform another query or exit the form. At that time, you
will be asked if the changes that were performed should be saved (see Figure
12.14).

Figure 12.14.
*User is asked if
changes should be
saved.*

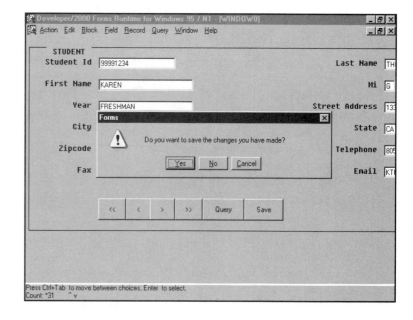

NOTE

By default, Oracle Forms does not automatically save the changes that the user makes. Behind the scenes, Oracle Forms is taking advantage of Oracle's ability to manage transactions. When you save the changes that you have made to the records in a form, Oracle Forms is performing a COMMIT on your behalf. When you indicate that you don't want to save any changes, Oracle Forms is performing a ROLLBACK on your behalf. Realize that if you don't save the changes that you have made, Oracle Forms will rollback all of the changes that have been made since the beginning of the forms session or since the last save.

To delete a record, navigate to that record and select Record I Remove from the menu. The previous record is then displayed. The record isn't actually removed from the table until you perform a save.

Saving a Form

Now that you've had an introduction to the behavior of a form, let's exit the form and return to the Forms Designer. To save the form that you've built, select File I Save as from the Forms Designer menu. By default, the Forms Designer saves the form in the FORMS45 directory beneath the Oracle home directory. Figure 12.15 shows the window that the Forms Designer uses to save the file. In the "Save as type" field, select Forms (*.fmb) from the list, enter **student** for the filename, and click Save. Notice that the Object Navigator now displays the form as STUDENT.

Figure 12.15.

Saving a form.

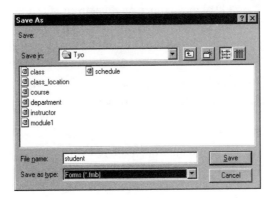

12

NOTE

> It's not a good idea to save application-specific files in the Oracle directory tree. If you do save the files in the Oracle directory tree, you'll lose track of which files belong with which application. Instead, you should create a separate directory for storing your application files.

Elements of Oracle Forms

There are actually three tools that are part of Oracle Forms—Forms Designer, Forms Generator, and Forms Runtime. The Forms Designer enables you to create and modify three types of modules: forms, menus, and libraries. Most Forms applications consist primarily of forms, with one or more menus and sometimes one or more libraries.

By default, the Forms Designer saves the modules that you design to either a file or to an Oracle database. To save a module to the database, you or your DBA need to install the database schema needed by Developer/2000. To learn more about this, read the Administrative Notes that are in the Developer/2000 Admin for Win95.

There are advantages and disadvantages to using an Oracle database for storing your application modules. If you're working with other developers who are geographically distributed, it may make sense to use an Oracle database as a common repository for your application modules. However, if you want to use a version control package, such as PVCS, for managing versions of your forms, reports, and graphics, you'll probably want to store your application modules to a file. If so, you'll probably want to modify the default options in the Forms Designer to open modules from a file or save modules to a file. To do this, select Tools | Options from the menu. In the Options window, change the Module Access radio button from File/Database to File (see Figure 12.16). You also should check the Save Before Generate checkbox—the forms generation process will be discussed in a moment.

The Forms Designer enables you to have multiple modules open simultaneously. For example, you could have five forms, one menu, and one library all open at the same time.

Forms

If you use the file system to open and save your forms, the Forms Designer uses a file extension of .fmb. An .fmb file is a binary file that is a complete description of the form. However, you cannot run an .fmb file—you must generate a runtime version of the file that has the extension .fmx. When you generate a form, the Forms Generator uses the .fmb file to generate an .fmx file. When you run a form, you use the Forms Runtime program to execute an .fmx file. You also can convert an .fmb file, which is binary, to an .fmt file, which is a text file. You can use a version control system to manage changes in the .fmt files. The .fmb and .fmt files are portable—you can transfer them from one environment to another and regenerate the .fmx file.

Figure 12.16.
Changing the Forms Designer options.

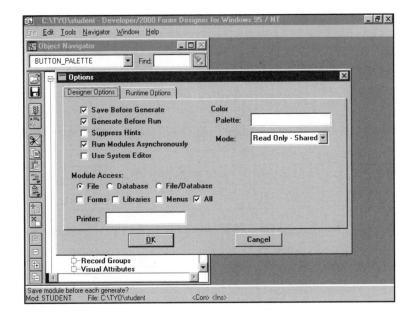

Menus

The Forms Designer stores a menu in a file with an extension of `.mmb`. When you generate a menu, the Forms Generator uses the `.mmb` file to generate an `.mmx` file. When you run a form that has a menu, the Forms Runtime program executes the `.mmx` file. You also can convert an `.mmb` file, which is binary, to an `.mmt` file, which is a text file. You can use a version control system to manage changes in the `.mmt` files.

Libraries

A library consists of PL/SQL procedures, functions, and packages. The Forms Designer stores a library in a file with an extension of `.pll`. When you generate a library, the Forms Generator uses the `.pll` file to generate a `.plx` file. When you run a form with an attached library, the Forms Runtime program executes the code contained in the `.plx` file. You also can convert a `.pll` file, which is binary, to a `.pld` file, which is a text file. You can use a version control system to manage changes in the `.pld` files.

Elements of a Form

A form is defined by a collection of objects. Some of these objects are mandatory, and some are optional. Each object can be one of the following:

☐ Block

☐ Canvas-Views

☐ Window

☐ Trigger

☐ List of Values (LOV)

☐ Record Group

☐ Alert

☐ Parameter

Later in the chapter, you get an in-depth look at each of these objects, but first, the following section examines the use of the Object Navigator.

Working with the Object Navigator

The Object Navigator is an intuitive, convenient interface for creating and manipulating forms, menus, and libraries. The Object Navigator displays objects in a hierarchical manner. For each module type—form, menu, or library—the Object Navigator displays a set of nodes beneath each module. For example, beneath each form, the following nodes are displayed: Triggers, Alerts, Attached Libraries, Blocks, Canvas-Views, Editors, LOVs, Object Groups, Parameters, Program Units, Property Classes, Record Groups, Visual Attributes, and Windows. You can use either the mouse or the up and down arrow keys to navigate between nodes.

To the left of each node is a box. If the box is empty, no objects of that node type exist for the form. If the box contains a +, the form does have objects of that node type. The + indicates that the node can be expanded—it is currently collapsed. There are a couple of ways to expand a node:

☐ You can click the box to expand the node.

☐ You can select Navigator | Expand from the menu.

If the box contains a -, there are objects of that node type but they are already fully expanded. There are a couple of ways to collapse a node:

☐ You can click the box to collapse the node.

☐ You can select Navigator | Collapse from the menu.

As an example, the Student form contains three nodes with objects: Blocks, Canvas-Views, and Windows (see Figure 12.17).

To expand each of these three nodes, click the box to the left of each node (see Figure 12.18). As you can see, the Student and Button_Palette blocks each have a + in the box, signifying that they can be further expanded.

Figure 12.17.

Expanding the nodes of the Student form.

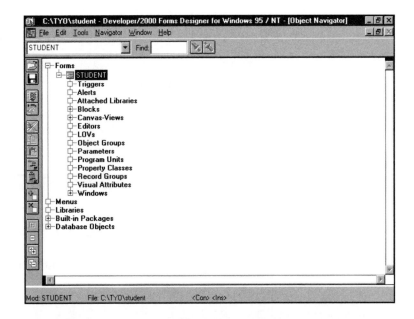

Figure 12.18.

Expanding the nodes with the Object Navigator.

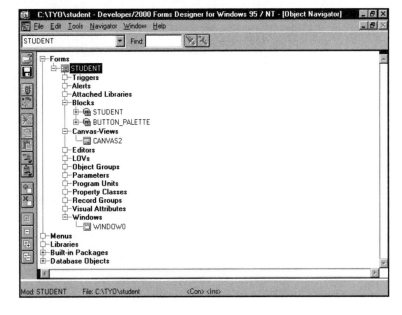

12

Each of these objects has a set of properties. To display the properties for a particular object, you can do one of the following:

- ☐ Right-click Properties.
- ☐ Select Tools | Properties from the menu.
- ☐ Click the icon to the left of the object name.

For example, to see the properties of the Student block, navigate to the Student block with the mouse or up/down arrow and right-click Properties (see Figure 12.19).

Figure 12.19.

Displaying the properties of the Student block.

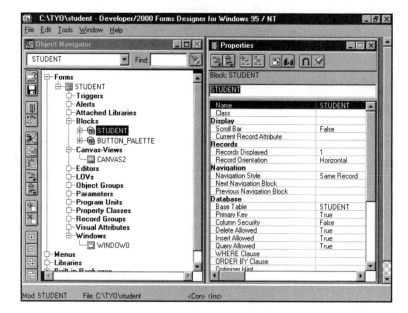

Object Properties

From the Object Navigator, you can examine and modify an object's properties. To access an object's properties, left-click the object node. Alternatively, you can select the object with the mouse and select Tools | Properties. You also can right-click Properties.

The properties that are displayed for an object depend on the type of object. You'll see some examples of object properties in the next few pages.

Blocks

Almost every form contains at least one block. There are two types of blocks: *base table* blocks and *control* blocks. A base table block is related to a specific table or view, and a control block isn't related to a table or view. Almost every block has one or more items. At least one item in a base table block is related to a column in the block's table or view.

12

NEW TERM A *base table block* is an Oracle Forms block that is associated with a database table or view.

NEW TERM A *control block* is an Oracle Forms block that is not associated with a database table and usually contains control objects such as buttons.

To access a block's properties, select the block and right-click Properties. A window displaying the block's properties will be displayed. For example, if you want to specify an ORDER BY clause for the Student block, use the arrow key to navigate to the ORDER BY clause property. At the top of the Properties window, you can then enter the ORDER BY clause or click the button containing the yellow balloon to the right of the field. For instance, if you want the records in the Student block ordered by year first and then the student's name, enter the ORDER BY clause as shown in Figure 12.20 and press Enter to assign the value to the property.

Figure 12.20.

Setting the ORDER BY *block property.*

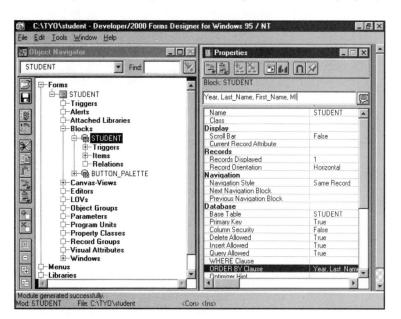

Base Table Block Items

A base table block contains items that are associated with the columns of a table or view. Each item has its own set of properties which can be accessed by selecting the item and right-clicking Properties. One important item property is the Item Type. To change an item's type, select the Item Type property, and select the item type that you want to use from the pop-up list at the top of the Properties window, as shown in Figure 12.21.

There are many other item properties that affect the appearance and behavior of an Oracle Forms application. Some of these item properties control what is entered in the item by the user. For instance, the Case Restriction item is set to Mixed by default. To change it, select the Case Restriction item, and click it until the property changes to Upper.

Figure 12.21.

Setting an item's type.

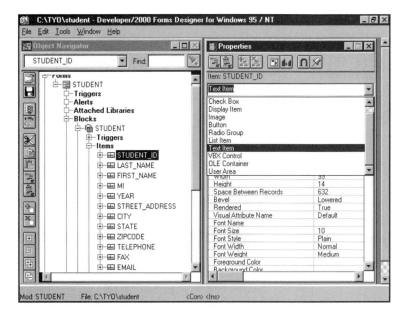

NOTE

If an item property has a pre-defined set of values, you can change the value of the selected property by repeatedly pressing Enter or by clicking the mouse. The property has a pre-defined set of values if there is a pop-up list to the right of the field at the top of the Properties window.

Control Block Items

To see the difference between a base table block item and a control block item, look at the properties of the Save item in the BUTTON_PALETTE control block. First, notice that the item type is Button (see Figure 12.22). Also, unlike a base table block item, a control block item doesn't have any properties related to the database.

Of course, given that the Save item is a button, the button must perform some action when it's activated. If you expand the Save item in the Object Navigator, you will see that a trigger, named WHEN-BUTTON-PRESSED, belongs to the item. Many control block items are buttons that "control" the behavior of other blocks in a form.

12

Figure 12.22.

Viewing a control block item type.

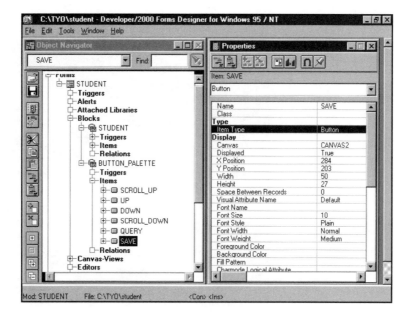

Canvas-Views

The canvas is a background object on which block items are placed. Each canvas has a view that defines how the canvas is viewed through a window. You can manipulate the items on the canvas with the Layout Editor. Select the Canvas-View that you want to change and right-click Layout Editor. When you create a new block, the Forms Designer creates a Canvas-View if one doesn't already exist and places the block items on it. Figure 12.23 shows the default layout for the Student form.

Windows

A window is an empty frame that "sits" on the Canvas-View. Every form has at least one window but may contain more. Figure 12.24 displays the Properties window for the default window, WINDOW0, which was created when the Student block was created. Some of the properties that are typically modified include the width, height, and title.

Triggers

A trigger is one or more PL/SQL statements that are executed when some action occurs that causes the trigger to fire. A trigger can be associated with many different levels of a form's object hierarchy. For instance, you can define a trigger that fires when a form is activated. You can define a trigger before a query is executed in a block. Or you can define a trigger that fires when the contents of an item changes. There are many pre-defined trigger events. Figure 12.25 displays the list of trigger events that are displayed if you select the pop-up list for the trigger Name property.

Figure 12.23.
Looking at a Canvas-View with the Layout Editor.

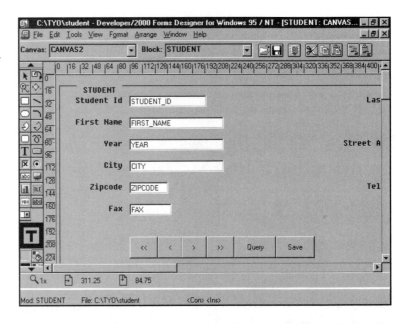

Figure 12.24.
Viewing the window properties.

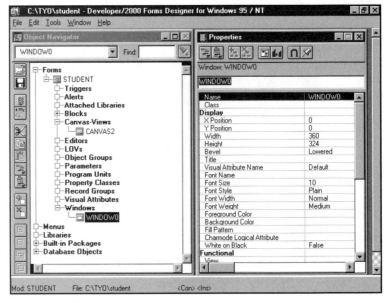

Figure 12.25.

Trigger events.

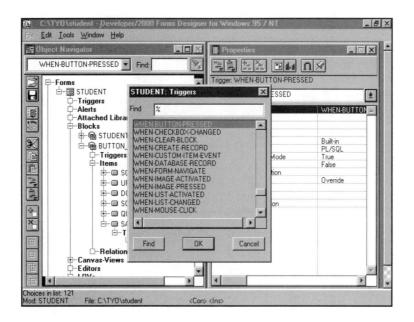

Record Groups

A record group is a set of values that can be defined:

☐ Dynamically by a SELECT statement that is executed at runtime

☐ Statically by a static set of values

☐ Programmatically by a PL/SQL subprogram that constructs a SELECT statement or a set of values at runtime

For example, suppose you want to create a record group based on the existing student IDs in the Student table. To do this, use the Object Navigator to select the Record Groups node in the STUDENT form, and click + in the vertical toolbar on the left-hand side of the window. A dialog window will be displayed in which you can enter the query that the new record group will be based on (see Figure 12.26).

After you enter the query and click OK, the record group is created. A record group is typically used by a List of Values (LOV).

LOVs

A List of Values (LOV) is an object based on a record group. A LOV is typically used to display a list of possible values from which a user can choose. There are several block item properties that are associated with an LOV. For example, you can indicate whether the LOV should also be used to validate the user input; that is, to ensure that the user cannot enter a value in a field unless that value exists in the specified LOV. You learn more about using LOVs on Day 13, "Developer/2000: Developing a User Interface with Oracle Forms," and Day 14, "Developer/2000: Application Development with Oracle Forms."

Figure 12.26.

Specifying a query for a new record group.

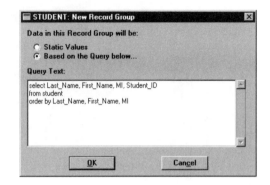

Alerts

An alert is a window that's used to inform the user about an event. The window is modal—the user must select one of the buttons on the window before proceeding.

Parameters

You can define parameters for a form that can be set from another form. Using a parameter, you can create a trigger that examines the value of a parameter and, depending on its value or lack thereof, takes a specific action. Suppose you wanted to be able to invoke the Student form from another form, pass a Student ID to the Student form, and have the corresponding student's record displayed. To do this, you would define a parameter named Student_ID of type CHAR. You would also write a trigger that fired when the window was activated and, if the parameter held a value, would retrieve the record that corresponded to the student ID contained in the parameter.

Using the Registry Editor to Change Oracle Components

It's a good idea to store your runtime forms, reports, and graphics files in a directory created specifically for your application. It is a bad idea to store these files in any of the Oracle directories for a couple of reasons:

☐ Because there are so many directories in the Oracle directory tree (Orawin95), it is easy to misplace your files.

☐ If you install a new version of the Oracle tools on your machine, your files may be removed.

If you do create another directory—for example C:\Tyo—you'll need to modify three values in the Windows 95 Registry. The runtime components of Developer/2000—Forms Runtime, Reports Runtime, and Graphics Runtime—don't use PATH to look for a form, report, or graphics file to execute. Instead, each runtime component of Developer/2000 uses a string value in the Oracle Registry key to search for the specified file. Specifically:

- ☐ Forms Runtime (F45run32) uses FORMS45_PATH
- ☐ Reports Runtime (R25run32) uses REPORTS25_PATH
- ☐ Graphics Runtime (G25run32) uses GRAPHICS25_PATH

By default, FORMS45_PATH, REPORTS25_PATH, and GRAPHICS25_PATH contain directories only in the Oracle directory tree. If you try to run a form that is in C:\Tyo, Forms Runtime displays an error message indicating that it can't open the form. To run your form, report, or graphics, you'll need to add the directory that contains these files with the Registry Editor.

1. To do this, select Start | Run.
2. Enter **regedit** and click OK. The Registry Editor is displayed.
3. Expand HKEY_LOCAL_MACHINE by clicking the + on its left (see Figure 12.27).

Figure 12.27.

Looking at
HKEY_LOCAL_MACHINE
with Registry Editor.

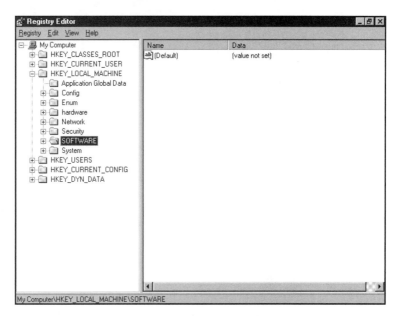

4. Expand SOFTWARE by clicking the + on its left. Click ORACLE.
5. On the right-side of the window, you should see a list of string values. Scroll down until you find FORMS45_PATH. Right-click on Modify—a window labeled Edit String is displayed. Click the mouse in the Value data field, and enter **;C:\Tyo**, as shown in Figure 12.28.

6. Follow the same steps to add the directory to GRAPHICS25_PATH and REPORTS25_PATH. When you're finished, exit the Registry Editor.

Figure 12.28.

Modifying
FORMS45_PATH *with*
Registry Editor.

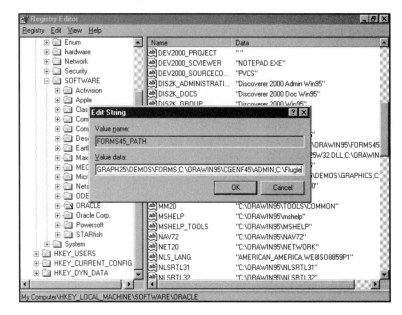

Summary

This was an in-depth introduction to Oracle Forms. The key concepts in this lesson were as follows:

☐ Developer/2000 consists of four primary components: Oracle Forms, Oracle Reports, Oracle Graphics, and Procedure Builder.

☐ The Forms Designer is used to design and test forms and the Forms Runtime is used to execute forms. The Forms Designer saves a form as an .fmb file, which is a binary file that's portable across different platforms. The Forms Designer can invoke the Forms Generator to create an .fmx file from an .fmb file. The Forms Runtime executes .fmx files.

☐ You use the Object Navigator to inspect a form's objects. Each object has a set of properties that can be viewed and modified.

☐ The Forms Designer can create three types of modules: forms, menus, and libraries.

☐ The Forms Designer can have multiple modules of all three types open simultaneously.

12

What Comes Next?

On Day 13, you learn how to customize the appearance and behavior of a form. You learn how to construct a menu, build a master-detail form, and change various object properties.

Q&A

Q Can a base table block include an item that isn't a part of the block's table?

A Absolutely. Such items are used to display values that are computed from other items in the block. For example, an order form typically has a line item total that you want to display for the user but isn't stored in a table.

Q Can a block be based on a view instead of a table?

A Yes. Often, such blocks are display-only; they aren't intended to be modified by the user.

Q Can a Forms application invoke other products, such as a report or chart?

A Yes. You can define menu items that will print a report or display a chart. You will see how this is done in Days 15, "Developer/2000: Developing Reports with Oracle Reports," and 16, "Developer/2000: Using Oracle Graphics and Procedure Builder."

Workshop

The purpose of the Workshop is to allow you to test your knowledge of the material discussed in the lesson. See if you can correctly answer the questions in the quiz and complete the exercise before you continue with tomorrow's lesson.

Quiz

1. True or false? Oracle Forms Runtime will only execute an `.fmb` file.
2. Name the three types of modules that the Forms Designer can create.
3. True or false? The Forms Designer can only save a form to an Oracle database if it contains a base table block.
4. True or false? You can create a block based on the contents of a table owned by another Oracle user.

Exercise

Create a form for the Instructor table. Specify an ORDER BY clause so that the records retrieved by a query are ordered by department ID, instructor last name, first name, and middle initial. Test the form.

Day 13

Developer/2000: Developing a User Interface with Oracle Forms

In the previous lesson, you were introduced to some basic concepts about Developer/2000 and started to work with Oracle Forms. You learned how to build a simple default form based on a single table. In this lesson, you continue with the Forms Designer and build a master-detail form. You also learn how to customize the appearance of a form with the Layout Editor.

NEW TERM A *master-detail form* is a form that contains two blocks, the master and detail blocks, which display database records. The master and detail blocks are synchronized; when a record is displayed in the master block, the detail records associated with the master record are displayed in the detail block. For example, a master-detail form might have a master block associated with the

Department table and a detail block associated with the Instructor table; when a particular department record is displayed in the Department block, the instructor records associated with that department are displayed in the Instructor block.

NOTE

> There are many properties for each object type in Oracle Forms. There simply aren't enough pages in this book to examine the nuances of each of these properties. Instead, I concentrate on the most important object properties.

Building a Master-Detail Form

On Day 12, "Developer/2000: Introduction to Oracle Forms," you used the Forms Designer to build a simple form for viewing and editing student information. Now, you're going to learn how to build a master-detail form. Specifically, you are going to build a form for scheduling a department's classes. The master block will contain the department, and the detail block will contain the classes to be offered by the department. To begin, invoke the Forms Designer by selecting Start | Programs | Developer/2000 for Win95 | Forms Designer. Next, connect to the Oracle database with the username, password, and database alias that you used in the previous lesson. By default, the Forms Designer creates a form named Module1.

Defining the Master Block

To define the master block for your form, follow these steps:

1. To begin, create the master block by selecting Tools | New Block from the menu. The New Block Options window will appear.

2. Click the Select button to the right of the Base Table field. Another window will appear in which you can specify which database objects will be displayed for tables to select from (see Figure 13.1).

3. Click OK. The tables owned by the current user—the username that you specified when you connected to the database—will be displayed.

4. Scroll down to the Department table, select it, and click OK (see Figure 13.2).

5. By default, the Forms Designer will name the block with the name of the table. Select the Items tab and click on Select Columns.

   By default, both columns in the table will be selected: Department_ID and Department_Name (see Figure 13.3).

Figure 13.1.
Restricting the list of database objects to tables owned by the current user.

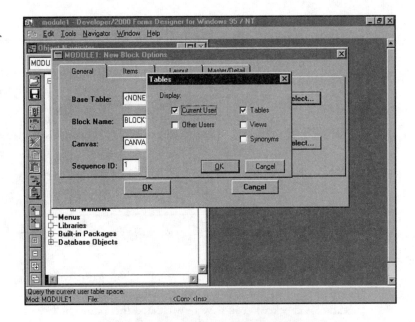

Figure 13.2.
Selecting the Department table for the master block.

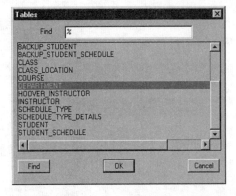

Figure 13.3.
Selecting the Department table columns to include in the master block.

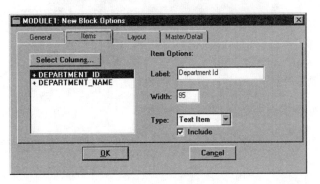

13

6. Now, select the Layout tab. In the Style field, select Form from the pop-up list. Check both the Integrity Constraints and the Button Palette, as shown in Figure 13.4. Click OK to complete the creation of the master block.

Figure 13.4.

Setting the layout options for the master block.

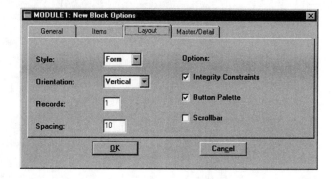

As you can see in Figure 13.5, the Object Navigator will display the two new blocks: Department and Button Palette (which is the control block created when the Button Palette checkbox is checked). You have now created the master block.

Figure 13.5.

Object Navigator displays the two new blocks.

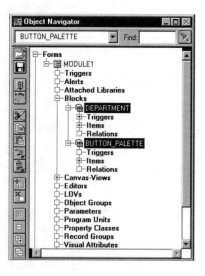

13

Notice that you didn't set any properties to indicate that this block is the master block. It is the master block because you are about to create another block that will identify Department as the master block.

Defining the Detail Block

To create the detail block, you'll follow many of the same steps needed to create the master block:

1. To begin, select Tools | New Block from the menu. Once again, click on Select to the right of the Base Table field to display the list of available tables.

2. In the Tables window, click OK to display the tables owned by the current user.

3. Select the Class table and click OK. You should see the New Block Options window, as displayed in Figure 13.6.

Figure 13.6.

New Block Options window for detail block.

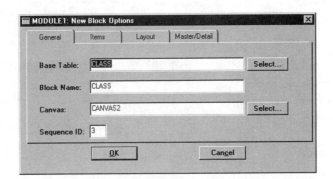

4. Select the Items tab and then select Select Columns. Click on the Semester and School Year columns to de-select them. You should see a - to the left of the two columns, indicating that the Forms Designer shouldn't create items for these columns; you won't need the Semester and School Year columns for this example.

Next, select the Layout tab. This time, be sure the Style field is set to Tabular and the Orientation is Vertical. Set Records to 10. Set the Integrity Constraints and Scrollbar checkboxes.

Defining the Relationship

Follow these steps to define the relationship between the master and detail blocks:

1. To select the master block, select the Master/Detail tab.

13

2. To the right of the Master Block field, click on Select. A window will appear and, by default, the Department block will be selected (see Figure 13.7). Click OK.

3. Using the foreign key that exists on the Class table, the Forms Designer will establish the join condition between the master and detail blocks, as shown in Figure 13.8. Click OK to create the detail block, Class.

Figure 13.7.

Choosing the master block.

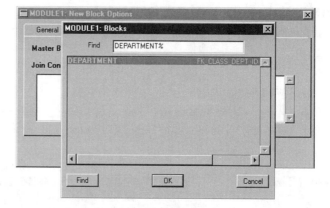

Figure 13.8.

Join condition created by the Forms Designer.

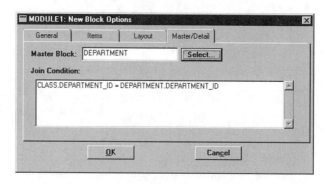

Let's look at the canvas that has been created. Select Tools | Layout Editor from the menu. Figure 13.9 displays what you should see with the Layout Editor. As you can see, there are a lot of changes you'll need to make to the form before you actually use it. In the next section, you learn how to use the Layout Editor to modify the appearance and properties of the block items.

Figure 13.9.

Looking at the canvas with the Layout Editor.

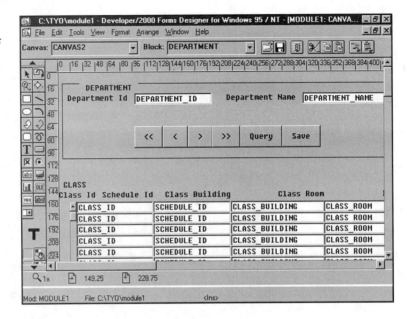

Working with the Layout Editor

When you invoke the Layout Editor, you'll notice that the menu items change. From the Layout Editor, there are several menu items that you can select under Format and Arrange. To begin with, let's change the font for all the text items.

Formatting Text

To select all the items on the canvas, press Ctrl+a. To change the font for all the selected items, select Format | Font, and the Font window will appear. Select MS Sans Serif, Regular font style, and 10 points (see Figure 13.10). Click OK for the change to take effect.

TIP To select multiple items, you can use the mouse to draw a rectangle around the items to be selected by holding the left button down and dragging the mouse until all the items are enclosed by the rectangle. Alternatively, you can select multiple items while holding down the Shift key.

13

Figure 13.10.

Changing the font for selected items.

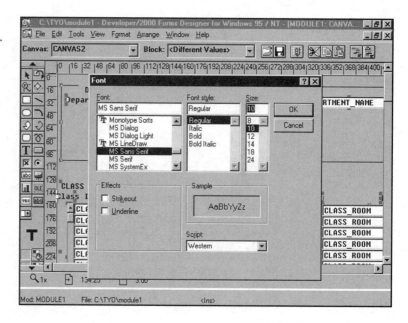

Sizing Objects

If you look at the layout, there are several fields that should be resized. For example, Class_Building and Class_Room can be made narrower. To change the width of a field, select the item with the mouse. Grab a point on the right side of the item and, holding down the left mouse button, drag the point to the left until the item is the desired width. Reduce the width of Class_ID, Schedule_ID, Class_Building, Class_Room, and Instructor_ID (see Figure 13.11). Don't worry if the items are no longer aligned with each other; you'll correct that in a little while.

Let's remove the rectangle around the master block. Select the bottom of the rectangle and press the Delete key. Reposition the fields and their text labels. Move the Button Palette items to the top of the canvas. Also, let's add a rectangle around the Button Palette items, the Department table fields, and their labels.

1. To do this, select the rectangle tool from the vertical toolbar.

2. Move the mouse to the position of the upper-left corner of the rectangle, hold the left mouse button down, drag the mouse to the lower-right corner of the rectangle, and release the mouse. Depending on your previous actions in the Layout Editor, you may or may not be able to see the rectangle.

3. To make the rectangle visible, select the Line Color tool, as shown in Figure 13.12 (notice the bubble help when the mouse is placed over the tool). You will see a window containing the available colors—select black (see Figure 13.13).

Figure 13.11.
Reducing the width of detail block items.

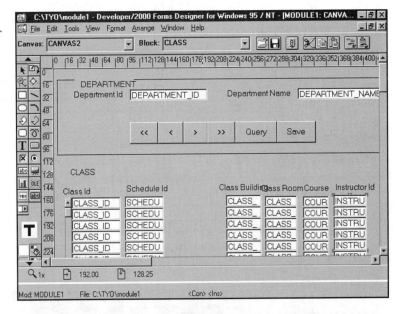

Figure 13.12.
Selecting the Line Color tool to make the rectangle visible.

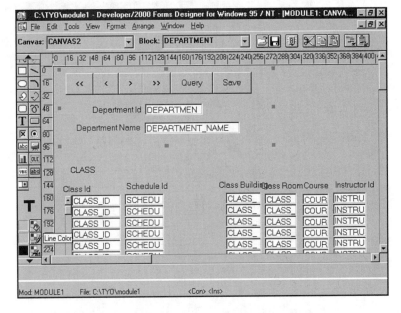

Figure 13.13.
Setting the line color for the rectangle.

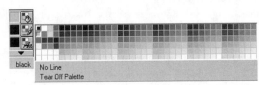

4. To give the rectangle an inset bevel, select Format | Bevel | Inset from the menu. The rectangle should now have an inset bevel as shown in Figure 13.14. Of course, this is a matter of personal taste; you can use whatever visual styles you prefer.

Figure 13.14.

Choosing the inset bevel for the rectangle.

Modifying Text

Some of the headings in the Class block need to be changed: in some cases, more appropriate headings should be used, or the headings need to be formatted. For example, to change `Class Building` to be simply `Building`, select the text with the mouse and then select the text tool. The pointer will become a crosshair. Move the crosshair to `Class Building` and left-click the heading; a box is formed around the heading, and an insertion point will indicate where you are editing the text (see Figure 13.15). Let's remove the word `Class` from the heading.

Figure 13.15.

Modifying the text heading.

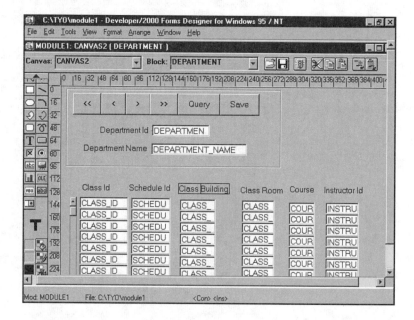

If a column heading is wider than the column that it covers, you may want to place the words onto separate lines. This will allow you to squeeze the columns more closely. For instance, you can change Instructor ID so that Instructor and ID are on two lines. To do this, select the column heading, select the text tool, and left-click the column heading. Move the insertion point to the beginning of ID and press Enter.

To center the column heading, select Format | Alignment | Center from the menu.

Sizing, Spacing, and Aligning Objects

When you were repositioning the items in the Class block, they became misaligned. Also, it is possible that you accidentally resized some of the items. To make a group of items the same size, select all of them, either by dragging a rectangle around the objects with the mouse or by clicking each object while holding down the Shift key.

For example, select these seven items in the Class block: the scrollbar, Class_ID, Schedule_ID, Class_Building, Class_Room, Course_ID, and Instructor_ID. To make these items the same vertical size, select Arrange | Size Objects from the menu. A window named Size Objects will appear. Because you don't want to change the width of any of these items, leave Width set to No Change. For Height, choose the Largest radio button; that will make all the items the same height as the largest item (see Figure 13.16). Click OK for the change to take effect.

Figure 13.16.

Sizing a group of items.

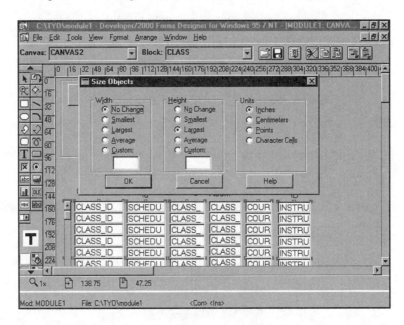

Now you'll align the items. Make sure that the items are still selected. Select Arrange | Align Objects. A window named Align Objects will appear. Set the Align To radio group to Each Other. Set the Horizontally radio group to Distribute; this will distribute the horizontal spacing evenly between the items. Set the Vertically radio group to Align Top, and then click OK (see Figure 13.17).

NOTE
If the items are not distributed evenly in the horizontal direction or aligned vertically at the top, you may accidentally have selected another item that is interfering with the alignment.

Figure 13.17.

Aligning a group of items.

Let's work on the column headings now. Because the text items in the Class block have been redistributed horizontally, you may need to reposition the column headings.

1. Be sure to select only the column headings.
2. Select Arrange | Align Objects from the menu.
3. In the Align Objects window, set the Align To radio group to Each Other.
4. Set the Horizontally radio group to None; you don't want to evenly distribute the spacing between the column headings because the headings will not be properly placed over the columns.
5. Set the Vertically radio group to Align Top and click OK.
6. Draw a rectangle around the Class block. Figure 13.18 displays the layout of the master-detail form that you should see on your screen.

Figure 13.18.

Layout of master-detail form.

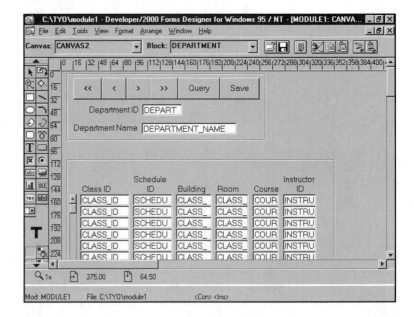

Running the Master-Detail Form

You are probably anxious to see the result of all this work. The best way to determine if the form is properly designed is to test it. Do this either by selecting File | Run from the menu or by pressing the green signal on the horizontal toolbar. First, the Forms Designer will generate an FMX file that can be executed. If there are no errors, the Forms Designer will invoke Forms Runtime to run the FMX file. You should see a window labeled Developer/2000 Forms Runtime for Windows 95/NT [WINDOW0]. Within that window, you should see another window labeled WINDOW0. Maximize both windows. Figure 13.19 shows what your screen should look like.

Figure 13.19.

Initial window when running the master-detail form.

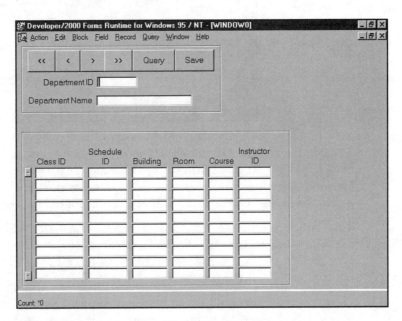

To run a query, click on the Query button twice; the first click enables you to enter query criteria and the second click executes the query. As you can see, the departments are not in any particular order. Also, the classes that belong to a department are not in any specific order either. In the next section, you'll change the Order By property for the master and detail blocks. To do this, exit Forms Runtime by selecting File | Exit.

Improving the Form

In the Forms Designer, go to the Object Navigator window by selecting Window | Object Navigator from the menu. Select the Department block, and right-click Properties. Scroll down to the Order By property and enter **Department_ID** (see Figure 13.20). Press Enter for the property to be set.

13

Figure 13.20.

Setting the Order By *property for the Department block.*

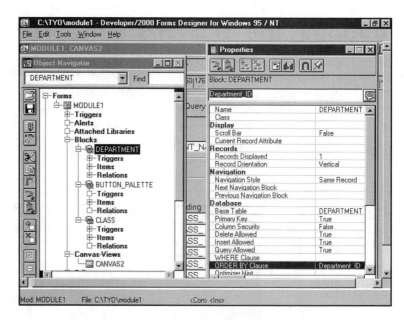

Select the Class block, and right-click Properties. It probably makes more sense to order the block by Course_ID rather than Class_ID because the Course ID is a familiar number to everyone: administrators, instructors, and students. Again, scroll down to the Order By property, and enter **Course_ID**. Press Enter for the property to be set.

There are several other things that should be changed in the form. First of all, some fields are too wide—namely, Class_ID, Schedule_ID, and Class_Room. One field is too narrow: Class_Building. Also, it probably would make more sense to put Course_ID directly to the right of Class_ID. Let's make these changes and run the form again.

Execute a query and scroll to the history department by clicking on > or by selecting Record | Next from the menu until you see the history department displayed in the Department block (see Figure 13.21).

If you want to change the room where Class 108400 (history course 115) is going to be held, you need to navigate to the Class block. By default, the current block is the first block, which happens to be Department. To go to the next block, press Ctrl+PageDown. However, when you do this, you'll notice that the focus is set to the left-most button on the Button Palette. This behavior can be explained by the order of the blocks.

If you use the Object Navigator to view the blocks, you'll notice that the blocks are in the order of Department, Button_Palette, and Class (see Figure 13.22); that is the order in which the blocks are navigated with the Next Block command. To change the order of the blocks, select a block and drag it until the pointer is over the block that you want to precede the selected block. For instance, to reposition the Class block, select it with the mouse and, holding down the left mouse button, position the pointer over the Department block and release the left mouse button.

Figure 13.21.
Viewing classes offered by the history department.

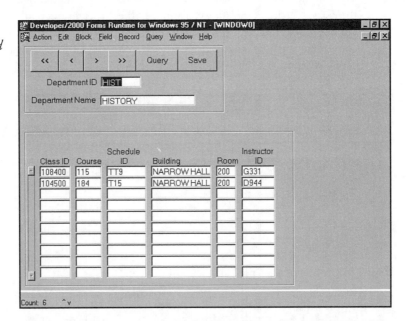

Figure 13.22.
Viewing the order of the blocks with the Object Navigator.

Controlling the Tab Order for Block Items

If you navigate to the Class block, you can move to the next item by pressing the Tab key. You can move to the previous item by pressing Shift+Tab. Notice that when the focus is on the Class_ID item, pressing Tab moves the focus to Schedule_ID. When you moved Course_ID to the right of Class_ID, the tab order of the fields didn't change. The most convenient way to change the tab order is to use the Object Navigator. Figure 13.23 shows the existing order of the items in the Class block.

Figure 13.23.

Viewing tab order of items in the Class block.

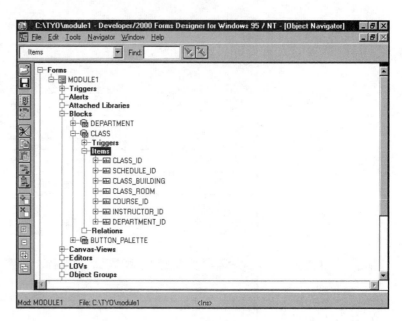

To make Course_ID the second tab item in the block, select it with the mouse and, holding down the left mouse button, position the pointer over the Class_ID item and release the left mouse button.

Creating a List of Values (LOV)

Let's think of other ways that this master-detail form can be improved. One way is to use an LOV for items that have a discrete set of values. For instance, Course_ID should be restricted to the values of Course_ID for the current Department_ID as found in the Course table. To create the LOV for Course_ID using the Object Navigator, select the LOVs node and click on + on the vertical toolbar. A window will appear in which you enter the query that you want executed for the new LOV. Actually, the Forms Designer will create a new record group based on the query that you enter. Figure 13.24 contains the text of the query. Notice that the Department_ID is restricted to the value contained in the Department_ID item in the Department block. Click OK to create the LOV.

NOTE

The code shown in this listing and figure is available for viewing in the .fmb file, which is on the CD-ROM. You can open the entire form and refer to all the objects and properties there.

Listing 13.1. Query used to create a new LOV for
INPUT Course_ID.

```
select Course_ID
from Course
where
Department_ID = :Department.Department_ID
order by Course_ID
```

Figure 13.24.

*Creating a new LOV
for Course_ID.*

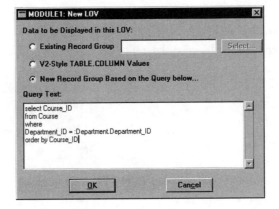

 NOTE

When you need to reference a block item in an SQL or PL/SQL statement, use the syntax :block.item.

13

Looking at the object nodes with the Object Navigator, you'll notice that there are two new objects: an LOV named LOV15 and a record group named LOV15. Please realize that you might see different default names given to these objects. To change the name of the record group, select the record group with the mouse and left-click it once more. The name will become blue, and the pointer will become an insertion point. Name the record group COURSE_ID_RG, and name the LOV COURSE_ID_LOV as shown in Figure 13.25.

Figure 13.25.

*Renaming the LOV
and record group.*

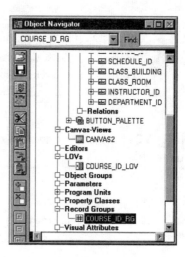

You'll want to modify a property of COURSE_ID_LOV. To do this, select COURSE_ID_LOV and right-click Properties. Scroll down until you reach the Column Mapping property. Click the button labeled More at the top of the Properties window (see Figure 13.26).

Figure 13.26.

*Modifying the
properties of an LOV.*

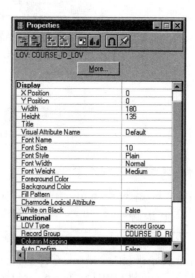

The LOV Column Mapping window will appear. There are four fields in this window. The Column Names field identifies the columns that are returned by the record group's query. The Return Item field is used to specify the block item in which the current value in the Column Names field is to be deposited. The Display Width field indicates the width of the field as displayed in the LOV. Finally, the Column Title field holds the title that will be displayed when the LOV is invoked.

As displayed in Figure 13.27, enter **Course_ID** in the Return Item field; this will cause the Course_ID selected the user to be placed in the Course_ID item. Increase the Display Width to 55 points so that the LOV heading for Course_ID isn't truncated. Change the Column Title to Course ID. Click OK for these changes to take effect.

Figure 13.27.

Modifying the Column Mapping *property of an LOV.*

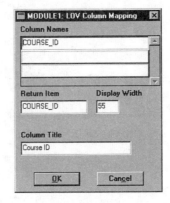

However, there are a few more steps that you need to perform before the LOV is actually used in the form.

1. Use the Object Navigator, and select the Course_ID item; right-click Properties.

2. Scroll down until you see a group of properties labeled Miscellaneous and select the LOV property.

3. Select COURSE_ID_LOV from the poplist at the top of the Properties window as shown in Figure 13.28.

4. Change the LOV for Validation property to True by clicking it; this will prevent a value from being entered into the field unless it exists in the LOV.

Let's test out the modified form.

1. Click on the green signal light from the vertical toolbar, or select File | Run from the menu.

2. When the runtime form is displayed, maximize both windows.

3. Execute a query by clicking twice on the Query button—once to enter query mode, and a second time to execute the query. You will see the first department appear in the Department block: Anthropology. However, there are no classes offered by this department.

4. Using the mouse, click on the first row in the Class block.

5. In Class_ID, enter **222333**.

13

Figure 13.28.

Modifying the Course_ID item properties to use the LOV.

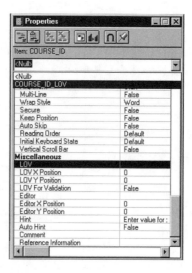

6. Press Tab to navigate to Course_ID. You should see `<List>` at the bottom of the screen in the status line; this indicates that there is an LOV for Course_ID.

7. To display the LOV, press F9. You will see the LOV displayed in the upper-left corner of the screen (see Figure 13.29).

Figure 13.29.

Displaying the LOV for Course_ID.

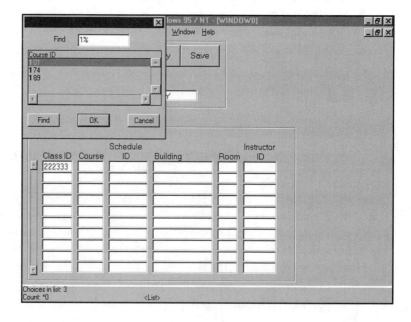

Scroll down to course 189 and press Enter; you will see 189 in the Course_ID item. If you enter a course that doesn't exist for this department, such as 1234, and press Tab to navigate to the next item, the form will display the LOV and also display a message in the message line stating FRM-40212: Invalid value for field COURSE_ID (see Figure 13.30).

Figure 13.30.
LOV enforces valid values for COURSE_ID.

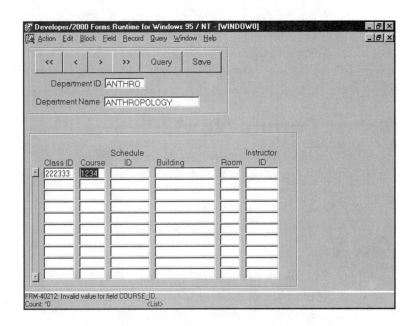

> **NOTE**
>
> Even if you don't use an LOV for validation, the Oracle database still enforces referential integrity. However, the advantage of an LOV is that it provides a set of legal values so the user doesn't have to remember what values can be entered in an item.

Before you complete this lesson, save this form as Department_Class.fmb by selecting File | Save as from the menu.

Summary

In this lesson, you learned the following:

☐ It is easy to construct master-detail forms with the Forms Designer.

☐ A master block is identified when the detail block is created.

☐ You use the Layout Editor to modify the form's appearance.

☐ You can modify the properties of several items at once by selecting them and, for example, changing their font.

☐ Using the Layout Editor, you can add graphical elements to a form by selecting tools from the vertical toolbar.

☐ When you create an LOV, you can automatically create the record group for the LOV by specifying the query for the record group.

☐ To use an LOV, the LOV property for an item must be set. If you want the LOV to validate user input in the item, you must set the LOV for Validation property to True.

What Comes Next?

On Day 14, "Developer/2000: Application Development with Oracle Forms," you learn how to construct a menu, add items to a block to display derived information, create form-level, block-level, and item-level triggers, and call a form from another form and pass a parameter to the invoked form.

Q&A

Q Can a master-detail form consist of more than one detail block?

A Yes. You simply create each detail block that you want and identify the master block in the Master/Detail tab.

Q Is it possible for several LOVs to reference the same record group?

A Yes. There is no restriction requiring each LOV to have its own record group.

Q Can a form have multiple windows and Canvas-Views?

A Yes, a single form can have multiple windows and Canvas-Views. However, as you will see in the next lesson, it usually makes more sense to create a multiple form application in which each form has a single Canvas-View and window.

Workshop

The purpose of the Workshop is to allow you to test your knowledge of the material discussed in the lesson. See if you can correctly answer the questions in the quiz and complete the exercises before you continue with tomorrow's lesson.

Quiz

1. True or false? A master block cannot be based on a view; it must be a table.

2. True or false? You can modify display characteristics of an item with the Layout Editor or by modifying the item's properties.

3. How can the tab order of a group of items be changed?

Exercises

1. Create a master-detail window for entering Schedule_Type and Schedule_Type_Details.

2. In the Department_Class form, create an LOV for Schedule_ID that will validate user input.

13

Day 14

Developer/2000: Application Development with Oracle Forms

In the previous two lessons, you built two forms: one form based on a single table and a master-detail form. You also learned how to modify the default layout that is generated by the Forms Designer when a new block is created.

This is your final lesson on Oracle Forms. In it, you investigate the use of PL/SQL to construct *application* triggers that serve a variety of purposes. You also go through the steps that can be used to develop a multi-form application. Along with that, you learn how to construct a menu that will invoke different forms.

An Overview of Triggers

NEW TERM A *trigger* is one or more PL/SQL statements that execute when an event occurs. The event may be directly related to an action performed by the user, such as pressing a button. Or the event may be indirectly related to an action performed by the user, such as the period before a query is executed.

A trigger can be defined at three levels:

- ☐ At the form level
- ☐ At the block level
- ☐ At the item level

Often, a single form will have one or more triggers at each level.

Default Triggers

In the previous lesson, you created a master-detail form named Department_Class. When you created each block, you checked a checkbox on the Layout tab to indicate that integrity constraints should be enforced. If you use the Object Navigator to expand the Department block, you will see three triggers that were created when you defined the Department block (see Figure 14.1):

- ☐ ON-CHECK-DELETE-MASTER
- ☐ ON-POPULATE-DETAILS
- ☐ KEY-DELREC

Figure 14.1.

Block-level triggers created to enforce integrity.

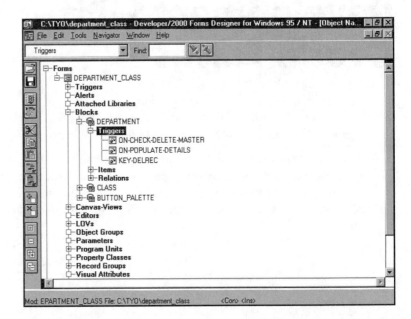

How do these triggers enforce referential integrity? Let's look at the KEY-DELREC trigger in detail. This trigger is fired when the user presses the Delete key. Listing 14.1 contains the text of this trigger. Notice that the trigger is composed of two anonymous PL/SQL blocks. The first block determines if there are any classes associated with the department to be deleted, and, if there are, issues an error message and raises an exception. The second block is very similar to the first block; it determines if any instructors belong to the department to be deleted and, if so, takes the necessary actions. You can view a trigger by double-clicking it in the Object Navigator.

Listing 14.1. KEY-DELREC trigger code for the Department block.

INPUT

```
declare
    cursor primary_cur is select 'x' from FLUGLE.CLASS
        where DEPARTMENT_ID = :DEPARTMENT.DEPARTMENT_ID;
    primary_dummy  char(1);
begin
    if ( ( :DEPARTMENT.DEPARTMENT_ID is not null ) ) then
        open primary_cur;
        fetch primary_cur into primary_dummy;
        if ( primary_cur%found ) then
            message('Cannot delete master record when matching detail
➥records exist.');
            close primary_cur;
            raise form_trigger_failure;
        end if;
        close primary_cur;
    end if;
end;

declare
    cursor primary_cur is select 'x' from FLUGLE.COURSE
        where DEPARTMENT_ID = :DEPARTMENT.DEPARTMENT_ID;
    primary_dummy  char(1);
begin
    if ( ( :DEPARTMENT.DEPARTMENT_ID is not null ) ) then
        open primary_cur;
        fetch primary_cur into primary_dummy;
        if ( primary_cur%found ) then
            message('Cannot delete master record when matching detail
➥records exist.');
            close primary_cur;
            raise form_trigger_failure;
        end if;
        close primary_cur;
    end if;
end;

declare
    cursor primary_cur is select 'x' from FLUGLE.INSTRUCTOR
        where DEPARTMENT_ID = :DEPARTMENT.DEPARTMENT_ID;
    primary_dummy  char(1);
```

14

continues

Listing 14.1. continued

```
begin
    if ( ( :DEPARTMENT.DEPARTMENT_ID is not null ) ) then
        open primary_cur;
        fetch primary_cur into primary_dummy;
        if ( primary_cur%found ) then
            message('Cannot delete master record when matching detail
➥records exist.');
            close primary_cur;
            raise form_trigger_failure;
        end if;
        close primary_cur;
    end if;
end;
delete_record;
```

Using a Trigger to Retrieve Values from Another Table

Let's work through an example of how a trigger can be used in the Department_Class form. If you look at the Class block, the Course_ID is displayed, but unless the user has memorized the Course IDs, he or she has no way of knowing anything else about the course. The user probably would benefit if the title of the course were displayed.

1. Using the Layout Editor, move Schedule_ID, Building, Room, and Instructor_ID to the right so that the course title can be displayed to the right of Course_ID.

2. Next, select the Text Item tool on the vertical toolbar, and left-click to the right of Course_ID (see Figure 14.2).

   Don't worry about the size and spacing of the new text item; you'll change it in a moment.

3. Right-click Properties to change the properties of the new text item.

4. In the Name property, enter **COURSE_TITLE**. Scroll down to the group of properties labeled Navigation. Set the Navigable property to False by pressing Enter.

5. The Course_Title text item will be used only to display the course title; there is no reason the user needs to navigate to it. Scroll down to the group of properties labeled Database.

6. Set the Base Table Item property to False by pressing Enter (see Figure 14.3).

   The reason you are setting the Base Table Item property to False is because the Class block is based on the Class table, and the Course_Title is not a column in the Class table.

Figure 14.2.

Adding a text item to the Class block.

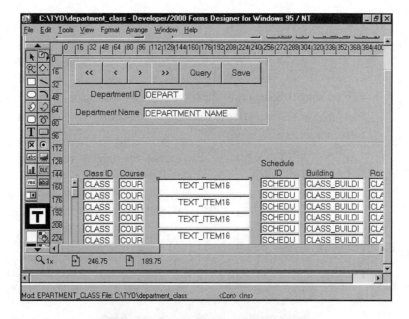

Figure 14.3.

Setting the properties for the Course_Title text item.

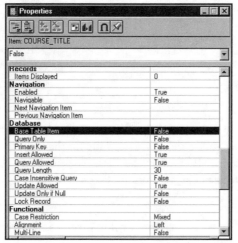

7. Let's return to the Object Navigator. Drag the COURSE_TITLE text item beneath the COURSE_ID text item.

8. Select the COURSE_ID text item, and right-click Properties. Scroll down to the Height property.

14

9. In the Object Navigator window, select the COURSE_TITLE text item by clicking it.

   Notice that the Properties window now displays the properties for COURSE_TITLE and that the focus is still on the Height property.

10. Change the height to the same value used for COURSE_ID: 14.

Now that you have a place to display the course title, you still need a trigger that will cause it to be displayed.

1. Use the Object Navigator to expand the triggers that belong to the Department block, and click + on the vertical toolbar to create a new block-level trigger.

2. A window will appear from which you can select the event that will cause the new trigger to fire; select POST-QUERY and click OK (see Figure 14.4).

Figure 14.4.

Creating a POST-QUERY trigger for the Department block.

3. The PL/SQL Editor will appear. As shown in Figure 14.5, enter a SELECT statement that will retrieve Course_Title for the value for Course_ID found in the Course_ID item in the Class block and the value for Department_ID found in the Department_ID item in the Department block.

NOTE

Notice that a colon precedes all references to blocks and items.

4. Enter the SELECT statement as shown in Listing 14.2, and click on Compile. If you've typed the statement correctly, you shouldn't see any error messages. Click on Close.

Figure 14.5.

Using the PL/SQL Editor to specify the POST-QUERY trigger.

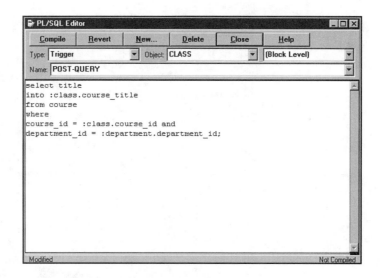

INPUT **Listing 14.2. Specifying a POST-QUERY trigger.**

```
select title
into :class.course_title
from course
where
course_id = :class.course_id and
department_id = :department.department_id;
```

Let's try running the form to see if the trigger works correctly.

1. Click on the green signal light on the vertical toolbar.

2. To execute a query against the Department block, click on the Query button.

3. In Department_ID, enter **HIST**.

4. Click on the Query button once more. As you can see in Figure 14.6, the trigger performed as expected—the title for each course was retrieved from the Course table.

Now, let's see what happens when a new class is entered.

1. Click the pointer in Class_ID. As illustrated in Figure 14.7, the title is *not* retrieved for Course_ID 199. As you can see, an item-level trigger is needed for Course_ID.

2. Exit the Forms Runtime.

14

Figure 14.6.

Testing the trigger.

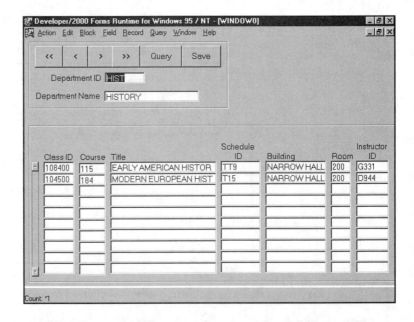

Figure 14.7.

Post-query doesn't work when a new record is inserted.

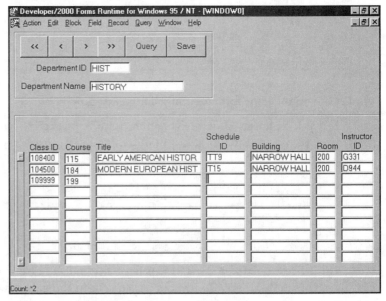

3. Using the Object Navigator, expand the Course_ID item.

4. In the Triggers node that belongs to Course_ID, click + in the vertical toolbar to add a trigger.

14

5. In the window that appears, select the WHEN-VALIDATE-ITEM trigger. Although the same SELECT statement that you used for the block-level trigger—POST-QUERY—is used for this item-level trigger, the statement is enclosed in an anonymous block, as shown in Figure 14.8.

Figure 14.8.

Specifying the WHEN-VALIDATE-ITEM *trigger for Course_ID.*

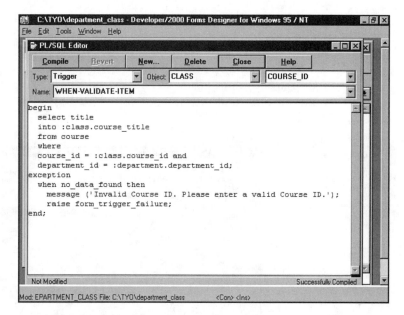

6. In addition, you should add an exception section to the trigger to handle the situation in which the user enters an invalid Course_ID. However, because you specified that the Course_ID_LOV be used to validate the Course_ID field, the exception should never be raised.

INPUT   **Listing 14.3.** WHEN-VALIDATE-ITEM **trigger for Course_ID field.**

```
begin
    select title
    into :class.course_title
    from course
    where
    course_id = :class.course_id and
    department_id = :department.department_id;
exception
    when no_data_found then
        message ('Invalid Course ID. Please enter a valid Course ID.');
        raise form_trigger_failure;
end;
```

14

Let's run the form again to test the item-level trigger.

1. Execute a query against the Department block by clicking Query.

2. In Department_ID, enter **HIST**.

3. Click Query once more.

4. Click the pointer in Class_ID.

5. Enter **109999** in Class_ID.

6. Tab to Course_ID, and enter **199**.

7. Press Tab once more. Figure 14.9 demonstrates that the trigger is working correctly; the correct title for History 199—"WORKSHOP ON JEFFERSON"—is displayed in Course_Title.

Figure 14.9.
Testing the WHEN -
VALIDATE - ITEM
trigger for Course_ID.

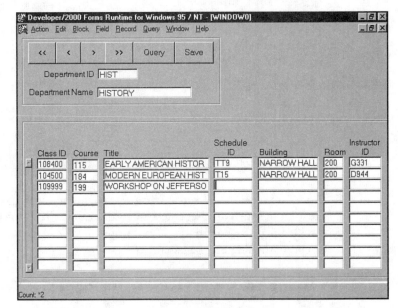

Using a Form-Level Trigger to Execute a Query

Let's work through another sample trigger. Follow these steps to create a form that, when invoked, will automatically execute a query:

1. Using the Forms Designer, create a new form by selecting File | New | Form from the menu.

2. Name the new form INSTRUCTOR, and create a new block based on the Instructor table. When you are finished designing your form, the layout should look similar to what is shown in Figure 14.10.

Figure 14.10.

Creating an Instructor form.

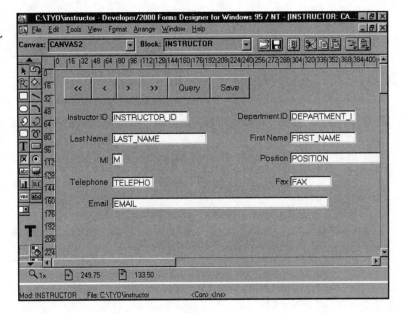

3. If you use the Object Navigator to view the Instructor form, you'll see that there aren't any triggers at the form level, which is directly beneath the form itself. To create a form-level trigger, select the Triggers node and click + on the vertical toolbar.

4. In the window that appears, select WHEN-WINDOW-ACTIVATED and click OK. This trigger will fire when the form is invoked.

5. The PL/SQL Editor will appear. You need to write only a single line of PL/SQL code for this trigger: a call to execute_query; which is a built-in Oracle Forms procedure. This built-in procedure will execute a query in the current block, which is Instructor.

6. Click Close, and test the form by clicking the green signal light on the vertical toolbar. As you can see in Figure 14.11, the form will automatically execute a query when it is invoked.

14

Figure 14.11.

Testing the WHEN-
WINDOW-ACTIVATED
trigger.

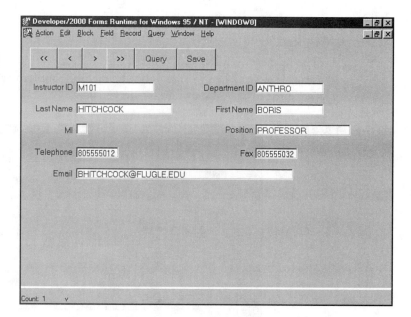

Using a Trigger to Validate User Input

In this section, you investigate another use for an item-level trigger: to validate user input. Suppose that the college president has told you that if an instructor is added to a department that already has at least one instructor who is a full professor, the new instructor cannot also be a full professor—he or she must be either an assistant or associate professor.

To do this, you will modify the existing WHEN-VALIDATE-ITEM trigger for the Position text item by expanding the Position text item and double-clicking the icon to the left of the WHEN-VALIDATE-ITEM trigger. As you can see in Figure 14.12, the existing trigger performs the same logic as the CHECK constraint on the Position column in the Instructor table. This trigger was automatically generated when you selected the Integrity Constraints when the block was created.

Listing 14.4 shows the WHEN-WINDOW-ACTIVATED trigger after it has been modified to perform this logic.

INPUT   **Listing 14.4. Modified** WHEN-WINDOW-ACTIVATED **trigger.**

```
declare
num_full_professors  integer;

begin
if not( :INSTRUCTOR.POSITION IN ('ASSISTANT PROFESSOR',
➡'ASSOCIATE PROFESSOR', 'PROFESSOR') ) then
  message( 'WHEN-VALIDATE-ITEM trigger failed on field - '
➡¦¦ :system.trigger_field );
```

```
    raise form_trigger_failure;
end if;

select count(*) into num_full_professors
from Instructor
where Department_ID = :Instructor.Department_ID and
➡Position = 'PROFESSOR';

if num_full_professors > 0 and :Instructor.Position = 'PROFESSOR' then
  message ('Cannot add another full professor to this department.');
  raise form_trigger_failure;
end if;

end;
```

ANALYSIS First, the PL/SQL statements are contained in an anonymous block. A variable named num_full_professors is declared. The first section of the block is used to enforce the CHECK constraint. Next, a SELECT statement is used to determine how many full professors exist in the department. If that number is greater than zero, a message is displayed, and a built-in exception, FORM_TRIGGER_FAILURE, is raised which prevents the user from continuing until the value is corrected.

Let's test the trigger. To create a new instructor, select Record | Insert from the menu. Try entering a new instructor for the anthropology department which already has two full professors, Boris Hitchcock and Ranier Poulson. As you can see in Figure 14.13, the trigger is working. As intended, the trigger will not prevent you from adding a full professor to the math department because that department does not already have a full professor.

Figure 14.12.

Existing code in the WHEN-WINDOW-ACTIVATED *trigger.*

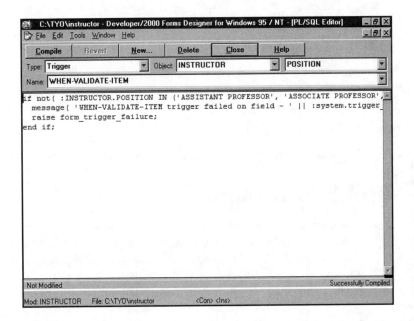

14

Figure 14.13.

Testing the WHEN -
WINDOW-ACTIVATED
trigger.

> **Developer/2000 Forms Runtime for Windows 95 / NT - [WINDOW0]**
>
> Action Edit Block Field Record Query Window Help
>
> `<<` `<` `>` `>>` Query Save
>
> Instructor ID X111   Department ID ANTHRO
>
> Last Name PATTERSON   First Name BO
>
> MI   Position PROFESSOR
>
> Telephone   Fax
>
> Email
>
> Cannot add another full professor to this department.
> Count: 1   ^ v

Elements of a Menu

Like a form, a menu is defined by a collection of objects. Some of these objects are mandatory, and some are optional. Each object may be one of the following:

- ☐ Menu
- ☐ Object Group
- ☐ Program Unit
- ☐ Parameter
- ☐ Property Class
- ☐ Attached Library
- ☐ Visual Attribute

You're now going to build a menu for your multi-form application and call it MAIN_MENU.

Building a Menu

To begin with, use the Forms Designer to open C:\Orawin95\Forms45\Demos\Dfltmenu\menudef by selecting File | Open from the menu (see Figure 14.14). This is the default path to use if you have installed Developer/2000 on Windows 95. Using the Object Navigator, expand the Menus object node. If you look at the Properties for MENUDEF, you'll see a property named Main Menu, which is set to Main_Menu. This property identifies the highest-level menu.

Figure 14.14.

Opening the default menu.

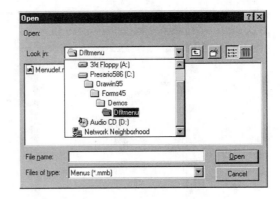

Beneath the Menus object node, you will see the following menus:

- [ ] ACTION
- [ ] BLOCK
- [ ] MAIN_MENU
- [ ] EDIT
- [ ] FIELD
- [ ] HELP
- [ ] QUERY
- [ ] RECORD

These menus constitute the highest-level menus. However, this is the default menu, and you'll want to add three high-level menus:

- [ ] A menu with items that enable the user to enter data into various tables
- [ ] A menu which contains items that enable the user to browse records in the database but not to modify them
- [ ] A menu for invoking reports and graphs

To add the three high-level menus to the default menu, select the Menus object node with the mouse or arrow keys, and click + on the vertical toolbar. A menu named MENU0 will appear; click the menu until it turns blue and change the name to DATA_ENTRY. Do the same to create the BROWSE and REPORTS menus (see Figure 14.15). Drag the three menus below RECORD.

14

Figure 14.15.

Creating new menus.

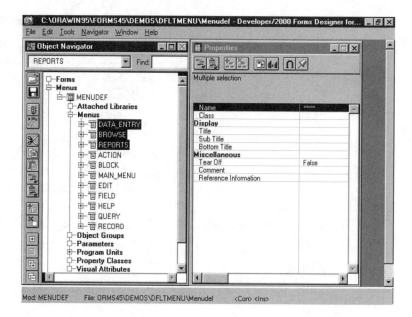

Incorporating New Menus

Although it is difficult to tell by looking at the menus with the Object Navigator, MAIN_MENU is the highest-level menu.

1. Expand the Items object node beneath MAIN_MENU.

2. To add the Data Entry menu to the main menu, select the Items object node and click + on the vertical toolbar. You will see a new item named ITEM followed by a number.

3. Click on the new item, and rename it as DATA_ENTRY.

4. If the properties are not displayed for DATA_ENTRY, right-click Properties, scroll down to the Command Type property, and change it to Menu (see Figure 14.16).

5. Scroll down to the Command Text property, and click the More button at the top of the Properties window. The Command Text property contains the command that will be executed when the menu item is selected. A window named Command Text will appear.

6. Enter **DATA_ENTRY**, and click OK (see Figure 14.17).

7. Scroll down to the Label property, and enter **Data Entry**. This will be the text that is displayed on the menu bar.

14

Figure 14.16.

Setting the Command Type property for the new menu item.

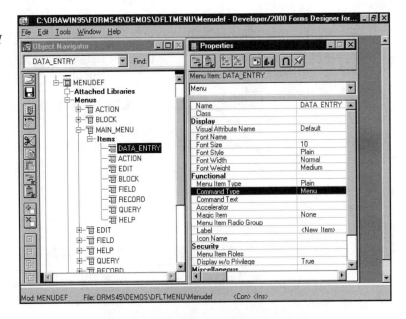

Figure 14.17.

Setting the Command Text property for the new menu item.

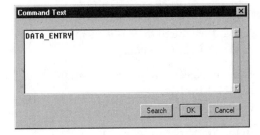

8. If you look at the items that belong to MAIN_MENU, you'll see that DATA_ENTRY is the first item. This isn't where you want it to appear on the menu bar.

   To move it between EDIT and BLOCK, select DATA_ENTRY with the mouse, hold down the left mouse button, drag it until the horizontal line appears below EDIT, and release the left mouse button.

9. To incorporate the Browse and Reports menus at the top level of MAIN_MENU, follow steps 3 through 8. To test the appearance of the menu, double-click the icon to the left of MENUDEF. Figure 14.18 displays what you should see.

14

Figure 14.18.

Testing the appearance of the menu.

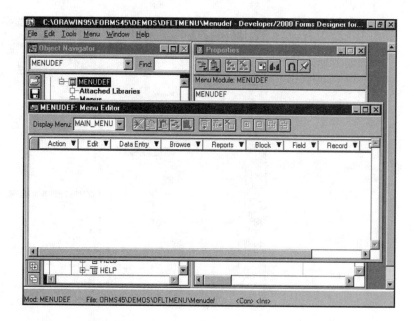

Adding Items to a Menu

Although you've created three new menus, none of the menus has any items. Let's add two items to the Data Entry menu.

1. Use the Object Navigator to expand the DATA_ENTRY menu (not item in MAIN_MENU).

2. Select the Items object node, and click + on the vertical toolbar.

3. In the Properties window, change the name of the item to INSTRUCTOR.

4. Scroll down to the Command Type property. As you can see, it is set to PL/SQL. Don't change it; this is the value that you want.

5. Scroll down to the Command Text property and click on More at the top of the Properties window. The PL/SQL Editor will appear.

6. Enter `call_form('Instructor',NO_HIDE,NO_REPLACE)`. This PL/SQL statement invokes the built-in Forms procedure, `call_form`, which will display the Instructor form.

7. Click Compile and Close.

8. In the Properties window, scroll down to the Label property, and enter `Instructor`.

You also will need to create an item for the Browse and Reports menu. If you don't, the Forms Generator will generate an error message when you try to generate an MMX file for the menu.

14

1. For the Browse menu, create an item named INSTRUCTOR_BROWSE.

2. In the Command Text property for this item, enter the following:

   ```
   call_form('Instructor_Browse',NO_HIDE,NO_REPLACE.
   ```

3. For the Reports menu, create an item named COURSE_CATALOG.

4. In the Command Text property for this item, enter **Null**; by specifying NULL, the menu item will appear in the menu but it won't perform any action—yet.

In the next lesson, you will learn how to invoke an Oracle Report from a menu item.

Saving the Menu

Before you go any further, you should rename the menu.

1. Select MENUDEF.

2. Select File | Save As from the menu.

3. Be sure to specify a directory designated for your application as the location for saving to.

4. In the Save As Type field, select Menus (*.mmb).

5. In the File name field, enter **Main_menu**.

6. Click Save.

Generating the Menu

When you save a menu in the file system, the file has an extension of .mmb. However, Forms Runtime can run only an MMX menu file, which is generated from an MMB file. To generate an MMX file for Main_menu, select File | Administration | Generate from the menu or press Ctrl+t.

Building a Multiform Application

NEW TERM Up to this point, you have only tested individual forms within the Forms Designer. Now, you are going to go through the steps of building a multiple-forms application. The first step is to create a form that will contain the *root window* for the application; this window will always display the menu and the console, consisting of the message and status lines.

1. To do this, select File | New | Form from the menu. A new form will appear in the Object Navigator.

2. Change the name of this form to MDI_FRAME.

3. Expand the Window object node, select the single window that was automatically created, and right-click Properties.

4. Change the name of the window to ROOT_WINDOW.

14

5. To properly display this window for a 600×480 size display, set Width to 473 and Length to 289. If you're planning to use a different screen resolution, you'll have to change Width and Length accordingly.

6. Scroll to the Title property, X and set it to `Flugle Information System`. Figure 14.19 illustrates what the window properties are set to.

Figure 14.19.

Setting the ROOT_WINDOW window properties.

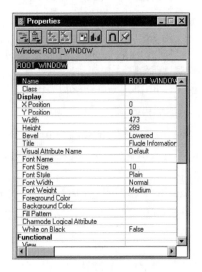

Now, you need to create a canvas for this form.

1. Select the Canvas-View object node, and click + on the vertical toolbar.

2. Select the canvas that was created, and right-click Properties.

3. Scroll the Width property to 473 and the Length property to 289. These are the same values that you specified for ROOT_WINDOW. Those are the only properties that you need to set for the canvas.

4. Now, select the form, MDI_FRAME, and right-click Properties.

5. Set the Title property to `Flugle Information System`.

6. Scroll down to the Menu Module property, and set it to MAIN_MENU. This is the menu that you have just created.

7. Scroll down to the Starting Menu property, and set it to MAIN_MENU. This will be the menu that is initially used when the MDI_FRAME form is invoked. Figure 14.20 displays the property values for the MDI_FRAME form.

8. Save the MDI_FRAME form as MDI_FRAME in the directory that you have created for storing application components.

9. Generate the `.fmx` file for the MDI_FRAME form by pressing Ctrl+t.

Figure 14.20.

Setting the properties for MDI_FRAME form.

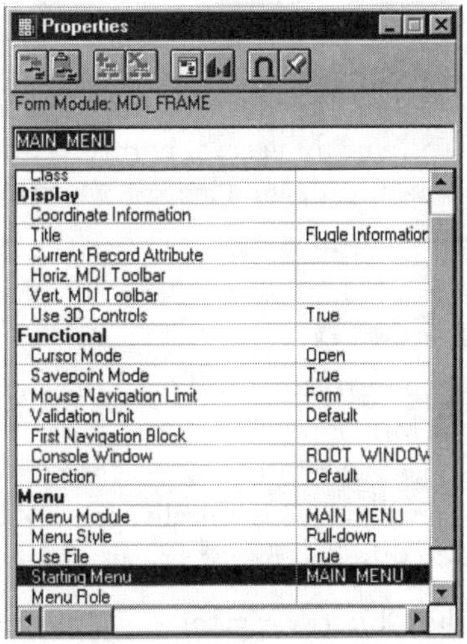

Creating a Windows Shortcut to Run an Application

Believe it or not, you've constructed the basic elements that are needed for a multiple-form application. To test your application, create a shortcut. To create the shortcut, right-click New | Shortcut on the Windows 95 desktop. You need to enter the command-line argument in the Create Shortcut window. Before you enter the command-line arguments for the shortcut, let's discuss a few arguments used by Forms Runtime:

☐ `userid` identifies the username, password, and database alias, if any, to be used to connect to the database.

☐ `module` identifies the form that you want to run (this should be the form that contains the root window: MDI_FRAME).

☐ `window_state` is an optional parameter that can be used to force the form specified in `module` to be MAXIMIZE, MINIMIZE, or NORMAL.

To run your forms application, enter the following line in the Command Line field:

```
c:\Orawin95\bin\F45run32 module=c:\Tyo\MDI_FRAME
➥userid=flugle/flugle@flugle window_state=maximize
```

Click on Next. Give the shortcut a name like `Flugle Information System`, and click Finish. You should see the new shortcut on your desktop. Try running the shortcut. Invoke Data Entry | Instructor from the menu; you should see the Instructor form.

14

NOTE

> One disadvantage of this shortcut is that the password is contained within the shortcut and could be viewed by others. If you don't specify a value for userid, Forms Runtime will prompt the user for username, password, and database when the shortcut is invoked.

Closing a Form

If you invoke the Instructor form from the Data Entry menu, you might discover that one way to close the form is to select Action | Exit from the menu. However, if you click the exit icon in the upper-right corner of the Instructor form (not the MDI_FRAME form), the Instructor form will not close. Ideally, you would like the form to close when the user clicks this icon. To do this, you need to create another trigger in the Instructor form.

1. Using the Object Navigator, open the Instructor form.
2. Expand the form, and select the Triggers object node at the form level.
3. Click + on the vertical toolbar to create a new trigger.
4. In the window that appears, select the WHEN-WINDOW-CLOSED event and click OK.
5. Double-click the icon to the left of the WHEN-WINDOW-CLOSED trigger displayed in the Object Navigator.
6. In the PL/SQL Editor, enter a single line: `exit_form`. This is a built-in procedure that will be invoked whenever the window is closed.
7. Click Close.
8. Save the Instructor form and regenerate it.
9. Use the shortcut to test the form and verify that the form closes when the exit icon is clicked.

Summary

The essential points in this lesson were the following:

☐ A trigger is a group of PL/SQL statements that is executed when a specified event occurs.

☐ A form can have triggers defined at different levels: the form level, the block level, and the item level.

☐ The events that can cause a trigger to fire vary depending on the level of the trigger. For example, certain window events will trigger only a form-level trigger.

☐ Some triggers are automatically generated by the Forms Designer when you request the enforcement of integrity constraints for a new block.

☐ You use the PL/SQL Editor to specify the PL/SQL statements for a trigger.

☐ A trigger can be used to retrieve values from other tables.

☐ A trigger can be used to validate user input. Such a trigger can raise the built-in exception, FORM_TRIGGER_FAILURE, if the user's input does not pass validation.

☐ A trigger can be used to automatically execute a query when a form is invoked.

☐ You use the Forms Designer to create and modify menus.

☐ A menu may consist of several object types, including a main menu and other menus, an object group, program unit, parameter, property class, attached library, and visual attribute.

What Comes Next?

On Day 15, "Developer/2000: Developing Reports with Oracle Reports," you learn about Oracle Reports. You'll go through the steps of creating two reports: a simple report based on a single table and a master-detail report. You'll also see how to specify a format trigger that uses PL/SQL statements to control the appearance of a report item, depending on its value.

Q&A

Q How does Oracle Forms handle triggers, associated with different levels, which respond to the same event?

A If two or more triggers are defined for the same event, the trigger associated with the *lowest* item level takes precedence. For example, suppose a form has two triggers, one at the block level and the other at the item level. If both triggers are defined for the WHEN-NEW-ITEM-INSTANCE event, the item-level trigger will fire when the event occurs.

Q What are some of the built-in procedures that are available in Oracle Forms?

A There are a number of built-in procedures that can be invoked from PL/SQL subprograms in triggers or library modules. These procedures include:

☐ Navigational procedures such as GO_BLOCK, GO_ITEM, and NEXT_ITEM

☐ Procedures that modify the contents of a block such as CLEAR_RECORD, DELETE_RECORD, and INSERT_RECORD

☐ Procedures that control query processing: ENTER_QUERY and EXECUTE_QUERY

Q What are some of the system variables that are available in Oracle Forms?

A There are several system variables that can be very useful in a trigger:

☐ $$DATE$$ and $$TIME$$ contain the current date and time, respectively.

☐ Variables that describe the current focus of the form such as SYSTEM.CURRENT_FORM, SYSTEM.CURRENT_BLOCK, and SYSTEM.CURRENT_ITEM.

14

Q Does Oracle Forms support the use of global variables?

A Yes. You can use global variables to store character strings up to 255 characters long. You don't declare a global variable; it is implicitly declared when you initially assign a value to it as in:

```
:GLOBAL.Instructor_ID := 'A1234';
```

Workshop

The purpose of the Workshop is to allow you to test your knowledge of the material discussed in the lesson. See if you can correctly answer the questions in the quiz and complete the exercises before you continue with tomorrow's lesson.

Quiz

1. True or false? An item-level trigger in one block cannot refer to items in a different block.

2. How are block items referenced in a trigger?

3. If you create an item-level trigger to validate user input, what exception should be raised if the user enters an invalid value?

Exercises

1. Modify the Instructor form so that it has the same width and height as the MDI_Frame form.

2. Create a menu item for the Browse menu that will invoke a form that displays Instructors in a tabular format, ordered by Instructor last name, first name, and middle initial.

14

WEEK 2

In Review

You've covered a considerable amount of material this week. Day 8 explored other forms of the SELECT statement such as joins, grouping rows by column value, and set operations. During Day 9, you were introduced to PL/SQL and learned about the three sections of a PL/SQL block and flow-of-control statements. Day 10 presented other PL/SQL datatypes; you also learned how to construct a PL/SQL package. The material on Day 11 discussed the use of cursors in retrieving rows, the construction of database triggers, and exception handling. Day 12 served as an introduction to Oracle Forms—you built a simple form and exercised it. Day 13 continued with a discussion of Oracle Forms in which you built a master-detail form, learned about object properties, and modified the appearance of a form. Finally, on Day 14, you continued to learn about Oracle Forms—how to use Forms triggers to validate user input and display derived values.

At A Glance

This is your final week, excluding the two Bonus Days that follow it. During Week 3, you'll continue to learn about the components of Developer/2000—Oracle Reports, Oracle Graphics, and Procedure Builder. During this week, two of the lessons focus on Oracle Power Objects. Here's a day-by-day summary of Week 3.

☐ **Day 15, "Developer/2000: Developing Reports with Oracle Reports"**
In this lesson, you'll learn about another component of Developer/2000: Oracle Reports. Step by step, you'll construct a simple report. You'll also learn about the various objects that compose an Oracle Report.

☐ **Day 16, "Developer/2000: Using Oracle Graphics and Procedure Builder"**
This lesson focuses on the other two components of Developer/2000: Oracle Graphics and Procedure Builder. You'll learn how to create a chart that reflects the values contained in a table. You'll also learn how to use Procedure Builder to construct a database trigger.

☐ **Day 17, "Introduction to Oracle Power Objects"**
This is the first of two lessons that talk about Power Objects. You'll gain a basic understanding of the properties used to create a simple form.

☐ **Day 18, "Developing an Application with Oracle Power Objects"**
Many important topics are addressed in this lesson, including using method code to validate input, creating a new class, inheritance, and report construction.

☐ **Day 19, "An Overview of Oracle Database Security and Tuning"**
In this lesson, you'll learn about Oracle users, roles, and privileges and how to manage them. The lesson briefly discusses the issue of performance tuning.

☐ **Day 20, "Using Oracle Database Designer and Oracle Designer/2000 in Application Development"**
During this lesson, you'll learn about a fairly new Oracle tool, Database Designer, and its use in the application development process. This lesson also presents Designer/2000 and some of its components.

☐ **Day 21, "Oracle: The Next Generation"**
In the last lesson for the week, you'll learn about the Oracle Web Application Server, including two special packages that are used to generate HTML tags from PL/SQL subprograms. You'll learn about the architecture and configuration of Developer/2000 for the Web. The lesson concludes with a discussion of Oracle's Network Computing Architecture.

Day 15

Developer/2000: Developing Reports with Oracle Reports

In this lesson, you'll learn about some basic features of Oracle Reports. You'll read about two basic report types—a tabular report based on a single table and a master-detail report. Oracle Reports is chock-full of features, and this lesson is intended to be an introduction to the most important of them.

Elements of an Oracle Report

Like Oracle Forms, Oracle Reports also has an Object Navigator that you can use to create and modify a report's objects. The Object Navigator displays objects in a hierarchical manner. For each report, the Object Navigator displays a set of nodes:

☐ Data Model
☐ Layout

☐ Parameter Form
☐ Report Triggers
☐ Program Units
☐ Attached Libraries

For directions on the use of the Object Navigator, refer to Day 12, "Developer/2000: Introduction to Oracle Forms." The next section looks more closely at some of the objects in a typical report.

Data Model

Every report must have a data model. The data model describes the queries that retrieve records from the database. A data model can be composed of one or more queries. A query can consist of any valid SELECT statement; in other words, you can select from multiple tables or even from a view. You also can use an ORDER BY clause to specify the order in which the rows are to be retrieved.

Layout

Every report must also have a layout. You can actually describe up to four layout components—header, body, footer, and margin. The examples in this chapter only define the body layout. However, you can define a layout for a report header that is printed only once at the very beginning of a report. An example of a report header might be a description of the report contents and a warning regarding the accuracy of the information contained within the body of the report.

The report layout may consist of many different elements, including frames, fields, text items, and graphical elements such as lines and rectangles. A frame is used to describe the characteristics of the items contained within it—for example, when they should be printed and in what direction. A frame can contain multiple fields. Each field may be associated with a column from a query—this is referred to as the *source* of the field. The field source also may be the current date or physical page number.

Parameter Form

Oracle Reports enables you to design a custom Runtime Parameter Form that may contain parameters whose values are specified by the user at runtime. For example, you can design a parameter form that enables the user to specify a Department ID that restricts the report output to that department. If you don't specify a parameter form, Oracle Reports displays the default Runtime Parameter Form.

15

Oracle Reports Programs

Oracle Reports contains two tools that are relevant to this lesson—Reports Designer and Reports Runtime. The Reports Designer enables you to create and modify three types of modules: reports, external queries, and libraries.

By default, the Reports Designer saves the modules that you design to either a file or to an Oracle database. To save a module to the database, you or your DBA need to install the database schema needed by Developer/2000. To learn more about this, read the Administrative Notes that are in the Developer/2000 Admin for Win95.

The Reports Designer saves a report as an RDF file: Reports Definition File. This is a binary file that is portable; that is to say, it can be read by the Reports Designer, whether on Windows 95, Mac OS, or UNIX. The Reports Designer generates an REP file that is a binary file used by the Reports Runtime program to actually run a report. An RDF file also can be converted to an REX file, which is a complete text description of the report that can be placed under source code control.

Building a Tabular Report Based on a Single Table

Let's begin using Oracle Reports to design a tabular report based on a single table. You will build a report that will present course information. To invoke the Reports Designer, from the Start button, click Oracle Designer for Win95 | Reports Designer. The Reports Designer program first displays the Object Navigator (see Figure 15.1).

Notice that a report titled UNTITLED is displayed in the Object Navigator. Before going any further, connect to the Oracle database.

Connecting to an Oracle Database

To connect Reports Designer to an Oracle database, follow these steps:

1. Select File | Connect from the menu. A dialog box is displayed, prompting you for the username, password, and database to use for establishing an Oracle database connection.

2. If you are using Personal Oracle for development, use `flugle` for the username and password. If you're using an Oracle server for development, use `flugle` for the username, password, and database.

3. For both cases, click the Connect button. If there are no error messages, you can assume that you have successfully connected to the database.

Figure 15.1.

Reports Designer first displays Object Navigator.

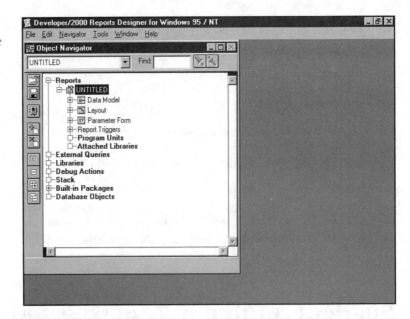

Creating a Data Model

The first step in creating any report is specifying the data model for the report. The Data Model Editor is used for this purpose. You can invoke the Data Model Editor by either clicking the icon to the left of the Data Model node in the Object Navigator or by selecting Tools | Data Model Editor from the menu. Maximize the window.

To create a query, click the button labeled SQL on the toolbar on the left-hand side of the window. Move the mouse to the main part of the window and hold down the left mouse button. You will see the outline of a rectangle. When the rectangle is a reasonable size, release the mouse button. You should now see a rounded black rectangle, labeled Q_1 (see Figure 15.2).

Double-click the rectangle that represents query Q_1. A window in which the SELECT statement for the query can be entered is displayed. Change the name of the query to Q_COURSE. Click the button labeled Tables/Columns. Another window, titled Table and Column Names, is displayed. This window enables you to choose the table and columns used for the query. In the listbox labeled Database Objects, scroll down to the COURSE table and select it. Select all of the columns in the Columns listbox (see Figure 15.3).

15

Figure 15.2.

Creating query Q_1.

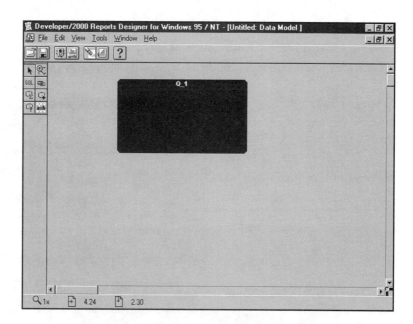

Figure 15.3.

Choosing the tables and columns for the query.

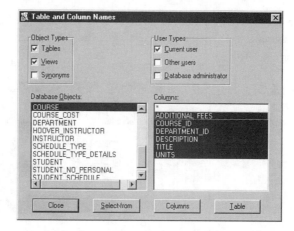

To use the selected table and columns in the query's SELECT statement, follow these steps:

1. Click SELECT-FROM and CLOSE. You'll see the SELECT statement that was constructed from the selected table and columns.

2. Rearrange the column names so that they are in the order you want to see on the report: Department_ID, Course_ID, Title, Description, Units, and Additional Fees.

3. Add an ORDER BY clause to the SELECT statement so that the rows are ordered by Department_ID and Course_ID, as shown in Figure 15.4.

4. Click OK to return to the Data Model Editor.

Figure 15.4.

Modifying the query's
SELECT *statement.*

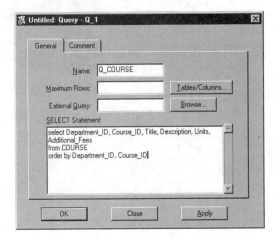

When you defined the SELECT statement for the query, the Reports Designer created a group for the query. As shown in Figure 15.5, the group's name is constructed from the query's name: G_COURSE.

Figure 15.5.

Group G_COURSE
created for query
Q_COURSE.

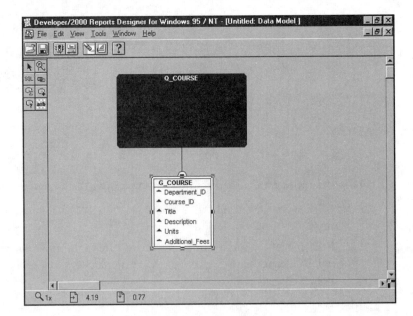

15

Specifying a Default Layout

You've successfully created the data model for the report. The next step is to specify the report layout.

1. To simplify this task, invoke the Default Layout dialog window either by clicking the green triangle on the horizontal toolbar or by selecting Tools | Default Layout from the menu.

2. The Default Layout window contains two tab folders. In the Style tab folder, select the Tabular style (see Figure 15.6).

Figure 15.6.

Default layout dialog window.

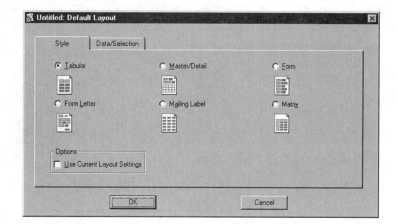

3. Select the Data/Selection tab folder. This tab folder contains each group and the columns that are associated with it.

By default, the Reports Designer constructs a label for each column by replacing each underscore in a column name with a blank. In addition, each word in the label has its initial character capitalized. As a result, the Department_ID column is given the label Department Id. You can change a label in the Data/Selection tab folder (see Figure 15.7).

4. Click OK to generate the default layout for the report. You should now see the default layout generated for the report (see Figure 15.8). Admittedly, what all the boxes and lines represent isn't intuitive. You can get another view of all the elements by looking at the layout in the Object Navigator (see Figure 15.9).

5. To navigate to the Object Navigator, select Window | Object Navigator from the menu. As you can see in the Object Navigator, a report layout may consist of a header, trailer, body, and margin. Only a body object was generated by the default layout. Beneath the body object is an object named M_COURSE_GRPFR—which is a

frame for the entire group. Beneath M_COURSE_GRPFR are two other objects—
M_COURSE_HDR and R_COURSE. M_COURSE_HDR is a frame that contains the header
objects, whereas R_COURSE is a repeating frame that contains the actual fields of each
record. R_COURSE is composed of three other objects:

F_ADDITIONAL_FEES	A field containing the value of Additional_Fees
M_COURSE_EXP	A frame that holds some other fields
M_COURSE_EXP1	Another frame that holds the re2maining fields that were specified for query Q_COURSE

Figure 15.7.

Changing a column label in the Data/ Selection tab folder.

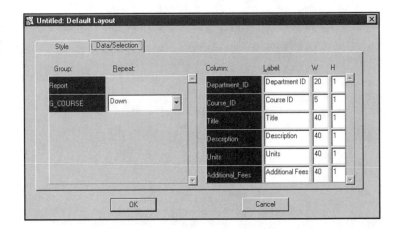

Figure 15.8.

Default layout generated for the report.

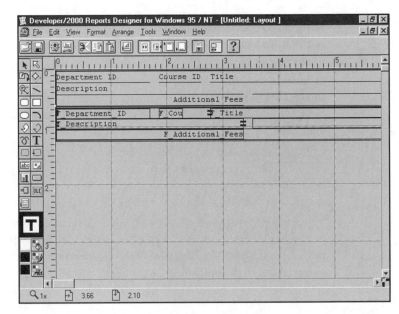

Figure 15.9.

Default layout hierarchy displayed by Object Navigator.

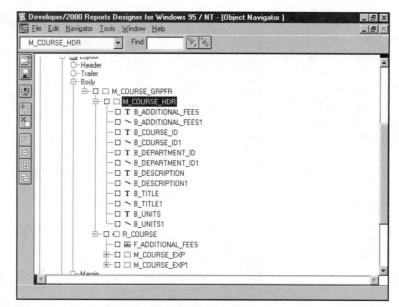

6. You wouldn't use this default layout without modifying it. For this report, you don't really need M_COURSE_EXP or M_COURSE_EXP1. So, using the Object Navigator, highlight each frame and press the Delete key.

7. Object Navigator asks you to confirm that you really want to delete the frame. Click Yes. As shown in Figure 15.10, the fields contained within M_COURSE_EXP and M_COURSE_EXP1 should now be directly beneath R_COURSE.

The next task is to reformat the layout. Follow these steps:

1. Return to the layout window by selecting Window | Untitled: Layout from the menu.

2. First, delete the lines in the header frame; you can distinguish the column headings from the report body by using a bold font.

3. Select each line and press the Delete key; be sure that you've selected a line and not a header.

4. Now, resize each column heading by selecting it and holding down the left mouse button until it's the proper size.

Figure 15.10.

Default layout hierarchy displayed by Object Navigator after deleting M_COURSE_EXP *and* M_COURSE_EXP1 *frames.*

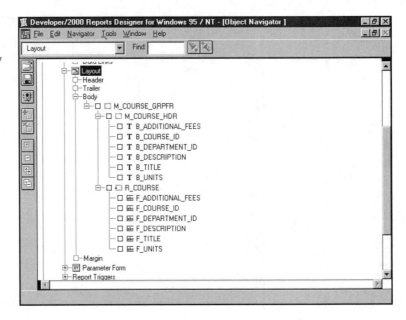

The next task is to resize all three frames so that there is a half-inch margin on both the right and left sides. Also, you'll want to reposition the column headings.

1. Resize the fields and place them beneath the column headings.

2. A few of the column headings are too long. For example, you can shorten Department ID to Dept by selecting the heading, clicking the text button on the toolbar (the large T) and clicking the heading once more. You can then shorten the column heading.

3. When you're done, the layout should look like that shown in Figure 15.11.

The layout appearance is still lacking. First, change all the column headings to a different font by following these steps:

1. Select all the column headings by holding down Shift as you select each one with the mouse.

2. Select Format | Font from the menu.

3. Choose MS Sans Serif, Bold, and 12 pt, and then click OK.

4. Repeat step 3 for each of the fields, but choose Normal instead of Bold.

5. Because the font has changed, you may need to resize some of the fields so that all the characters are visible.

6. You'll also want to change the format mask for the field that displays Additional_Fees. By default, no dollar sign is displayed. Double-click the field labeled F_ADDITIONAL_FEES.

7. In the Format Mask field, select $NNN,NN0 from the drop-down list and click OK.

Figure 15.11.
Layout after repositioning and resizing the objects.

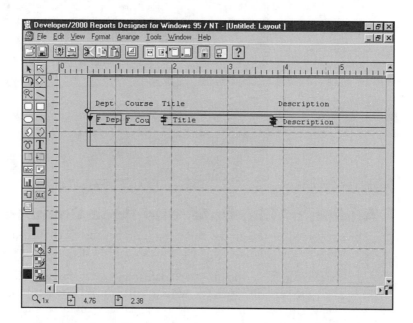

Sizing and Aligning Objects

You can make the column headings and fields the same height by increasing the height of one of them so that all of the characters are completely visible.

1. Select the other objects that you want to have the same height, and select Arrange | Size Objects from the menu.

2. Set the Width radio button to None and the Height radio button to Largest.

3. Click OK. Your layout should look fairly similar to what is shown in Figure 15.12.

Figure 15.12.

Layout after reformatting the objects.

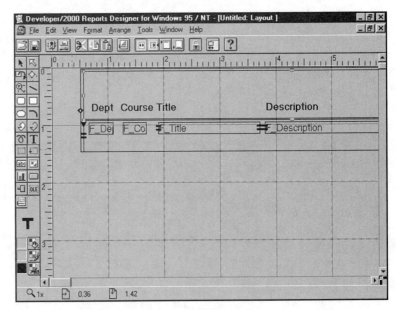

Adding a Title, Date, and Page Count to the Report

Before you add a title to the report, be sure that there's enough space above the column headings for the title, date, and page count. To add the title, follow these steps:

1. Select the Text Tool from the toolbar and, while holding the left mouse button, drag the area in which you want to enter the title—**FLUGLE COLLEGE Course Catalog**. Between FLUGLE COLLEGE and Course Catalog, press the Enter key so that FLUGLE COLLEGE appears above Course Catalog.

2. To center the text in the box, select Format | Alignment | Center from the menu.

3. Format the title so that FLUGLE COLLEGE is MS Sans Serif, Bold, 14 points and Course College is MS Sans Serif, Bold, 12 points.

To add the current date to the report, follow these steps:

1. Select the Field Tool from the toolbar and, while holding the left mouse button, drag the area in which you want the date to appear.

2. Double-click the field, causing a window to be displayed.

3. Change the name of the field from F_1 to **F_CURRENT_DATE**.

4. In the drop-down list labeled Source, select &Current Date.

5. In the Format Mask, select Month DD, YYYY from the formats in the drop-down list (see Figure 15.13).

6. Also, set the font for the date to MS Sans Serif, Bold, 10 points.

7. Click OK for these settings to be used for the field.

15

Figure 15.13.

Specifying the date for the report.

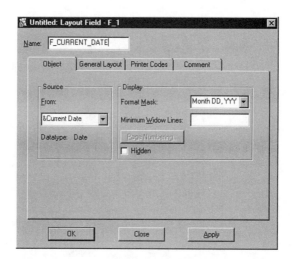

To add the page number to the report, follow these steps:

1. Select the Field Tool from the toolbar and, while holding the left mouse button, drag the area in which you want the page number to appear.

2. Double-click the field, and a window labeled "Course: Layout Field - F_1" will be displayed.

3. Change the name of the field from F_1 to **F_PAGE**.

4. In the drop-down list labeled Source, select &Physical Page Number.

5. In the Format Mask, enter **NNN**.

6. Also, set the font for the page number to MS Sans Serif, Bold, 10 points. At this point, your report layout should look very similar to that shown in Figure 15.14.

7. Click OK for these settings to be used for the field.

Testing the Report

It's time to test the report.

1. Click the green light on the horizontal toolbar. You should see a window titled Runtime Parameter Form (see Figure 15.15).

2. By default, the Destination Type for the report is set to Screen.

3. Click Run Report. You will see a window—Report Progress—that displays the activity that is occurring on both the client and the server. After a short time, you should see the first page of the report as shown in Figure 15.16.

4. Click Close when you are finished reviewing the report.

Figure 15.14.
Current report layout.

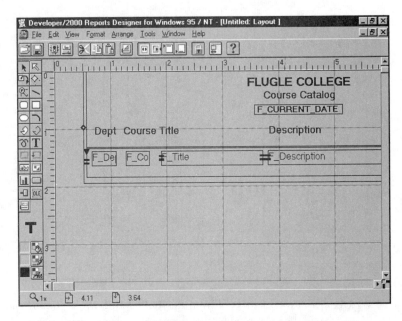

Figure 15.15.
The Runtime Parameter Form is displayed.

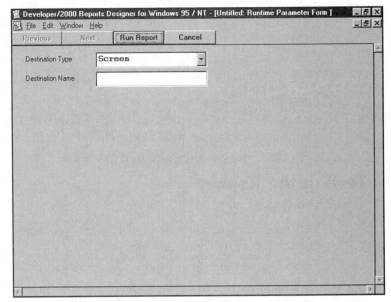

Figure 15.16.

First page of report is displayed.

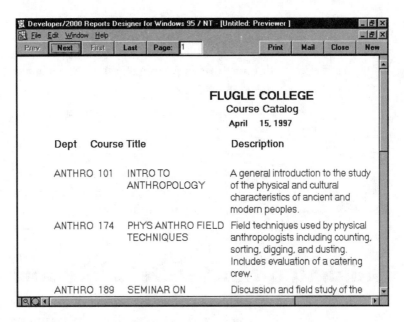

Printing a Report

There are several ways to print a report. By default, the Runtime Parameter Form sets the report destination to the screen; in other words, the default behavior is that the user will see a report preview. You can create your own parameter form in which the default destination is the printer. However, even in preview mode, you can print a report by clicking the Print button.

Saving the Report

This is a good time to save your report. Like the Forms Designer, the Reports Designer can use the Oracle database as a repository. To save a module to the database, you or your DBA need to install the database schema needed by Developer/2000. To learn more about this, read the Administrative Notes that are in the Developer/2000 Admin for Win95.

However, for the examples in this book, save the reports to a file. To set this as the default in the Reports Designer, select Tools | Tools Options from the menu. In the Object Access group, there is a field labeled Storage Type. By default, it's set to File/Database. Select File from the drop-down list and click OK.

To save this new report, follow these steps:

1. Select File | Save As from the menu.
2. Select the directory that you're using for storing your application-specific files.
3. Enter **Course** for the File Name.
4. Click OK. The Reports Designer will save a file named **Course.rdf** in the designated directory.

NOTE

The Reports Designer enables you to have multiple reports open simultaneously. You'll find this is a real convenience for copying objects from one report to another.

Building a Master-Detail Report

Another common type of report is the master-detail. An example of this is a report that lists each department and the instructors associated with the department. The Department table is the master record while the Instructor table is the detail record.

Creating a Data Model

To begin with, you need to create the data model for the report.

1. Invoke the Data Model Editor by either clicking the icon to the left of the Data Model node in the Object Navigator or by selecting Tools | Data Model Editor from the menu.
2. To create the master query, click the button labeled SQL on the toolbar on the left-hand side of the window.
3. Move the mouse to the main part of the window and hold down the left mouse button, drag the mouse to the lower right, and release the mouse button. Double-click query Q_1.
4. Change the name of the query to **Q_DEPARTMENT**.
5. Click the button labeled Tables/Columns. Another window is displayed, titled Table and Column Names, enabling you to choose the table and columns used for the query.
6. In the listbox labeled Database Objects, scroll down to the DEPARTMENT table and select it.
7. Select each of the columns in the Columns listbox (see Figure 15.17).

Figure 15.17.
Choosing the tables and columns for the master query.

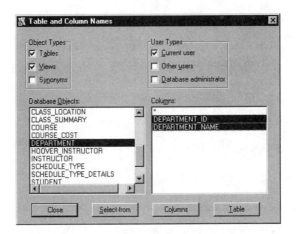

8. To use the selected table and columns in the query's SELECT statement, click SELECT-FROM and CLOSE. You'll see the SELECT statement that was constructed from the selected table and columns.

9. Rearrange the column names so that they are in the order that you want to see on the report: Department_ID and Department_Name.

10. Also, add an ORDER BY clause to the SELECT statement so that the rows will be ordered by Department_ID, as shown in Figure 15.18.

Figure 15.18.
Modifying the master query's SELECT statement.

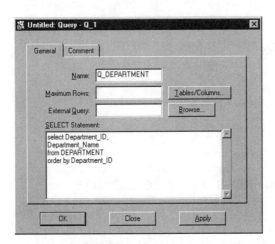

11. Click OK to return to the Data Model Editor. When you defined the SELECT statement for the query, the Reports Designer created a group for the master query—G_DEPARTMENT.

Now you can create the detail query by following these steps:

1. Click the SQL tool from the vertical toolbar. Initially, this query will be named Q_1 because you renamed the master query.

2. Double-click query Q_1.

3. Change the name of the query to **Q_INSTRUCTOR**.

4. Click the button labeled Tables/Columns.

5. In the Table and Column Names window, scroll down to the INSTRUCTOR table and select it.

6. Select each of the columns in the Columns listbox.

To use the selected table and columns in the query's SELECT statement, follow these steps:

1. Click SELECT-FROM and CLOSE.

2. Rearrange the column names in the SELECT statement so that they're in the order that you want to see on the report: Department_ID, Instructor_ID, Last_Name, First_Name, MI, Position.

   Even though Department_ID is already part of the master query, it's also needed in the detail query so that the two queries can be joined based on the common column.

3. Also, add an ORDER BY clause to the SELECT statement so that the rows will be ordered by Last_Name, First_Name, and MI, as shown in Listing 15.1.

4. Click OK to return to the Data Model Editor.

INPUT　**Listing 15.1. The detail query's SELECT statement.**

```
Select Department_ID, Instructor_ID,
Last_Name, First_Name, MI, Position
from Instructor
order by Last_Name, First_Name, MI;
```

When you defined the SELECT statement for the query, the Reports Designer created a group for the master query: G_INSTRUCTOR.

To join the master query to the detail query, select the data link tool from the vertical toolbar. Place the pointer over Q_DEPARTMENT, hold down the left-mouse button, drag the pointer over Q_INSTRUCTOR, and release the mouse button. The Data Model Editor should create a link between Q_DEPARTMENT and Q_INSTRUCTOR, using Department_ID (see Figure 15.19).

Figure 15.19.
Master query is linked to detail query.

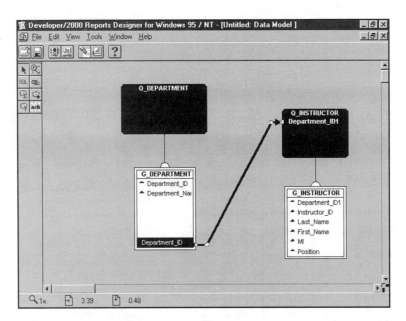

Specifying a Default Layout

Now that you've created the data model for the master-detail report, the next task is to specify the report layout.

1. Invoke the Default Layout dialog window by either clicking the green triangle on the horizontal toolbar or by selecting Tools | Default Layout from the menu.

2. In the Style tab folder, select the Master/Detail style (see Figure 15.20).

Figure 15.20.
Specifying Master/Detail report style.

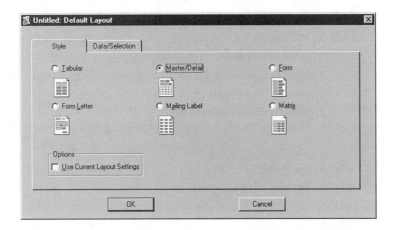

3. Select the Data/Selection tab folder. You can change a label in the Data/Selection tab folder. For example, you can reduce the width of a field or abbreviate its name, as shown in Figure 15.21.

4. Click OK to generate the default layout for the report.

Figure 15.21.

Modifying labels and field widths.

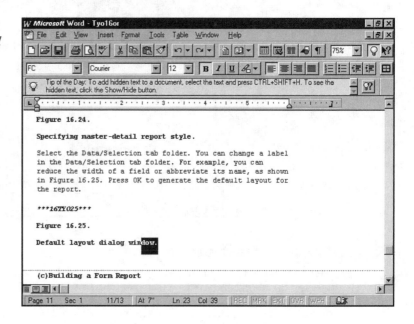

The resulting layout needs to be modified.

1. Using the Object Navigator, delete the detail column heading for Department ID.

2. Delete all the lines beneath the column headings.

3. In the Layout Editor, reposition all of the fields so that they're aligned with the column headings and with each other.

4. Change the fonts for all objects to MS Sans Serif, Normal, 12 points.

5. Change the column labels and headings to Bold. Figure 15.22 illustrates what the report layout should look like.

There's one more thing that needs to be changed. The detail frame—Q_INSTRUCTOR—contains Department_ID so that the detail query can be linked to the master query. But it would be redundant to display Department_ID in the detail frame because it's already displayed in the master frame.

1. To hide this field, double-click F_Department_ID1 in the detail frame. A window appears in which you can specify that the field should be hidden is displayed (see Figure 15.23).

2. Check the field labeled Hidden.

3. Click OK.

Figure 15.22.

Completed layout for master-detail report.

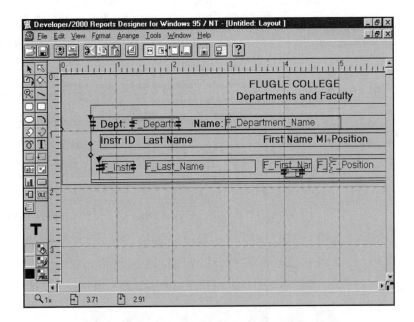

Figure 15.23.

Hiding the Department ID in the detail group.

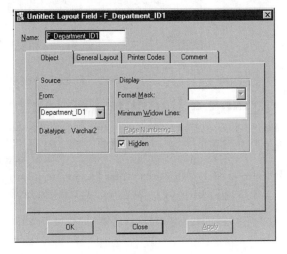

Testing the Report

This section walks you through testing the master-detail report.

1. Click the green light on the horizontal toolbar.

2. In the Runtime Parameter Form, click Run Report. The Report Progress window displays the activity that's occurring on both the client and the server. Shortly, you will see the first page of the report as shown in Figure 15.24.

3. Click Close when you're finished reviewing the report. If you like, you can save this report in the application directory as `Dept_Instructor.rdf`.

Figure 15.24.

The first page of Master/Detail report is displayed.

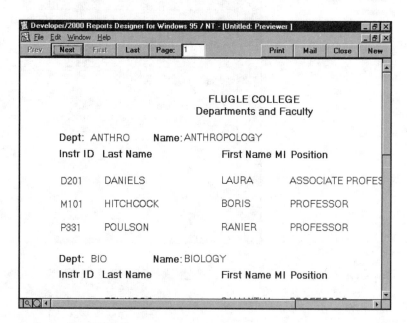

Generating a Runtime Version of a Report

To run a report from a forms application or from a shortcut on the Desktop, you need to generate a runtime version of the report—which is an REP file. While you have a report open in the Reports Designer, you can generate a runtime version of the report by pressing Ctrl+t or by selecting File | Administration | Generate from the menu. By default, the Reports Designer assumes that you want to use the same name for the REP file that you used for the RDF file.

Using a Format Trigger

There are many things that you can do to customize a report with Reports Designer. For example, you can specify a format trigger for a field so that the field's appearance depends on its contents. Let's explore an example using the master-detail report that you constructed.

Suppose you want the report to emphasize when an instructor is a professor by increasing the font of the Instructor ID field. To do this, double-click the field named F_Instructor_ID. In the window that is displayed, select the General Layout tab folder. In the lower-left corner of the General Layout tab folder, click the key labeled Edit. The Program Unit Editor is displayed; by default, the editor displays a function named F_Instructor_IDFormatTrigger. The layout field properties window will still be displayed. Reposition it so you can modify the function as shown in Figure 15.25.

Figure 15.25.

Specifying a format trigger for a layout field.

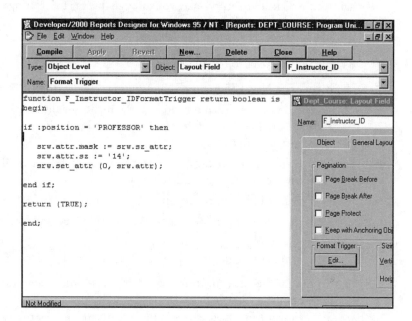

The function makes use of a built-in package named SRW, which is used to modify the format characteristics of the field associated with the format trigger. Specifically, the `if` statement checks to see if the current value for the `Position` field is `PROFESSOR`; if so, the three calls to SRW are executed. The first line identifies the format attribute that's being modified—`sz_attr`—which represents the field's font size. The second line sets the font size attribute to 14 points. Finally, the third line calls the set_attr function, which modifies the field's attributes by passing two arguments:

- ☐ 0, which indicates that the attributes apply to the current field
- ☐ srw.attr, which contains the attributes to be modified

The function returns a Boolean value. If it is true, the field is displayed on the report with whatever attributes were modified by the format trigger; if it's false, the field is not displayed on the report.

Creating a Shortcut to Run a Report

A shortcut can be a real convenience for a user who wants to be able to run a report with a single mouse click. This section takes you through the steps of creating a shortcut. Before you create the shortcut, you will need to generate the REP file from the RDF file as previously described.

To create the shortcut, follow these steps:

1. Right-click New | Shortcut on the Windows 95 desktop.
2. You need to enter the command-line arguments for the shortcut in the Create Shortcut window, but before you do, you need to look over a few arguments used by Reports Runtime:
   - ☐ userid identifies the username, password, and database alias, if any, to be used to connect to the database.
   - ☐ report identifies the report that you want to run.
   - ☐ paramform determines whether the Runtime Parameter Form should be displayed.
   - ☐ destype specifies the report destination: screen, printer, file, or mail.
3. To run the Department Instructors report at runtime, enter the following line in the Command Line field:

   ```
   c:\Orawin95\bin\r25run32 report=c:\Tyo\Dept_Instructor paramform=no
   ➥destype=screen
   ```
4. Click Next.
5. Give the shortcut a name like **Report - Department with Instructors**.
6. Click Finish.

You should see the new shortcut on your desktop. Try running the shortcut. You will be prompted for your username, password, and database. If you don't want the user to be prompted for these values, modify the shortcut in the following way:

```
c:\Orawin95\bin\r25run32 userid=flugle/flugle
➥report=c:\Tyo\Dept_Instructor paramform=no destype=screen
```

> **NOTE**
>
> One disadvantage to this shortcut is that the password is contained within the shortcut and could be viewed by others.

Invoking a Report from an Oracle Form

As discussed, Developer/2000 is an integrated application development environment. In this section, you'll learn how to run a report from a forms application. As an example, you'll see how modify your menu, MAINMENU, to run the Course Catalog report.

To begin, use the Forms Designer to open MAINMENU. Use the Object Navigator to look at the Course_Catalog_Report item; it's located in the REPORTS menu. Display the Properties window for Course_Catalog_Report as shown in Figure 15.26.

Figure 15.26.

Properties of Course_Catalog_Report menu item.

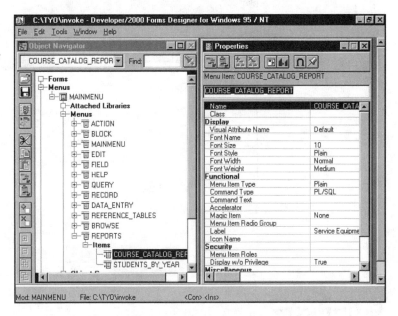

Next, navigate to the Command Text property and click More at the top of the window. A PL/SQL Editor window is displayed. As shown in Figure 15.31, use the Run_Product built-in procedure to invoke Oracle reports. The Run_Product procedure requires seven arguments:

☐ Product to run: Reports

☐ Object to be run: Course

☐ Mode that is either synchronous (meaning that the forms application will wait until the invoked product has completed before continuing) or asynchronous (meaning that the forms application will continue to be active while the invoked product performs its task): Synchronous

☐ Execution mode, either batch or runtime: Runtime

☐ Object location, either filesystem or database: filesystem

☐ Parameter list, if any: null, because you aren't using any parameters

☐ Name of chart item to display an Oracle Graphics chart: null, because it isn't applicable

Once you've entered the line shown in Figure 15.27, click Compile and Close. Save and generate the menu and test it to verify that it works correctly.

Figure 15.27.

Using Run_Product to invoke another Developer/2000 program from a menu item.

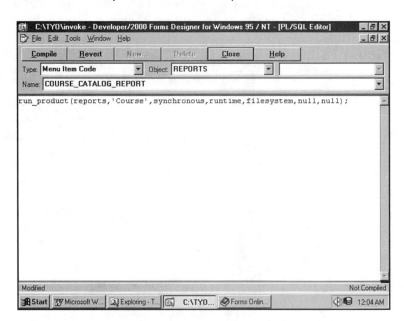

Summary

Here are the important points covered in this lesson:

☐ Oracle Reports, a part of Developer/2000, consists of several programs including Reports Designer and Reports Runtime.

☐ You can use the Reports Designer to develop a wide range of reports from simple to complex. The Reports Designer can save a report as a binary file known as an RDF file.

15

☐ The Reports Designer uses an Object Navigator that displays a report's components in a hierarchical structure.

☐ At the highest level, a report is defined by a data model, a layout, a parameter form, and report triggers. At a minimum, a report contains a data model and a layout.

☐ The Reports Designer contains specialized editors for defining a report's components. These editors include the Data Model Editor and the Layout Editor.

☐ A data model consists of one or more queries that retrieve the records that constitute the report. Using the Data Model editor, you can link queries based on a common column.

☐ You use the Layout Editor to construct the appearance of a report. The layout includes four components: the header, footer, body, and margin. Generally, a report contains the layout for the body.

What Comes Next?

On Day 16, "Developer/2000: Using Oracle Graphics and Procedure Builder," you will learn about the two other components of Developer/2000: Oracle Graphics and Procedure Builder. You'll learn how to create a chart from the contents of a table. You'll also see how Procedure Builder can help you create and maintain PL/SQL modules in an Oracle database.

Q&A

Q Is it possible to record the execution of a report?

A Yes. Although it wasn't discussed in this lesson, you can define a report trigger that's executed once when the report is run. The report trigger could insert a row into a table that recorded the name of the report, who requested it, and when it was executed. You also could save other details about the report.

Q Can you prevent a user from printing a report after hours?

A Yes. Again, you can create a report trigger that looks at the day of the week or time of day and determines if the report should be printed at that time.

Q Is it feasible for more than one user to execute the same report at the same time?

A Yes. Unless the report has triggers that modify the data in some unusual way, multiple users can run the same report simultaneously without any adverse outcome.

Workshop

The purpose of the Workshop is to allow you to test your knowledge of the material discussed in the lesson. See if you can correctly answer the questions in the quiz and complete the exercise before you continue with tomorrow's lesson.

Quiz

1. True or false? You can store your RDF files in a source code control system such as PVCS.

2. Name the four elements of a report layout.

3. True or false? A report cannot have more that two queries linked together.

Exercise

Create a master-detail report that lists each classroom and the classes that are scheduled for that room, regardless of meeting time (for example, all of the classes that are scheduled to use a particular room).

Day 16

Developer/2000: Using Oracle Graphics and Procedure Builder

In the previous four lessons, you worked with Oracle Forms and Reports to develop pieces of an application. In this lesson, you work with the other two components of Developer/2000: Oracle Graphics and Procedure Builder.

The Role of Oracle Graphics

Oracle Graphics provides a method for generating charts whose values are derived from the contents of one or more tables in an Oracle database. Remember that old saying, "A picture is worth a thousand words?" The purpose of Oracle Graphics is to streamline the graphical presentation of the contents of a database so that trends can be quickly identified, large quantities of data summarized, and comparisons made between sets of data.

The Elements of Oracle Graphics

Oracle Graphics uses the same paradigm as Forms and Reports. A tool named Graphics Designer is used to design a chart and generate a runtime version of the chart. Another program named Graphics Runtime runs the generated chart. As you will see in this lesson, you can add a menu item to a Forms menu that will run a chart.

Like Forms and Reports, Oracle Graphics also uses an Object Navigator to create, modify, and view the elements of a chart. Oracle Graphics uses the term *display* to refer to a graphics object. The object nodes for a display are as follows:

- [ ] Layout
- [ ] Template
- [ ] Query
- [ ] Parameter
- [ ] Sound
- [ ] Timer
- [ ] Program Unit
- [ ] Attached Library

At a minimum, a chart will include a query and a layout.

Building a Chart with the Graphics Designer

Let's start off using Graphics Designer by designing a pie chart based on a single table. You will build a chart that will present the breakdown of students based on year. To invoke the Graphics Designer, select Oracle Designer for Win95 | Graphics Designer from the Start menu. The Graphics Designer program will first display the Object Navigator (see Figure 16.1).

Notice that a chart titled UNTITLED is displayed in the Object Navigator. Before going any further, you need to connect to the Oracle database.

Connecting to an Oracle Database

To connect Graphics Designer to an Oracle database, select File | Connect from the menu. A dialog box will appear, prompting you for the username, password, and database to use for establishing an Oracle database connection. Connect to the Oracle database; refer to Day 12, "Developer/2000: Introduction to Oracle Forms," for details on how to do this with Developer/2000.

Figure 16.1.
Graphics Designer first displays Object Navigator.

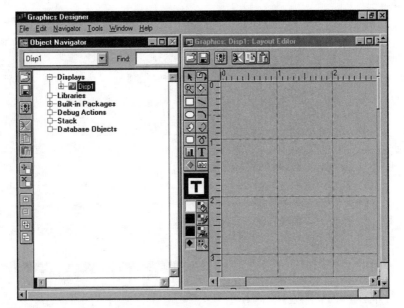

Creating a New Chart

To create a new chart, follow these steps:

1. Select Window | Graphics: Disp1: Layout Editor from the menu. Notice that the menu changes.

2. Select Chart | Create Chart from the menu—the Chart Genie will appear.

3. In the Name field, change the name of the query from `query0` to `Student_Query`.

4. You want to construct a pie chart that shows the relative percentage of students in a given year. To do this, you need to use the `GROUP BY` clause in the `SELECT` statement (see Figure 16.2). In the SQL Statement list box, enter

```
select Year, Count(*)
from Student
group by Year;
```

Choosing the Chart Type

Next, the Chart Genie will display a window in which you specify the Chart Properties.

1. In the Name field, enter `Students_by_Year`.

2. In the Title field, enter `Students by Year`.

3. In the Type selection, select the pie chart. Another grouping, labeled Subtype, will be displayed; select the 3D pie chart. Figure 16.3 shows what the tabbed dialog should look like.

4. Click OK.

Figure 16.2.

Specifying the query in the Chart Genie.

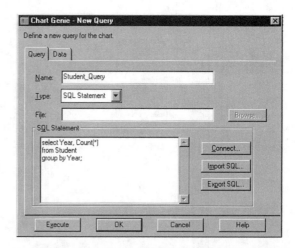

Figure 16.3.

Specifying the Chart Properties in the Chart Genie.

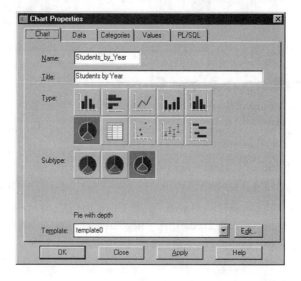

The layout for the 3D pie chart will appear, per your specifications (see Figure 16.4). However, realize that this is only the initial layout. Let's look at some of the changes you might want to add.

16

Figure 16.4.
Layout of the pie chart.

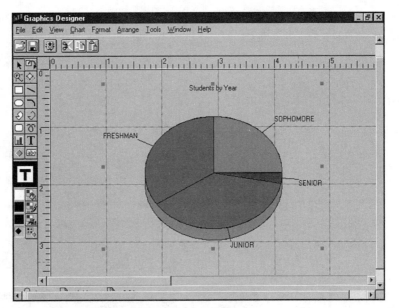

Customizing the Chart Layout

As you can see in Figure 16.5, there are no percentage labels for the pie segments. To add them, follow these steps:

1. Select the center of the pie, right-click, and select Frame from the menu. A window labeled Frame Properties will appear.
2. Select the Pie Frame tab folder.
3. Enable the checkbox labeled Show Percent Values, as shown in Figure 16.5.
4. Click OK.

You should now see the percent values displayed in the layout. Let's increase the size of the title.

1. Select the title with the mouse.
2. Select Format | Font from the menu.
3. Set the title to MS San Serif, Bold, 12 points (see Figure 16.6).

Figure 16.5.

*Changing the frame
properties to display
percent values.*

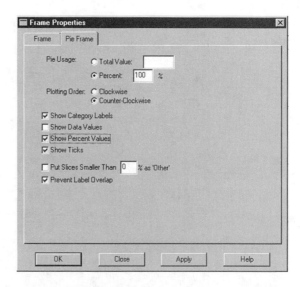

Figure 16.6.

*Formatting the chart
title.*

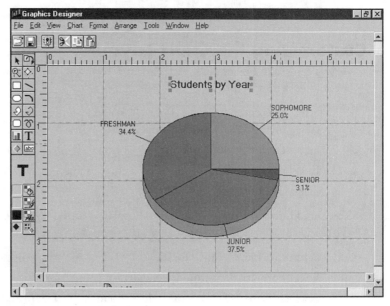

Saving the Chart

To save the pie chart, select File | Save As | File System from the menu. A dialog window will
prompt you for the name of the file; enter **Students_by_Year**. The Graphics Designer saves
a file with an extension of .ogd which is shorthand for Oracle Graphics Designer. However,
to create a graph with Graphics Runtime, you must generate an .ogr file from the equivalent

.ogd file (.ogr is shorthand for Oracle Graphics Runtime). To do this, select File | Administration | Generate | File System from the menu; alternatively, press Alt+t. By default, the Save As dialog window will give the .ogr file the same filename as the .ogd file. Click OK so that the Graphics Designer will save the file as Students_by_Year.ogr. You can exit the Graphics Designer—the next step is to create a shortcut to run the chart with Graphics Runtime.

TIP

Be sure to save your graphics files in a directory that isn't part of the Oracle directory tree (beneath c:\Orawin95). Also, remember to use the Registry Editor to add that directory to GRAPHICS25_PATH, or Graphics Runtime won't be able to open your graphics files.

Creating a Shortcut to Run a Chart

Users are always happy if you can make it simple for them to achieve the desired results. Creating a Windows shortcut is one way to do this. It may not be as seamless as an integrated Developer/2000 application, but it is a "cheap and dirty" way to help a user.

Before you create the shortcut, you should set a preference in Graphics Runtime so that it tries to log on to the database at startup. This will cause Graphics Runtime to prompt you for your username, password, and database if you haven't supplied those on the command line. To do this, follow these steps:

1. Invoke Graphics Runtime by selecting Start | Developer/2000 for Win95 | Graphics Runtime.

2. Select Edit | Tools Options from the menu.

3. Enable the checkbox labeled Logon at Startup.

4. Click Save and OK.

5. Exit the program.

To create the shortcut, do this:

1. Right-click New | Shortcut on the Windows95 desktop. The Create Shortcut window appears.

2. To run the Students by Year chart at runtime, enter the following line in Command Line field:

   ```
   c:\Orawin95\bin\g25run32 openfile=c:\Tyo\Students_by_Year.ogr
   ```

3. Click Next.

4. Give the shortcut a name like Chart - Students by Year.

5. Click Finish.

You should see the new shortcut on your desktop. Double-click the shortcut. You will be prompted for your username, password, and database. If you don't want the user to be prompted for these values, modify the shortcut in this way:

```
c:\Orawin95\bin\g25run32 openfile=c:\Tyo\Students_by_Year.ogr
↪userid=flugle/flugle
```

NOTE One disadvantage to this shortcut is that the password is contained within the shortcut and could be viewed by others.

The Role of Procedure Builder in the Application Development Process

The last component of Developer/2000 to discuss is Procedure Builder. Procedure Builder is designed to ease the initial development and maintenance of PL/SQL code contained on both the client and the server.

NOTE Procedure Builder doesn't support the use of PL/SQL Version 2 features such as PL/SQL tables in client-side PL/SQL modules used by Oracle Forms, Reports, or Graphics.

Elements of Procedure Builder

Procedure Builder contains several tools:

- ☐ A Program Unit Editor for creating, modifying, and deleting program units such as procedures and functions that are used in libraries attached to Oracle Forms applications
- ☐ A PL/SQL Interpreter that enables you to author and test a block of PL/SQL code
- ☐ A Stored Program Unit Editor that supports the creation and maintenance of a package, procedure, or function stored in an Oracle database to which Procedure Builder is connected
- ☐ A Database Trigger Editor for creating and maintaining database triggers

16

To invoke Procedure Builder, select Start | Programs | Developer/2000 for Win95 | Procedure Builder. Figure 16.7 shows the initial window displayed by Procedure Builder. Notice that Procedure Builder, like the other components of Developer/2000, supplies an Object Navigator for selecting PL/SQL objects and modifying their properties.

Figure 16.7.

Initial window displayed by Procedure Builder.

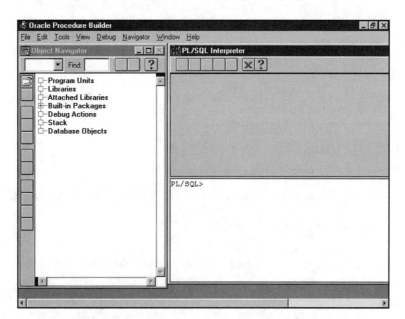

NOTE

Like the other components of Developer/2000, Procedure Builder also uses the Object Navigator. Please refer to the lesson on Day 12 for details on using the Object Navigator.

Before you start using these Procedure Builder tools, you'll want to connect to an Oracle database.

Connecting to an Oracle Database

Connect Procedure Builder to an Oracle database using the method shown in Day 12.

Using the Procedure Builder's Object Navigator

The Object Navigator for Procedure Builder functions in the same way as in the other components of Developer/2000. It displays seven object nodes:

- ☐ Program Units
- ☐ Libraries
- ☐ Attached Libraries
- ☐ Built-in Packages
- ☐ Debug Actions
- ☐ Stack
- ☐ Database Objects

In this lesson, you'll focus on Program Units and Database Objects.

Program Unit Editor

You can use the Program Unit Editor to view, create, modify, and delete packages, procedures, and functions. You can invoke the Program Unit Editor by selecting Tools | Stored Program Unit Editor from the menu. For example, to create a new function, click New; a window will appear, prompting you for the name and type of the program unit (see Figure 16.8). After you click OK, the Program Unit Editor creates a template for the function, as shown in Figure 16.9).

PL/SQL Interpreter

You can invoke the PL/SQL Interpreter by selecting Tools | PL/SQL Interpreter from the menu. The PL/SQL Interpreter operates in two states:

- ☐ Modeless, meaning that you have invoked the PL/SQL Interpreter directly. In this state, you provide input via a command line. The input could be the lines of an anonymous PL/SQL block. Figure 16.10 displays an example of an anonymous PL/SQL block that was entered manually at the command line and executed by the PL/SQL Interpreter.
- ☐ Modal, meaning that the PL/SQL Interpreter is invoked at breakpoints that you have set in PL/SQL modules.

Figure 16.8.

Creating a new function with the Program Unit Editor.

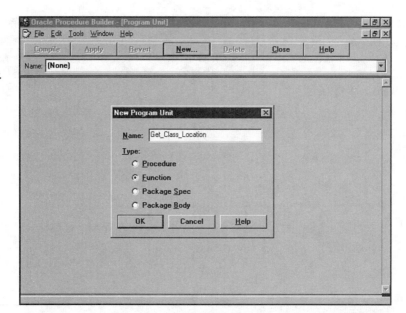

Figure 16.9.

Function template created by the Program Unit Editor.

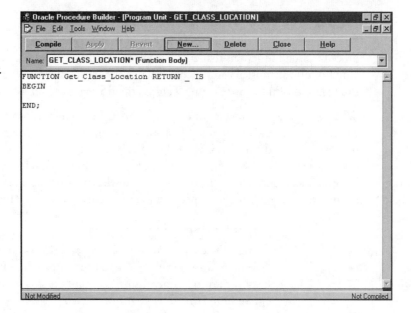

Figure 16.10.

Using the PL/SQL Interpreter to enter and execute an anonymous block.

```
Oracle Procedure Builder - [PL/SQL Interpreter]                    _ 8 X
  File  Edit  Tools  View  Debug  Navigator  Window  Help          _ 8 X

PL/SQL> declare
     +> i number := 0;
     +>
     +> begin
     +>
     +> while i <= 10 loop
     +>   text_io.put_line('i: ' || to_char(i));
     +>   i := i + 1;
     +> end loop;
     +> end;
i: 0
i: 1
i: 2
i: 3
i: 4
i: 5
i: 6
i: 7
i: 8
i: 9
i: 10
PL/SQL>
```

Stored Program Unit Editor

You can use the Stored Program Unit Editor to view, create, modify, and delete packages, procedures, and functions that are stored in an Oracle database. To use the Stored Program Unit Editor, you must already be connected to an Oracle database. You can invoke the Stored Program Unit Editor by selecting Tools | Stored Program Unit Editor from the menu.

When the editor window appears, you'll notice that there are two fields at the top of the window: Owner and Name. The Owner text box contains a dropdown list of the Oracle users that exist in the database to which Procedure Builder is connected. The Name text box contains a list of stored program units that are owned by the Oracle user displayed in Owner. For example, Figure 16.11 illustrates how you select a particular stored program unit in the Name text box after you have specified the Oracle user, which is flugle.

NOTE

> Not every Oracle user owns packages, procedures, and functions; some Oracle users won't own any. In that case, Procedure Builder will display (None) in Name. Also, your ability to create and modify stored program units owned by your own Oracle account or others will depend on the system and object privileges possessed by your Oracle account.

16

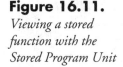

Figure 16.11.

Viewing a stored function with the Stored Program Unit Editor.

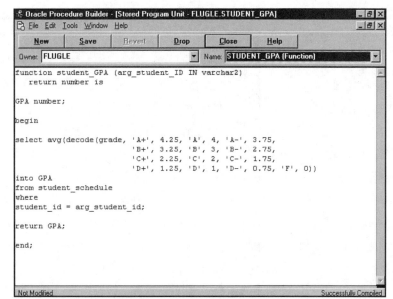

Database Trigger Editor

There are two ways to invoke the Database Trigger Editor: you can use the Object Navigator to view or modify an existing database trigger, or you can select Tools | Database Trigger Editor from the menu.

To use the Object Navigator to view or modify an existing database trigger, expand the Database Objects node; the Object Navigator will display a list of Oracle accounts. If you select an Oracle account and expand it, you will see another level of nodes, including Stored Program Units, Libraries, Tables, and Views (see Figure 16.12).

If you expand the Tables node, a list of the tables owned by the selected Oracle account will appear. If you select a table and expand the node, you will see two nodes beneath the table: Triggers and Columns. Expand the Triggers node and double-click the icon to the left of a specific trigger.

Figure 16.12.
Viewing the nodes
belonging to the
`flugle` *Oracle*
account.

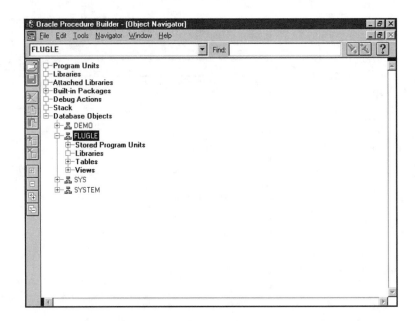

Viewing and Editing a Stored Program Unit

Let's look at an example of how you view or modify a stored program unit. Suppose you want to modify the `Student_GPA` stored function which is owned by the `flugle` Oracle account. As you may recall, the `Student_GPA` function is used to translate the letter grades that a student has received—A, B, C, and so on—and return a numeric grade point average. From the Object Navigator, expand the Database Objects node and also expand the Flugle node. Select the Student_GPA node (see Figure 16.13).

Double-click the icon to the left of the Student_GPA node. You should now see the PL/SQL code for the `Student_GPA` function, displayed by the Stored Program Unit Editor (see Figure 16.14).

Let's look at some of the user interface elements of the Stored Program Unit Editor. At the top of the window, there are two poplists: Owner and Name. If you click on Owner, the poplist will display a list of all the Oracle accounts that exist in the database to which Procedure Builder is connected, whether or not that account owns any stored program units (see Figure 16.15). Similarly, the Name poplist will display a list of all of the stored program units—package specifications, package bodies, procedures, and functions—that are owned by the Oracle account shown in the Owner field (see Figure 16.16).

16

Figure 16.13.

Selecting a stored program unit with the Object Navigator.

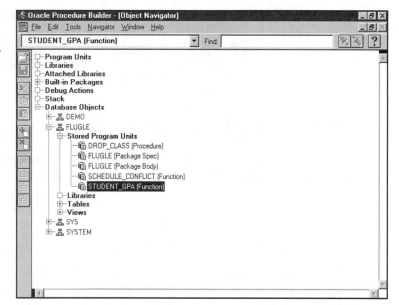

16

Figure 16.14.

Viewing a stored function with the Stored Program Unit Editor.

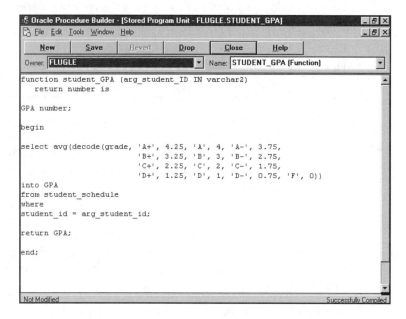

Figure 16.15.

Owner poplist displays all Oracle accounts.

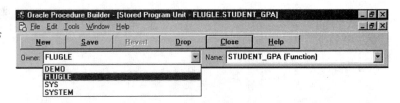

Figure 16.16.

Name poplist displays all stored program units owned by the Oracle account in Owner.

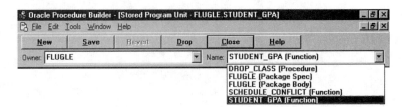

Also, there are six buttons at the top of the window:

New   Creates a new program unit.

Save   Saves any changes that have been made to a program unit.

Revert   Undoes any changes that have been made to a program unit.

Drop   Drops the current program unit.

Close   Closes the Stored Program Unit Editor.

Help   Displays online help for the Stored Program Unit Editor.

NOTE

The Revert button will not be enabled until you actually make a change to a program unit. And if you have made changes and click Close, you will be prompted by the Stored Program Unit Editor either to apply the changes to the program unit or to revert to the original version of the program unit.

If you add a line to the Student_GPA function that isn't valid and click Save, the Stored Program Unit Editor will try to compile the function and display any errors in the bottom of the window (see Figure 16.17). If you look at the line after begin, you'll see an invalid statement: not a valid line.

Let's remove the offending line. In addition, let's modify the function by removing F grades from the calculation of a GPA (see Listing 16.1). Click Save to compile the changes and save the function. Click Close to exit the Stored Program Unit Editor.

16

Figure 16.17.

*Stored Program
Unit Editor displays
PL/SQL errors.*

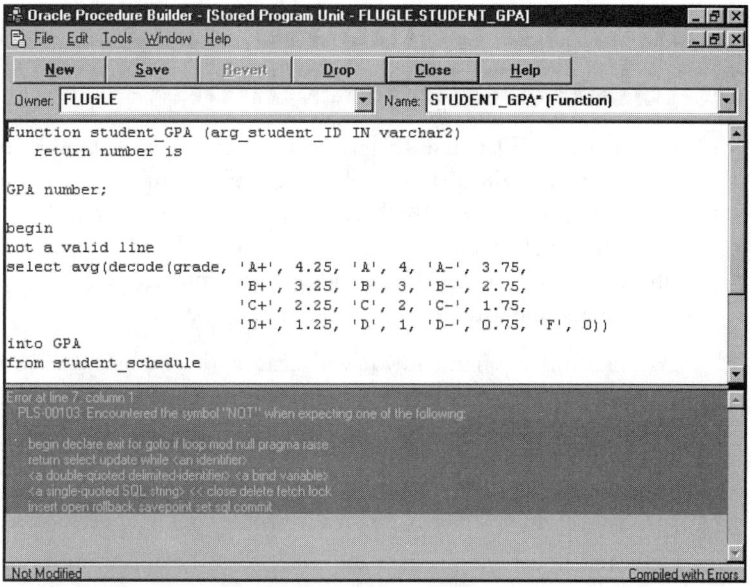

16

INPUT   **Listing 16.1. Modifying a stored function.**

```
function student_GPA (arg_student_ID IN varchar2)
    return number is

GPA number;

begin

select avg(decode(grade, 'A+', 4.25, 'A', 4, 'A-', 3.75,
                         'B+', 3.25, 'B', 3, 'B-', 2.75,
                         'C+', 2.25, 'C', 2, 'C-', 1.75,
                         'D+', 1.25, 'D', 1, 'D-', 0.75))
into GPA
from student_schedule
where
student_id = arg_student_id;

return GPA;

end;
```

Creating a Database Trigger with the Database Trigger Editor

You can use the Database Trigger Editor to create, view, modify, or drop a database trigger. Let's work through an example. Suppose that a requirement of the Flugle College Information System is that a journal record be kept of every grade that is assigned to a student, including any changes that are made to an assigned grade. As you recall, the Student_Schedule table contains each class that a student has completed, including the grade that the student received and the date that the grade was assigned.

To satisfy this requirement, you will create another table named Student_Schedule_Journal that contains all the columns of the Student_Schedule table and three additional columns:

Operation   A single letter that corresponds to the DML operation: I for insert, U for update, and D for delete

Changed_by   The name of the Oracle user who performed the operation

Changed_date   The date and time when the operation was performed

You will use the Database Trigger Editor to create a database trigger on the Student_Schedule table that will insert a record into the Student_Schedule_Journal table that records all information about the row in the Student_Schedule table that is being either inserted, updated, or deleted.

1. Invoke the Database Trigger Editor by selecting Tools | Database Trigger Editor from the menu.
2. Select FLUGLE from the poplist under the Table Owner label (see Figure 16.19).
3. Select STUDENT_SCHEDULE from the poplist under the Table label (see Figure 16.18).
4. Click New to create a database trigger. By default, this trigger has been given a name that you'll want to change.
5. In the upper-right corner of the window, beneath the Name field, change the name of the trigger to AIUD_STUDENT_SCHEDULE, which is shorthand notation to signify that this trigger is an *After Insert Update Delete* trigger for the Student_Schedule table.
6. Set the Triggering radio button to After.
7. In the Statement group, check all three checkboxes, UPDATE, INSERT, and DELETE.
8. Check the checkbox labeled For Each Row.

Figure 16.19 illustrates what you should see in the Database Trigger Editor when you are finished.

Figure 16.18.

Preparing to create a database trigger on the Student_Schedule table.

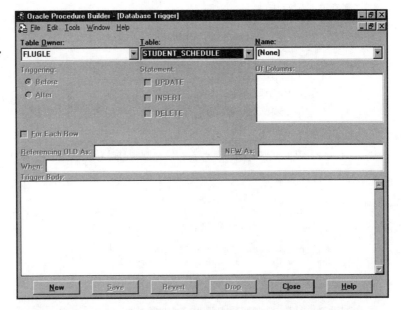

Figure 16.19.

Setting the options for the new database trigger.

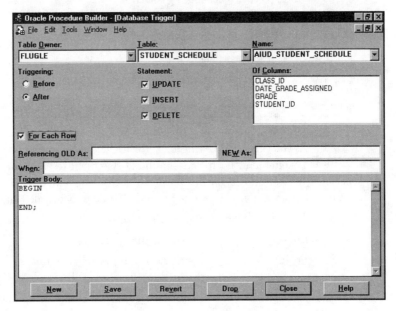

Type Listing 16.2 into the list box labeled Trigger Body, and click Save to compile and save the trigger.

INPUT **Listing 16.2. PL/SQL block for the database trigger body.**

```
begin

if inserting then

  insert into student_schedule_journal
  (operation, student_ID, Class_ID, Grade, Date_Grade_Assigned,
   Changed_By, Changed_Date)
  values
  ('I', :new.Student_ID, :new.Class_ID, :new.Grade,
   :new.Date_Grade_Assigned, user, sysdate);

elsif updating then

  insert into student_schedule_journal
  (operation, student_ID, Class_ID, Grade, Date_Grade_Assigned,
   Changed_By, Changed_Date)
  values
  ('U', :new.Student_ID, :new.Class_ID, :new.Grade,
   :new.Date_Grade_Assigned, user, sysdate);

elsif deleting then

  insert into student_schedule_journal
  (operation, student_ID, Class_ID, Grade, Date_Grade_Assigned,
   Changed_By, Changed_Date)
  values
  ('I', :new.Student_ID, :new.Class_ID, :new.Grade,
   :new.Date_Grade_Assigned, user, sysdate);

end if;

end;
```

ANALYSIS As you can see in Listing 16.2, the trigger body consists of a PL/SQL block with an IF statement. Each clause in the IF statement tests for the operation that is being performed. For instance, the first portion of the IF statement tests to see if the triggering event is an INSERT; if so, a row is inserted into the Student_Schedule_Journal with the following values. Click Close to exit the Database Trigger Editor.

Operation	I, because the operation is an INSERT
Student_ID	:new.Student_ID, which contains the value for Student_ID that is being inserted in the Student_Schedule table
Class_ID	:new.Class_ID, which contains the value for Class_ID that is being inserted in the Student_Schedule table
Grade	:new.Grade, which contains the value for Grade that is being inserted in the Student_Schedule table

16

Date_Grade_Assigned	:new.Date_Grade_Assigned, which contains the value for Date_Grade_Assigned that is being inserted in the Student_Schedule table
Changed_By	USER, a built-in function that returns the name of the Oracle user that is executing the statement
Changed_Date	SYSDATE, a built-in function that returns the current date and time

Testing the New Database Trigger

Let's test the trigger. You can do this by using either SQL*Plus or SQL Worksheet.

1. Connect to the `flugle` account.

2. To begin with, verify that the Student_Schedule_Journal table is empty (see Figure 16.20).

Figure 16.20.

Student_Schedule_Journal table is empty.

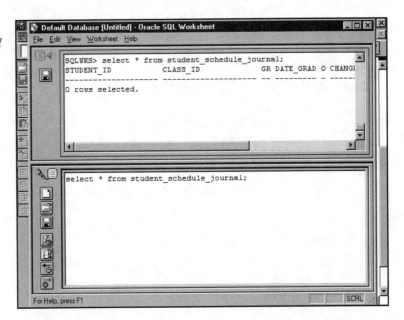

3. Retrieve all records from the Student_Schedule table in which the Student_ID is 10231324 (who happens to be Anna Anastatia). As you can see in Figure 16.21, there is only one class listed: 109100 (which happens to be Biology 101).

4. Anna worked hard this semester—she deserves an A in the class. To assign her an A in the course, use an UPDATE statement to set the value of GRADE to an A (see Listing 16.3).

Figure 16.21.

Viewing records in the Student_Schedule table.

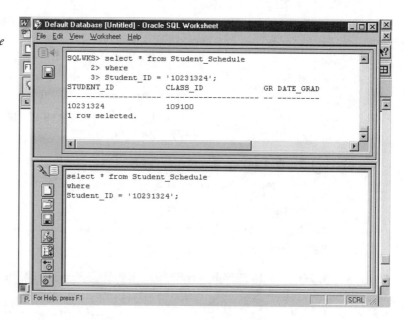

INPUT   **Listing 16.3. Assigning a grade with an UPDATE statement.**

```
update Student_Schedule
set
Grade = 'A',
Date_Grade_Assigned = sysdate
where
Student_ID = '10231324' and
Class_ID = '109100';
```

As shown in Figure 16.22, the Student_Schedule_Journal now has a single row with the expected values, including:

Operation	U, which corresponds to the UPDATE statement that was executed
Grade	A, which is the grade that was changed
Date_Grade_Assigned	04-MAY-97, which is when the row was updated

16

Figure 16.22.
Verifying that the trigger has fired.

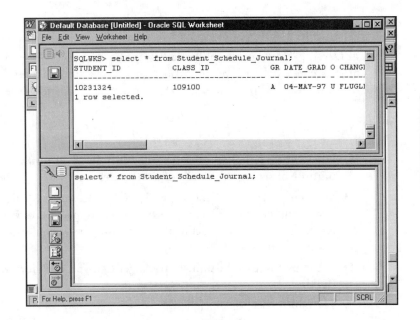

Summary

This lesson explored these key concepts regarding Oracle Graphics and Procedure Builder:

☐ Oracle Graphics consists of two programs: Graphics Designer and Graphics Runtime.

☐ You design a chart by defining a query and a chart type. A query can be based on a single table, a join of two or more tables, or a view.

☐ Oracle Graphics provides many options for customizing the appearance and layout of a chart.

☐ Procedure Builder is a convenient tool for modifying PL/SQL subprograms in a variety of sources, including stored program units, libraries, and database triggers.

☐ The Stored Program Unit Editor enables you to create, view, modify, and drop stored procedures, stored functions, package specifications, and package bodies.

☐ If you are connected to an Oracle account with the proper privileges, you can view the stored program units and database triggers owned by other Oracle accounts.

☐ You can create, modify, and drop a database trigger with the Database Trigger Editor. You can specify the operations that will cause a database trigger to fire, as well as when the trigger will fire (before or after the operation).

What Comes Next?

On Day 17, "Introduction to Oracle Power Objects," you will learn about this intuitive, object-oriented tool for developing client/server applications. Power Objects differs significantly from Oracle Forms. It uses a scripting language named Oracle Basic.

Q&A

Q Does Oracle Graphics offer the capability to "drill-down" into a chart for the purpose of seeing the details of a chart element?

A Yes. You can specify a detail query that will be executed when the user clicks on an element in the chart. The main chart is referred to as the *master chart*. A parameter is created that is used to define the relationship between the master and detail charts.

Q What are some of the built-in packages that you can view with Procedure Builder?

A The built-in packages include

- ☐ TEXT_IO for reading from and writing to files
- ☐ DDE, which provides Dynamic Data Exchange support within Oracle Forms, Reports, Graphics, and other Windows-based programs
- ☐ TOOL_ENV for obtaining the values of Oracle environment variables

Workshop

The purpose of the Workshop is to allow you to test your knowledge of the material discussed in the lesson. See if you can correctly answer the questions in the quiz and complete the exercises before you continue with tomorrow's lesson.

Quiz

1. What are the two file types used by Oracle Graphics?
2. Name three chart types that can be specified with the Graphics Designer.
3. True or false? You can use the Stored Program Unit Editor to modify a package specification but not a package body.

Exercises

1. Create a bar chart that displays the number of courses offered by each department at Flugle College.
2. Modify the trigger on the Student_Schedule table so that it records changes to the Student_Schedule table only if the value of the Grade column is A, B, or C.

Day **17**

Introduction to Oracle Power Objects

Power Objects is supported on all three Windows platforms (Windows 3.11, Windows 95, and Windows NT) and the Macintosh platform (System Software Version 7.1.1, 7.1.2, or 7.5.3 and later). The material in this lesson and the next one will emphasize the use of Power Objects Version 2.0 on Windows 95.

Elements of an Oracle Power Objects Application

To construct a Power Objects application, you will manipulate these objects:

☐ **Database session:** A database session is defined as a connection to an Oracle database (or ODBC Data Source) via a username, password, and database alias. A database session provides access to tables, views, sequences, synonyms, and indexes. A database session is stored as a file with an extension of .pos.

☐ **Application:** A collection of forms, reports, classes, bitmap files, and OLE objects that communicate with a database through a database session. An application is stored as a file with an extension of .poa.

☐ **Library:** A collection of classes and bitmap files that can be shared by many applications. A library is stored as a file with an extension of .pol.

The best way to learn about Power Objects is going through the steps of building an application. To start the Power Objects Designer, select Start | Programs | Oracle Power Objects 2.0 | Power Objects Designer; Figure 17.1 displays the initial window presented by Power Objects Designer. The Power Objects desktop is composed of four main areas:

☐ The menu bar

☐ The toolbar

☐ The main window

☐ The status area at the bottom of the screen

Figure 17.1.

Power Objects Designer initial window.

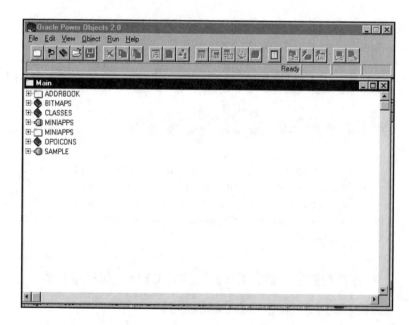

Creating a New Session

The starting point in creating a new application is to create a new database session. To do this, you can either select File | New Session from the menu or click on the New Session icon on the toolbar (it looks like an electrical plug). A window will appear, labeled Create Session, which contains four fields:

Database   By default, it will be set to Oracle.

Username   The name of the Oracle account you want to connect to (enter **Flugle**).

Password   The password for the Oracle account contained in Username (enter **Flugle**).

Connect string If you are using Personal Oracle, leave this field blank. If you are connecting to an Oracle server on another machine, enter the appropriate database alias.

Once you have entered the appropriate values in the fields, click OK to create the database session.

Figure 17.2.

Creating a new session.

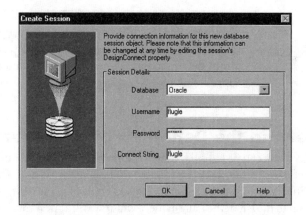

Once the new session is created, the property sheet for the Flugle database session will appear on the desktop (see Figure 17.3).

In the Main window, you will see the new database session. As usual, click the +. As you can see in Figure 17.4, all the database objects owned by the Flugle account are displayed in the Main window.

Figure 17.3.

Power Objects session property sheet.

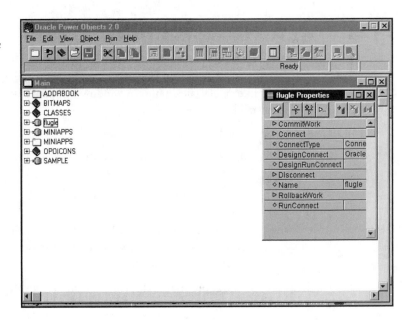

NOTE

> It's important to realize that each object has its own set of properties. For example, the properties defined for a session object are distinct from the properties defined for an application object. (Of course, an application object property might name a session object.)

Viewing the Definition of a Database Object

Each object type is displayed with a different icon. For example, the icon for a table looks like a grid (Schedule_Type, for instance). The icon for a view looks like two tables joined together (Student_No_Personal, for instance). To display the definition of a table, double-click the icon to the left of the table name; a window will appear that contains the table definition. For instance, Figure 17.5 displays the definition for the Schedule_Type table. Notice the key icon to the left of the Schedule_ID column, signifying that the column is the primary key. You can modify the definition of a table, subject to the restrictions that were discussed in the lesson in Day 4, "Implementing Your Logical Model: Physical Database Design." If you do modify the table definition, Power Objects will ask you to confirm that you want to save the changes you have made.

17

Figure 17.4.

Power Objects application property sheet.

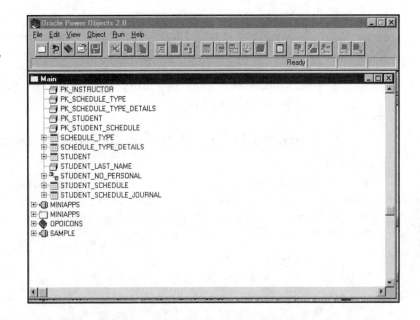

Figure 17.5.

Viewing a table definition in the Main window.

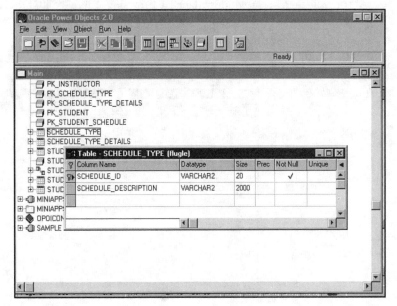

NOTE

When you expand a database session, you can create new database objects, such as tables, indexes, and views, by either making a menu selection (such as Object | New Table) or by pressing the appropriate icon on the toolbar (the fourth group of icons from the left).

Viewing and Modifying the Contents of a Database Object

Power Objects also will let you view or modify the contents of a database object, such as a table. As an example, if you double-click on the table icon to the left of the Student table, Power Objects will display the definition for the Student table. If you want to view or modify the contents of the Student table, you can do any of the following:

☐ Press Ctrl+r

☐ Select Run | Run from the menu

☐ Click on the Run icon on the toolbar (it looks like a lightning bolt)

You will then see a window, labeled Browsing Table - STUDENT, which contains the contents of the Student table (see Figure 17.6).

Figure 17.6.

Viewing the contents of the Student table.

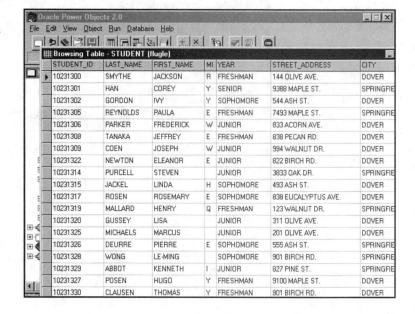

From this window, you can also modify the contents of a table. For example, if you wanted to set Anna Anastatia's middle initial to *Q* (for Quinn), you would click on the MI field in that record and make the change. As shown in Figure 17.7, Power Objects enables you to make the change and also locks the record, as evidenced by the lock icon placed on the left of the record. You can also insert a row or delete a row either by selecting the appropriate menu item within the Database menu item or by clicking the + or - icon on the toolbar.

NOTE

When you modify a record either by creating it, changing one of its fields, or deleting it, Power Objects will place a row-level lock on it. This lock won't prevent other users from viewing the record, but it will prevent them from modifying it until you commit or rollback the changes you have made.

Figure 17.7.

Changing a row in the Student table with Power Objects Designer.

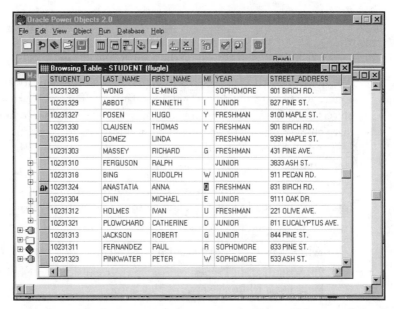

If you try to close the window labeled Browsing Table after you have changed the contents of the table, Power Objects will inform you that a transaction is pending—you must either commit the changes that you have made or roll back the changes (see Figure 17.8). You can perform a commit or rollback either by selecting the appropriate menu item within the Database menu item or by pressing the appropriate icon on the toolbar (the commit icon is a green checkmark, and the rollback icon is a purple curved arrow).

Figure 17.8.

*Power Objects Designer
requires commit or
rollback before closing the
window.*

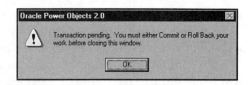

To exit the Browsing Table window, you can either close the window using typical Windows 95 methods or click on the Stop icon on the toolbar.

Creating a New Application

Now that you've created a new database session, let's see how a new application object is created. To create the new application object—which you will name Flugle—you can choose from these three methods:

☐ Press Ctrl+n

☐ Select File | New Application from the menu

☐ Click on the folder icon on the toolbar (the left-most icon)

A window, labeled Create as, will appear, prompting you for the directory where the application object should be stored. By default, the Power Objects Designer will save your objects in the Power Objects directory; however, you should save your objects in a directory that you have created for storing application-specific files. Enter Flugle in the File name field and click Save. You will then see the Flugle application object in the Main window (application objects are represented by a folder).

To view the property sheet for the application that you have just created, select the Flugle application in the Main window and perform one of the following steps:

☐ Right-click Property Sheet

☐ Select View | Property Sheet from the menu

☐ Click on the Edit Properties icon on the right side of the horizontal toolbar (it looks like a white sheet with a blue border)

Figure 17.9 displays the property sheet for the Flugle application.

Figure 17.9.

Power Objects application property sheet.

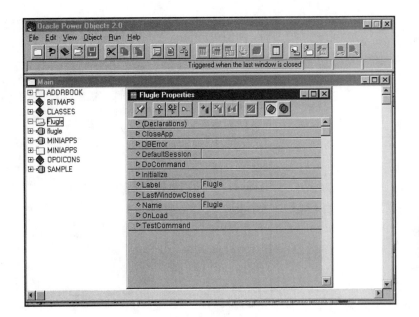

Creating a Form

Now that you've created the application object, you're ready to create your first form. You are going to create a simple form that will display the Student ID, last name, and first name, sorted by last name and first name. Before you create a form, you must select the application to which it will belong. Therefore, select the Flugle application in the Main window, and click the New Form icon on the left side of the horizontal toolbar (it looks like a miniature form with a blue band on top). You will see a window, labeled Form1, appear (see Figure 17.10). On the left side of the screen, you should also see the Object Palette.

There are certain form properties that you'll typically want to set. To change the properties for the new form, be sure that the form is selected, and then right-click the Property Sheet menu item. The properties dialog box appears (see Figure 12.11). Scroll down the property list until you see the RecSrcSession property. In the field to the right of the RecSrcSession label, enter **Flugle**. Scroll up the property list until you see the RecordSource property. In the field to the right of the RecordSource label, enter **Student**; the RecordSource identifies the table or view from which the form retrieves records.

Figure 17.10.

New form is displayed.

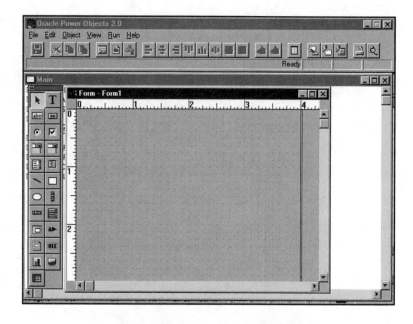

Figure 17.11.

Setting the `RecSrcSession` *and* `RecordSource` *form properties.*

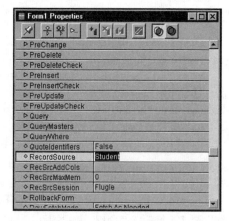

Of course, the form is still empty—it contains no objects. There are three categories of objects that can be placed on a form:

Containers   These are objects that can contain other objects such as embedded forms, repeater displays, classes, OLE objects, and rectangles/ovals.

Static objects   These are graphical elements such as lines, ovals, and static text.

Controls	These are objects that hold data values that are either retrieved from the database, derived from the database, or entered by the user. For example, text fields, list boxes, combo boxes, and popup lists are examples of this type of control. Controls also include objects that affect the behavior of the form such as pushbuttons and scrollbars.

Adding Controls to a Form

Using the Object Palette, let's add some controls to your form.

1. Select the Text Item icon from the Object Palette (it is directly below the red pointer icon in the left corner of the palette), and left-click the mouse on the form.

2. Do this three times so that you have three fields on the form.

3. Align the fields so that the form appears as shown in Figure 17.12.

Figure 17.12.

Adding text fields to the form.

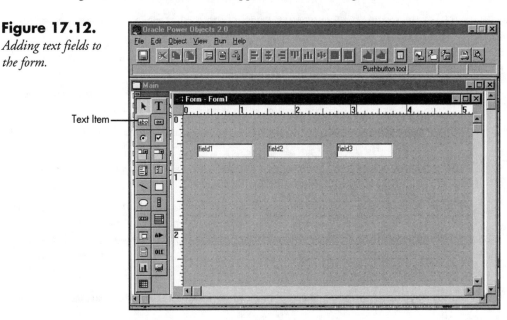

However, these text fields know nothing about the Student table; you need to display the property sheet for each field.

4. Select the first field, and right-click Property Sheet.

5. In the DataSource property, enter **Student_ID** (see Figure 17.13). You should also change the name of the field; scroll down to the Name property and enter **Student_ID**. Exit the property sheet for this field.

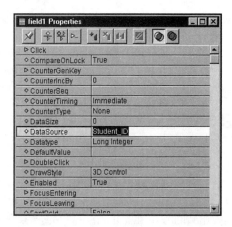

Figure 17.13.

Setting the
DataSource *property*
for the text field.

6. For the second field, enter **Last_Name** in both the DataSource and Name properties. Also, set the Datatype property to String.

7. For the third field, enter **First_Name** in both the DataSource and Name properties. As with the second field, set the Datatype property to String.

8. To add column headings for the three fields, select the Static Text tool from the Object Palette (it is to the right of the red pointer icon).

9. Left-click the mouse over the Student_ID text item. Change the text from static1 to Student ID.

10. In the same way, create two other column headings: one over the Last_Name text field and the other over the First_Name text field.

11. To format the static text objects, select them by pressing Shift and clicking all three objects. Right-click Property Sheet; the property sheet will appear with a label of Multiple Selection Properties, signifying that the properties will be applied to all three static text objects. Set the FontSize property to 10 and the FontBold property to True (see Figure 17.14).

When you close the property sheet, your form should look like the one displayed in Figure 17.15.

Figure 17.14.

Setting the FontSize *and* FontBold *properties for multiple static text objects.*

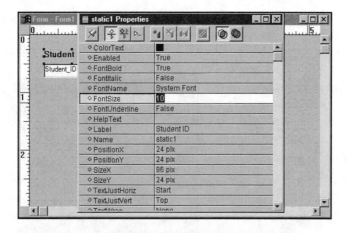

Figure 17.15.

Form with text fields and headings.

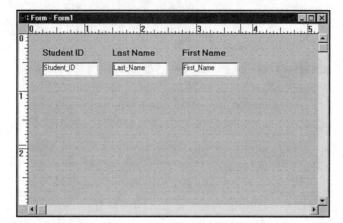

Testing the Form

The Power Objects Designer provides a convenient method for testing a single form (it is very similar to the same feature provided in Oracle Forms). To run the current form, you can right-click Run Form or click on the Run Form button on the toolbar (appropriately, it resembles a lightning bolt striking a form). If you've made any changes to the form since it was last saved, Power Objects Designer will ask you to confirm that you want to save the changes that you have made. After you click Yes, the Power Objects Designer will run the form. As you can see in Figure 17.16, the fields contain a record from the Student table. However, there is no way to navigate to the next or the previous record! Exit test mode either by clicking the Terminate button (which resembles a red traffic signal) or by closing Form1.

Figure 17.16.

Testing the form—the form retrieves a record from the Student table.

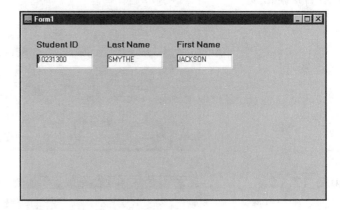

Adding a Scrollbar to the Form

Power Objects provides an easy way to add navigation to a form. From the Object Palette, select the horizontal scrollbar icon and left-click on the form where you want the scrollbar to appear. Reposition and resize the scrollbar as you like.

Now, test the form again by right-clicking Run Form. Try navigating to the next and previous records by clicking each end of the scrollbar. As you can see, you were able to add the scrollbar to the form without setting any properties or writing any code.

There are some other features that Power Objects provides that are "freebies"; for instance, you can run a query by selecting Database | Query by Form from the menu. Another window, titled "Find What?" will appear. If you want to find all students whose last name begins with an *A*, enter **A%** in the Last Name field in the Find What? form (see Figure 17.17). To execute the query with the search criterion, select Database | Apply Form Query. You will find two students who satisfy the criterion—Anna Anastatia and Kenneth Abbot. You can also update a record, insert a record, and delete a record by right-clicking the mouse and selecting the appropriate menu item. Exit the form to return to design mode.

Specifying the Retrieval Order for the Form

You'll want to specify the order in which the records are retrieved and displayed on the form. As you recall, the form should present the records from the Student table ordered by last name and first name. Select the form, and right-click Property Sheet. Scroll down to the `OrderBy` property and enter **Last_Name, First_Name**. Once again, try testing the form. The records should be presented in the order that you specified: `Last_Name, First_Name`.

17

Figure 17.17.

Enter a search criterion in Query by Form.

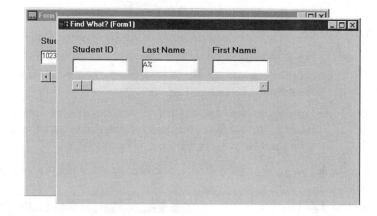

Naming the Form

Unlike Oracle Forms, Power Objects doesn't save a form in its own file; a form is saved as part of the application object. To change the name of the form to Student, set the Label property to Student and the Name property to frmStudent.

Creating a Master-Detail Form

Creating a master-detail form in Power Objects is easy. As an example, let's create the Department Class form that you created using Oracle Forms. To begin, create a new form in the Flugle application object.

First, you're going to create the objects that are associated with the master table, which is Department.

1. Select the form by clicking it, and right-click Property Sheet.
2. Set these properties for the form:

Name	frmDepartment_Class
RecSrcSession	Flugle
RecordSource	Department
OrderBy	Department_ID

3. Exit the form property sheet.
4. Select the text field icon from the Object Palette, and place the text field in the upper portion of the form.
5. Right-click Property Sheet, and set the DataSource and Name properties to Department_ID. Also, you'll need to set the Datatype property to String (by default, it is set to Long Integer).

17

6. Exit the text field property sheet.

7. Select the static text tool from the Object Palette, and place a text label to the left of the Department_ID text field.

8. Set the name of the label to Department; change the FontBold property to True and the FontSize property to 10.

9. Finally, you'll need a scrollbar to navigate between departments. Select the horizontal scrollbar tool from the Object Palette, and create the horizontal scrollbar on the form just below the Deparment_ID text field.

At this point, your form should look like the one displayed in Figure 17.18.

Figure 17.18.

Master portion of the form.

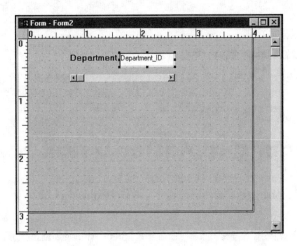

Next, you're going to create the detail portion of the form. Select the repeater tool on the Object Palette—it is in the right column, fourth from the bottom, and looks like a gray form with white borders. Place the repeater on the form beneath the Department_ID text field. The repeater will be used to display the detail records from the Class table that correspond to the currently displayed Department_ID. A repeater is a container that is composed of these elements:

Frame	This is the object that encloses the entire object.
Primary panel	This is the panel at the top of the repeater in which you place other controls and static objects. Typically, the primary panel is where you place the text fields that will be displayed in the repeater.
Secondary panel	These are the panels that display additional instances of the objects that are contained in the primary panel.
Scrollbar	The repeater contains a vertical scrollbar on its right side.

17

Once you've placed the repeater on the form, right-click Property Sheet. There are several properties that you need to set for the repeater to function properly:

RecordSource	**Class** (this is the table from which the records are retrieved)
RecSrcSession	**Flugle** (this is the database session to be used in accessing the database)
LinkDetailColumn	**Department_ID** (this is the name of the column in the detail recordset that will be used to link to the master recordset)
LinkMasterColumn	**Department_ID** (this is the name of the column in the master recordset that the detail recordset will be linked to)
LinkMasterForm	**DepartmentClass** (this is the name of the form that contains the master records)
OrderBy	**Class_ID** (the column/columns that should be used in ordering the detail records)

Figure 17.19 displays the property sheet for the repeater. Close the repeater property sheet.

Figure 17.19.
Property sheet for the repeater.

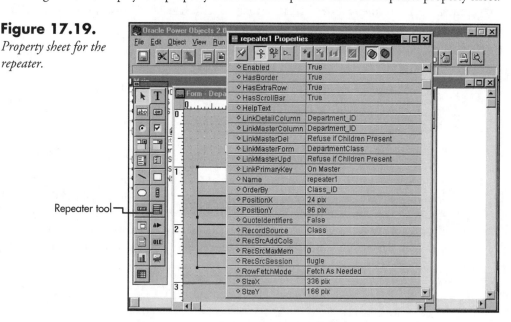

Repeater tool

Next, you need to add the text fields to the repeater's primary panel. Select the primary panel as illustrated in Figure 17.20.

Figure 17.20.

Selecting the repeater's primary panel.

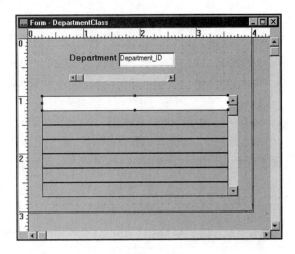

Select the text field tool on the Object Palette, and create a text field by clicking within the primary panel of the repeater. Create a total of six text fields. For each text field, do the following:

- [ ] Set the DataSource property to the column name that you want to display in that text field.
- [ ] Set the Datatype property to the appropriate value for the column's datatype.
- [ ] Set the Name property to the column name.
- [ ] Set the FontName property to MS Sans Serif.

As an example, Figure 17.21 displays the property sheet for the Class_ID text field.

Once you have specified the properties for each of the text items in the repeater's primary panel, add a heading to each column by selecting the static text tool on the Object Palette and placing a static text object above the repeater text field. When you have finished, test the form by right-clicking Run Form. Figure 17.22 illustrates what your form should look like when it displays the classes for the psychology department. Exit test mode, and open the Student form for the next exercise.

17

Figure 17.21.

Property sheet for a text field within the repeater's primary panel.

Figure 17.22.

Testing the Master/Detail form.

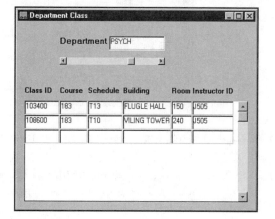

Using Radio Buttons

Let's look at two other objects that you can incorporate in your forms: the radio button frame and the radio button. A radio button frame typically contains two or more radio buttons. For example, suppose you wanted to modify the Student form by incorporating the student's year displayed as a group of radio buttons.

The first step is to add a radio button frame to the form.

1. Select the radio button frame icon on the Object Palette (it's in the right column, fifth from the top).

2. Left-click on the form where you want to place the radio button frame (see Figure 17.23).

Figure 17.23.

Adding a radio button frame to a form.

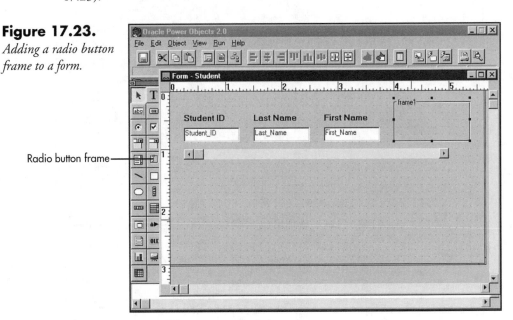

Radio button frame

3. Once the radio button frame is created, you can resize it by grabbing a corner and dragging it.

4. Align it with the other fields on the form. Right-click Property Sheet to specify the properties for the radio button frame (see Figure 17.24). Specifically, you'll need to set these properties:

DataSource   **Year** (the column that is represented in the radio buttons contained by the radio button frame)

Datatype   **String**

FontBold   **True**

FontName   **MS Sans Serif**

FontSize   **10**

Label   **Year**

Name   **StudentYear**

Figure 17.24.

*Specifying the radio
button frame properties.*

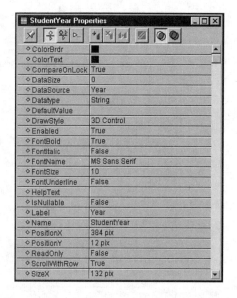

5. When you have set all the properties, close the property sheet.

 NOTE

You cannot name the radio button frame "Year" because it is an Oracle
Basic reserved word.

The next step is to add four radio buttons to the radio button frame—Freshman, Sophomore,
Junior, and Senior. To add a radio button, select the radio button icon from the Object
Palette (it's in the left column, third from the top). Position the pointer inside the radio
button frame and left-click. Your form should look like the one displayed in Figure 17.25.

You'll need to set the properties for the radio button by left-clicking Properties. For the first
radio button, you'll want to set these properties:

DataSource   **Year**

Datatype   **String**

Label   **Freshman**

Name   **Freshman**

ValueOn   **FRESHMAN** (this property contains the value that is actually stored in the
              column when the radio button is set)

Figure 17.25.

Adding a radio button to the radio button frame.

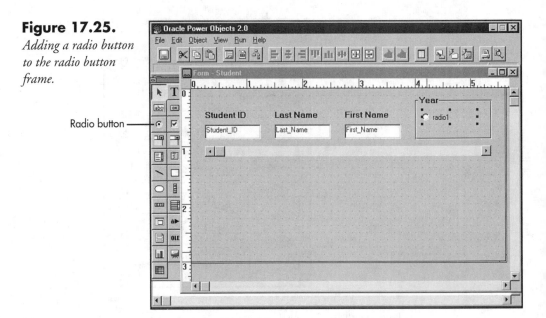

Radio button ⟶

Figure 17.26 displays the Property Sheet for the radio button. When you have finished setting the properties, close the Property Sheet. Perform the same steps to add radio buttons for Sophomore, Junior, and Senior. When you are finished, your form should look similar to the one displayed in Figure 17.27.

Figure 17.26.

Setting properties for the Freshman radio button.

Freshman Properties	
◇ DataSource	Year
◇ Datatype	String
◇ DefaultValue	
◇ DrawStyle	3D Control
◇ Enabled	True
◇ FontBold	False
◇ FontItalic	False
◇ FontName	System Font
◇ FontSize	8
◇ FontUnderline	False
◇ HelpText	
◇ Label	Freshman
◇ Name	Freshman
◇ PositionX	12 pix
◇ PositionY	24 pix
◇ ReadOnly	False
◇ ScrollWithRow	True
◇ SizeX	96 pix
◇ SizeY	24 pix
◇ TabEnabled	True
◇ TabOrder	1
◇ ValidateMsg	
◇ ValueOff	
◇ ValueOn	FRESHMAN

17

Figure 17.27.
Student form with radio button frame and four radio buttons.

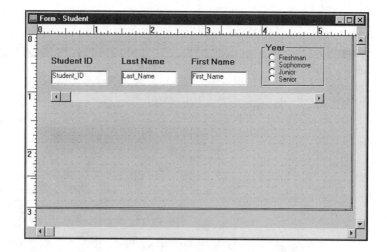

Try testing the modified Student form. As you can see in Figure 17.28, the student's year is displayed in the correct radio button.

Figure 17.28.
Testing the form with the radio button frame and four radio buttons.

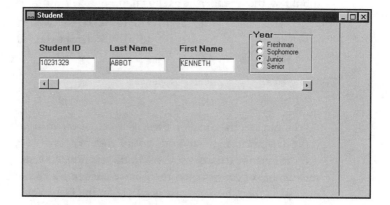

Displaying a Lookup Field

You will often need to add a lookup field to a form. Power Objects provides a built-in function named SQLLOOKUP that is used to execute a query and return a single column. As an example, let's look at the DepartmentClass form. Suppose that, in addition to the department ID, you also want to display the number of courses that the department offers.

1. Add a text field to the form (see Figure 17.29).

Figure 17.29.

Adding a text field that will display a lookup value.

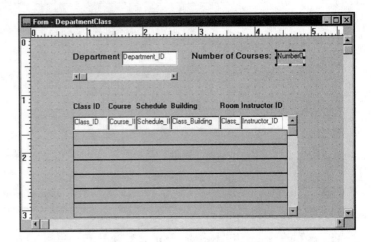

2. Set the properties for the new text field by right-clicking Property Sheet. You should set these properties as shown in Figure 17.30:

DataSource	`=sqllookup(flugle,"select count(*) from course where department_id = '" + department_id.value + "'")`
Datatype	`Long Integer`
Name	`NumberOfCourses`
ReadOnly	`True`

As you can see, the function SQLLOOKUP contains two arguments. The first argument is the database session, and the second argument is the SELECT statement to be executed via the database session. In this example, the SELECT statement will return the number of courses from the Course table in which the Department_ID column is equal to the value currently displayed in the Department_ID text field.

NOTE

If you set the DefaultSession property for an application, you don't have to specify the database session when invoking SQLLOOKUP, unless you want to use a different database session.

3. Test the form. As you can see in Figure 17.31, the NumberOfCourses field displays the correct value; if you check the contents of the Course table, you will see that there are three courses offered by the Anthropology department. However, the detail portion of the form is empty because none of the Anthropology courses is offered as a class this semester.

Figure 17.30.

Setting the properties of the lookup field.

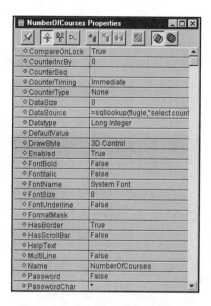

Figure 17.31.

Testing the form with the lookup field.

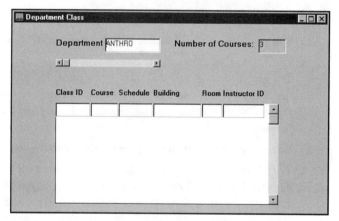

Summary

The main ideas presented in this lesson are the following:

☐ Power Objects is an application-development tool that is supported on the Windows and Mac platforms.

☐ Power Objects is more closely related to Visual Basic and PowerBuilder than to Oracle Forms. Its object orientation is manifested by the capability to create a new class and inherit from a class.

☐ Power Objects uses Oracle Basic as a scripting language for specifying the methods defined for an object.

☐ At the highest level, Power Objects manages three types of objects: applications, sessions, and libraries.

☐ An application consists of forms, reports, and classes.

☐ Power Objects provides a property sheet for each type of object that it supports.

☐ Power Objects uses two modes: Design mode and Run-Time mode. In Design mode, you assemble the objects that constitute an application. In Run-Time mode, you are able to test the behavior of a form.

What Comes Next?

On Day 18, "Developing an Application with Oracle Power Objects," you learn more about Power Objects such as the fundamentals of Oracle Basic, developing reports, creating a class object, and other topics.

Q&A

Q **Is it possible to simultaneously set the properties for a group of objects?**

A Yes. To do this, select all the objects whose properties you want to set either by dragging a rectangle around them or by pressing Shift and clicking each object with the mouse. When you right-click Property Sheet, you will notice that the property sheet window is titled Multiple Selection Properties. You will be able to set the properties that the objects have in common—for instance, FontSize or FontName.

Q **What files are necessary to generate an executable application?**

A With Power Objects, you can generate a runtime file (.PO) which can be executed with the Power Objects Run-Time executable named PWRRUN.EXE. Alternatively, you can generate a standalone executable file that doesn't require PWRRUN to execute. If you are generating a standalone executable file, you also will need the appropriate database drivers and DLLs.

Workshop

The purpose of the Workshop is to allow you to test your knowledge of the material discussed in the lesson. See if you can correctly answer the questions in the quiz and complete the exercises before you continue with tomorrow's lesson.

Quiz

1. True or false? A Power Objects application connects to an Oracle database through an application transaction object.

2. Name three types of objects that you can place on a form.

3. Give an example of a container object.

Exercises

1. Build a form for displaying and modifying information about each instructor. Display the number of classes, if any, that the instructor is scheduled to teach.

2. Modify the Student form to display the GPA of the current student.

17

Day **18**

Developing an Application with Oracle Power Objects

In the previous lesson, you became acquainted with Oracle Power Objects. You learned how to define a database session, how to create an application object, and how to create a simple form and a master-detail form. In this lesson, you continue exploring some of the features of Power Objects including the following:

☐ Using some standard methods for various objects

☐ Specifying method code

☐ Displaying a calculated value in a form

☐ Creating a class

☐ Inheriting from a class

☐ Developing a report

Methods and Method Code

NEW TERM A method is a set of instructions that are executed by an object in response to an event or a call to the object. Each type of object has a set of predefined methods called *standard methods*. The set of instructions—which are Oracle Basic statements—executed for a method is known as *method code*. Some methods may have default processing that is executed if a developer has not written any method code.

The methods for an object are listed on the object's property sheet below the properties. On the property sheet, a small diamond is displayed to the left of each property, and a small arrowhead is displayed to the left of each method. Let's look at an example of a method for a form.

1. To begin, create another form and name it MyForm.

2. Add two text fields to the form: XPos and YPos.

3. Bring up the property sheet for the form and scroll down to the MouseOver method. The MouseOver method is triggered when the mouse moves over the object.

4. As shown in Figure 18.1, click on the MouseOver method and enter:

```
XPos.value = x
YPos.value = y
```

Figure 18.1.

Method code for MouseOver.

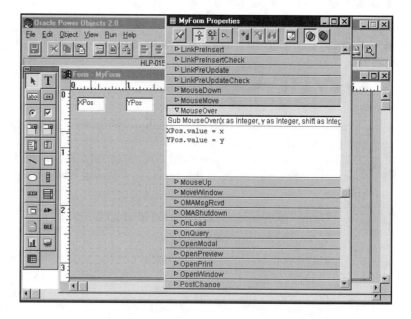

This script will assign the current x and y positions to the XPos and YPos fields, respectively. Click on the MouseOver method title to close the window. Alternatively, you can invoke the Code Editor window by clicking the Code Editor button at the top of the property sheet (it resembles a yellow pencil on a page). As you can see in Figure 18.2, the Code Editor window can be resized, making it convenient for entering a large block of method code.

Figure 18.2.

Using the Code Editor window to specify the method code for MouseOver.

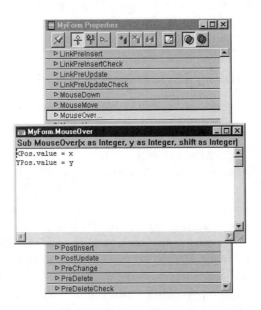

Close the property sheet and test the form by right-clicking Run Form. Figure 18.3 illustrates what your form should display in Run-Time mode.

Figure 18.3.

Testing the method code for MouseOver.

Validating User Input

Let's look at a commonly used method for a control: the Validate method. This method is used to enforce the business rules for an object. For example, suppose that one of the business rules for Flugle College is that the student ID must begin with a 1. To specify this business rule, select the Student_ID text field on the Student form, and bring up its property sheet. Scroll down to the Validate method—it's the last method for the object. Enter the Oracle Basic statements shown in Listing 18.1.

INPUT

Listing 18.1. Enforcing a business rule in the method code for Validate.

```
IF LEFT(newval,1) = "1" THEN
    Validate = TRUE
ELSE
    Validate = FALSE
    MSGBOX("Student ID must begin with a 1"
END IF
```

The business rule is expressed in the Oracle Basic statement, IF-THEN-ELSE. The first line uses the LEFT function to return the first character of the Student_ID being validated. If the first character is equal to 1, the Validate function will return TRUE, indicating that the new value passes validation; otherwise, the Validate function will return FALSE, preventing the user from navigating to another control or committing the change. Also, the MSGBOX function is used to display an error message to the user.

Let's test the method code.

1. Close the property sheet for Student_ID.

2. Click the Run Form button on the toolbar to test the form.

3. In the first record, try setting the first character of Student_ID to 2.

4. Try clicking another field. As you can see in Figure 18.4, the method code displays an error message, as expected.

5. To exit the form, click on the Rollback button on the toolbar (it resembles a purple arrow) and then the Stop button.

18

Figure 18.4.

Testing the method code for Validate.

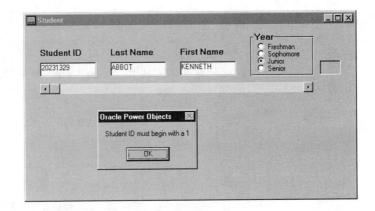

Displaying Calculated Values in a Form

In the previous lesson, you learned how to display a lookup field that used the built-in function SQLLOOKUP. Now, you'll see how you can construct a field which will display a value that is calculated from the value of other controls in the form.

As an example, let's construct a form that displays information about each course.

1. Set the following properties for the form:

RecSrcSession	**Flugle**
RecordSource	**Course**
OrderBy	**Department_ID, Course_ID**
Label	**Course Information**
Name	**CourseInformation**

2. Also, add text fields and static text to the form, as shown in Figure 18.5.

3. The calculated field is named Total_Cost; it will reflect the cost of a course, which is based on the cost per unit, $350, plus any additional fees. Select the calculated field, named Total_Cost, and right-click Property Sheet. As shown in Figure 18.6, set these properties:

DataSource	**= Units.value*350 + Additional_Fees.value**
Datatype	**Long Integer**
Name	**Total_Cost**

18

Figure 18.5.

The CourseInformation form.

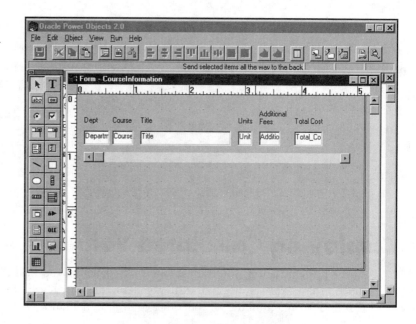

Figure 18.6.

Setting the DataSource *property for the calculated field.*

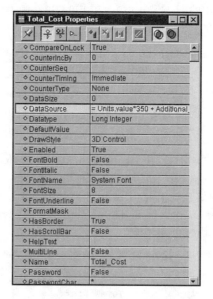

4. Exit the property sheet; it's time to test the form and see if the calculated field is working.

5. Click on the Run Form button on the toolbar. As you can see in Figure 18.7, the calculated field is displaying the correct amount for each record.

Figure 18.7.

Testing the form that displays a calculated value.

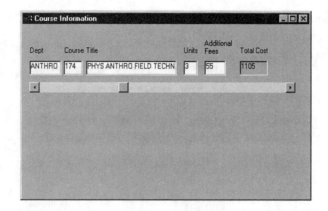

Creating a Class

A major feature of Power Objects is its support for classes.

1. You can add a class to an application by pressing the New Class button on the toolbar or by selecting Object | New Class from the menu. Figure 18.8 illustrates what the new class looks like—as you would expect, it is initially empty.

Figure 18.8.

Creating a new class.

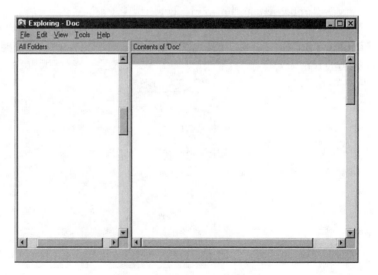

2. You're going to add a button to this class. On the Object Palette, select the pushbutton icon and create a button on the class. Power Objects will assign a name to the button, as shown in Figure 18.9.

Figure 18.9.

Adding a pushbutton to the new class.

Pushbutton ————

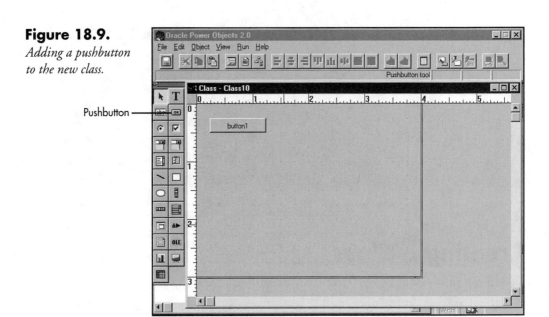

3. Reduce the size of the class by grabbing the lower-right corner and dragging to the upper-left, as shown in Figure 18.10.

Figure 18.10.

Reducing the size of the class.

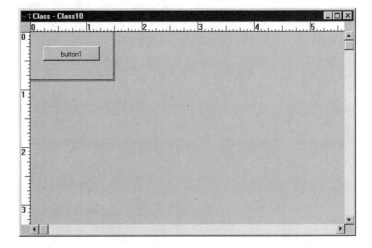

Let's change some of the properties of the pushbutton. Select the pushbutton, right-click Property Sheet, and set these properties:

    Label   **Close**

    Name   **btnClose**

Close the property sheet. Before you add an instance of the class to an existing form, you'll want to give the new class a name. Therefore, select the class by clicking anywhere within the class's defining border except the pushbutton and then right-clicking Property Sheet. Set the Name property for the class to MyFirstClass, and exit the property sheet. Click the Save button on the toolbar to save the changes to the class. Press Ctrl+w to close the class.

Adding an Instance of a Class to a Form

If you look at the Main window, you should now see the class that you've created—MyFirstClass—in the collection of objects that belong to the Flugle application (see Figure 18.11).

Figure 18.11.

Main Window displays MyFirstClass *class.*

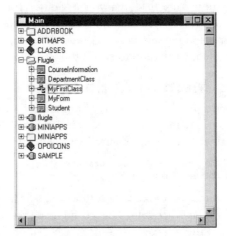

You're going to add an instance of MyFirstClass to MyForm. To do this, select the icon next to MyFirstClass, and hold down the left mouse button. Drag the icon onto the icon for MyForm; you should see a + near the pointer. Release the mouse button. Power Objects will display MyForm with the class instance in the upper-left corner (see Figure 18.12).

Figure 18.12.

MyForm *contains an*
instance of
MyFirstClass.

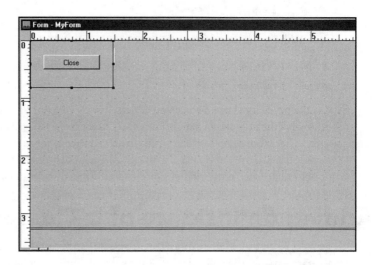

You can reposition MyFirstClass on MyForm by selecting it and dragging it to the right, revealing the two text fields that you previously created, XPos and YPos. Try running the form by selecting Run | Run Form from the menu. Try clicking on Close. Did you expect anything to happen? Nothing should because you haven't provided any method code for the button's Click method. Click Stop to return to Design mode.

Adding Method Code to the Class

To make the pushbutton close the form in which it is placed, open MyFirstClass, select the pushbutton, and right-click Property Sheet. Scroll down to the Click method, and click the method title. As shown in Figure 18.13, enter two lines of Oracle Basic:

```
MSGBOX("Closing " + GetTopContainer.Name)
GetTopContainer.CloseWindow()
```

The first line invokes the MSGBOX function. The argument to MSGBOX is a concatenation of Closing with another item. The second item uses the GetTopContainer to obtain an object reference to the top container—form, report, or class—in which the object is contained. GetTopContainer.Name returns the name of the top object in which the pushbutton is contained. The net effect of this line is to issue a message box that will display the name of whatever form contains an instance of MyFirstClass. The second line will close the form that contains this pushbutton.

To test MyForm again, double-click MyForm on the Main Window. Click on Close. As you can see in Figure 18.14, a message box appears, informing you that the button is about to close MyForm. Click OK on the message box. Click Stop to return to Design mode.

Figure 18.13.

Specifying method code for the Click *method in* btnClose.

Figure 18.14.

Testing the Click *method in* btnClose.

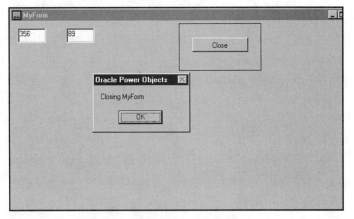

Changing a Property in a Class Object

You've now seen a simple example on the use of classes. By changing the method code for an object in the class, you affect the behavior of other objects that contain an instance of the modified class.

Let's look at the effect of changing the property of an object in a class. As you may have noticed in MyForm, there is a border surrounding the Close button. The border is defined in the class. Invoke MyFirstClass by double-clicking its icon in the Main Window. Select the MyFirstClass window, and right-click Property Sheet. Scroll down to the HasBorder property, and click it so that it changes to False. Exit the Property Sheet.

Invoke MyForm from the Main Window by double-clicking its icon. Notice that there is no longer a border surrounding the Close button.

Overriding an Inherited Class Property

In the last example, you changed the HasBorder property for MyFirstClass by setting it to False; as a result, an instance of MyFirstClass on another form inherits the property of having no border. However, you can override a property or method in a class instance. For example, invoke MyForm and select the instance of MyFirstClass that you placed on it. Right-click Property Sheet. The HasBorder property is set to False, the value that you set for the class property. However, you can override that property for this instance of MyFirstClass by clicking False; the value will become True. The diamond to the left of the property name will become black, signifying that the inherited property has been overridden (see Figure 18.15).

Figure 18.15.

Overriding an inherited class property.

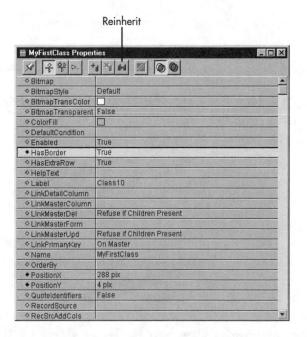

NOTE

If you look at the PositionX and PositionY properties for the instance of MyFirstClass on MyForm, you'll notice that the black diamond indicates that their inherited values have been overridden. This happened automatically when you dragged MyFirstClass to the right on the MyForm.

You *can* reinherit a property or method that you have overridden by selecting the property (or method) and pressing the Reinherit button at the top of the property sheet (it is two buttons to the right of the + button). When you do this, the property (or method) will revert to its inherited value, and the diamond will revert from black to gray.

Overriding an Inherited Class Method

As an object-oriented programming environment, Power Objects allows you to override a method that has been inherited. You can see how this is accomplished by referring to MyForm and MyFirstClass. As you recall, MyFirstClass contains a pushbutton named btnClose, which has method code specified for the Click method.

When you added an instance of MyFirstClass to MyForm, that class instance inherited the Click method code. Let's see how you can override the processing that was specified in btnClose.

1. Open MyForm by double-clicking its icon on the Main Window.
2. Select btnClose, and right-click Property Sheet.
3. Scroll down to the Click method, and enter a single line:

   ```
   MSGBOX("Override the Click method")
   ```

4. Click on the method title. Notice that the method is a solid black triangle, indicating that it overrides its inherited method code.
5. Close the property sheet and test MyForm. When you click on Close, a message box appears informing you that the Click method has been overridden (see Figure 18.16).
6. When you click OK in the message box, nothing else happens. As you would expect, the inherited method code does not execute.

Figure 18.16.

Testing the overridden method.

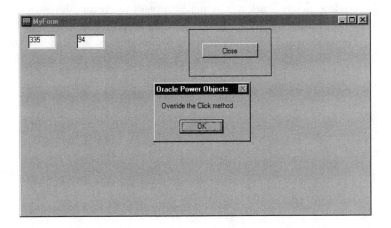

Power Objects will also permit you to override the method code *and* invoke the inherited method code. The statement `Inherited.Method_name()` is used to execute the default processing for a method. Using the example of `MyForm` and `MyFirstClass`, suppose that you have decided that you want to display a message box when Close is clicked but also want the inherited method code to execute. To achieve this, select `btnClose` on `MyForm`, and right-click Property Sheet. Scroll down to the `Click` method, and enter these two lines of Oracle Basic:

```
MSGBOX("Override the Click method")
Inherited.Click()
```

The first line will display a message box containing the specified message. The second line will invoke the method code for `btnClose` that specified in the class, `MyFirstClass`. Exit the property sheet, and test the form. When you click on Close, the message box displays the message about overriding the `Click` method. When you click OK, another message box appears, demonstrating that the inherited code is executing.

As you learn more about the use of classes and inheritance, you'll discover that you'll benefit from their use in several ways:

- [ ] With inheritance, you'll actually write less code.
- [ ] You'll be able to apply your classes to a variety of applications.
- [ ] If you've created a sensible set of classes and inherited them in an appropriate manner, you will find it easier to maintain your application; you will have a smaller amount of code to modify than if you didn't use classes.

Building an Oracle Power Objects Report

The last object you're going to explore in Power Objects is the report object. An application can contain zero or more reports. To add a report to an application, open the Main Window, select the application in which you want to create the report, and press the New Report button on the toolbar. As an alternative, you can select Object | New Report from the menu. A window will appear, containing the new report. If you look at the Main Window, you will see that the new report belongs to the application (see Figure 18.17).

Figure 18.17.

New report object belongs to application.

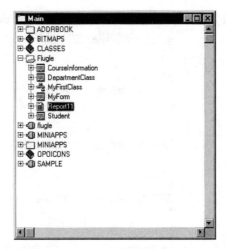

Sections of a Report

If you maximize the window that contains the new report, you will see that the report contains five sections (see Figure 18.18):

ReportHeader	The objects that you place in this area will be displayed once, at the beginning of the report.
PageHeader	The objects that you place in this band will be displayed at the top of each page.
Detail	This band contains the objects that constitute the body of the report. These objects are repeated once for each record retrieved by the report.
PageFooter	The objects that you place in this band will be displayed at the bottom of each page.
ReportFooter	The objects that you place in this band will be displayed once, at the end of the report.

Increase the width of the report by dragging the right edge of the report to the right.

18

Figure 18.18.
New report layout.

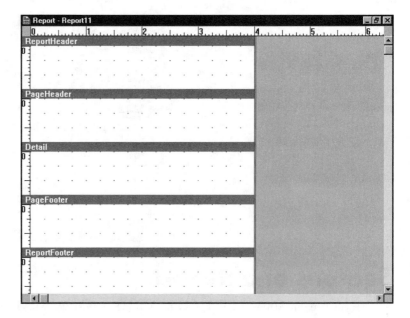

Specifying Report Objects

Let's set some properties for the new report:

1. From the report window, right-click Property Sheet, and specify these properties:

Label	**Course Catalog**
Name	**rptCourseCatalog**
RecordSource	**Course**
RecSrcSession	**Flugle** (this is the database session to be used by the report)

2. Exit the property sheet.

3. Let's add a group section to the report. On the Object Palette, click on the Report Section button (it resembles a page containing red rectangles), and click in the Detail band on the report. You'll notice that the report now has two additional bands: a GroupHeader band and a GroupFooter band (see Figure 18.19).

18

Figure 18.19.

Group header and footer bands added to report layout.

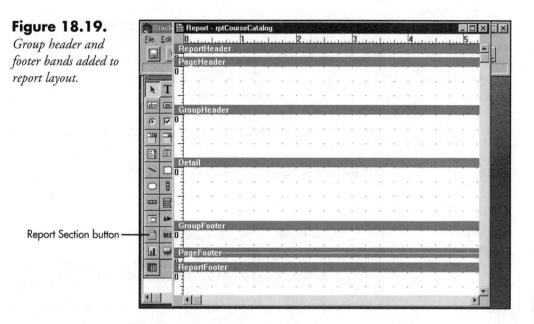

Report Section button —

Specifying the PageHeader Area

The objects in the PageHeader area will be printed at the top of each report page. Therefore, this is where you want to specify the report title and any other information you want to appear on every report page. Select the PageHeader by clicking on the dark gray band and right-click Property Sheet. By default, the PageHeader has a property named FirstPgHdr that is set to False, causing the objects in the PageHeader to be suppressed for the first page. Set this property to True, and close the property sheet. As shown in Figure 18.20, add a title and subtitle for the report. Click the Static Text button on the Object Palette, and click in the PageHeader where you want the title to appear. You will see a highlighted field labeled static1; enter the title that you want to appear on the report. Follow the same steps to add the subtitle.

Figure 18.20.

Properties for the Department_ID field in the GroupHeader area.

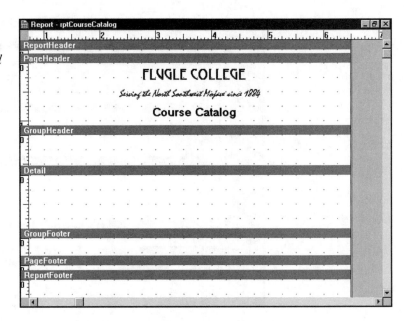

Specifying the GroupHeader Area

A Group area is used to "break" the report output. For this sample report, you want the report to "break" whenever the department changes so that a new column heading for department is printed.

1. Select the Text Field button on the Object Palette, and click in the GroupHeader area. Right-click Property Sheet to set these properties for this text field (see Figure 18.21):

DataSource	**Department_ID**
Datatype	**String**
DrawStyle	**Standard Control** (assuming that you don't want a report item to appear recessed)
HasBorder	**False** (assuming that you don't want a border around report items)
Name	**Department_ID**

2. Exit the property sheet.

3. On the report, add a label for the Department_ID field by clicking the Static Text button on the Object Palette and clicking to the left of the Department_ID text field.

4. Set the properties for the static text such as Name and FontBold.

5. Also, you need to set a property for the GroupHeader band itself.

6. Select the GroupHeader band, and right-click Property Sheet.

7. There is a single property you need to set—GroupCol—which should be set to Department_ID.

There is another property you may want to set for some reports: PageOnBreak. By default, this property is set to False, meaning that Oracle Objects will *not* go to the next page when there is a new value for Department ID. If you do want this behavior, set PageOnBreak to True.

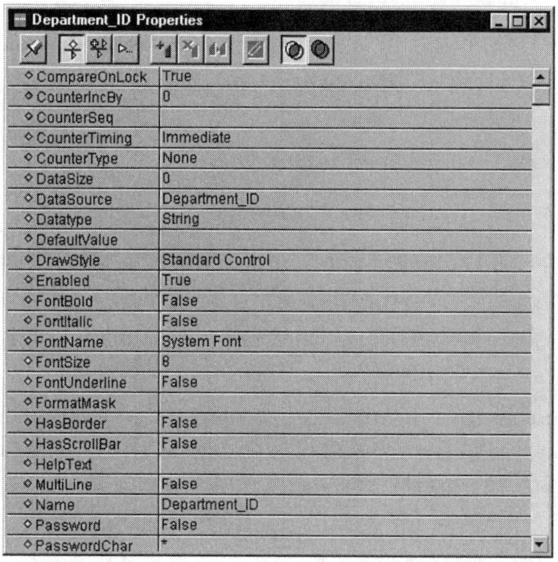

Figure 18.21.

Properties for the Department_ID field in the GroupHeader area.

Specifying the Detail Area

You still need to add three objects to the Detail area: the course ID, the course title, and the course description. These will all be text fields. To add these three objects to the Detail area, select the Text Field button on the Object Palette, and add three text fields in the detail area.

Select the first text field, invoke its property sheet, and set these properties:

DataSource	**Course_ID**
Datatype	**String**
DrawStyle	**Standard Control**
HasBorder	**False**
Name	**Course_ID**

Select the second text field, invoke its property sheet, and set these properties:

DataSource   **Title**

Datatype   **String**

DrawStyle   **Standard Control**

HasBorder   **False**

Name   **Title**

Select the third text field, invoke its property sheet, and set these properties:

DataSource   **Description**

Datatype   **String**

DrawStyle   **Standard Control**

HasBorder   **False**

Name   **Description**

However, there are two other properties that you must specify for the Description field:

DataSize   **2000** (this allows the field to accommodate the contents of the Description column, which can be up to 2000 characters)

Multiline   **True** (this allows the Description field to wrap to multiple lines, as needed)

Close all the property sheets. At this point, your report should look much like the one displayed in Figure 18.22. Try testing the report by right-clicking Run Form. Figure 18.23 illustrates what the finished report looks like.

As you can see, the courses appear below the department that offers them. Also, notice that the Run-Time mode toolbar for a report is different from the Run-Time mode toolbar for a form. In the upper-left corner, there are two buttons that will go to the previous or next pages in the report. To exit Run-Time mode, click Stop on the toolbar.

18

Figure 18.22.
Final report layout.

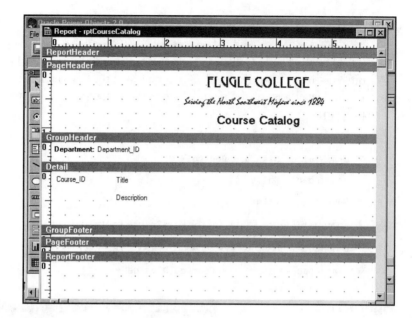

Figure 18.23.
Testing the report.

Next page

Previous page

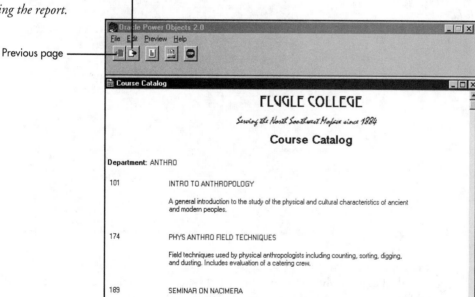

Adding a Lookup Field to a Report

As with forms, you can add a lookup field to a report. For example, suppose you want to add a field to the Flugle College Course Catalog that indicated whether or not a course was offered—in other words, whether or not it was in the Class table. To do this, add a text field to the Detail area of the report. Invoke the property sheet for the new field. Set these properties:

Datatype	**String**
DrawStyle	**Standard Control**
HasBorder	**False**
Name	**Offered**

As shown in Figure 18.24, set the DataSource property to:

```
=sqllookup(Flugle,"select decode(count(*),0,null,'Offered') from Class
where Department_ID = '" + Department_ID.value +
➥"' and Course_ID = '" + Course_ID.value + "' ")
```

Figure 18.24.

Setting the properties for a report lookup field.

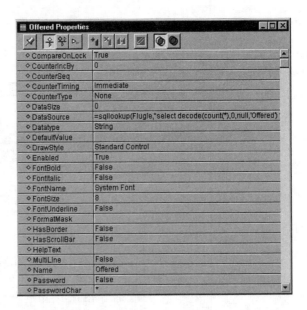

Let's examine this statement. The SQLLOOKUP function is used to execute a SELECT statement against the Flugle database session. The SELECT statement uses the DECODE function to decode the value count(*), which is the number of classes that have the same value as the Department ID and Course ID fields. If count(*) is equal to 0, the DECODE function will return null; nothing will appear in the report. If count(*) is not equal to zero, this means that there are classes offered for this department and course, and the DECODE function will return the string Offered.

Let's test the revised report. Click on Run Form on the toolbar. On the first page of the report, scroll down to the courses offered by the Biology department. As you can see in Figure 18.25, BIO 101 is offered this semester.

Figure 18.25.

Testing the lookup field in the report.

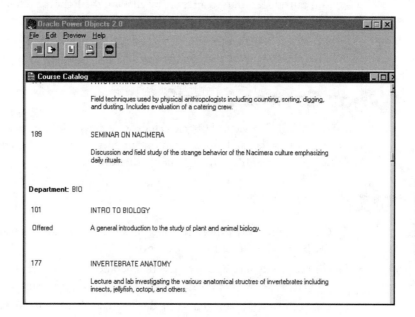

Summary

In this lesson on Power Objects, you learned these important concepts:

- [ ] You can create a class in Power Objects. A class consists of a collection of one or more objects in which you define each object's properties and methods.

- [ ] To use a class, you add an instance of the class to a form, report, or even another class. The instance inherits the properties and methods of the class from which it is inherited.

- [ ] You can override one or more inherited properties in the instance of a class on a form, report, or another class.

- [ ] You can override one or more inherited methods in the instance of a class on a form, report, or another class.

- [ ] In the method code for a class instance, you can both override the inherited method code and invoke it using the Inherited.*Method_Name*() statement.

☐ An application can include zero or more reports.

☐ A Power Objects report contains five areas in which you place objects, such as static text and text fields: ReportHeader, PageHeader, Detail, PageFooter, and ReportFooter. In general, you will add objects to the Detail area, but you may or may not have objects in the other report areas.

☐ You can add a group to a report by clicking the Report Section button on the Object Palette and adding it to the report.

☐ When you add a group to a report, two areas are also added to the report: GroupHeader and GroupFooter.

What Comes Next?

On Day 19, "An Overview of Oracle Database Security and Tuning," you will learn how to create database roles and users, granting privileges, using synonyms, determining the execution plan for a SQL statement, and other topics.

Q&A

Q Can you view the inherited code for a method in an instance of the class that has been added to a form or report?

A Unfortunately, no. You can view the method code for a class only by invoking the property sheet for the class that contains the code you want to see.

Q Can a Power Objects report be designed so that the format of a field depends on its contents?

A Yes. You can use a method, such as Validate, to inspect the field value and change another field property, such as FontBold.

Q Are there any other products included with the Oracle Power Objects 2.0 CD-ROM?

A Yes! The Oracle Power Objects 2.0 CD-ROM includes a full version of Crystal Reports Professional Version 5.0. Using your Web browser, you can order Power Objects from the Oracle Store at www.oracle.com; these products are not included on the CD-ROM accompanying this book.

Workshop

The purpose of the Workshop is to allow you to test your knowledge of the material discussed in the lesson. See if you can correctly answer the questions in the quiz and complete the exercises before you continue with tomorrow's lesson.

Quiz

1. True or false? A report's `RecordSource` property must reference a single table or view; it cannot join two or more tables.

2. True or false? Power Objects supports a maximum of three levels of inheritance. In other words, you can create class A, add an instance of class A on class B, and add an instance of class B on class C.

3. If you can validate user input in a Power Objects application with the `Validate` method, why would you need to use database constraints and triggers to enforce data integrity?

Exercises

1. Power Objects includes a number of predefined classes. If you examine the contents of the `Classes` folder, you'll see a class named `clsMeter`. Add an instance of it to `MyForm`. See if you can figure out how to link the meter to the X position of the mouse on the form.

2. Use Power Objects to build a report which contains a list of the instructors that belong to each department. Add a lookup field to each instructor line that indicates whether the instructor is not teaching any classes for the semester.

18

Day 19

An Overview of Oracle Database Security and Tuning

Today's lesson covers two topics that can't be ignored during the development of Oracle database applications—security and tuning. Many of the tasks discussed in this lesson are typically performed by a dedicated database administrator. Even if you're never responsible for the security and tuning of an Oracle database, it's a good idea for you to understand some of the issues that are involved. This lesson begins with a discussion of users, roles, and the privileges granted to them.

Users and Roles

During Day 3, "Logical Database Design," you went through the steps of adding a new user to an Oracle database. In addition to a user, Oracle also enables you to create a database *role*—a set of Oracle privileges that can correspond with a functional role in an organization. For example, you may want to allow a data entry clerk to insert and update rows in a particular table but prevent him or her from deleting any rows. To enforce this security scheme, you would create a database role named DATA_ENTRY, which would be granted these privileges.

On the other hand, the data entry manager should be able to insert, update, and delete rows in the tables. Therefore, you would create a separate role named DATA_ENTRY_MANAGER to implement this security policy. Once a database role is created, it can be granted to an individual user as needed. In addition, a role also can be granted to another role. Database roles not only help to ensure appropriate security, they also simplify database administration.

For an application environment with many tables, many users, and distinct functional roles, the implementation and maintenance of a security scheme is a major task. If the database administrator grants privileges directly to individual users, it's very easy for things to fall through the cracks in the long run. The DBA might forget to give some people a privilege they need to do their work or might give others a superfluous privilege. Also, if a change to the database application requires that the privileges of users also change, the DBA will have far more work to accomplish this without roles.

By defining a database role for each functional role that exists in the organization, you significantly reduce the task of managing users and their privileges. For instance, suppose you have 10 database users—three belong to the marketing department and the other seven are in the engineering department. You would create two database roles, Marketer and Engineer, and grant the appropriate privileges to each role; the Marketer role needs access to one set of tables, whereas the Engineer role requires access to a different set. You would then grant the appropriate role to each user. If the database changes—for instance, the addition of a table— you simply update the privileges of the role, not the user.

Pre-Defined Users: SYS and SYSTEM

Every Oracle database has two pre-defined accounts that serve a special purpose—SYS and SYSTEM. The SYS account owns the Oracle data dictionary tables and associated database objects. The SYSTEM account owns tables that are used by Oracle application development tools such as Oracle Forms or Reports. You should not create any database objects such as tables or indexes while connected as SYS or SYSTEM, except for Oracle-supplied SQL scripts that specifically indicate that they should be installed as SYS or SYSTEM.

Pre-Defined Roles

When an Oracle database is installed, the five database roles are created:

- [ ] CONNECT has the capability to connect to the Personal Oracle database (by means of the system privilege, CREATE SESSION).
- [ ] RESOURCE has the capability to create tables, indexes, views, and other Oracle objects.

- [ ] DBA consists of all system privileges needed to create, alter, or drop users and manage the database objects that they own.
- [ ] IMP_FULL_DATABASE consists of all system privileges needed to perform a full database import.
- [ ] EXP_FULL_DATABASE consists of all system privileges needed to perform a full database export.

NOTE

The historical reason for these pre-defined roles is that Oracle version 6 had only three privileges—connect, resource, and DBA. Because Oracle re-defined these privileges as roles in Oracle7, SQL*Plus scripts developed for Oracle version 6 can be processed in Oracle8. These roles also simplify the assignment of system privileges to other roles and users.

System and Object Privileges

A role isn't useful unless it has been granted at least one privilege. Oracle privileges belong in two categories:

- [ ] *System* privileges enable an Oracle user to execute statements such as CREATE TABLE, CREATE USER, or ALTER INDEX.
- [ ] *Object* privileges are associated with a particular operation (such as SELECT or UPDATE) on a specified database object (such as a table or index).

You can grant many different system privileges to a role or user—in fact, Oracle has more than 80 system privileges. One system privilege that almost every Oracle user needs is CREATE SESSION—the capability to establish an Oracle session.

Creating and Using a Role

To make these concepts more concrete, this section walks you through the process of creating a role and assigning it to an individual. You will also grant system privileges to the role. To do this, you'll need an account that has been granted the DBA role. Please realize that what you see on your screen may differ from the figures in this lesson because you may have users and roles already defined.

1. To start, invoke Security Manager from the Oracle Enterprise Manager program group.
2. Enter the username, password, and service as appropriate.

3. Once Security Manager has connected to the Oracle database, click the Roles folder on the left-hand window.

4. In the right-hand window, you should see the existing database roles (see Figure 19.1).

Figure 19.1.

Viewing existing database roles with Security Manager.

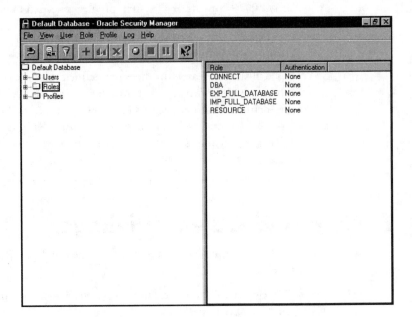

5. To create a new role, you may either click the + button on the toolbar or select the menu item Role | Create. A dialog window is displayed, prompting you for the new role's name (see Figure 19.2).

6. Enter **Department_Administrator**.

7. Leave the Authentication radio button set to None.

Next, grant the CONNECT and RESOURCE roles to the new database role.

1. Press the tab folder named Privileges. By default, Security Manager displays the roles that are currently granted to the new database role. At the bottom of the dialog window, you will see the existing roles.

2. Holding down the Control key, select CONNECT and RESOURCE and click Add (see Figure 19.3). You should now see the CONNECT and RESOURCE roles in the upper portion of the dialog window.

19

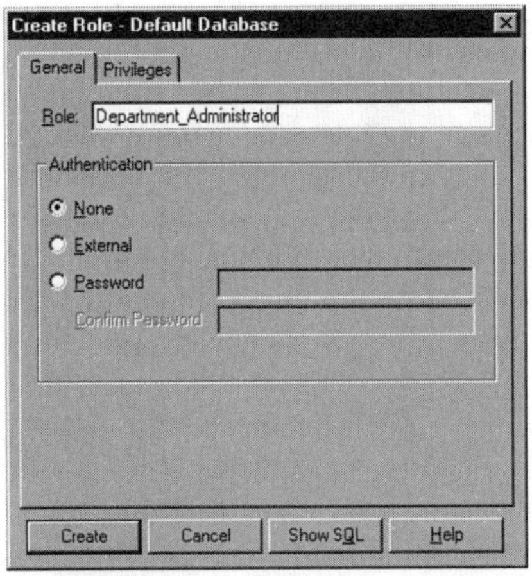

Figure 19.2.

*Creating a new role
with Security Manager.*

Figure 19.3.

Granting the CONNECT
and RESOURCE *roles to
the new role.*

3. Once you click the Create button, the Department_Administrator role is created, and you should see it in the lists of database roles on the right-hand side of the window.

4. Now, add a user—Terri Greenglass, the English department administrator—to the database.

5. Click the Users folder, and click the + button on the toolbar.

6. In the User field, enter **tgreenglass**.

7. In the Password and Confirm Password fields, enter the password you wish to give the new user (see Figure 19.4).

Figure 19.4.

Creating the new database user.

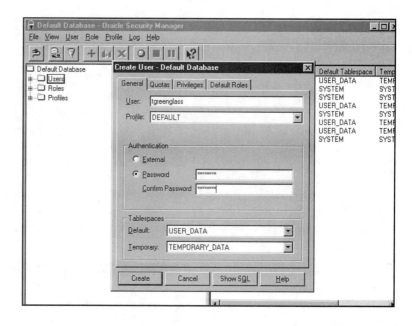

8. For the purpose of this example, ignore the Tablespaces section of the window.

9. To grant the Department_Administrator role to Terri Greenglass, select the Privileges tab.

10. Using the mouse, select the Department_Administrator role, and click the Add button (see Figure 19.5).

Figure 19.5.

Granting the Department_Administrator *role to the new user.*

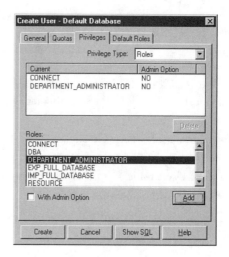

11. To complete the creation of the Oracle account for Terri Greenglass, click the Create button. Security Manager submits the SQL statements to the Oracle database to create the new user and grant the role.

Limiting a User's Resources with a Profile

In addition to providing a quota on the use of storage in a tablespace, Oracle also provides other system-level quotas that can be established for a user. These quotas include the following:

☐ CONNECT_TIME is the number of elapsed minutes since the user has connected to an Oracle database

☐ IDLE_TIME is the number of elapsed minutes since the user last performed an action resulting in an Oracle call

☐ LOGICAL_READS_PER_CALL is the number of Oracle blocks read from memory or disk to satisfy an Oracle call

The mechanism that you use for specifying these quotas is the *profile*. For example, you might want to create a profile for a casual user that limits his or her connect time to two hours or less. In addition, you might also want to limit a casual user's idle time to 10 minutes. On top of that, you might also fear that a casual user—particularly, one who has access to an ad hoc query tool—could inadvertently construct queries that produce a Cartesian product of several tables. By setting a fairly high limit on LOGICAL_READS_PER_CALL, you can prevent the user's query from consuming memory and CPU time needed by other users.

To enforce the resource limits specified in a user's profile, the DBA must perform either one of the following tasks:

☐ Set the resource_limit initialization parameter to TRUE. The new value for resource_limit won't take effect until you restart the database.

☐ Modify the database by issuing the following command in SQL*Plus: ALTER SYSTEM SET RESOURCE LIMIT = TRUE; or by setting the RESOURCE_LIMIT=TRUE in the init.ora file for the database.

Obstacles to Optimal Performance

One of the goals of this lesson is to address performance issues related to an Oracle database. The material in this lesson is an introduction to some of the issues you may encounter during the database development process. Here are some general suggestions.

19

Keep these guidelines in mind as you read about the performance characteristics that occur in an Oracle client/server environment.

Synonyms

A synonym is another name for a table. Actually, the term *table synonym* is more accurate. Synonyms come in two flavors: private and public. A private synonym is visible only to the Oracle user who created it. A public synonym is visible to all Oracle users. Any Oracle user who has been granted the RESOURCE role can create a private synonym. On the other hand, only an Oracle user who has been granted the DBA role—or the Create Public Synonym system privilege—can create a public synonym.

 A *synonym* is another name for a table or view. A synonym that is visible only to its owner is referred to as a *private synonym*. A synonym that is visible to all Oracle users is referred to as a *public synonym*.

In one way, a synonym is similar to a view: both objects enable a table to be referenced by a different name. However, a synonym doesn't enable you to restrict columns or rename them.

A synonym provides an additional name for referencing a table. For example, you may not be able to rename a table because existing applications reference the current table name. However, a synonym that provides a more intuitive and meaningful name might be ideal for use in an ad hoc query tool.

Synonym Syntax

You should see how you can manage synonyms with the Personal Oracle Navigator or with Schema Manager. However, there is an advantage to using an SQL script for creating and dropping synonyms.

Therefore, take a look at the syntax for creating a synonym:

```
CREATE [PUBLIC] SYNONYM synonym-name
FOR owner.object-name;
```

The variables are defined as follows:

> synonym-name is the synonym name and is subject to Oracle database object-naming requirements.
>
> owner is the name of the Oracle account that owns the referenced table or view.
>
> object-name is the name of the table or view referenced by the synonym.

You might want to create a synonym to reference a table whose name is inappropriate or difficult to remember. In this example, the synonym p_artifact is used to point to the table parthaginian_artifacts, which belongs to the same Oracle user.

```
SQL> create synonym p_artifact for parthaginian_artifacts;

Synonym created.
```

A private synonym also can point to a table owned by another Oracle user. Suppose Oracle user RJOHNSON has created the Project table and wants to enable Oracle user KCHOW to read the Project table. First, RJOHNSON grants the select privilege on the Project table to KCHOW. However, each time KCHOW wants to look at the table, she has to remember to qualify the table name with RJOHNSON—the table owner. Consequently, she creates a private synonym that enables her to reference the table by the Project name alone, as shown in Listing 19.1.

INPUT/OUTPUT Listing 19.1. Using a private synonym.

```
SQL> select Project_Number
  2  from Project;
from Project
     *
ERROR at line 2:
ORA-00942: table or view does not exist

SQL> create synonym Project for RJOHNSON.Project;

Synonym created.

SQL> select Project_Number
  2  from Project;

PROJECT_NUMBER
--------------
          1201
          2143
          4310
```

19

Dropping Synonyms

Oracle provides a statement for eliminating a synonym—the DROP SYNONYM statement.

SYNTAX

Its syntax is as follows:

```
DROP [PUBLIC] SYNONYM synonym-name;
```

The variable is defined as follows:

synonym-name is the name of the existing synonym that you want to eliminate.

Hiding Table Ownership with Public Synonyms

Consider the following example. You've developed a project accounting application at your company. You now must support two groups of users: those users who are running version 1.0 and those running version 2.0. However, version 2.0 requires some database changes; the database used by version 1.0 cannot be used by version 2.0. The tables used by both versions can be stored in the same Oracle database, provided that they are owned by separate Oracle accounts.

Suppose that the version 1.0 tables are owned by an Oracle account named PAV10. The version 2.0 tables are owned by another Oracle account named PAV20. If you wanted to support a group of software testers who need to switch back and forth between the two versions, you could construct two SQL*Plus scripts. The first script drops the existing synonyms and creates synonyms that point to the version 1.0 tables, as shown in Listing 19.2.

Listing 19.2. Using synonyms to point to the first version of the tables.

INPUT

```
drop synonym Account_Number;
...
drop synonym Task_Header;
drop synonym Task_Detail;
...
...
create synonym Account_Number for PAV10.Account_Number;
...
create synonym Task_Header for PAV10.Task_Header;
create synonym Task_Detail for PAV10.Task_Detail;
```

The second script, shown in Listing 19.3, also drops the existing synonyms but creates synonyms that point to the version 2.0 tables.

INPUT **Listing 19.3. Using synonyms to point to the second version of the tables.**

```
drop synonym Account_Number;
...
drop synonym Task_Header;
drop synonym Task_Detail;
...
...
create synonym Account_Number for PAV20.Account_Number;
...
create synonym Task_Header for PAV20.Task_Header;
create synonym Task_Detail for PAV20.Task_Detail;
```

With these two scripts, a user can switch back and forth between the two versions of the project accounting tables.

Synonyms, the Navigator, and Schema Manager

Personal Oracle for Windows 95 enables you to manipulate synonyms with the Navigator. To look at a list of the existing synonyms in your local database, double-click the Synonym folder. A list of all synonyms is displayed on the right side of the Main window. (See Figure 19.6.)

Figure 19.6.

The Navigator displays a list of synonyms in the Local database.

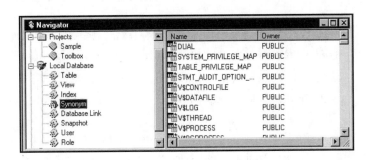

19

NOTE

If you're using an Oracle server, you can use Schema Manager to manage private and public synonyms. In fact, you also can use Schema Manager with a Personal Oracle database.

Examining a Synonym with the Navigator

To examine the definition of a synonym, select the synonym and right-click Properties. The Navigator displays a window that identifies the name of the synonym, its owner, and the table (or view) that it references (see Figure 19.7). However, if the owner name and table name are lengthy, you may not be able to read the full table name.

Figure 19.7.

The Navigator displays the definition of a synonym.

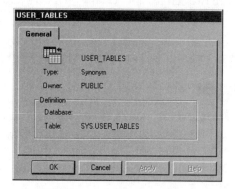

Creating a Synonym with the Navigator

Follow these steps to create a synonym with the Navigator:

1. Select the Synonym folder and right-click New.

2. In the Create Synonym window, enter a name for the new synonym in the Name field.

3. You have a choice for the synonym type—it may either be public or private.

4. In the Database field, select Personal Oracle and select the table from the drop-down list in the Table field. Click OK to create the synonym. Figure 19.8 illustrates how a public synonym is created.

5. If you want to create a private synonym, you must select the Private To radio button and identify the user that will own the synonym in the drop-down list to the right.

Figure 19.8.

Creating a public synonym with the Navigator.

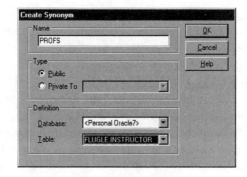

Deleting a Synonym with the Navigator

To delete a synonym, select the synonym that you want to delete, and right-click Delete. The Navigator will ask you to confirm that you really want to delete the synonym.

Where's the Bottleneck?

Users are the best judges of the performance of an information system. Users measure performance in terms of response time, report turnaround time, and data transfer speed. A very inefficient system may be perceived by users as providing excellent turnaround time. Conversely, a group of users might consider the performance of a very efficient information system to be inadequate. Ignore the perception of the users at your peril.

Suppose you have to analyze a system that's the object of complaints about lackluster performance. You will need to examine four elements of a client/server architecture:

- ☐ The network
- ☐ The server
- ☐ The Oracle database
- ☐ The application

Your goal in performance tuning should be to make the biggest immediate improvement with the least amount of disruption to existing software, hardware, and procedures. The following sections look at each of the four elements in some detail.

Network

The network used in a client/server architecture may be a LAN, WAN, or a combination of both. Seek the help of a networking expert to determine the saturation level of the network. Characterize the network demands of a single client. If the network appears to be the performance bottleneck, investigate the client application software to discover whether you can reduce the number of SQL requests to the server. Changing the client application software has a huge impact; this strategy should be your last resort!

If you're just beginning to design an application, you can reduce the network traffic by identifying functionality that can be implemented with stored procedures and functions in the database.

Identifying Application Bottlenecks

Oracle furnishes two optimizers—the rule-based optimizer and the cost-based optimizer. Both optimizers are concerned with maximizing the performance of queries. The rule-based optimizer looks at the structure of the SQL statement to be optimized, determines what indexes exist for the table, and constructs an execution plan; it doesn't use any information about the contents of the table to be queried, or its index values.

NEW TERM The *rule-based optimizer* is a mechanism in the Oracle RDBMS that looks at the database objects referenced by a SQL statement to determine the most efficient plan for performing the tasks specified by the SQL statement. The *cost-based optimizer* is an alternative to the rule-based optimizer; it uses the characteristics of the table and index contents to determine the most efficient plan for performing the tasks specified by the SQL statement.

The *cost-based optimizer* looks at statistics regarding the table, its columns, and its indexes and then calculates an execution plan based on the lowest cost path—the number of database blocks that must be read to retrieve the query results. Oracle stores these statistics in the data dictionary tables whenever an analysis of the tables and indexes is performed.

An initialization parameter named `OPTIMIZER_MODE` controls the choice between the rule-based and cost-based optimizer; this parameter has three possible values:

CHOOSE   If the data dictionary doesn't contain any table or index statistics, Oracle uses the rule-based optimizer. However, if table and index statistics are available, Oracle uses the cost-based optimizer. The default for `OPTIMIZER_MODE` is `CHOOSE`.

RULE   Oracle will always use the rule-based optimizer.

COST   Oracle will always use the cost-based optimizer.

NOTE
> Measuring the performance of a query isn't as simple as it sounds. If you perform the same query twice against a large table, the second query will probably retrieve the results more quickly because the SGA already contains the database blocks that the query needs to read. Fewer disk reads are needed so the second query takes less time to complete. You can accomplish this by using the following SQL statement:
>
> ```
> SQL> alter system flush shared_pool;
> ```

Determining the Execution Plan for an SQL Statement with EXPLAIN PLAN

If you don't analyze tables and indexes, Oracle will use the rule-based optimizer to determine the best execution plan for each query. You can use the EXPLAIN PLAN statement to obtain the execution plan for a query.

SYNTAX

The syntax for EXPLAIN PLAN is as follows:

```
EXPLAIN PLAN FOR sql-statement
```

The variable is defined as follows:

> sql-statement is the SQL statement for which an execution plan is to be generated.

Before you use the EXPLAIN PLAN statement, you'll need to run a script from SQL*Plus that creates the PLAN_TABLE in your Oracle account. This is displayed in Listing 19.4.

INPUT/OUTPUT   **Listing 19.4. Creating the PLAN_TABLE table.**

```
SQL> @c:\orawin95\rdbms73\admin\utlxplan.sql

Table created.

SQL> desc plan_table
 Name                            Null?     Type
 ------------------------------- --------- ----
 STATEMENT_ID                              VARCHAR2(30)
 TIMESTAMP                                 DATE
 REMARKS                                   VARCHAR2(80)
 OPERATION                                 VARCHAR2(30)
 OPTIONS                                   VARCHAR2(30)
 OBJECT_NODE                               VARCHAR2(128)
 OBJECT_OWNER                              VARCHAR2(30)
 OBJECT_NAME                               VARCHAR2(30)
 OBJECT_INSTANCE                           NUMBER(38)
 OBJECT_TYPE                               VARCHAR2(30)
 OPTIMIZER                                 VARCHAR2(255)
 SEARCH_COLUMNS                            NUMBER(38)
 ID                                        NUMBER(38)
 PARENT_ID                                 NUMBER(38)
 POSITION                                  NUMBER(38)
 OTHER                                     LONG
```

After the PLAN_TABLE has been created, you can begin using the EXPLAIN PLAN statement. Whenever the EXPLAIN PLAN statement is executed, Oracle inserts rows into the PLAN_TABLE; as a result, you need to delete the contents of PLAN_TABLE before each use of EXPLAIN PLAN. For example, suppose you create a table that records the day of the year and the maximum temperature in degrees Fahrenheit for each day. As a developer, you want to determine the efficiency of a query's execution plan. Listing 19.5 contains the steps that you would follow to determine a statement's execution plan.

19

INPUT/
OUTPUT **Listing 19.5. Using the EXPLAIN PLAN statement.**

```
SQL> delete from plan_table;

0 rows deleted.

SQL> explain plan for
  2  select day_number, temp_deg_f
  3  from day_temp
  4  where day_number = 100;

Explained.

SQL> select operation, options, object_name, id, parent_id, position
  2  from plan_table
  3  order by id;
```

OPERATION	OPTIONS	OBJECT_NAME	ID	PARENT_ID	POSITION
SELECT STATEMENT			0		
TABLE ACCESS	FULL	DAY_TEMP	1	0	1

EXPLAIN_PLAN is looking for the word FULL that is displayed in the OPTIONS column in conjunction with the TABLE ACCESS operation. FULL signifies that the query performs a full table scan to retrieve the data. If a query involving Day_Number is a fairly common operation, you should consider adding an index on the Day_Number column. Listing 19.6 shows how to create the index and rerun EXPLAIN_PLAN.

INPUT/
OUTPUT **Listing 19.6. Determining the execution plan after creating an index.**

```
SQL> create index day_temp_day_number_ck
  2  on day_temp (day_number);

Index created.

SQL> delete from plan_table;

2 rows deleted.

SQL> explain plan for
  2  select day_number, temp_deg_f
  3  from day_temp
  4  where day_number = 100;

Explained.

SQL> select operation, options, object_name, id, parent_id, position
  2  from plan_table
  3  order by id;
```

OPERATION	OPTIONS	OBJECT_NAME	ID	PARENT_ID	POSITION
SELECT STATEMENT			0		
TABLE ACCESS	BY ROWID	DAY_TEMP	1	0	1
INDEX	RANGE SCAN	DAY_TEMP_DAY_NUMBER_CK	2	1	1

As you can see, by creating the index, you've changed the optimizer's execution plan for the query. Instead of performing a full table scan, the optimizer performs an index range scan, which is almost always a more efficient operation (although not for a table with a small number of rows). Even though the EXPLAIN PLAN statement supplies useful information about the methods used by the optimizer, it doesn't provide any hard performance numbers. To retrieve performance data, you should use the tkprof utility.

Using tkprof to Analyze a Statement

If you're using Personal Oracle, you'll find an executable file c:\orawin95\bin\tkprof73.exe (the directory and filename will depend on the Oracle version that you're using). If you're using an Oracle server, a version of tkprof can be found in the bin directory beneath the Oracle home directory. tkprof's command line arguments are the same for any version of Oracle7 or higher. tkprof processes Oracle trace files to produce a text file that describes the SQL activity that occurred during a particular Oracle session. A trace file is extremely useful for performance analysis and tuning for these reasons:

- [ ] It contains the exact SQL statements that were executed by a given user during a particular Oracle session.
- [ ] If the initialization parameter TIMED_STATISTICS is enabled, the trace file will contain statistical information about the execution of each SQL statement.

By default, an Oracle database won't produce trace files. To produce a trace file with performance data, you'll need to have your DBA set an initialization parameter named TIMED_STATISTICS to TRUE and restart the Oracle instance. You must stop the database and restart it for this parameter to take effect.

If you wanted to analyze the performance of a group of SQL statements processed by SQL*Plus, you can enable a trace file for the Oracle session in the following way:

```
SQL> alter session set sql_trace true;

Session altered.
```

You may then process any SQL statements that you were interested in analyzing. If you're using Personal Oracle, you'll find the trace files in c:\orawin95\rdbms73\trace. If you're using an Oracle server, the trace files can be found in the directory named rdbms73/trace and beneath the Oracle home directory. You should end the Oracle session before you try to analyze the trace file.

19

Next, open an MS-DOS window. If you type **tkprof73** at the prompt, the program displays a list of its command-line arguments. At a minimum, you should specify the name of the trace file, the name of the output file, and the Oracle user and password whose PLAN_TABLE will be used to determine the statement execution plan.

By default, the output file will have an extension of .prf. You may then use an editor to display and print the contents of the output file. The summary portion of a sample tkprof output file is shown in the following code segment.

```
OVERALL TOTALS FOR ALL NON-RECURSIVE STATEMENTS

call      count      cpu    elapsed      disk      query    current      rows
-------   ------   -------  --------   ------   --------   --------   --------
Parse         7     0.00       1.59        2          0          4          0
Execute       8     0.00       0.49        2         13         38         10
Fetch         5     0.00       0.04        2          3          9         35
-------   ------   -------  --------   ------   --------   --------   --------
total        20     0.00       2.12        6         16         51         45

Misses in library cache during parse: 4
Misses in library cache during execute: 1

    8  user  SQL statements in session.
   26  internal SQL statements in session.
   34  SQL statements in session.
    4  statements EXPLAINed in this session.
*****************************************************************************
Trace file: c:\orawin95\rdbms73\trace\ora63171.trc
Trace file compatibilty: 7.02.01
Sort options: execpu
    1  session in tracefile.
    8  user  SQL statements in trace file.
   26  internal SQL statements in trace file.
   34  SQL statements in trace file.
   18  unique SQL statements in trace file.
    4  SQL statements EXPLAINed using schema:
       FLUGLE.prof$plan_table
          Default table was used.
          Table was created.
          Table was dropped.
  382  lines in trace file.
```

As you can see, the trace file provides a wealth of statistical information about the SQL statements that were processed during the Oracle session. This tool is particularly powerful in helping you solve the so-called 80-20 problem: identifying and improving the 20 percent of the SQL statements that represent 80 percent of the work.

Creating Indexes to Improve Performance

A significant portion of database activity consists of SELECT statements. Accordingly, improving query performance results in better overall application performance. A query generally is processed more quickly if it uses an index to access the qualified rows. A *full table scan* is a query in which all of a table's rows are read to find the qualified rows. To determine whether a query performs a full table scan, you must obtain the query's *execution plan.* When an execution plan indicates that a full table scan is being performed, consider creating an index that the query can use.

NEW TERM An *execution plan* is the method that the Oracle RDBMS uses to perform the tasks for an SQL statement. For example, if a table has no indexes, the execution plan to query the table will require that every row in the table be read; this is known as a *full table scan.*

Be alert to the possibility of *overindexing* a table. Remember that Oracle automatically maintains a table's indexes whenever the contents of the table change because of an INSERT, UPDATE, or DELETE statement. Your goal should be to optimize the most frequent queries without forcing Oracle to maintain an inordinate number of indexes.

Tuning an Oracle Database

Oracle performance-tuning efforts can be classified in three ways:

- [ ] Efforts that are application independent. For example, you don't have to modify or rebuild any software to tune the System Global Area.
- [ ] Efforts that are mostly application independent. For instance, by inspecting an application's queries, you may identify indexes that you should create to improve query performance.
- [ ] Efforts that affect the application software. You might discover that the underlying database design is inefficient or that the application software makes unnecessary SQL requests. Making such changes is very expensive in terms of budget and schedule. Trying to restructure a system after it's been constructed is very difficult!

Your best bet is to focus on tuning efforts that have a minimal effect on the existing application.

Increasing the Size of the SGA

Among its other uses, the SGA functions as Oracle's cache. If you increase the number of data block buffers in the SGA, you increase the higher probability that an SQL statement will find the block that it needs in memory—thereby reducing the number of disk reads it needs to locate a block. However, be sure that the SGA isn't so large that it's swapped out of memory by the operating system. The number of database buffers used by an Oracle database is one of the initialization parameters that are used when an Oracle database is started. The new value for an initialization parameter doesn't take effect until the next time the database is started.

Reducing Disk Contention

To tune disk I/O, you must first determine if disk I/O requests are balanced across all the server's disk drives. Use operating system commands and utilities to identify the average

number of I/O requests serviced by each disk drive. Your objectives should include the
following:

☐ Lower the overall number of disk I/O requests by adding more memory to the
server. By adding more RAM, you'll be able to increase the size of the Oracle SGA
and thereby reduce overall disk I/O, assuming no other changes are made to the
database.

☐ Lower the average number of I/O requests per drive by adding disk drives to the
server. You can then relocate a tablespace's datafiles to a new disk drive by using
the ALTER TABLESPACE statement with the RENAME option.

☐ Lower the average number of I/O requests per disk controller by adding another
disk controller to the server.

☐ Balance disk I/O requests so that each drive is servicing the same number of I/O
requests. This tuning method requires both analysis and experimentation to
determine the optimal distribution of Oracle datafiles and redo log files.

Summary

This lesson covers the following principles regarding the management of Oracle users,
database roles and privileges, and performance tuning:

☐ You can manage users, roles, and privileges with the point-and-click interface
offered by Personal Oracle Navigator and Security Manager. You also can use SQL
commands in SQL Worksheet or SQL*Plus to create and modify users, roles, and
privileges.

☐ A profile is a set of system-level quotas that can be levied on a user or role. These
quotas include the amount of idle time and the number of logical reads performed
for a single query.

☐ To maximize network performance before implementing an application, plan to
use stored procedures and functions in the database to reduce the number of SQL
requests on the network, and minimize superfluous SQL requests from the client
application.

☐ To improve Oracle database performance, tune the SGA, reduce data segment
fragmentation, and add non-unique indexes where appropriate.

☐ To improve the server's performance, add memory so that more data block buffers
can be added to the SGA; also add more disk drives to reduce the average number
of I/O requests per disk drive.

☐ Oracle uses two optimizers: the rule-based optimizer and the cost-based optimizer.

☐ The rule-based optimizer looks at a query's syntax and the existence of indexes to
determine the most efficient method for retrieving the qualified rows.

☐ The cost-based optimizer looks at a query's syntax, the existence of indexes, and the table and index statistics to determine the most efficient method for retrieving the qualified rows.

☐ Use the EXPLAIN_PLAN statement to determine a query's execution plan.

☐ You can generate a trace file for a specific Oracle session by executing ALTER SESSION SET SQL_TRACE TRUE when the Oracle session begins.

☐ tkprof is a utility that converts a binary Oracle trace file to a listing file containing each SQL statement executed during an Oracle session.

What Comes Next?

On Day 20, "Using Oracle Database Designer and Oracle Designer/2000 in Application Development," you will learn about the use two database design tools. Oracle Database Designer is used to develop a logical data model and automatically implement the physical database by generating the SQL DDL statements that create tables, indexes, and other objects. Oracle Designer/2000 is a comprehensive, multi-user design tool that enables you to design and create databases and applications for a large, complex enterprise.

Q&A

Q Can a database role be granted to another database role?

A Yes. You can grant a role to another role or to an Oracle user. However, you should avoid creating an unnecessarily complex set of roles; the use of roles should simplify the management of database privileges, not make it more complex.

Workshop

The purpose of the Workshop is to allow you to test your knowledge of the material discussed in the lesson. See if you can correctly answer the questions in the quiz and complete the exercise before you continue with tomorrow's lesson.

Quiz

1. True or false? A database role can be granted to both users and other database roles.

2. True or false? Adding an index to a table always improves the performance of an application.

3. True or false? Any Oracle user can create a public synonym as long as the synonym points to a table that is owned by that user.

Exercise

You can answer this question descriptively, without using SQL statements: If you were the DBA at Flugle College, what database roles would you create? What privileges would you grant to those roles?

Day **20**

Using Oracle Database Designer and Oracle Designer/2000 in Application Development

Although this lesson comes near the end of the book, you may want to think of this lesson as the starting point for developing an Oracle database application. In this lesson, you examine the use of Database Designer and Designer/2000.

Database Designer was announced by Oracle Corporation in 1997. It is an entity-relationship (ER) design tool, designed to compete with Logic Works' ERwin and Sybase's S-Designor. All three tools provide a graphical interface for creating an entity-relationship diagram which can generate the DDL statements that create a working database. Database Designer, and its competitors, are appropriate for projects where it is practical for one person to create and maintain the data model. Also, these tools focus only on the development of a logical data model and its implementation as a physical database; they do not help the application designer with process modeling, dataflow modeling, and other facets of large application design.

In contrast, Designer/2000 is a comprehensive suite of tools that supports the analysis, design, and implementation phases of a large project. You can think of Designer/2000 as a "cradle-to-grave" development methodology. These tools can help an entire team to gather, document, and verify the requirements for an application on many levels—data model, process model, and data flow, to name a few. These tools work together such that the outputs produced by one tool become the inputs used by another tool. At the heart of Designer/2000 is an Oracle-based repository that contains a description of the elements of the application to be built.

You can order Database Designer and Designer/2000 directly from Oracle Corporation or an Oracle reseller. You can also download a trial version of Database Designer from the Oracle Web site at www.oracle.com. To get the most from this lesson, you'll want to have a copy of Database Designer so you can follow the steps in each exercise.

 A *repository* is a set of database objects that contains metadata—that is, data about data. For example, the Designer/2000 repository contains information about the data model, the process model, and many other design aspects of an application.

 Database Designer is a 16-bit application. As a result, if you are using the product on Windows 95 or Windows NT, you must install the Windows version of SQL*Net, which is a 16-bit version.

A natural question is: Which tool is better—a tool like Database Designer (including ERwin or S-Designor) or Designer/2000? The answer is: It depends on "where you are going." To use an analogy, if you are planning a long weekend in your mountain cabin, it might suffice to pack a small overnight bag. However, if you are planning a six-month expedition to a remote region in Central Asia, packing an overnight bag would be a grave mistake; instead, it would be prudent to pack a dozen large crates with gear that might be needed to deal with unforeseen circumstances.

Similarly, Database Designer, ERwin, or S-Designor are good choices for a project that is

- ☐ Intended for a small organization
- ☐ Not too ambitious in terms of the features to be provided by the application
- ☐ Staffed by a handful of developers who have access to the end users

However, by themselves, Database Designer, ERwin, or S-Designor would be inadequate for a project that is

☐ To be implemented for a large enterprise, spanning many departments and divisions

☐ Seen as a threat by influential political players in various parts of the organization

☐ Very ambitious in terms of the features to be provided by the application and the technologies to be employed

☐ Staffed by many individuals—analysts, designers, developers, testers, technical writers, and trainers

If you haven't worked with Designer/2000, don't expect to receive the software on Monday and begin building finished applications on Tuesday. This is a complex suite of tools that requires significant training to exploit. Also, don't expect a single person to become intimately familiar with every feature in every component; that just isn't realistic. Instead, it makes much more sense for each member of the development team to focus on the components that are associated with his or her role in the development process. In this lesson, you get only a glimpse of the Designer/2000 components; a thorough tour of Designer/2000 would require a book in itself.

Creating an Entity-Relationship Diagram with Database Designer

There are many advantages to using a tool such as Database Designer instead of maintaining a script containing SQL statements. You are far less likely to make typographical errors with Database Designer; for example, it validates that the column referenced by a foreign key is itself a primary key. You can print the Entity Relationship Diagram and present it in a meeting; it is much more difficult to visualize the data model represented by a script.

Let's look at the steps that are required to create a new ER diagram. To invoke Database Designer in Windows 95, press Start | Programs | Database Designer | Database Designer. When the program is first started, you will see a menu and toolbar at the top of the screen. To create a new diagram, select File | New from the menu. A window will appear in which you have two choices: you can either create a new diagram or reverse engineer an existing database. The default option is to create a new diagram (see Figure 20.1). Click OK. You should see a window labeled ODD1—the default name for the first diagram you create.

20

Figure 20.1.

Creating a new diagram.

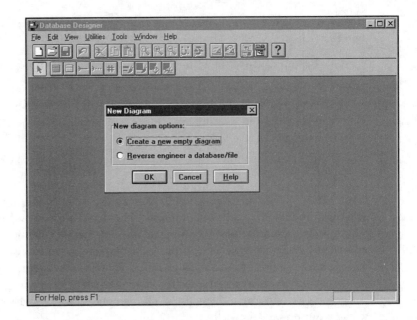

Adding a Table to the Diagram

To begin with, let's add the Student table to the diagram. In the bottom row of the toolbar, there are five buttons that correspond to these elements in an ER diagram:

- ☐ Table
- ☐ View
- ☐ Mandatory foreign key
- ☐ Optional foreign key
- ☐ Primary key

For example, to create a new table, you would click the Table button on the toolbar, position the pointer on the diagram where you want the table to be placed, and left-click (see Figure 20.2).

To specify details about the new table, move the pointer over the table and double-click. A window, labeled Edit Table, will appear, and it contains six tab folders:

- ☐ Table
- ☐ Column Definition
- ☐ Column Display (optionally used with Designer/2000 Application Generators to specify the display characteristics of the table's columns)

20

☐ Constraints

☐ Validation

☐ Index

Figure 20.2.

Creating a table.

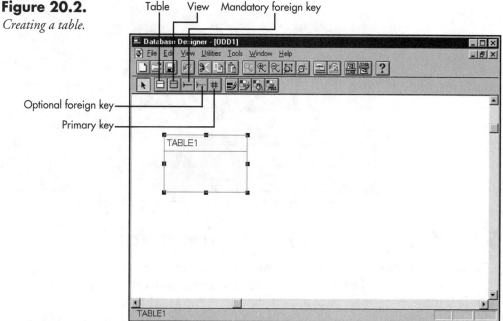

As shown in Figure 20.3, fill in these fields in the Table folder:

Name	STUDENT
Display Title	Student
Number of Rows, Start/End	An estimate of the number of rows that will initially/ultimately be stored in the table (used to estimate the size of the initial extent for the table)
Comment	Contains basic information about students.
Journal	Checked. When used with Designer/2000, it indicates that a journal table should be created for this table (a journal table is used to store all changes to a table, including who was responsible for the change and when it was made).

20

Figure 20.3.

Specifying the table characteristics.

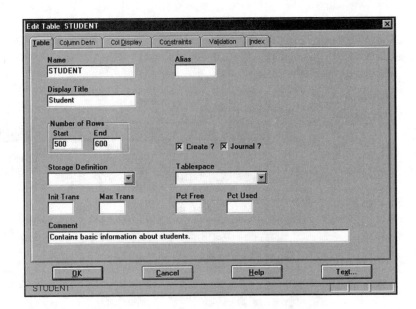

Specifying the Columns for a Table

To specify the columns in the Student table, select the tab folder labeled Column Defn. You will see five column headings displayed: Column Name, Seq, Domain, Datatype, and Avg Len. However, there are more fields to the right of Avg Len that can be displayed by using the horizontal scrollbar. In this form, each row represents information about a single column (see Figure 20.4). To add a column to the Student table, specify a value for these fields:

Column Name	The name of the column (for example, Student_ID)
Seq	The order in which the columns should be specified in the CREATE TABLE statement generated by Database Designer
Domain	May be left blank (can be used with Designer/2000 to define each domain and the attributes that are associated with the domain)
Datatype	The datatype of the column can be specified from the popup list
Avg len	Average length of the column (this is used for estimating the size of the initial extent for the table)

If you scroll to the right, you will see some other fields displayed, including (see Figure 20.5):

Max Len	The maximum length for the column (which you may or may not specify, depending on the datatype of the column).
Opt	If checked, the column is optional (the default); if not checked, the column is mandatory (NOT NULL).

20

Figure 20.4.

Defining a column.

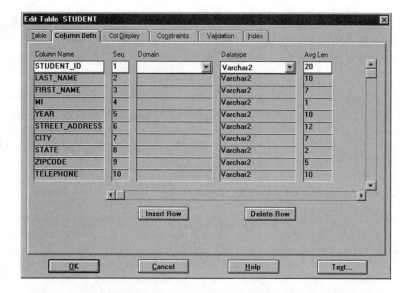

Figure 20.5.

Additional fields for defining a column.

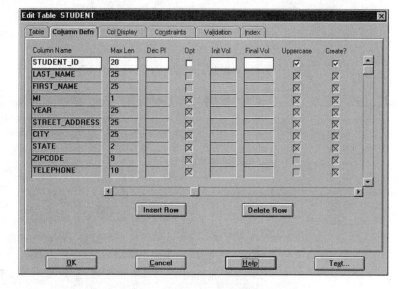

Specifying a Table's Constraints

To specify a table's constraints, select the Constraints tab folder. Within the Constraints tab folder, you will see four other tab folders that correspond to the four types of constraints: Primary, Foreign, Unique, and Check. To specify the primary key for the Student table, enter the constraint name, and select the Student_ID column from the poplist labeled Column Name (see Figure 20.6).

Figure 20.6.

Specifying the primary key.

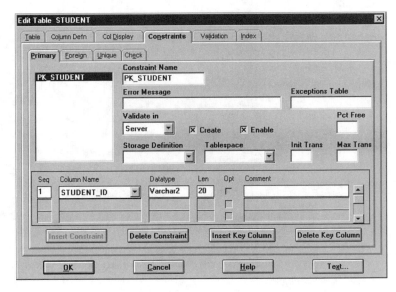

The Student table has another constraint: a CHECK constraint on Year to ensure that it is either FRESHMAN, SOPHOMORE, JUNIOR, or SENIOR. To create this constraint, select the Validation tab folder. Select the column whose values you want to validate—in this case, YEAR. Enter each valid value for the column, as shown in Figure 20.7.

Figure 20.7.

Specifying the validation for a column.

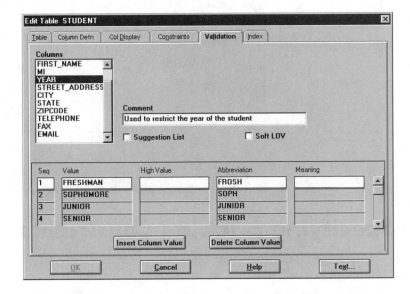

When you are finished specifying the table's characteristics, click OK. The table will be displayed in the diagram with the characteristics that you specified. As you can see in Figure 20.8, the # is displayed to the left of Student_ID, signifying that the column is the primary key. Also, all mandatory columns have a * displayed to their left.

Figure 20.8.

The created table is displayed in a diagram.

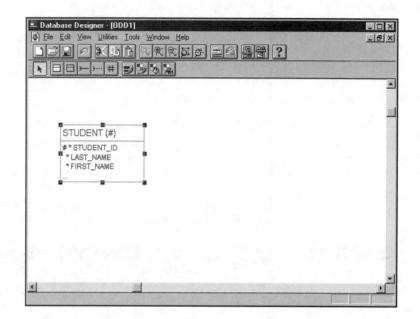

Specifying a Foreign Key

To follow the steps that are used to create a foreign key, let's refer to an existing diagram that has two tables: Department and Instructor. As you can see in Figure 20.9, the Instructor table doesn't contain Department_ID, which identifies the department with which the instructor is associated.

To create a mandatory foreign key in the Instructor table, select the Mandatory Foreign Key button on the tool bar (it is commonly referred to as a *crow's foot*). Notice that the mouse pointer has now changed to the crow's foot. Move the crow's foot over the Instructor table. Left-click on the Instructor table; drag the crow's foot over the Department table and left-click. You should now notice two things (as shown in Figure 20.10):

- [ ] A mandatory foreign key labeled DEPARTMENT_FK connects the Department and Instructor tables.

- [ ] The Department_ID has been added to the Instructor table.

20

Figure 20.9.

Existing diagram containing two tables without a relationship.

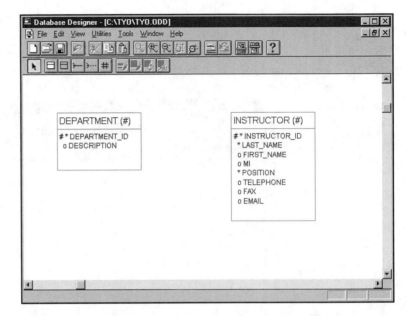

Figure 20.10.

The foreign key is created.

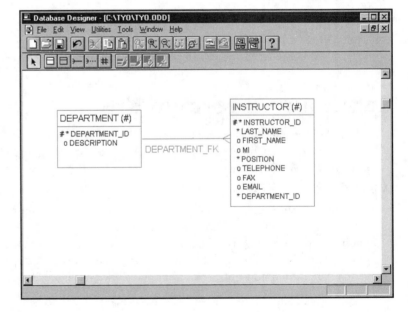

To edit the foreign key, double-click the line that defines the foreign key. A window, labeled Edit Foreign Key, will appear (see Figure 20.11). For this foreign key, the default values do not need to be changed.

Figure 20.11.

Editing the foreign key.

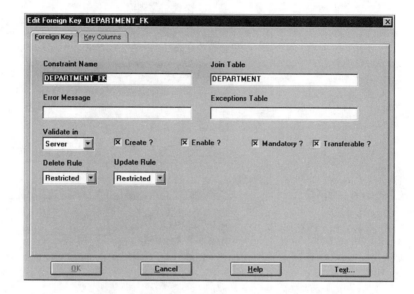

Generating the DDL Statements for the Diagram

Database Designer provides a Generation Wizard that guides you through the process of generating a database schema from your ER diagram. To invoke the Generation Wizard, you can select Tools | Generation Wizard from the menu. The first window displayed by the Generation Wizard simply informs you that you can generate database objects to a file or to a database (see Figure 20.12). Click Next to proceed to the next window.

In the next window, you must indicate where you want to create the database objects—to a file that contains the DDL statements which will build your database or directly to a database. By default, the DDL statements will be directed to an SQL file (see Figure 20.13). Click Next to proceed to the next window.

In the next window, you can restrict the generation of database objects to specific object types. However, by default, all database objects will be generated (see Figure 20.14).

20

Figure 20.12.

First window displayed by Generation Wizard.

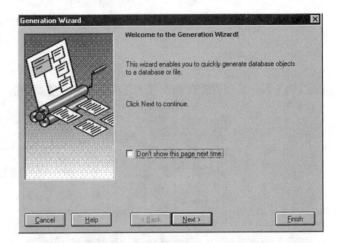

Figure 20.13.

Sending DDL statements to a file.

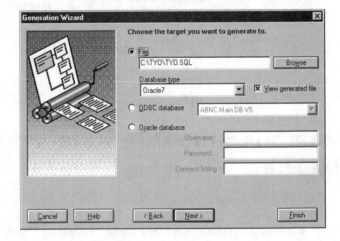

At this point, you can click Finish to generate the SQL file. If no errors occurred, a dialog window will indicate that no processing errors occurred. On the progress meter, click Done to proceed (see Figure 20.15).

20

Figure 20.14.

Specifying the database objects to be generated.

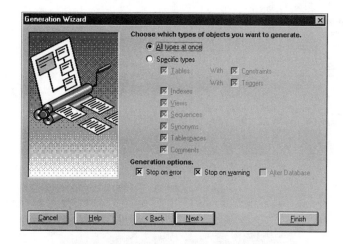

Figure 20.15.

Progress meter displayed by Generation Wizard.

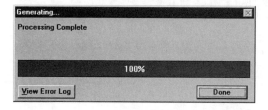

If you look on the Taskbar, you will see that Database Designer has opened the Notepad with the generated SQL file (see Listing 20.1).

INPUT   **Listing 20.1. SQL file generated by Generation Wizard.**

```
-- C:\TYO\TYO.SQL
--
-- Generated for Oracle 7 on 12/5/1997 17:47:07 by Oracle Database
➥Designer v1.00
/* Source Diagram Details:
 * Name C:\TYO\TYO.ODD  created 6/4/1997 18:55:25
 * Last modified 11/5/1997 22:51:13
 */


CREATE TABLE DEPARTMENT
 (DEPARTMENT_ID  VARCHAR2(20) NOT NULL
 ,DESCRIPTION  VARCHAR2(25)
 );

CREATE TABLE INSTRUCTOR
 (INSTRUCTOR_ID  VARCHAR2(20) NOT NULL
 ,LAST_NAME  VARCHAR2(25) NOT NULL
```

continues

20

Listing 20.1. continued

```
,FIRST_NAME  VARCHAR2(25)
,MI  VARCHAR2(1)
,POSITION  VARCHAR2(25) NOT NULL
,TELEPHONE  VARCHAR2(10)
,FAX  VARCHAR2(10)
,EMAIL  VARCHAR2(100)
,DEPARTMENT_ID  VARCHAR2(20) NOT NULL
);

ALTER TABLE DEPARTMENT
 ADD CONSTRAINT DEPARTMENT_PK PRIMARY KEY
  (DEPARTMENT_ID) ;

ALTER TABLE INSTRUCTOR
 ADD CONSTRAINT INSTRUCTOR_PK PRIMARY KEY
  (INSTRUCTOR_ID) ;

ALTER TABLE INSTRUCTOR
 ADD CONSTRAINT DEPARTMENT_FK
 FOREIGN KEY
  (DEPARTMENT_ID)
 REFERENCES DEPARTMENT
  (DEPARTMENT_ID)
 ;
```

Using Database Designer to Reverse Engineer an Oracle Database

Database Designer will also reverse engineer a data model from several sources—an SQL file containing DDL statements, an ODBC data source, or an Oracle database. The capability to reverse engineer a data model is sometimes necessary. As a developer, you may be provided with a legacy database without any accompanying documentation. By reverse engineering the legacy database, Database Designer can construct a diagram that will aid you in your understanding the legacy data model. You are then able to reengineer the model—perhaps adding additional entities and attributes—by using the legacy data model as a baseline. Let's go through the steps that are needed to reverse engineer a data model from an SQL file.

1. To invoke the Reverse Engineer Wizard, select Tools | Reverse Engineer Wizard from the menu.

2. On the window that appears, you can select the source to be used for reverse engineering:

   ☐ An SQL file

   ☐ An ODBC Data Source

   ☐ An Oracle database

3. By default, the Reverse Engineer Wizard assumes that you want to reverse engineer a data model using an SQL file as the source. To select a particular SQL file, you can enter the filename directly or use Browse to select the SQL file.

4. As you can see in Figure 20.16, the Reverse Engineer Wizard also assumes that the source reflects an Oracle7 database—in other words, the DDL statements in the SQL file were intended to be applied against an Oracle7 database.

Figure 20.16.

Reverse Engineer Wizard prompts for the source to be used to reverse engineer a data model.

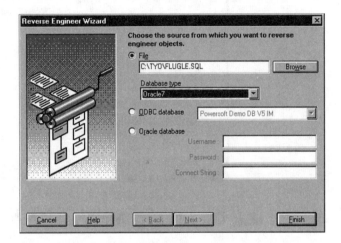

5. After you have specified an SQL file, click Finish to proceed with the reverse-engineering process.

6. A progress meter will appear, displaying messages about the objects that it is constructing from the SQL file. If there are no errors during the reverse-engineering process, a window will notify you that there were no processing errors.

7. To view the data model, click Done on the progress meter.

TIP

As you can see in Figure 20.17, the Reverse Engineer Wizard will construct the objects based on the objects referenced in the SQL file. However, you may need to rearrange some of the objects; some of them may be overlapping, making it difficult to read the diagram. You may want to print the diagram to see all the objects and their relationships.

20

Figure 20.17.

Diagram constructed by Reverse Engineer Wizard.

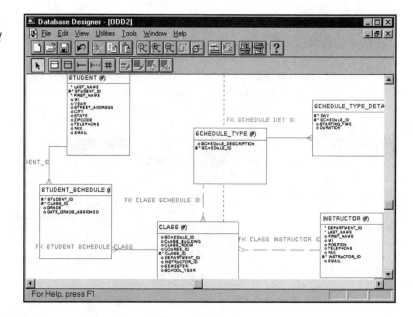

The Basics of Designer/2000

The components of Designer/2000 can be grouped into these categories:

- ☐ **Process Modeling:** Consists of Process Modeller
- ☐ **Systems Modeling:** Includes Entity Relationship Diagrammer, Function Hierarchy Diagrammer, and Dataflow Diagrammer
- ☐ **Design Wizards:** Includes Database Design and Application Design Wizards
- ☐ **Systems Design:** Includes Data Diagrammer, Module Structure Diagrammer, Module Data Diagrammer, Preferences Navigator, and Module Logic Navigator
- ☐ **Generation:** Includes Server Generator, Forms Generator, Reports Generator, Graphics Generator, Visual Basic Generator, Webserver Generator, MS Help Generator, and C++ Object Layer Generator
- ☐ **Repository Administration:** Includes Repository Administration Utility

Let's discuss the role that some of these components play in the application-development process. To initially create a new application, you use the Repository Object Navigator and select File | New from the menu. A new application is created, which is named Flugle (see Figure 20.18).

20

Figure 20.18.

Creating a new application with the Repository Object Navigator.

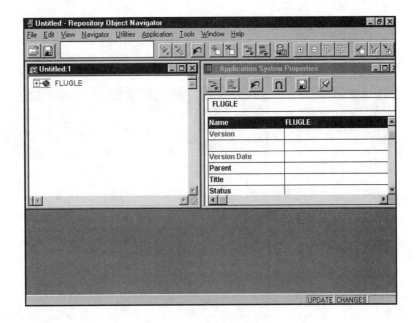

Process Modeller

Process Modeller is a tool that enables you to graphically describe the business processes that you are interested in modeling. Initially, Process Modeller is used to understand the processes as they currently exist. The tool is able to animate a process, making the dynamics more easily understood. From an understanding of the current processes, the processes can be redesigned to reduce cycle time or eliminate unnecessary steps.

Entity Relationship Diagrammer

Entity Relationship Diagrammer is similar to Database Designer but offers more features. Specifically, Entity Relationship Diagrammer distinguishes between the logical data model—composed of entities, attributes, domains, and relationships—and the physical database design—composed of tables, columns, views, constraints, and other objects. Like Database Designer, Entity Relationship Diagrammer enables the designer to graphically depict the data model. Like the other components of Designer/2000, Entity Relationship Diagrammer uses the Designer/2000 Repository for storing the data models for each application.

Function Hierarchy Diagrammer

You use the Function Hierarchy Diagrammer to graphically describe the hierarchy of business functions performed by an organization. For example, at the highest level, you might describe a function named Manage Human Resources. Within that function, there are lower-level functions such as Recruit New Instructors, Hire New Instructors, and so on. With the

20

Function Hierarchy Diagrammer, you can identify the usage of entities and attributes by each function. As an example, Figure 20.19 illustrates a simple function hierarchy for the administrative function at Flugle College.

Figure 20.19.

Function hierarchy created with Function Hierarchy Diagrammer.

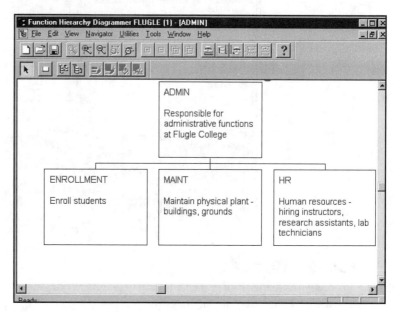

Database Design and Application Design Wizards

The Database Design Wizard is a tool that generates SQL statements from an entity relationship diagram, thereby implementing the physical database from the logical model that Designer/2000 maintains in its repository. Similarly, the Application Design Wizard will generate a module or menu from a function, implemented in one of the Developer/2000 components—such as Forms or Reports.

Module Structure Diagrammer

The Module Structure Diagrammer is used to create and modify modules and their details. This tool also enables you to describe how modules are related to one another. A module may be one of the following:

- ☐ Screen
- ☐ Report
- ☐ Menu
- ☐ PL/SQL subprogram (package, procedure, or function)
- ☐ Chart

For example, Figure 20.20 displays a tabbed folder for specifying the Flugle College Course Catalog, which is a report.

Figure 20.20.

Specifying the module details for a report in the Module Structure Diagrammer.

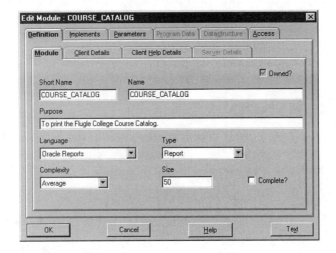

Summary

In this final lesson, the key concepts to remember are the following:

☐ Database Designer is a database diagramming tool that can help you develop a database design and build it for a variety of databases—for example, Oracle, RDB, DB2, and SQL Server.

☐ With Database Designer, you graphically describe your database design: tables, columns, constraints, and indexes.

☐ Database Designer can generate a physical database from the design that you specify.

☐ Database Designer enables you to document each table and column, thereby capturing a complete database design in one source.

☐ Database Designer saves a database design in a file with an extension of .ODD.

Q&A

Q Can Database Designer and Designer/2000 exchange information?

A Yes. Of course, Database Designer uses a small subset of the information that Designer/2000 maintains in its repository. As an example, Database Designer lets you specify the display characteristics of a column. It can pass this information to Designer/2000, which will use it in the generation of screens and reports.

20

Q If I'm developing a small application, do I even need to use a tool like Database Designer or ERwin?

A It really is a good idea to use an ER diagramming tool like Database Designer or ERwin. As you may already know, small projects are typically subject to "scope creep"; that is, the scope of the project is enlarged by many of the participants. Database Designer or ERwin *will* help you manage a growing number of entities, attributes, and relationships.

Workshop

The purpose of the Workshop is to allow you to test your knowledge of the material discussed in the lesson. See if you can correctly answer the questions in the quiz before you continue with tomorrow's lesson.

Quiz

1. True or false? One drawback to Database Designer is that it supports only Oracle databases.

2. Name three advantages of using Database Designer instead of a text editor to create the DDL statements that implement a database design.

Day 21

Oracle: The Next Generation

The purpose of this last lesson is to explore three topics:

- ☐ The Oracle Web Application Server, version 3.0—the latest version of Oracle's Web Server that significantly increases the accessibility of an Oracle database from a Web application through the use of cartridges

- ☐ Developer/2000 for the Web, release 1.4W—a new release of Developer/2000 that supports the deployment of Forms and Reports applications as both client/server and Web applications

- ☐ Oracle's Network Computing Architecture—a major computing initiative that emphasizes the role of the Internet and the World Wide Web, the growing importance of distributed objects, and support for open standards

Also, you probably will want to read Bonus Day 23, "Oracle8: New Features," which discusses new features of the Oracle8 server that are of interest to database designers and application developers.

Connecting an Oracle Database to the Web: Using Oracle WebServer

In 1995, Oracle Corporation introduced a product that allowed access to an Oracle database from a Web browser: Oracle WebServer. The initial version of WebServer consisted of several components:

☐ One or more Web Listeners that listened for HTTP connection requests

☐ Web Agents that connected to a local or remote Oracle database via a specified Oracle account

☐ Two built-in PL/SQL packages containing procedures and functions that generate HTML tags

NOTE

The examples shown in this lesson are based on creating a WebServer application that invokes a stored procedure written in PL/SQL. This stored procedure will dynamically generate the HTML needed to display the contents of the Student table.

Since then, Oracle WebServer has been significantly enhanced. The current version, 3.0, is designed to support the Network Computing Architecture, Oracle's major initiative to provide an open, platform-independent, object-based, Web-based, distributed computing architecture.

Today, you look at the configuration of WebServer 3.0. You also build a few dynamic Web pages through the use of Oracle stored procedures that invoke components of the htp and htf packages.

Elements of the Oracle WebServer

The Oracle WebServer consists of several major components:

☐ **Web Listener:** A Web Listener named admin is created during the installation of the product. By default, the admin listener listens on port 8888. A second Web Listener named www is also created during the WebServer installation. By default, the www listener listens on port 80. However, you can modify its configuration, including the ports that it will service.

☐ **Web Request Broker:** This program forms the heart of the WebServer product. It dispatches HTTP requests to other WebServer programs, depending on the type of request.

☐ **Database Access Descriptor:** A file that describes how a PL/SQL Agent connects to an Oracle database. The Database Access Descriptor includes the name of the Oracle account that is to be used for the connection and the Oracle SID that identifies the database to which the agent will connect. Alternatively, the Database Access Descriptor can describe a SQL*Net2 database alias to be used for the Oracle connection.

☐ **Cartridges:** WebServer includes several cartridges, each supporting a different language. Included with the product are cartridges for PL/SQL, Java, Perl, and ODBC (allowing you to access non-Oracle databases via the Oracle WebServer).

☐ **Web Agent:** A given cartridge type can support one or more Web Agents. Each Web Agent is associated with a particular Database Access Descriptor that identifies how a connection to an Oracle database is to be made.

The Oracle WebServer must be installed on a server such as Solaris, HP-UX, or Windows NT. After you perform the initial installation, you can complete the installation and configuration with a Web browser. To do this, the initial URL you should use is `http://server-name:8888` where `server-name` is the name of the server, including its domain. As you can see in Figure 21.1, the initial Web page will display nine links that you can choose from.

Figure 21.1.

Initial WebServer administration page.

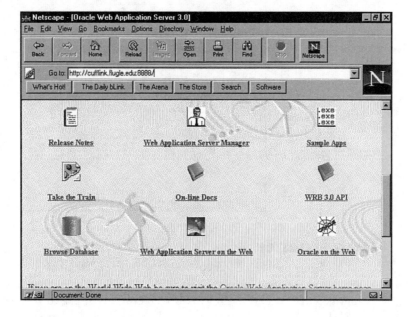

NOTE

> To access the Web pages shown in this lesson, you need to know the admin password that was specified during the installation of Oracle WebServer.

If you select the Web Application Server Manager link, another Web page will appear containing three links (see Figure 21.2):

☐ Oracle Database (enables you to start up or shut down an Oracle database on the server where Oracle WebServer is installed)

☐ Oracle Web Listener

☐ Oracle Web Application Server

Figure 21.2.

Viewing the Web Application Server Manager.

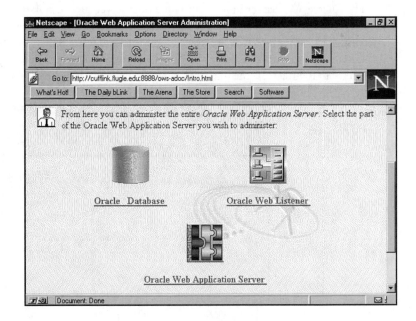

Web Listener

To configure the Web Listeners, select the Oracle Web Listener link as displayed on Figure 21.2. The page that appears is labeled Oracle Web Listener Administration. If you scroll down on that page, you will see two Web Listeners displayed: admin and www. Both of these Web Listeners are created during product installation. However, the admin Web Listener must be running to perform any other administrative tasks.

You can reconfigure the www Web Listener by selecting the CONFIGURE link. A page, titled Oracle Web Listener Advanced Configuration for Listener www, will appear. If you want to add another Directory Mapping, you can scroll down the frame on the right until you see the heading Directory Mappings. You probably will want to add a directory mapping to this list for each Web Agent that you plan to create. For example, Figure 21.3 displays a directory mapping, /flugle/owa, that will be used for the Flugle College Web agent that will be created shortly. Scroll down to the Modify Listener button and click it. To return to the previous page, you can click the Admin button on the bottom frame.

NOTE   After you modify a Web Listener, you must restart the Web Listener—stop it and start it—for the changes to take effect.

Figure 21.3.

Creating a directory mapping for the www *Web Listener.*

Web Application Server Administration

To access the Web Application Server Administration page, select the Web Application Server link (as shown previously on Figure 21.2). Another page, titled Oracle Web Application Server Administration, will appear. As you can see in Figure 21.4, there are nine links displayed on this page:

Authorization Server   With this component, you can define Authentication Schemes to be used with the Web Application Server, including Basic, Digest, and IP-based.

21

Logger	This component automatically collects statistics regarding HTTP requests. You can also configure the Logger to trace the execution of other WebServer components.
Log Analyzer	With this component, you can view HTTP-request log entries and run various reports that summarize the execution of Oracle WebServer.
Migration	In addition to migrating from WebServer 2.0 to WebServer 3.0, this component enables you to configure the Netscape Server for use with the Oracle Web Broker.
DAD Administration	This component enables you to create and modify Database Access Descriptors.
Web Request Broker	This is a link to the Web Request Broker Administration page.
Default Configuration	By selecting this link, you can install a set of default users and PL/SQL packages in an Oracle database.
Support	This link enables you to fill out an Oracle Support form.
Cartridge Administration	With this link, you can select a cartridge type such as PL/SQL, Java, or Perl. Once you've selected a cartridge type, you can view, create, reconfigure, or delete a Web Agent for that cartridge type.

The following sections present a closer look at some of these links.

Figure 21.4.

Choices for configuring the Web Application Server.

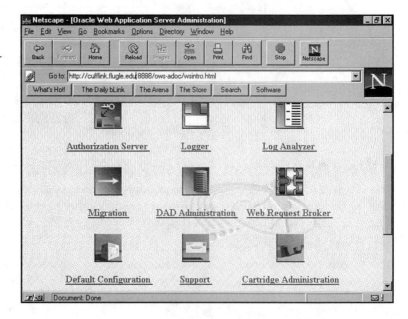

Database Access Descriptor (DAD) Administration

Before you can create a new Web Agent based on a particular cartridge type (such as PL/SQL), you probably will want to create a new DAD. To do this, select the DAD Administration link from the Web Application Server Administration page. From the DAD Administration page, you will see another link titled Create New DAD. Select this link. Another page, titled Database Access Descriptor Creation will appear (see Figure 21.5). On this page, there are several fields for which you will enter information:

DAD Name	The name of the new Database Access Descriptor (flugle).
Database user	The name of the Oracle account that the new DAD should use when connecting to the Oracle database (flugle).
Database User Password	The password for the database user (flugle).
Confirm Password	A confirmation of the database user's password (flugle).
ORACLE_HOME	The server directory that is defined as ORACLE_HOME for the ORACLE_SID (the next parameter in the form). Ask your DBA for the correct value for ORACLE_HOME.
ORACLE_SID	The name of the Oracle database to which the new DAD should connect. This assumes that the Oracle database resides on the same machine as the Oracle WebServer. If this is not the case, you will need to enter a value in the field titled SQL*Net V2 Service.

Figure 21.5.

Creating a new Database Access Descriptor.

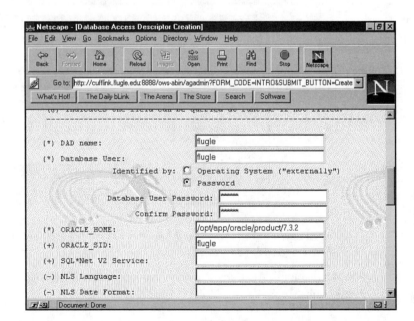

When you have entered values for all of the required fields, click the Submit New DAD button at the bottom of the page.

Web Request Broker Administration

You'll want to reconfigure the Web Request Broker for at least one reason: to specify a virtual directory for your application.

1. Select the Web Request Broker link from the Web Application Server Administration page.

2. In the page that appears—Web Request Broker Administration—select Applications and Directories in the left-hand frame.

3. In the right-hand frame, scroll down to the first empty entry in the table and enter these values (see Figure 21.6):

    Virtual Directory   `/flugle/owa`

    Application   `PLSQL`

    Physical Path   `%ORACLE_HOME%/bin`

Figure 21.6.

Specifying a virtual directory for an application for the Web Request Broker.

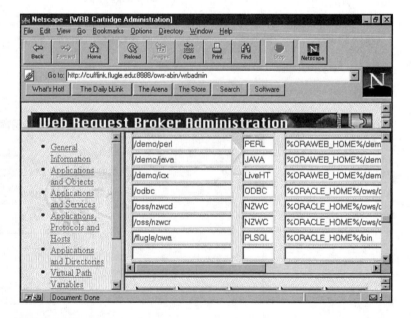

4. Scroll down until you see the Modify WRB Configuration button. Click it so that the changes will take effect.

For an actual application, you may want to modify other WRB parameters such as Protecting Applications.

Cartridge Administration

You can select the Cartridge Administration link from the Web Application Server Administration page. As you can see in Figure 21.7, several cartridge types will be displayed, including:

- [ ] PLSQL
- [ ] Java
- [ ] Perl
- [ ] ODBC

Figure 21.7.

Selecting a cartridge type.

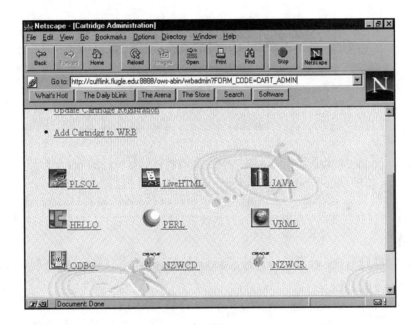

Select the PLSQL cartridge type. Another page, titled PL/SQL Agent Administration, will be displayed (see Figure 21.8).

On this page, you can select the link named Create New PL/SQL Agent. In the next page that appears—PL/SQL Agent Creation—enter these values in the fields:

Name of PL/SQL Agent   `flugle`

Name of DAD to be used   `flugle`

Scroll down and click the button labeled Submit New PL/SQL Agent. Oracle WebServer should create the new PL/SQL Agent.

21

Figure 21.8.
*PL/SQL Agent
Adminstration.*

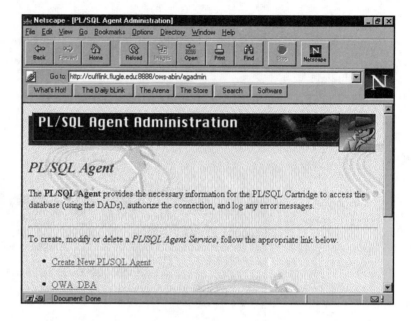

Special PL/SQL Packages `htp` and `htf`

Included with Oracle WebServer are several PL/SQL packages that are installed by default.
One package, `htp`, contains a large number of procedures that generate HTML tags. Another
package, `htf`, includes a large number of functions that can be used as arguments to many
of the procedures in the `htp` package.

Using a Stored Procedure to Generate Dynamic HTML

As an example, let's look at a very elementary example of how a dynamic Web page is
generated from a stored procedure. The following code is a stored procedure named
`StudentList` that displays a subset of student information, one student per line, in a Web
browser.

INPUT

```
PROCEDURE StudentList IS
cursor GetStudents is
select Student_ID, Last_Name, First_Name
from Student
order by Student_ID;
```

21

```
S_ID  Student.Student_ID%type;
LName Student.Last_Name%type;
FName Student.First_Name%type;

begin

open GetStudents;

htp.HTMLOpen;
htp.BodyOpen;

loop
  fetch GetStudents into S_ID, LName, FName;
  exit when GetStudents%NOTFOUND;

  htp.print ('Student ID: ' || S_ID);
  htp.print ('Last Name:  ' || LName);
  htp.print ('First Name: ' || FName);

  htp.para;

end loop;

htp.BodyClose;
htp.HTMLClose;

END;
```

ANALYSIS A cursor, named GetStudents, is declared which selects the student ID, last name, and first name from the Student table. Three other variables are declared—S_ID, LName, and FName—which will contain the values from the cursor's columns as each row is fetched.

At the beginning of the procedure, the cursor is opened. Two procedures are invoked in the htp package: HTMLOpen and BodyOpen. These packages generate the <HTML> and <BODY> tags, respectively.

In the cursor loop, each row is fetched from the cursor. A procedure, named htp.print, is used to print each row's value for student ID, last name, and first name. A call to htp.para is used to generate the <P> tag, signifying a paragraph. Finally, when the loop is closed, htp.BodyClose and htp.HTMLClose are called, generating </BODY> and </HTML> tags, respectively.

Figure 21.9 displays the output of the StudentList stored procedure.

21

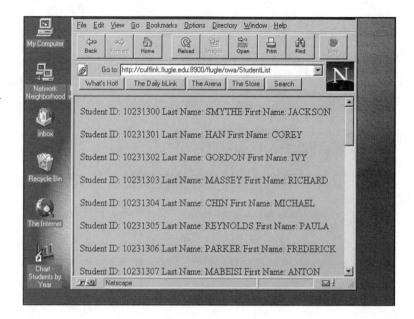

OUTPUT

Figure 21.9.
*Example of PL/SQL
stored procedure that
generates dynamic
HTML.*

Developer/2000 for the Web

In May 1997, Oracle Corporation announced the production release of Developer/2000 for the Web, release 1.4W. At the time this book was published, a trial version of Developer/2000 for the Web could be downloaded from the Oracle Web site. However, be warned—the Developer/2000 release 1.4W download file is 159MB and expands to almost 500MB. This section will focus on the Windows NT version of Developer/2000 for the Web (it is also available for the Solaris operating system).

Developer/2000 for the Web supports the deployment of Oracle Forms and Oracle Reports applications as Web applications. Developer/2000 requires the use of either the Oracle Web Server 2.1 or the Oracle Web Application Server 3.0. Developer/2000 for the Web includes a new component, the Forms Server Listener, that must reside on the same server with the Web Application Server. Let's take a closer look at the architecture in Figure 21.10.

Figure 21.10.
*Architecture Support-
ing Developer/2000
for the Web.*

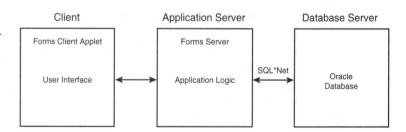

As you can see in Figure 21.10, the architecture consists of three tiers:

- [ ] The Forms client, which consists of a Web browser that downloads the forms application as a Java applet
- [ ] The application server, where the Web Server and Forms Server Listener both reside
- [ ] The database server, where the Oracle database that supports the Forms application

The client machine only requires a Web browser that has been Java enabled (specifically, it must support the Java Development Kit 1.1.2 or higher). The user enters a URL that contains the following:

- [ ] The name of the application server
- [ ] The port that the Web Listener is monitoring
- [ ] The name of the Web application
- [ ] The name of the module
- [ ] The user ID and the database alias

NOTE

> The current version of Developer/2000 for the Web, release 1.4W, is labeled *Limited Production*. This release fully supports the deployment of client/server applications written in Oracle Forms, Reports, and Graphics. However, Developer/2000 for the Web has limited production capabilities for the deployment of Web applications. Specifically, this release requires the use of a Web browser that supports the Java Development Kit (JDK) version 1.1.2 or higher; at the present time, there are no commercially available browsers that provide this support. As a result, the installation of Developer/2000 for the Web includes an appletviewer that must be used to launch the Java applet that runs the Oracle Forms or Reports application. In addition, there are known restrictions and bugs involving the use of the applet viewer. Refer to the Developer/2000 for the Web Release Notes for further details.

The application server (Solaris and Windows NT are currently supported) contains these components:

- [ ] Oracle WebServer 2.1 or Oracle Web Application Server 3.0
- [ ] Forms Server Listener
- [ ] Java Development Kit (JDK) 1.1.2 or higher
- [ ] Oracle Forms .FMX files and Oracle Reports .RDF files

21

The Forms Server Listener is responsible for reading the .FMX file referenced in the URL and downloading the necessary Java classes and applet to mimic the functionality that the form provides in a client/server environment.

Finally, the database server hosts the Oracle database that is accessed by the Forms Web application. Of course, the Oracle database could reside on the application server.

Configuring Oracle Forms for the Web

To configure Oracle Forms for the Web, you need to perform three tasks:

☐ Generate and deploy the Oracle Forms .FMX files on the application server.

☐ The Forms Server Listener must be started on the application server.

☐ The WebServer must be configured so that the Forms application is available to the client machine. Refer to the Developer/2000 for the Web Installation Guide for further details.

Let's look at the detailed steps needed to complete each task.

Generating and Deploying Oracle Forms .FMX Files

When you install Developer/2000 for the Web, release 1.4W, Oracle Forms 4.5.8 is also installed. For each .FMB file that you want to run as a Forms Web application, you must regenerate the .FMX file using Oracle Forms 4.5.8. If there are no errors during the generation of the .FMX file, place the .FMX file on the application server. You can place the .FMX files in any directory on the application server as long as you specify the directory path and filename in the cartridge or HTML file that users reference to run the Web application.

Invoking the Forms Server Listener

The Forms Server Listener must be running before a user can run an Oracle Form as a Web application. There are two ways to invoke the Forms Server Listener on Windows NT:

☐ You can choose Start | Programs | Developer/2000 for NT | Forms Server Listener.

☐ You can choose Run, enter `C:\ORANT\bin\f45srv32 port=5555`, and click OK.

To verify that the Forms Server Listener is running, move the mouse so the pointer is on a blank region of the Taskbar and right-click `Task Manager` from the popup menu. Select the Processes tab and scroll through the list of processes. If the Forms Server Listener is running, you will see a process named `f45srv32.exe` in the list.

Running a Form from the Applet Viewer

To make the applet viewer available on the client machine, you will need to install JDK 1.1.2 which is available on the Developer/2000 for the Web CD-ROM. By default, JDK 1.1.2 will be installed beneath the Oracle home directory as JDK1.1.

21

You should also set two system variables:

☐ CLASSPATH, which should be set to `C:ORACLE_HOME\jdk1.1\jdk\lib\classes.zip` (where *ORACLE_HOME* is the directory where the Oracle products are installed on the application server).

☐ PATH, which should include `C:\ORACLE_HOME\jdk1.1\jdk\bin` (where *ORACLE_HOME* is the directory where the Oracle products are installed on the application server).

To run the applet viewer, you will need to open a DOS window on the client machine.

Development Considerations Regarding Developer/2000 for the Web

If you or your organization are already using Developer/2000 to build client/server applications, Developer/2000 for the Web offers a direct path to deploying your Oracle Forms and Reports applications as Web applications (subject to the caveats discussed in the previous note). On the positive side, Developer/2000 for the Web enables you to avoid the burden of coding a Java applet that has the equivalent functionality as your Forms or Reports application. On the other hand, with Developer/2000 for the Web, you have little control over the Java code that is generated; it may be quite difficult to integrate a Forms application with other Java applets. However, if you aren't currently using Developer/2000 and have no plans to begin using it, there are other alternatives available to you:

☐ Develop PL/SQL subprograms using PL/SQL packages supplied with the Web Application Server to dynamically generate HTML

☐ Develop a Java applet using a Java development environment such as Symantec Cafe

☐ Use third-party software packages such as Cold Fusion or Tango that enable you to access an Oracle database via ODBC

Let's look at the advantages and disadvantages of these alternatives.

Developing Web Applications with PL/SQL

Oracle's Web Application Server includes several packages, including htp and htf, which you can use to construct a Web application. There are several advantages to this approach:

☐ Because you are using PL/SQL to code your application, you have access to all the built-in packages and other capabilities of the Oracle database.

☐ With the responsibility of coding each Web form, you also have control over the appearance and behavior of your Web application.

☐ Through the use of the Web Application Server 3.0 PL/SQL Cartridge, you can ensure that transactions are properly rolled back or committed.

21

There are also some disadvantages to coding your Web application in PL/SQL:

☐ Unlike a Java applet, a PL/SQL subprogram that dynamically generates HTML tags is limited to the user interface available in HTML. In other words, a user's input will not be validated until the user submits the form by pressing a button.

☐ PL/SQL does not offer the object-oriented features that exist in languages like Java. Even with the object-relational features introduced in the Oracle8 server and PL/SQL 3.0, this remains true.

☐ Except for Designer/2000, there are no development environments that will allow you to graphically construct a Web form and generate the PL/SQL code to implement it. And Designer/2000, version 1.3, is limited to the generation of Web forms that only query an Oracle database.

Developing Web Applications with Java

There are several Java development environments, such as Symantec Café, that can be used to develop a Java applet which can be invoked from a Web browser. These products typically use a JDBC driver—similar to an ODBC driver—to access a relational database. There are some advantages to this development approach:

☐ You have control over the look and feel of the applet user interface.

☐ By including field-level validation, the applet user interface can be less frustrating for the user. The applet can prevent the user from navigating to the next field if the current field contains an invalid value.

☐ The applet can support a heterogeneous environment. With a JDBC driver, the applet can simultaneously connect to different vendor databases and present a cohesive view of related information.

Let's ponder the negative aspects of this development approach:

☐ By using a JDBC driver, the applet is not as well integrated with the Oracle database as Developer/2000 for the Web or PL/SQL. You may not be able to use as many features as are available through the Oracle-supplied tools.

☐ Because you have responsibility for the user interface, you have to write a considerable amount of Java code.

Developing Web Applications with Other Software Packages

There are several software packages, such as Cold Fusion and Tango, that provide a graphical interface for developing a Web application. Generally, these products require the installation of an application server on either a Sun Solaris or Windows NT server. The application server accesses an Oracle database via an ODBC driver. There are some clear advantages to these packages:

☐ They are quite easy to use. An inexperienced developer can build an application in a matter of days.

☐ Because the generated HTML code includes calls to the application server, the resulting applications can include field-level validation.

There are also some aspects of these tools that you should be aware of:

☐ Because these packages typically use an ODBC driver to access an Oracle database, you may not be able to use many features available in the Oracle server.

☐ Depending on the product that you choose, the resulting Web application may not prevent two users from modifying the same record at the same time. If you are building a query-only application, this isn't a concern. However, if you are building a Web application that will allow a user to add, modify, or delete database records, you need to investigate the support that the software package provides for record locking.

Oracle's Network Computing Architecture

In September 1996, Oracle Corporation introduced a strategy for future software development: the Network Computing Architecture (NCA). The key factors that influenced the creation of the NCA are as follows:

☐ Explosive growth of the Internet and the World Wide Web

☐ Increasing complexity and expense to administer client/server applications on a variety of client platforms such as PCs, Macs, and UNIX workstations

☐ Support for objects

☐ Support for multiple programming languages

☐ Support for distributed application and database servers

☐ Continued support for legacy applications (for example, client/server)

NOTE Don't confuse the NCA with Oracle Corporation's development of a network computer via Network Computer, Inc., a subsidiary of Oracle Corporation. The Network Computing Architecture is a software architecture, whereas the network computer is a hardware/software platform that plays a role in the NCA.

21

Overview of the Network Computing Architecture

It is important to understand that the NCA is a strategy for commercial software development that will be implemented over time by specific Oracle products. As stated by Oracle Corporation, the goals of this strategy include:

- ☐ **Scalability:** A principal goal of the NCA is to overcome many of the limitations associated with client/server applications such as performance, administration, and deployment. For instance, by enabling the deployment of Web-based applications, the NCA significantly reduces the administration of client machines; a network administrator no longer needs to worry about the logistics of installing the latest version of an executable program and its associated libraries on hundreds of PCs.

- ☐ **Portability:** The goal of the NCA is to support enterprise software development, regardless of programming language, computing platform, or operating system. The use of Java is central to this goal. Java offers developers the possibility of writing software once and deploying it in a variety of computing environments.

- ☐ **Interoperability:** The NCA assumes that customers want the flexibility of choosing separate components, regardless of vendor, and expecting them to integrate; a customer might want to use the Oracle database server, a Netscape Web server, and a combination of Microsoft Windows 95 and Mac clients. By adhering to two common standards—CORBA 2.0 and HTTP/HTML—the NCA supports a heterogeneous environment.

- ☐ **Support for component-based software development:** Oracle Corporation has stated that the NCA will support the CORBA 2.0 specification, which addresses the use of distributed objects, regardless of their location on the network—client, application server, or database server. This support will be implemented in future releases of Oracle products.

Let's examine some of the benefits provided by the CORBA 2.0 specification.

CORBA

CORBA is the acronym for the Common Object Request Broker Architecture which is an architecture and specification produced by the Object Management Group, an industry consortium that was established in 1989. The current version of CORBA is 2.0, which was initially released in July 1995 and updated in July 1996. The principal goal of CORBA is to foster the use and integration of objects, regardless of the language used to construct the object and the operating system where it resides. CORBA accomplishes this goal through the use of an Object Request Broker (ORB) which is a piece of software that handles requests for object services. You can think of an ORB as an object bus. There are a number of ORB vendors, including Iona, Visigenic, Sun, HP, and IBM.

Another important part of CORBA 2.0 is the specification for Interface Definition Language (IDL), which provides a language-independent description of the services provided by an object. The ORB vendors provide software that will generate language-specific bindings from IDL. The intent of CORBA 2.0 is to reduce the external specification for an object to its IDL. A developer doesn't need to know about the language used to implement an object or the operating system on which it was developed; everything that a developer needs to know about an object is contained in its IDL specification. IDL is a subset of the proposed C++ ANSI specification with extensions to support the invocation of object services.

CORBA 2.0 also includes a specification for Internet Inter-ORB Protocol (IIOP). This protocol specifies the communication mechanism, via TCP/IP, that allows one ORB to communicate with another ORB. Essentially, IIOP is a mechanism whereby a client on a computing platform can issue a request for a service from object *abc* which is handled by an ORB. Acting as a client, object *abc* issues a request, sent via TCP/IP, for a service from object *xyz* which is managed by an ORB on a different computing platform.

Components of the Network Computing Architecture

Because a picture is worth a thousand words, please look at Figure 21.11 for a diagram of the Network Computing Architecture. As you can see, the components of the NCA are as follows:

☐ The Oracle Universal Server

☐ The Oracle Universal Application Server

☐ Cartridges that may interface with the client, application server, or universal server

☐ The Inter-Cartridge Exchange that allows cartridges to communicate with one another

☐ A client that may be a PC, a Mac, or a network computer

Cartridges

As envisioned by the NCA, a cartridge is a software component that interfaces with the client, application server, or the database itself. The purpose of a cartridge is to provide a specialized capability that is made available to other components and cartridges in the NCA. For example, an organization might develop a cartridge to handle the processing of some external data feed such as commodity prices. A cartridge can utilize the services that are provided by the NCA such as installation, registration, instantiation, administration, and security. You can write a cartridge in many different languages such as Java, C++, or PL/SQL.

21

Figure 21.11.

Diagram of Network Computing Architecture.

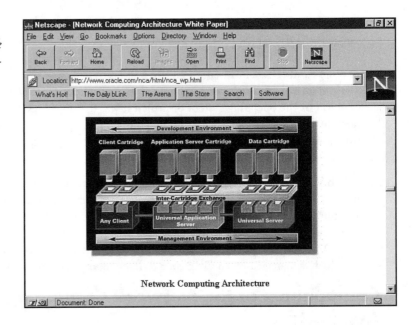

Inter-Cartridge Exchange

The NCA includes a component called the Inter-Cartridge Exchange (ICX) that acts as a clearinghouse for the services provided by cartridges wherever they exist on the network—on the client, on the application server, or on the database server. In addition to functioning as an ORB, the ICX also integrates the NCA with the Microsoft Component Object Model (COM) so that ActiveX clients can communicate with NCA cartridges. The ICX will also provide integration with Java components and legacy system interfaces. If you are using Oracle server version 7.3.3 or above, you can communicate with the ICX via the PL/SQL Cartridge.

Summary

In this final lesson, the key concepts to remember are the following:

☐ Oracle Web Application Server can be used to provide access to an Oracle database from a Web browser.

☐ The components of the Web Application Server are the Web Listener, the Database Access Descriptor, the Web Request Broker, and cartridges for various languages.

☐ Developer/2000 for the Web allows an Oracle Forms or Reports application to be deployed either as a client/server application or a Web application.

☐ Developer/2000 for the Web utilizes a Forms Server which translates the contents of an .FMX or .RDF file into calls to various Java components.

☐ The Network Computing Architecture is Oracle's strategy for the future of commercial software development. It emphasizes support for open standards such as CORBA 2.0 and HTTP/HTML.

Q&A

Q Can the Web Application Server be used to access a non-Oracle database?

A Yes. This can be accomplished through the use of a gateway. Oracle offers gateway products for popular databases such as DB2 and Sybase. Another alternative is to use the ODBC cartridge to access a non-Oracle database, assuming that an ODBC driver is available for the non-Oracle database.

Workshop

The purpose of the Workshop is to allow you to test your knowledge of the material discussed in the lesson.

Quiz

1. What is the role of the htp and htf PL/SQL packages?

2. True or false? The Network Computing Architecture is available only for Sun Solaris and Microsoft Windows NT Server.

21

WEEK

3

15

16

17

18

19

20

21

In Review

This was your last week; if you've been following the material in each lesson, you've gained a serious introduction to a variety of Oracle tools.

Day 15 presented the use of Oracle Reports—you built a simple report and a master-detail report. During Day 16, you used Oracle Graphics to create a chart based on the values in a table; you also learned how to use Procedure Builder to create a database trigger. Day 17 served as an introduction to Power Objects. On Day 18, you continued to learn about Power Objects: using method code to control the behavior of an application, creating a class, and constructing a report. The material on Day 19 included a discussion of Oracle users, roles, and privileges. Day 20 presented Database Designer and demonstrated its use in the database design process. Finally, Day 21 discussed three topics: the Web Application Server, Developer/2000 for the Web, and Oracle's Network Computing Architecture.

Day 22

Using PowerBuilder with an Oracle Database

This Bonus Day deals with the use of PowerBuilder and Oracle. PowerBuilder is an application-development environment that can be compared to Oracle Power Objects. It is the principal product of Powersoft, a wholly owned subsidiary of Sybase.

PowerBuilder's features include:

- ☐ The DataWindow, a flexible and intuitive mechanism for mapping a database table to an object that can be manipulated in an application
- ☐ Support for most desktop and server databases including Oracle, Sybase, SQL Server, Informix, and SQL Anywhere
- ☐ Excellent integration with Windows via DDE and OLE
- ☐ Support for distributed objects

☐ A pipeline object that supports data transfer between different database platforms (for example, from Sybase to Oracle)

☐ Support for classes, inheritance, and polymorphism

NOTE

The examples in this lesson are based on PowerBuilder Enterprise Edition. To learn more about PowerBuilder, visit the Powersoft Web site at www.powersoft.com.

Like Developer/2000 and Power Objects, PowerBuilder uses a scripting language named PowerScript for event-driven programming. Each object has a set of predefined events for which you can write a script. This script is executed when the event is triggered by an external event—for example, a user pressing Delete—or by another object's script. In addition, you can define additional events for an object and invoke PowerBuilder's comprehensive set of built-in functions from an event script.

Today, you will look at three specific areas:

☐ Defining a database profile for an Oracle database

☐ Creating a DataWindow for an Oracle table or join

☐ Handling Oracle errors

Defining a Database Profile

The first phase in using PowerBuilder with an Oracle database is setting up a database profile.

1. Open the PowerBuilder application in which you want to add the database profile.

2. To add a database profile, click on the DB Profile icon on the toolbar (it looks like four green cylinders). A window will appear, displaying the existing database profiles (see Figure 22.1).

3. Click on New to add a database profile. The Database Profile Setup window will appear.

4. Enter **Flugle** in the Profile Name field (see Figure 22.2).

5. In the DBMS field, select the current version of your database. This example shows O72 ORACLE v7.2 from the dropdown list (see Figure 22.2).

6. Click on More to specify the other fields for the Oracle database profile.

22

Figure 22.1.

The Database Profiles window displays existing database profiles.

DataWindow   DB Profile

Figure 22.2.

Specifying the Profile Name and DBMS for the new database profile.

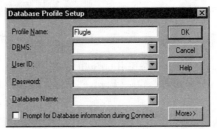

NOTE

If you do not see your current version in the dropdown list, you may need to reinstall some components. During the installation of PowerBuilder Enterprise Edition, you can select Typical or Custom installation options. The Typical installation option will not install the current version's native database driver. If you are using Windows 95 or Windows NT, you must be using SQL*Net V2.2 or above, and you must install the Oracle 7.x or higher's PowerBuilder native database driver.

7. If you are connecting to an Oracle server, enter the database alias that you use in the Server Name field. If you are using Personal Oracle, leave this field blank.

8. In Login ID, enter the Oracle username that you want to use for accessing the database.

9. In Login Password, enter the password for the Oracle user, as displayed in Figure 22.3.

Figure 22.3.

Specifying the Server Name, Login ID, and Login Password for the new database profile.

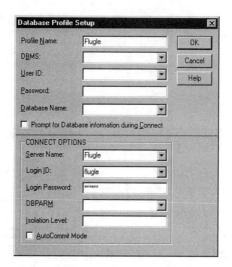

10. Click OK. PowerBuilder will create the database profile and display it in the list of available profiles (see Figure 22.4).

Figure 22.4.

The new database profile is displayed in the list of database profiles.

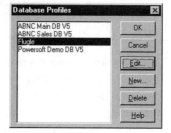

11. After you've created the new database profile, you will see it displayed in the list of available database profiles. To use the database profile, select it and click OK.

NOTE

> The first time you create a database profile for an Oracle database, PowerBuilder tries to create a repository—a set of five tables that are used to store additional information about each table's columns, such as format or validation. The tables are PBCATCOL, PBCATEDT, PBCATFMT, PBCATTBL, and PBCATVLD.
>
> By default, PowerBuilder tries to create these tables in the Oracle SYSTEM account. Normally, PowerBuilder will return an Oracle error ORA-01031, insufficient privileges, if the Oracle user specified in Login ID doesn't have the privilege to create a table in the SYSTEM account.
>
> There are a couple ways to create the repository if it doesn't already exist. You can create the new database profile and specify SYSTEM for Login ID and the SYSTEM password for Login Password. From SQL*Plus or SQL Worksheet, you then can grant the SELECT, INSERT, UPDATE, and DELETE privileges on the five repository tables to the Oracle user that you want to specify in Login ID.

BD 22

Creating a DataWindow

To create a new DataWindow, follow these steps:

1. Click the Datawindow button on the toolbar (it looks like a form and is the ninth button from the left). A window, labeled Select DataWindow, will appear, displaying all the existing DataWindows for the application (see Figure 22.5).

2. Click New to create a new DataWindow. You will then see the New Datawindow window.

3. You must make two choices for the New DataWindow—its data source and presentation style. Choose SQL Select for the data source and Tabular for the presentation style (see Figure 22.6).

4. Click OK.

Another window, labeled Select Tables, will appear. By default, this window will display all the tables that are accessible to the Oracle user associated with the current database profile. This list of tables will include tables owned by other Oracle users. Scroll down to the STUDENT table and click Open (see Figure 22.7).

Figure 22.5.

*Existing Data-
Windows are dis-
played.*

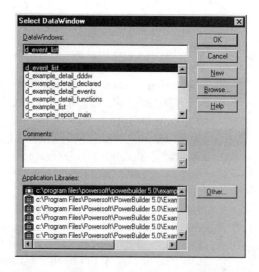

Figure 22.6.

*Specifying the data
source and presenta-
tion style for the new
DataWindow.*

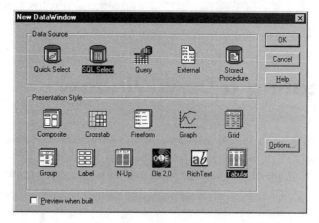

You are now using the DataWindow Painter. PowerBuilder provides a "painter" for each object type. In the DataWindow Painter, you will see each column in the Student table, along with its datatype. Using the mouse, select each column that you want to include in the DataWindow. As you select each column, you will see that column listed in the Selection List displayed near the top of the DataWindow window. Select all the columns as illustrated in Figure 22.8.

Figure 22.7.
List of available tables is displayed.

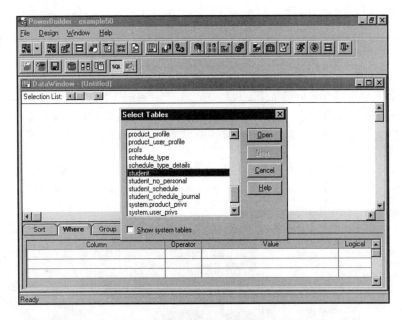

Figure 22.8.
Selecting the columns to be included in the new DataWindow.

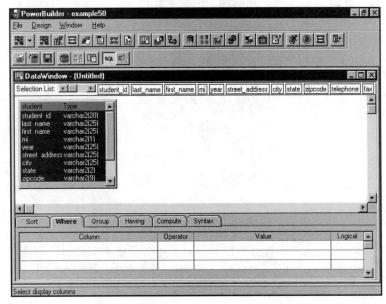

BD
22

Next, you should specify the order in which you want the records displayed in the DataWindow. Near the bottom of the DataWindow Painter, you should see six tab folders: Sort, Where, Group, Having, Compute, and Syntax.

1. Select the Sort tab. The list on the left of the tab contains a list of the columns in the Student table.

2. Drag each column and drop it onto the right-hand window, in the order in which you want the records sorted. By default, each column will be sorted in ascending order.

3. Select Student_ID in the list on the left and drag it to the list on the right. Figure 22.9 illustrates what you should see in the DataWindow Painter.

Figure 22.9.

Specifying the sort order for the DataWindow.

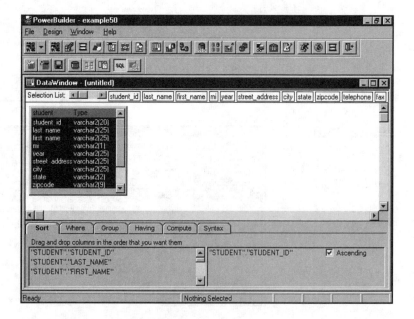

If you want to see the SQL statement that has been constructed by the DataWindow Painter, select the Syntax tab folder. You can scroll through the SQL statement with the scrollbar. As you can see in Figure 22.10, the DataWindow Painter, by default, specifies the table and column names within double quotes. Also, each column reference includes the table to which it belongs, even if a single table is being queried.

To construct the DataWindow, select Design | Data Source from the menu. You'll now see the default DataWindow layout that the DataWindow Painter has constructed (see Figure 22.11). The DataWindow Painter enables you to place objects in four bands: Header, Body, Summary, and Footer. As you can see, the default column headings have been created by removing the underscores in each column name and capitalizing each word. Each column is placed in the body band.

Figure 22.10.

The new database profile is displayed in the list of database profiles.

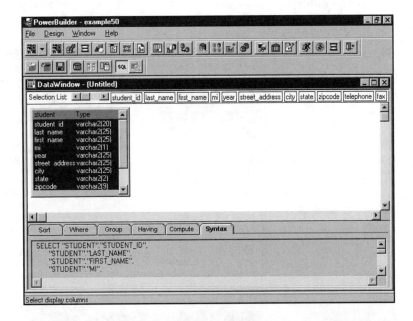

Figure 22.11.

Default layout for the new DataWindow.

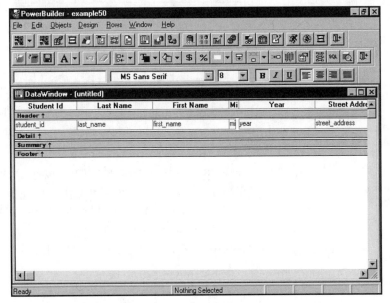

To preview the DataWindow, select Design | Preview from the menu. PowerBuilder will execute the query that the DataWindow uses and display the results (see Figure 22.12). In Preview mode, you can also insert, delete, and update rows in the DataWindow. To exit Preview mode, select Design | Preview from the menu.

Figure 22.12.

Previewing the new DataWindow.

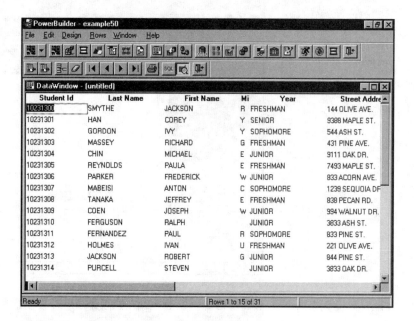

Error Handling with Oracle

To communicate with an Oracle database from a PowerBuilder application, you must have successfully connected a transaction object to the database. By default, PowerBuilder uses a transaction object named SQLCA to communicate with a database. The transaction object has a set of properties that must be set to the proper values to establish an Oracle connection. These properties are

ServerName	The database alias to be used when connecting to an Oracle database
DBMS	O72 Oracle v7.2 (it is critical that this string exactly match what PowerBuilder displays in the Database Profile window)
LogID	The Oracle user to be used for the connection
LogPass	The password associated with the Oracle user assigned to LogID

Once the correct transaction properties have been set, you can use the CONNECT statement to connect to the Oracle database. Because it is an embedded SQL statement, the CONNECT statement is terminated with a semicolon. After the CONNECT statement is executed, you will need to examine another transaction object property to determine if the connection was successful. There are several transaction object properties whose values can be examined after each SQL statement:

SQLCode   This is a DBMS-independent error code whose value is zero if there were no errors in processing the previous SQL statement.

SQLDBCode   This is a DBMS-specific error code whose value is zero if there were no errors in processing the previous SQL statement. However, if SQLDBCode is not equal to zero, it will contain a vendor-specific error code.

SQLErrText   This is a DBMS-specific error message that corresponds to the value of SQLDBCode.

SQLNRows   If you are connecting to an Oracle database, this value will indicate the number of rows that were affected by the previous SQL statement.

Listing 22.1 displays the script for the open event for an application that connects to an Oracle server. The first portion of the script assigns a value to the properties of SQLCA, the default transaction object. The CONNECT statement is used to connect to the Oracle database. SQLDBCode is examined to determine if it is less than 0; if it is, an Oracle error has occurred during the connection attempt.

INPUT   **Listing 22.1. Open script for application object.**

```
SQLCA.ServerName = ""
SQLCA.DBMS = "O72 Oracle v7.2"
SQLCA.LogID = "flugle"
SQLCA.LogPass = "flugle"

Connect;

if SQLCA.SQLDBCode < 0 then
    messagebox("Unable to connect to the database", &
        "SQLDBCode: " + string(SQLCA.SQLDBCode))
end if

open (w_genapp_frame)
```

NOTE   The open script is intended to illustrate the use of the transaction object; in a real application, you would not want to "hardcode" these values in the script.

Summary

PowerBuilder is an excellent application development environment that integrates nicely with the Oracle database, as well as other databases. The Usenet newsgroup, `comp.soft-sys.powerbuilder`, is an excellent source of information—examples, answers, and tips—about PowerBuilder and its use with an Oracle database.

22

Day **23**

Oracle8: New Features

On June 24, 1997, Oracle Corporation formally announced the next major release of the Oracle RDBMS: Oracle8. This new release is one of the major components of Oracle's Network Computing Architecture. Oracle Corporation is emphasizing several new characteristics of the Oracle8 server, such as:

- [ ] **Improved scalability:** The maximum size of an Oracle database has been increased to support hundreds of terabytes, depending on the operating system on which it resides.

- [ ] **Improved security administration:** As an example, the Oracle8 server now includes password management so that a password has a limited lifetime, and must meet certain complexity criteria, such as minimum length. An account can be locked after a specified number of failed login attempts.

- [ ] **Improved performance via partitioning:** A table or index can be divided into smaller pieces, called partitions, based on the value of one or more columns. A table's partitions can be individually managed so that operations in one partition do not affect the availability of data in the other partitions. Also, insert, update, and delete operations against partitioned tables can be processed in parallel; in other words, the

Oracle8 server can assign a portion of the work to execute a single DML statement to multiple processes, which may then be allocated to multiple processors by the server operating system. As a result, the parallel DML operation is completed more quickly.

☐ **Enhanced support for database replication:** The performance and manageability of database replication has been significantly improved.

☐ **Capability to handle a much larger number of concurrent users:** By pooling database connections, the Oracle8 server is able to service a much larger number of concurrent users—up to 3,000, depending on the server operating system and server hardware resources.

☐ **New and improved datatypes:** Some existing datatypes have been enhanced, and new datatypes have been introduced.

☐ **Improved SELECT statement:** A new feature of the SELECT statement allows a subquery to be used in place of a table in a FROM clause.

☐ **Object-relational features via the Oracle Objects Option:** A new RDBMS option supports the definition and use of new datatypes.

NOTE

> Oracle Corporation has stated that the Oracle8 Migration Tool can migrate an Oracle7 database (version 7.1, 7.2, or 7.3) to Oracle8. In addition, an application that currently works with an Oracle7 database will work properly with an Oracle8 database. Therefore, all the features of SQL and PL/SQL discussed throughout this book will continue to work in Oracle8.

Many of these new features are of primary interest to database administrators and system architects. However, this lesson will focus on new features of Oracle8 that are of interest to database designers and application developers. The material in this lesson is based on Oracle8 for Windows NT, version 8.0.2.0.1 Beta2.

Enhancement of Existing Datatypes and Some New Datatypes

Oracle8 has increased the maximum size of some existing Oracle datatypes:

☐ The capacity of a RAW column has been increased from 255 bytes to 2,000 bytes.

☐ The capacity of a VARCHAR2 column has been increased from 2,000 characters to 4,000 characters.

In addition, a single table can now have up to 1,000 columns.

Two new datatypes, NCHAR and NCHAR VARYING, can be used with Oracle8. These datatypes can be used for national character sets that require more than one byte per character; this is needed for many Asian languages.

NOTE

> The examples in this lesson were performed with SQL*Plus and SQL Worksheet.

BD 23

Large Objects, or LOBs

Oracle8 provides much more support in the area of large objects. In fact, a new category of datatypes, called LOB, or Large Object, is introduced with Oracle8.

LOBs can be one of four datatypes:

- [ ] BLOBs, which store unstructured binary data
- [ ] CLOBs, which store character data
- [ ] NCLOBs, which store character data using a multibyte national character set (primarily designed to support Asian languages)
- [ ] BFILEs, which reference binary files in the filesystem

There are several advantages to using LOBs. First, a LOB can accommodate 4GB or twice the capacity of the LONG or LONG RAW column. Second, a table can contain more than one LOB column, whereas it can contain only a single LONG or LONG RAW column. Also, the data stored in a LOB column is kept in a storage area separate from the table that contains the LOB column, resulting in better overall performance. Let's look at some examples of how these datatypes can be used.

Using BLOBs

You can think of the BLOB datatype as a new, improved version of the LONG RAW datatype. A BLOB column can store twice as much as a LONG RAW column. Unlike a LONG RAW column, an INSERT statement with a subquery may contain a BLOB column. Listing 23.1 is an example of the creation of a table that contains a BLOB column. The BLOB column is used to store a scanned image of a potential instructor's resume.

INPUT/OUTPUT **Listing 23.1. Creating a table that contains a BLOB column.**

```
SQL> create table Instructor_Application (
  2  Application_Number  number,
  3  Last_Name           varchar2(30),
```

continues

Listing 23.1. continued

```
4  First_Name       varchar2(30),
5  MI               varchar2(1),
6  Resume           blob,
7  Status           varchar2(30));

Table created.
```

Using CLOBs

The CLOB datatype is similar to the LONG datatype. Like the LONG datatype, the CLOB datatype is used for storing long strings. However, the CLOB datatype has twice the capacity of the LONG datatype—4GB instead of 2GB.

In Listing 23.2, you can see an example of how a CLOB column, named OCR_Resume, is added to the Instructor_Application table. The purpose of the OCR_Resume column is to store the text recognized by the scanning software after the resume has been scanned.

 Listing 23.2. Altering a table to add a CLOB column.

```
SQL> alter table Instructor_Application add
  2  (OCR_Resume  clob);

Table altered.

SQL> update Instructor_Application
  2  set OCR_Resume = 'Resume of A. Einstein - Born in Ulm, Germany in 1879'
  3  ;

1 row updated.

SQL> select OCR_Resume from Instructor_Application;

OCR_RESUME
--------------------------------------------------------------------------
Resume of A. Einstein - Born in Ulm, Germany in 1879
```

ANALYSIS   After the CLOB column has been added to the table, an UPDATE statement is used to set the value of OCR_Resume. A SELECT statement illustrates that the contents of OCR_Resume can be retrieved from the table.

Another important distinction between the CLOB and LONG datatypes is that there are fewer restrictions on referencing a CLOB column in a SQL statement. Refer to Listing 23.3 to see an example.

Listing 23.3. Inserting a row into a table with a LONG column.

INPUT/
OUTPUT

```
SQL> create table New_Instructor_Application
  2  as
  3  select * from Instructor_Application;

Table created.

SQL> create table Old_Instructor_Application (
  2  Application_Number  number,
  3  Last_Name           varchar2(30),
  4  First_Name          varchar2(30),
  5  MI                  varchar2(1),
  6  Resume              long,
  7  Status              varchar2(30));

Table created.

SQL> create table Another_Instructor_Application
  2  as
  3  select * from Old_Instructor_Application;
select * from Old_Instructor_Application
       *
ERROR at line 3:
ORA-00997: illegal use of LONG datatype
```

ANALYSIS   As you can see in Listing 23.3, a table named New_Instructor_Application is created with a subquery that retrieves all the columns in Instructor_Application, including OCR_Resume. The next statement creates a table named Old_Instructor_Application, which contains a column named Resume that is a LONG datatype. If you try to create another table named Another_Instructor_Application via a subquery of Old_Instructor_Application, Oracle rejects the statement.

Specifying a NULL for a BLOB or CLOB

There are two new built-in functions that are used to assign a NULL to a LOB: EMPTY_BLOB and EMPTY_CLOB. There are no arguments for either function. Listing 23.4 illustrates the use of EMPTY_BLOB in an INSERT statement.

Listing 23.4. Inserting a row into a table with a BLOB column.

INPUT/
OUTPUT

```
SQL> insert into Instructor_Application
  2  (Application_Number, Last_Name, First_Name, MI, Resume, Status)
  3  values
  4  (1001, 'EINSTEIN', 'ALBERT', NULL, EMPTY_BLOB(), 'REJECTED');

1 row created.
```

Using BFILEs

A BFILE column is used to reference a binary file that is stored in the filesystem where the Oracle8 server resides; that is, the binary file is external to the Oracle8 database. As an example, Listing 23.5 demonstrates how to create a table that contains a BFILE column.

INPUT/OUTPUT **Listing 23.5. Defining and using a BFILE column.**

```
SQL> create table Instructor_Photo
  2  (Instructor_ID  varchar2(5),
  3   Recent_Photo   bfile);

Table created.

SQL> insert into Instructor_Photo
  2  (Instructor_ID, Recent_Photo)
  3  values
  4  ('E251', BFILENAME ('C:\Flugle\Photos', 'E251.jpg'));

1 row created.
```

ANALYSIS The Instructor_Photo table is created with a BFILE column named Recent_Photo. The purpose of this column is to identify the location and name of the .JPG file that contains a photograph of the instructor identified by Instructor_ID. A row is inserted into the Instructor_Photo table. As you can see, the BFILENAME function is used to supply a literal value for the BFILE column; the directory and filename are enclosed in single quotes. The contents of the binary file referenced by a BFILE column cannot be modified by a SQL statement; however, the directory and filename as contained in the BFILE column can be modified.

The CREATE DIRECTORY Statement

A new SQL statement introduced with Oracle8 is CREATE DIRECTORY. This statement is designed to work with BFILE columns. The purpose of CREATE DIRECTORY is to create an alias for a filesystem directory. Once the directory alias is defined, the privilege to read the contents of a file in that directory can be granted to a role or user.

SYNTAX

Here's the syntax for the CREATE DIRECTORY statement:

```
CREATE DIRECTORY directory_alias  as 'directory';
```

The variables are defined as follows:

> directory_alias is the name that Oracle users will use to reference the directory.
>
> directory is the fully qualified directory where the binary files that are referenced by a BFILE column reside.

For example, Listing 23.6 illustrates how a directory is created. The privilege to read files from that directory can then be granted to a database role.

INPUT/ OUTPUT **Listing 23.6. Creating a directory.**

```
SQL> create directory instructor_photos as 'C:\Flugle\Photos';

Directory created.
```

BD 23

In addition to the CREATE DIRECTORY statement, another new statement—DROP DIRECTORY— is used to drop a directory alias so that no privileges can be granted to read a directory from an Oracle8 application.

New Datatypes Available with the Oracle Objects Option

The Oracle Objects Option is an optional component of the Oracle8 server. You must have this option to be able to use these datatypes:

☐ The object datatype
☐ Nested tables
☐ VARRAY
☐ REF

We'll be examining the object datatype, nested tables, and the VARRAY datatype in this section. To begin with, let's look at the object datatype.

NOTE   Inheritance is an important concept in object-oriented languages. At the present time, neither SQL nor PL/SQL supports inheritance.

The Object Datatype

Oracle8 Objects Option provides a new statement, CREATE TYPE, which can be used to create a new datatype that can then be used when creating a table or another datatype. For example, if you wanted to create a table which described the equipment that an instructor might want to use in a classroom, you could create a new datatype called Classroom_Equipment for this purpose. Once the datatype is created, you can then create a table that uses the datatype (see Listing 23.7).

Listing 23.7. Creating a new datatype.

```
SQL> create type Available_Room as object
  2  (building     varchar2(20),
  3   room         varchar2(6));

Type created.
```

Once you define a new datatype, you can specify the datatype for a column as demonstrated in Listing 23.8.

Listing 23.8. Creating a table that contains an object datatype.

```
SQLWKS> create table Seminar (
    2> Seminar_ID     varchar2(6),
    3> Instructor_ID varchar2(6),
    4> Location       Available_Room);
Statement processed.
```

An object consists of attributes (the columns defined for it) and methods (the functions and procedures that manipulate the object and return information about it). By default, Oracle creates a constructor method for each object type. This constructor method creates an instance of the object. When you want to specify a value for an object column, you must use this constructor method, which consists of the name of the object type followed by the attribute values enclosed in parentheses. Listing 23.9 provides an example.

Listing 23.9. Using a constructor method to specify a value for an object datatype.

```
SQLWKS> insert into Seminar
    2> (Seminar_ID, Instructor_ID, Location)
    3> values
    4> ('1001', 'A101', Available_Room('NARROW HALL', 'B200'));
1 row processed.
```

Once you've created a table that contains an object column, you can use a SELECT statement to retrieve the values from the object column. However, you must specify each object attribute that you want to retrieve (see Listing 23.10).

**INPUT/
OUTPUT**

Listing 23.10. Qualifying an attribute with the name of the object column.

```
SQLWKS> select Location.Building, Location.Room from Seminar;
LOCATION.BUILDING     LOCATI
-------------------   ------
NARROW HALL           B200
1 row selected.
```

Nested Tables

Oracle8 also supports the use of nested tables. Suppose you create an object datatype called Test_Score which is designed to store a student's ID and a score on a particular test (see Listing 23.11). You can also create another datatype called Test_Score_Table which is a table based on the Test_Score datatype. Finally, you can use the Test_Score_Table datatype to specify a column's datatype when you create or alter a table.

**INPUT/
OUTPUT**

Listing 23.11. Creating a table that contains a nested table column.

```
SQLWKS> create type Test_Score as object (
    2> Student_ID   varchar2(6),
    3> Score        number);
Statement processed.

SQLWKS> create type Test_Score_Table as table of Test_Score;
Statement processed.

SQLWKS> create table Test_Results (
    2> Instructor_ID     varchar2(6),
    3> Class_ID          varchar2(6),
    4> Test_Name         varchar2(30),
    5> Scores            Test_Score_Table)
    6> nested table Scores store as Test_Scores;
Statement processed.
```

ANALYSIS   The last SQL statement in Listing 23.11 is a CREATE TABLE statement. When you create a table that contains a column that is a nested table, you must specify a storage table that is identified for the nested table.

When you specify a set of values for a nested table in a DML statement, you must specify the constructor method for the nested table datatype, and, as arguments to that constructor method, you can specify the constructor method for the datatype on which the nested table datatype is based. Listing 23.12 presents an example; a single row is inserted in the Test_Results table. Even though a single row is inserted in the Test_Results table, three test scores are stored in the column Scores, which is a nested table.

Listing 23.12. Inserting a row into a table which contains a nested table column.

```
SQLWKS> insert into Test_Results
    2> (Instructor_ID, Class_ID, Test_Name, Scores)
    3> values
    4> ('E101', '123456', 'Final exam',
    5>  Test_Score_Table
    6>  (Test_Score ('A12345', 98),
    7>   Test_Score ('E13111', 87),
    8>   Test_Score ('F13999', 84)));
1 row processed.
```

 On line 5, the constructor method for the nested table type Test_Score_Table is specified. On lines 6, 7, and 8, the constructor method for Test_Score is specified with each set of attribute values.

The VARRAY Datatype

A new datatype available in Oracle8 is the VARYING ARRAY or VARRAY. This datatype represents an ordered set of elements of the same datatype.

 Here's a simplified version of the VARRAY syntax:

```
CREATE TYPE type_name  as VARRAY (limit) of datatype;
```

The variables are defined as follows:

   type_name is the name of the VARRAY type to be created.

   limit is the maximum number of elements in the array.

   datatype is either a predefined or user-defined datatype.

The VARRAY limit must be an integer literal; you cannot use an expression to specify the limit. As you can see in Listing 23.13, once a VARRAY type is declared, it can be used as the datatype for a column.

Listing 23.13. Creating a table that contains a VARRAY column.

```
SQL> create type Available_Rooms as varray (100) of Available_Room;

Type created.

SQL> create table Class_Scheduling (
  2  Administrator_ID  varchar2(6),
  3  Semester          varchar2(6),
  4  Year              number,
  5  Room_Assignments  Available_Rooms);

Table created.
```

23

Let's look at how you specify values for a VARRAY column in an INSERT statement. If you want to specify a null value for the VARRAY column, you can specify the constructor method for the VARRAY datatype with a NULL argument (see Listing 23.14).

**INPUT/
OUTPUT**

Listing 23.14. Specifying a null value for a VARRAY column in an INSERT.

```
SQL> insert into Class_Scheduling
  2  (Administrator_ID, Semester, Year, Room_Assignments)
  3  values
  4  ('101', 'FALL', '1998', Available_Rooms(NULL));

1 row created.
```

If you want to specify a value for an object column in a DML statement, you must specify the constructor method for the base object type enclosed within the constructor method for the VARRAY type. For example, Listing 23.15 contains an INSERT statement that attempts to store an available room in the column Room_Assignments. Oracle rejects the first INSERT statement because Available_Rooms is a VARRAY. The second INSERT statement uses the constructor method for Available_Room enclosed within the constructor method for Available_Rooms.

**INPUT/
OUTPUT**

Listing 23.15. Specifying a value for a VARRAY column in an INSERT.

```
SQL> insert into Class_Scheduling
  2  (Administrator_ID, Semester, Year, Room_Assignments)
  3  values
  4  ('101', 'FALL', '1998', Available_Rooms('FLUGLE HALL', 100));
('101', 'FALL', '1998', Available_Rooms('FLUGLE HALL', 100))
                                        *
ERROR at line 4:
ORA-00932: inconsistent datatypes

SQL> insert into Class_Scheduling
  2  (Administrator_ID, Semester, Year, Room_Assignments)
  3  values
  4  ('101', 'FALL', '1998',
  5  Available_Rooms(Available_Room('FLUGLE_HALL', '100')));

1 row created.
```

BD
23

Data Dictionary Views for User-Defined Types

To help the user inspect user-defined types, Oracle8 includes some new data dictionary views:

☐ USER_TYPES presents basic information about datatypes that have been created by a user—in other words, datatypes other than predefined.

☐ USER_TYPE_ATTRS provides detailed information about each datatype listed in USER_TYPES.

Listing 23.16 contains a description of the columns returned by USER_TYPES and a sample query against USER_TYPES.

<table>
<tr>
<td>**NOTE**</td>
<td>Many of the Oracle data dictionary views are categorized as USER_, ALL_, and DBA_. Those views that begin with USER provide information on the applicable objects owned by the user who is querying that data dictionary view. Those views that begin with ALL provide information on all applicable objects that the user who is querying that data dictionary view has the privilege to see. Finally, those views that begin with DBA provide information on all applicable objects in the database. Although this section discusses only the USER_TYPES and USER_TYPE_ATTRS data dictionary views, the Oracle8 server also provides four other related data dictionary views: ALL_TYPES, ALL_TYPE_ATTRS, DBA_TYPES, and DBA_TYPE_ATTRS.</td>
</tr>
</table>

| INPUT/
OUTPUT | **Listing 23.16. Looking at the contents of USER_TYPES.** |

```
SQLWKS> desc USER_TYPES
Column Name                       Null?     Type
--------------------------------  --------  ----
TYPE_NAME                         NOT NULL  VARCHAR2(30)
TYPE_OID                          NOT NULL  RAW(16)
TYPECODE                                    VARCHAR2(30)
ATTRIBUTES                                  NUMBER
METHODS                                     NUMBER
PREDEFINED                                  VARCHAR2(3)
INCOMPLETE                                  VARCHAR2(3)

SQLWKS> select type_name, typecode, attributes, methods from user_types;
TYPE_NAME                         TYPECODE           ATTRIBUTES METHODS
--------------------------------  ------------------ ---------- ----------
AVAILABLE_ROOM                    OBJECT                      2          0
AVAILABLE_ROOMS                   COLLECTION                  0          0
CLASS_PRESIDENTS                  COLLECTION                  0          0
```

```
TEST_SCORE                    OBJECT              2        0
TEST_SCORE_TABLE              COLLECTION          0        0
5 rows selected.
```

ANALYSIS   As you can see in the previous query, the TYPECODE column will return OBJECT
if a type is defined as an object or COLLECTION if a type is defined as a VARRAY or a nested
table. For example, AVAILABLE_ROOM was defined as an object so its TYPECODE is OBJECT,
whereas AVAILABLE_ROOMS was defined as a VARRAY of AVAILABLE_ROOM so its TYPECODE is
COLLECTION.

If you want to look at the attributes that have been defined for a type, you can query the
USER_TYPE_ATTRS data dictionary view. Listing 23.17 provides a description of the
USER_TYPE_ATTRS view and a sample query which returns the attributes that have been defined
for the TEST_SCORE type.

**INPUT/
OUTPUT**   **Listing 23.17. Looking at the contents of USER_TYPE_ATTRS.**

```
SQLWKS> desc user_type_attrs
Column Name                   Null?    Type
----------------------------- -------- ----
TYPE_NAME                     NOT NULL VARCHAR2(30)
ATTR_NAME                     NOT NULL VARCHAR2(30)
ATTR_TYPE_MOD                          VARCHAR2(7)
ATTR_TYPE_OWNER                        VARCHAR2(30)
ATTR_TYPE_NAME                         VARCHAR2(30)
LENGTH                                 NUMBER
PRECISION                              NUMBER
SCALE                                  NUMBER
CHARACTER_SET_NAME                     VARCHAR2(44)

SQLWKS> select attr_name, attr_type_name, length
    2> from user_type_attrs
    3> where
    4> type_name = 'TEST_SCORE';
ATTR_NAME                          ATTR_TYPE_NAME                       LENGTH
---------------------------------- ------------------------------------ --------
STUDENT_ID                         VARCHAR2                             6
SCORE                              NUMBER
2 rows selected.
```

Changes to the SELECT Statement

A new feature provided with the Oracle8 server is the capability to supply a subquery in the
FROM clause of a SELECT statement in place of a table or view. Listing 23.18 presents an
example.

INPUT/OUTPUT **Listing 23.18. Using a subquery in the FROM Clause.**

```
SQLWKS> select Operating_Room, Surgeon_ID, Last_Name
    2> from (select Patient_ID, Last_Name from Patient
    3> where Status != 'MORGUE') P, Surgery_Schedule S
    4> where
    5> P.Patient_ID = S.Patient_ID;
OPERAT SURGEO LAST_NAME
------ ------ ------------------------------
A10    G101   JOHNSON
1 row selected.
```

ANALYSIS In line 2 of Listing 23.18, a subquery of the Patient table is enclosed in parentheses; it returns `Patient_ID` and `Last_Name` only for those patients whose value for `Status` is not equal to `'MORGUE'`. In line 3, the subquery is joined with the Surgery_Schedule table based on the join criterion found on line 5.

Referencing External Procedures

Oracle8 gives a developer the capability to call routines written in other languages from a PL/SQL subprogram. These routines, written in a 3GL and residing in a shared library, are referred to as *external procedures*. To register an external procedure, Oracle8 includes a new statement that will let a developer reference an external library which contains the *external procedures*: CREATE LIBRARY (see Listing 23.19).

NOTE

> At the present time, only external procedures must be written in C.

SYNTAX

Here is the syntax to create a library that contains external procedures:

```
CREATE LIBRARY library_name  as 'file_name';
```

The variables are defined as follows:

library_name is the name of the library that can be referenced from PL/SQL subprograms.

file_name is the directory and name of the shared library.

INPUT/OUTPUT **Listing 23.19. Creating a library alias for referencing external procedures.**

```
SQLWKS> create library flugle_lib as '/opt/flugle/lib/flugle_lib.so';
Statement processed.
```

23

Object Views

Oracle8 also introduces a new feature called *object views*. An object view is an extension of the relational view that you've learned about. One of Oracle's goals with Oracle8 is to begin supporting object-relational applications; the object view is part of this strategy. Object views can coexist with relational views of the same tables; therefore, users can continue to use traditional relational applications that work with a set of tables in an Oracle database while developers experiment with object-oriented applications that rely on object views against the same tables.

Listing 23.20 presents an example of an object view. First, the Patient table is created. Next, the Patient_Type datatype is created which mirrors the Patient table. Finally, the object view Patient_View is created which uses Patient_ID as the object ID.

INPUT/OUTPUT

Listing 23.20. Looking at the contents of USER_TYPES.

```
SQLWKS> create table Patient (
    2> Patient_ID      varchar2(6),
    3> Last_Name       varchar2(30),
    4> First_Name      varchar2(20),
    5> MI              varchar2(1),
    6> SS_Number       varchar2(9),
    7> Location        varchar2(6),
    8> Status          varchar2(20),
    9> Admittance_Date date,
   10> Discharge_Date  date,
   11> Carrier         varchar2(30));
Statement processed.

SQLWKS> create type Patient_Type (
    2> Patient_ID      varchar2(6),
    3> Last_Name       varchar2(30),
    4> First_Name      varchar2(20),
    5> MI              varchar2(1),
    6> SS_Number       varchar2(9),
    7> Location        varchar2(6),
    8> Status          varchar2(20),
    9> Admittance_Date date,
   10> Discharge_Date  date,
   11> Carrier         varchar2(30));
Statement processed.

SQLWKS> create view Patient_View of Patient_Type
    2> with object oid (Patient_ID) as
    3> select Patient_ID, Last_Name, First_Name, MI, SS_Number,
    4> Location, Status, Admittance_Date, Discharge_Date, Carrier
    5> from Patient;
Statement processed.
```

BD 23

Development Considerations

Although Oracle has provided an easy migration path to Oracle8, it is difficult to predict how quickly existing Oracle customers will migrate their databases from Oracle7 to Oracle8. In any event, if you are planning to develop an application that will be used with Oracle7 databases, you won't be able to use the new features discussed in this chapter in that version of the application. Of course, you could develop a separate version for an Oracle8 database that incorporates some of the new features. However, at the present time, support for the new features described in this chapter is limited to use in:

- PL/SQL stored programs
- C/C++ programs that use the Oracle Call Interface (OCI), a library of callable functions
- C/C++ programs developed with the Oracle Pro*C/C++ Precompiler, a tool that allows a developer to embed SQL statements in a C/C++ program that is then translated to the native C/C++ statements for a particular C/C++ compiler

However, Oracle Corporation and other third-party software tool vendors will soon provide tools that are able to take advantage of the new datatypes and the features provided by the Object Option. Until then, you have an opportunity to learn how these features can be utilized in an application.

Summary

This lesson was a brief introduction to some of the new features provided by the Oracle8 server, such as the following:

- The LOB datatypes, which consist of the BLOB, CLOB, NCLOB, and BFILE datatypes. The BLOB datatype can store up to 4GB of unstructured binary data. The CLOB and NCLOB datatypes can store up to 4GB of character data. The BFILE datatype is used to reference an external file that contains binary data.
- With the optional Oracle Objects Option, you can create your own datatypes such as an object datatype, a varying array of some base datatype, or a nested table datatype.
- Oracle8 supports the use of a subquery in the FROM clause of a SELECT statement.

APPENDIX

A

Answers to Quizzes and Exercises

Day 1, "Exploring the World of Relational Databases"

Quiz

1. Name two advantages that relational databases offer over file management systems.

   Answer: A relational database provides declarative integrity. The term *declarative* means that the integrity is enforced simply by declaring the integrity rules when a table is created or modified. A relational database also provides an ad hoc query capability, making it easy to pose complex questions without programming.

2. Name three advantages of the client/server computing architecture when compared to the mainframe computing architecture.

   Answer: Advantages of the client/server computing architecture are the capability to support different client operating systems, independence from networking protocol, and partitioning of processing between client and server (for example, client controls the user interface, whereas server provides data storage and retrieval).

3. What is the name of the Oracle middleware product?

   Answer: The Oracle middleware product is named SQL*Net.

4. What is a "fat" client? What is a "thin" client?

   Answer: Today, a "fat" client refers to a traditional client/server architecture in which a client machine hosts a fairly large executable, required libraries, and a middleware product. A "thin" client describes a client machine in which a Web browser is used to execute an application, either via HTML or by downloading Java applets as required.

Exercise

As I mentioned, this book uses a sample database for a small college. Start thinking about what kinds of information you think the college will want to store and retrieve. Ask yourself what kinds of questions a student, a professor, or an administrator might ask of the database. Jot down how you might organize this information. You'll return to this information on Day 3, "Logical Database Design."

Answer: A college would certainly want to maintain information about:

- ☐ Students
- ☐ Departments
- ☐ Instructors
- ☐ Courses
- ☐ Facilities, such as buildings and equipment

A student would want to know about which classes are available, where they will be taught and by whom; the cost of each class.

An instructor would want to know about the classes that they are assigned to teach. An instructor needs to be able to assign a grade to each student in a class.

An administrator would want to be able to assign each class to an appropriate location (e.g. seating capacity or lab resources). An administrator might also want to be able to compare one department to another in various ways—teaching load, instructor seniority, or average grade given in classes.

Day 2, "Guidelines for Developing an Oracle Application"

Quiz

1. True or false? If you use an application-development tool that supports object-oriented development, there is a greater chance of implementing a successful application.

   Answer: False. An object-oriented development tool might reduce the effort to develop and maintain the application. However, this doesn't imply that this will result in a successful implementation; there are many other factors that will influence the course of a project.

2. Name three types of requirements that are needed when designing a system.

   Answer: Data requirements, functional requirements, and performance requirements.

3. True or false? You shouldn't begin developing software until you have a complete set of requirements.

   Answer: False. You *should* wait to develop software until you have a large number of requirements identified. However, if you wait until all the requirements are identified, you'll be waiting a long time. Many requirements will emerge when end-users see each prototype of the application. Also, requirements are not static; they definitely will change over time.

Exercise

What types of risks might exist during the development of an Oracle application? What factors could contribute to these risk categories? What steps could be taken to mitigate these risk categories?

Answer: You could categorize the risks during the development of an Oracle application as follows:

- [ ] **Schedule risk:** The risk that the application fails to meet its development milestones.

  One obvious reason a project often fails to meet its development milestones is because the milestones were unrealistic to begin with. Often, the pressure on project management is simply too great; individuals are compelled to underestimate the time and resources needed to complete a task.

  Also, a project may appear to meet early milestones, such as requirements analysis, but fail in achieving milestones that provide the actual application. What has often happened on such projects is that the early milestones *appeared* to have been met but careful scrutiny would have uncovered problems. Therefore, on a large project, it is prudent for the customer to engage an independent audit of the project for each early milestone.

- [ ] **Budget risk:** The risk that the application fails to meet the budget that has been allocated to it.

  Often, if a project fails to meet its schedule, it also fails to meet its budget. The reason is simple: the largest component of a project's budget is usually for labor. If the estimate for the labor required to complete a task was low, the corresponding budget estimate will also be low. One exception to this is a project that is late in acquiring the people that are needed; in this case, the budget is within its limit but the schedule isn't met.

- [ ] **Technical risks:** The technical risks on a project could have many sources. New products or technology may have been selected without careful analysis. Developers may not have received enough training or have sufficient experience to build a reliable application. The project designers may have underestimated the server computing resources (for example, CPU speed, storage requirements) or networking resources needed for the production environment. Each of these elements require careful thought. Often, it's worth the time and money to conduct a simple benchmark to characterize the application performance in a production environment.

Day 3, "Logical Database Design"

Quiz

1. True or false? If an attribute that isn't part of the primary key is a foreign key, it must be mandatory; it cannot allow a null value.

   Answer: False. Sometimes a foreign key is mandatory and sometimes it isn't. It really depends on the business rules that are being modeled.

2. Will the Student Schedule table handle the situation in which a student needs to repeat a course? Why or why not?

Answer: Yes. Each class is uniquely identified by class ID. But each offering of the same course will have a different class ID. For instance, suppose a student takes Biology 101 during the Fall 1997 semester and fails the course—which is class ID 109230. In Spring 1997, he repeats the course—which is now class ID 110330. Because the two classes have unique IDs, a row can be inserted into the Student Schedule for both classes.

3. What characteristic of a relational database will prevent a class from being deleted from the Class table if there are rows in the Student Schedule table that contain the Class ID to be deleted?

Answer: Referential integrity.

4. From an entity-relationship perspective, there is a relationship between the Class and Instructor tables. Is it identifying or non-identifying?

Answer: Non-identifying. Instructor ID is not part of the primary key in the Class table.

5. True or false? If you create the proper index for a table, its rows will always be retrieved in the ascending order of the indexed columns.

Answer: False. There is no implied order to the rows in a table. To guarantee that rows are retrieved in a particular order, you must specify that order in a SQL statement.

Exercises

1. Suppose you want to identify the instructor who is the head of a department. Can you think of at least two ways of doing this? What are the strengths and weaknesses of each approach?

Answer: There are two obvious choices. One choice is to add an attribute to the Department entity that identifies the instructor who is the head of the department. Of course, this attribute would be a foreign key to the Instructor entity. So, the Department entity would consist of three attributes:

☐ Department ID

☐ Department Name

☐ Department Head

The other choice is to add an attribute to the Instructor entity that indicates whether or not an instructor is the head of the department. You could also name this attribute Department Head and allow it to have the value Y if the instructor was the head of the department (it could be null if the instructor was not the department head). The problem with this approach is that this information is a characteristic of a department; therefore, it makes more sense to incorporate it in the Department entity.

2. The Student Schedule table currently holds both current classes and previous classes that a student has taken. Propose an alternate design using two tables—one table contains the current schedule and the second table contains classes that the student has previously taken. Identify each attribute in the two tables. What are the advantages of this design?

   Answer: The current definition of the Student_Schedule entity is:

   - ☐ Student ID (foreign key to Student table)
   - ☐ Class ID (foreign key to Class table)
   - ☐ Grade
   - ☐ Date Grade Assigned

   Primary key: Student ID, Class ID

   As an alternative, the Student_Schedule entity can be broken into two entities: Current Student Schedule and Student Class History. The student's current schedule would be stored in Current Student Schedule; it would not include the student's grade. As soon as a student's grades were assigned, records would be added to the Student Class History entity. At the beginning of each semester, the contents of Current Student Schedule would be deleted.

   The definition for Current Student Schedule could be this:

   - ☐ Student ID (foreign key to Student table)
   - ☐ Class ID (foreign key to Class table)

   The definition for Student Class History could be this:

   - ☐ Student ID (foreign key to Student table)
   - ☐ Class ID (foreign key to Class table)
   - ☐ Grade
   - ☐ Date Grade Assigned

   For a large university, this design makes more sense. For example, suppose a university has twenty thousand enrolled students. Suppose that each student is enrolled in an average of 3.5 classes per semester. At the beginning of each semester, the Current Student Schedule entity would therefore contain 20,000×3.5 = 70,000 records. At the end of each semester, another 70,000 records would be added to the Student Class History. If all of these records were kept in a single entity, Student_Schedule, the performance of the system would degrade over time. For example, in about fourteen years, the Student_Schedule entity would contain almost a million rows, which could really slow down the process of class enrollment.

Day 4, "Implementing Your Logical Model: Physical Database Design"

Quiz

1. What is wrong with this statement?

```
CREATE TABLE new_table (
first_col number,
second_col date
third_col number default sysdate);
```

Answer: There are two problems with the statement. First, a comma is needed at the end of the definition for second_col. Second, third_col is a number and cannot have a default value—sysdate—that is a date datatype.

2. Describe an SQL statement that might result in the following Oracle error message?

```
ORA-02266: unique/primary keys in table referenced by
↳enabled foreign keys
```

Answer: You will see this error if you try to drop a table whose primary key is referenced by another table's foreign key.

3. What is the difference between a column and table check constraint?

Answer: A column CHECK constraint is defined at the column level and cannot reference any other columns in the table. A table CHECK constraint is defined at the table level and can reference any of the table's columns.

Exercise

The Instructor table has a column named Position. In the current design of this table, there is a CHECK constraint on the Position column that restricts the value to ASSISTANT PROFESSOR, ASSOCIATE PROFESSOR, and FULL PROFESSOR. Modify the database design so that an additional table, Instructor_Position, is used to specify legal values for instructor position.

Answer: Create a table named Instructor_Position:

```
create table Instructor_Position
(Position         varchar2(25),
 constraint PK_Instructor_Position Primary Key (Position));
```

Redefine the Instructor table as follows:

```
create table Instructor
(Instructor_ID    varchar2(20),
 Department_ID    varchar2(20)
 constraint NN_Instructor_Dept_ID NOT NULL,
 Last_Name        varchar2(25)
 constraint NN_Instructor_Last_Name NOT NULL,
 First_Name       varchar2(25),
 MI               varchar2(1),
 Position         varchar2(25),
```

```
Telephone        varchar2(10),
Fax              varchar2(10),
Email            varchar2(100),
constraint PK_Instructor Primary Key (Instructor_ID),
constraint FK_Instructor_Department_ID
Foreign Key (Department_ID) references Department (Department_ID),
constraint FK_Instructor_Position
Foreign Key (Position) references Instructor_Position (Position));
```

Day 5, "Introduction to Structured Query Language (SQL)"

Quiz

1. True or false? You must include a column in the select list if you want to sort the rows returned by the SELECT statement by that column.

   Answer: False. You can specify a column in the ORDER BY clause that is not in the select list.

2. What is wrong with this statement:

   ```
   select First_Name
   from Student
   order by Last_Name
   where
   Last_Name like '%IN%';
   ```

   Answer: The ORDER BY clause occurs before the WHERE clause.

3. True or false? A column must be indexed before it can be specified in the ORDER BY clause.

   Answer: False. Oracle and other relational databases don't require that a column be indexed before it can be used to sort the rows retrieved from a table.

Exercise

Using the COURSE table that was discussed in this lesson, construct a SELECT statement that will return the Department ID, Course ID, and Course Title, sorted by Department ID and Course ID, for any course whose description contains the phrase introduc, regardless of capitalization.

Answer: Here is the SELECT statement that will accomplish this. Note that the lower function is used to convert all course descriptions to lowercase so that a consistent comparison can be made with introduc.

```
SQL> select Department_ID, Course_ID, Title
  2  from Course
  3  where
  4  lower(Description) like '%introduc%'
  5  order by Department_ID, Course_ID;
```

```
DEPARTMENT_ID        COURS  TITLE
----------------     -----  --------------------------------------------
ANTHRO               101    INTRO TO ANTHROPOLOGY
BIO                  101    INTRO TO BIOLOGY
ECON                 101    INTRO TO ECONOMICS
ENG                  101    INTRO TO STRUCTURES
ENG                  102    INTRO TO CIRCUIT THEORY
ENG                  103    INTRO TO DYNAMICS
ENGL                 101    INTRO TO ENGLISH LIT
ENGL                 193    SEMINAR ON THEME ANALYSIS
MATH                 101    GENERAL CALCULUS
MATH                 189    NUMBER THEORY
PHILO                101    INTRO TO PHILOSOPHY
PSYCH                101    INTRO TO PSYCHOLOGY

12 rows selected.
```

Day 6, "Using SQL to Modify Data"

Quiz

1. Construct an SQL statement that adds a course with the following characteristics: Department ID = BIO, Course ID = 137, Title = INSECT BEHAVIOR, Description = In-depth study of insect societies and their behavior patterns, Units = 3, no additional fees.

   Answer: Here is the INSERT statement:

   ```
   insert into Course
   (Department_ID, Course_ID, Title, Description, Units)
   values
   ('BIO', '137', 'INSECT BEHAVIOR',
   'In-depth study of insect societies and their behavior patterns', 3);
   ```

2. Construct an SQL statement that charges $50 in additional fees for all courses in the philosophy department.

   Answer: Here is the UPDATE statement:

   ```
   update Course
   set Additional_Fees = 50
   where
   Department_ID = 'PHILO';
   ```

3. Construct an SQL statement that eliminates a scheduled class if it is offered by the English department or is going to be held in Flugle Hall.

   Answer: Here is the DELETE statement:

   ```
   delete from Class
   where
   Department_ID = 'ENG' or
   Class_Building = 'FLUGLE HALL';
   ```

Exercise

Several of the instructors at Flugle College have decided to create a new department called Integrated Studies. As a result, the English, History, and Philosophy departments will merge to become the Integrated Studies department. The department ID for this new department will be INTSTD. In the database, create the Integrated Studies department (without deleting the existing departments). Also, modify the contents of the Instructor table so that instructors in the English, History, and Philosophy departments are now associated with the Integrated Studies department.

Answer: You can determine that six instructors are associated with the English, History, and Philosophy departments with this query:

```
SQL> select Instructor_ID
  2  from Instructor
  3  where
  4  Department_ID in ('ENGL', 'HIST', 'PHILO');

INSTRUCTOR_ID
--------------------
G331
L391
E491
T149
D944
B331

6 rows selected.
```

First, create the new department:

```
SQL> insert into Department
  2  (Department_ID, Department_Name)
  3  values
  4  ('INTSTD', 'Integrated Studies');

1 row created.
```

Next, update the Instructor table so that any instructor in the English, History, and Philosophy departments is now associated with Integrated Studies:

```
SQL> update Instructor
  2  set
  3  Department_ID = 'INTSTD'
  4  where
  5  Department_ID in ('ENGL', 'HIST', 'PHILO');

6 rows updated.
```

If you query the Instructor table, you will see that the same six instructors now belong to the Integrated Studies department:

```
SQL> select Instructor_ID
  2  from Instructor
  3  where
  4  Department_ID = 'INTSTD';
```

```
INSTRUCTOR_ID
-------------------
G331
L391
E491
T149
D944
B331

6 rows selected.
```

Finally, do a ROLLBACK so that the changes aren't permanent.

```
SQL> rollback;

Rollback complete.
```

Day 7, "Taking Advantage of SQL Built-In Functions"

Quiz

1. Construct an SQL statement that will retrieve each row from the Instructor table as shown in this example:

   ```
   Professor Parker
   ```

   Answer: The SELECT statement is

   ```
   SQL> select initcap(position ¦¦ ' ' ¦¦ last_name)
      2  from instructor;
   ```

2. Construct an SQL statement that will retrieve the instructor whose last name appears first in an alphabetic order.

   Answer: The SELECT statement is

   ```
   SQL> select min(Last_Name)
      2  from Instructor;

   MIN(LAST_NAME)
   -------------------------
   ANGELO
   ```

Exercise

Create a table, named NEW_CLASS, using a CREATE TABLE <xyz> AS ... statement based on a join of the Class, Schedule_Type, and Schedule_Type_Details tables that contains the following columns:

- ☐ Class_ID
- ☐ Department_ID
- ☐ Course_ID

☐ Day of the week spelled out

☐ Time spelled out (for example, 11:00 a.m.)

Answer:

```
SQL> create table New_Class as
  2  select Class_ID, Department_ID, Course_ID,
  3  decode(day,1,'Sunday',2,'Monday',3,'Tuesday',4,'Wednesday',
  4  5,'Thursday',6,'Friday',7,'Saturday') Day_of_Week,
  5  to_char(Starting_Time,'HH:MI PM') Starting_Time
  6  from Class, Schedule_Type_Details
  7  where
  8  Class.Schedule_ID = Schedule_Type_Details.Schedule_ID;

Table created.

SQL> select Class_ID, Department_ID, Course_ID, Day_of_Week, Starting_Ti
  2  from New_Class
  3  order by Class_ID;
```

CLASS_ID	DEPARTMENT_ID	COURS	DAY_OF_WE	STARTING_TIME
103400	PSYCH	183	Monday	01:00 PM
103400	PSYCH	183	Wednesday	01:00 PM
103400	PSYCH	183	Friday	01:00 PM
103600	MATH	50	Monday	03:00 PM
103600	MATH	50	Friday	03:00 PM
103600	MATH	50	Wednesday	03:00 PM
104200	PHILO	198	Friday	09:00 AM
104500	HIST	184	Monday	03:00 PM
104500	HIST	184	Wednesday	03:00 PM
104500	HIST	184	Friday	03:00 PM
108300	ENGL	101	Monday	10:00 AM
108300	ENGL	101	Wednesday	10:00 AM
108300	ENGL	101	Friday	10:00 AM
108400	HIST	115	Tuesday	09:00 AM
108400	HIST	115	Thursday	09:00 AM
108600	PSYCH	183	Monday	10:00 AM
108600	PSYCH	183	Wednesday	10:00 AM
108600	PSYCH	183	Friday	10:00 AM
109100	BIO	101	Monday	03:00 PM
109100	BIO	101	Wednesday	03:00 PM
109100	BIO	101	Friday	03:00 PM
110300	ENG	199	Friday	09:00 AM
120200	ECON	199	Tuesday	09:00 AM
120200	ECON	199	Thursday	09:00 AM

```
24 rows selected.
```

Day 8, "More Sophisticated Queries with SQL"

Quiz

1. Construct an SQL statement that retrieves the last name of an instructor who is teaching a course with additional fees greater than $50.

   Answer: Here is a three-table join that returns the information:

```
SQL> select Last_Name
   2  from Class CL, Instructor I, Course CO
   3  where
   4  CL.Instructor_ID = I.Instructor_ID and
   5  CL.Department_ID = CO.Department_ID and
   6  CL.Course_ID    = CO.Course_ID and
   7  Additional_Fees > 50;

LAST_NAME
-----------------------
WEISS
```

2. Construct an SQL statement that retrieves a list of cities in which students reside and the number of students that reside in each city.

   Answer: Here is the SELECT statement that produces the desired results:

```
SQL> select City, count(*)
   2  from Student
   3  group by City;

CITY                     COUNT(*)
------------------------ --------
DOVER                         14
SPRINGFIELD                   17
```

3. Create a view that lists each class—its Class_ID, Department_ID, and Course_ID—for those classes that meet on Mondays.

   Answer: Here is the CREATE VIEW statement that performs the requested action. Before you actually try to create the view, you should experiment until you have defined the SELECT statement on which the view will be based:

```
SQL> select Class_ID, Department_ID, Course_ID
   2  from Class CL, Schedule_Type ST, Schedule_Type_Details STD
   3  where
   4  CL.Schedule_ID = ST.Schedule_ID and
   5  ST.Schedule_ID = STD.Schedule_ID and
   6  STD.Day = 2;
```

A

CLASS_ID	DEPARTMENT_ID	COURS
104500	HIST	184
109100	BIO	101
108300	ENGL	101
108600	PSYCH	183
103400	PSYCH	183
103600	MATH	50

6 rows selected.

Then, you can create the view:

```
SQL> create view Classes_on_Monday as
  2    select Class_ID, Department_ID, Course_ID
  3    from Class CL, Schedule_Type ST, Schedule_Type_Details STD
  4    where
  5    CL.Schedule_ID = ST.Schedule_ID and
  6    ST.Schedule_ID = STD.Schedule_ID and
  7    STD.Day = 2;
```

View created.

```
SQL> select Class_ID, Department_ID, Course_ID
  2    from Classes_on_Monday;
```

CLASS_ID	DEPARTMENT_ID	COURS
104500	HIST	184
109100	BIO	101
108300	ENGL	101
108600	PSYCH	183
103400	PSYCH	183
103600	MATH	50

6 rows selected.

Exercise

The number of instructors is 18. The number of classes being offered is 10. However, the number of distinct Instructor_IDs in the Class table is 9. Using these tables and SQL, provide a complete explanation.

Answer: There are 10 classes being offered as you can see:

```
SQL> select count(*) from Class;
```

```
 COUNT(*)
---------
       10
```

There are nine instructors for these classes:

```
SQL> select distinct Instructor_ID from Class;
```

```
INSTRUCTOR_ID
- - - - - - - - - - - - - - - - - - - -
D944
E405
E491
G331
J505
R983
S131
T149
W490

9 rows selected.
```

Let's see if any of the instructors are teaching more than one class:

```
SQL> select Instructor_ID from Class
  2  having count(*) > 1
  3  group by Instructor_ID;

INSTRUCTOR_ID
- - - - - - - - - - - - - - - - - - - -
J505
```

Instructor J505, who happens to be Jerrold Jason, is teaching more than one class:

```
SQL> select Class_ID from Class
  2  where Instructor_ID = 'J505';

CLASS_ID
- - - - - - - - - - - - - - - - - - - -
108600
103400
```

Day 9, "Programming an Oracle Database with PL/SQL"

Quiz

1. Name the three sections of a PL/SQL subprogram.

   Answer: The three sections of a PL/SQL subprogram are the declaration, executable, and exception sections.

2. True or false? A PL/SQL variable that stores a column value must have the same name as the column.

   Answer: False. A PL/SQL variable that stores a column value may have any legal name.

3. Why is it a good practice to use %TYPE when declaring variables?

Answer: It is a good practice to use %TYPE when declaring a variable because it reduces the effort needed to maintain PL/SQL code. If you declare a variable without using %TYPE and the corresponding column's definition changes, you will have to modify the variable declaration. If you use %TYPE, you won't have to modify the variable declaration.

Exercise

Construct an anonymous block that declares a procedure that will set the additional fees for a course to $50 if there are no current additional fees. The procedure should have only one argument—Department_ID—and should perform this action only for the value of Department_ID supplied to the procedure.

Answer: Let's interpret "no current additional fees" as meaning that the additional fees are either zero or null. Let's look at a possible solution.

As you can see in the following query, the math department has three courses without additional fees: Course IDs 50, 101, and 189.

```
SQL> select Course_ID, Additional_Fees
  2  from Course
  3  where
  4  Department_ID = 'MATH';

COURS ADDITIONAL_FEES
----- ---------------
50                  0
101                 0
189                 0
51                 10
```

Here is the anonymous block that contains a procedure (see line 2) that is invoked on line 13. As specified, the procedure contains a single argument: Department_ID.

```
SQL> declare
  2
  2  procedure Set_Default_Course_Fees (arg_Department_ID varchar2) is
  3
  3  begin
  4
  4  update Course
  5  set Additional_Fees = 50
  6  where
  7  Department_ID = arg_Department_ID and
  8  Additional_Fees is null or
  9  Additional_Fees = 0;
 10
 10  end;
 11
 11  --   Main block.
 12
```

```
12  begin
13
13  Set_Default_Course_Fees ('MATH');
14
14  end;
15  /
```

PL/SQL procedure successfully completed.

You can see from the following query that the procedure has set the additional fees to $50 for the three courses:

```
SQL> select Course_ID, Additional_Fees
  2  from Course
  3  where
  4  Department_ID = 'MATH';

COURS ADDITIONAL_FEES
----- ---------------
50                 50
101                50
189                50
51                 10
```

Day 10, "Program Development with PL/SQL"

Quiz

1. True or false? A stored procedure can call a stored function but a stored function cannot call a stored procedure.

   Answer: False. A stored procedure can call other procedures or functions. A stored function also can call other procedures and functions.

2. Name three reasons for using stored procedures, functions, and packages in an application.

   Answer: Efficiency, reusability, and portability.

3. What tools can be used to develop PL/SQL subprograms?

   Answer: SQL*Plus, SQL Worksheet, Procedure Builder, and other third-party tools. Procedure Builder makes the task of PL/SQL development much easier than using SQL*Plus or SQL Worksheet.

4. If "x > 32" is assigned to a PL/SQL variable, what is the datatype of the variable?

   Answer: Boolean. Only a Boolean expression can be assigned to a Boolean variable.

Exercises

1. Create an anonymous PL/SQL block that will call the `Assign_Grade` procedure in the Flugle package and assign a B to Anna Anastatia for Biology 101.

   Answer: If you query the Student and Class tables, you'll find the following:

   ☐ Anna Anastatia's student ID is 10231324.

   ☐ The class ID for Biology 101 is 109100.

   As you can see in the following query, Anna has not yet received a grade for Biology 101:

   ```
   SQL> select * from Student_Schedule;

   STUDENT_ID            CLASS_ID              GR DATE_GRAD
   -------------------   -------------------   -- ---------
   10231311              104200                B  02-JUN-97
   10231311              104500                B- 03-JUN-97
   10231324              109100
   10231311              109100
   ```

   Here is an anonymous block that will invoke the Assign_Grade procedure in the Flugle package:

   ```
   SQL> set serveroutput on
   SQL>
   SQL> declare
     2
     2   Status        number;
     3
     3   --   Main block.
     4
     4   begin
     5
     5   dbms_output.enable;
     6
     6   Flugle.Assign_Grade('10231324','109100','B',status);
     7
     7   dbms_output.put_line('status: ' || to_char(status));
     8
     8   end;
     9   /
   status: 0

   PL/SQL procedure successfully completed.
   ```

   Once again, if you inspect the Student_Schedule table, you'll see that Anna has now been assigned a B for the class:

   ```
   SQL> select * from Student_Schedule;

   STUDENT_ID            CLASS_ID              GR DATE_GRAD
   -------------------   -------------------   -- ---------
   10231311              104200                B  02-JUN-97
   10231311              104500                B- 03-JUN-97
   10231324              109100                B  04-JUN-97
   10231311              109100
   ```

2. A student, Jackson Smythe, has created a stored function named `Change_My_Grade` with two arguments: Student ID and Class ID. The function changes the grade for any specified student and class to an A+. Write out the statements that will create this function.

Here is the function that will perform this dastardly deed:

```
SQL> create or replace function
  2  change_My_Grade(arg_student_ID IN  varchar2,
  3                         arg_class_ID   IN  varchar2)
  4  return number is
  5
  5  counter number;
  6  status  number;
  7
  7  normal  CONSTANT number := 0;
  8  unsuccessful CONSTANT number := -1;
  9
  9  not_registered exception;
 10
 10  begin
 11
 11  status := normal;
 12
 12  --  Determine if the student is registered for this class.
 13
 13  select count(*) into counter
 14  from student_schedule
 15  where
 16  student_id = arg_student_id and
 17  class_id   = arg_class_id;
 18
 18  if counter = 0 then
 19  --
 20  -- The student is not taking this class.
 21  --
 22    raise not_registered;
 23    status := unsuccessful;
 24  else
 25  --
 26  --  Assign the grade for this class.
 27  --
 28    update student_schedule
 29    set
 30    grade = 'A+',
 31    date_grade_assigned = sysdate
 32    where
 33    student_id = arg_student_id and
 34    class_id   = arg_class_id;
 35  end if;
 36
 36  return status;
 37
 37  exception
 38    when not_registered then
 39      raise_application_error (-21003, 'Student not registered for
         ➥class');
```

A

```
40    when others then
41       null;
42
42  end;
43  /
```

Function created.

To test the function, create an anonymous block that will invoke Change_My_Grade for Paul Fernandez's grade in History 184.

```
SQL> declare
  2
  2  Status       number;
  3
  3  -- Main block.
  4
  4  begin
  5
  5  dbms_output.enable;
  6
  6  status := Change_My_Grade('10231311','104500');
  7
  7  dbms_output.put_line('status: ' || to_char(status));
  8
  8  end;
  9  /
status: 0
```

PL/SQL procedure successfully completed.

As you can see from the following query, the function works as advertised:

```
SQL> select * from Student_Schedule;

STUDENT_ID            CLASS_ID               GR DATE_GRAD
-------------------   -------------------    -- ---------
10231311              104200                 B  02-JUN-97
10231311              104500                 A+ 04-JUN-97
10231324              109100
10231311              109100
```

Day 11, "More Programming Techniques with PL/SQL"

Quiz

1. How are SQLCODE and SQLERRM used in PL/SQL subprograms?

   Answer: SQLCODE returns the Oracle error that resulted from the last SQL operation. An error code of 0 indicates the normal completion of the operation. SQLERRM returns the text of the Oracle error message that corresponds to the value in SQLCODE.

2. True or false? A PL/SQL subprogram may have multiple cursors open at the same time.

   Answer: True. In a PL/SQL subprogram, there is no restriction on having more than one cursor open at the same time.

3. What are the benefits of using database triggers?

   Answer: Triggers serve several purposes. A trigger can perform complex validation when a row is added or modified. A trigger can modify a column's value before it is stored in the table. A trigger in one table can be used to modify the contents of a different table.

4. What kind of database trigger would you use if you wanted to modify the value to be stored in a column when a new row is added to a table?

   Answer: A before-insert trigger which will fire for each row.

Exercises

1. Create a stored function, Teaching_Load, that has a single argument—a Department_ID. Teaching_Load should return the average number of courses that instructors in the specified department are currently teaching.

   First, you need to create the stored function:

```
SQL> create or replace function Teaching_Load(arg_Department_ID IN
varchar2)
  2
  2  return number is
  3
  3  number_of_instructors  number;
  4  number_of_classes      number;
  5  avg_teaching_load      number;
  6
  6  begin
  7
  7  --  Get the number of instructors for this department.
  8
  8  select count(*) into number_of_instructors
  9  from Instructor
 10  where
 11  Department_ID = arg_Department_ID;
 12
 12
 12  --  Get the number of classes for this department.
 13
 13  select count(*) into number_of_classes
 14  from Class
 15  where
 16  Department_ID = arg_Department_ID;
 17
 17  avg_teaching_load := number_of_classes / number_of_instructors;
 18
 18  return avg_teaching_load;
 19
 19  exception
```

```
20    when others then
21      null;
22
22  end;
23  /
```

Function created.

To test the function, you can invoke it in a SELECT statement that references the DUAL table. As you can see, the instructors in the Biology department are teaching an average of 0.5 classes:

```
SQL> select Teaching_Load('BIO') from dual;

TEACHING_LOAD('BIO')
--------------------
                  .5
```

2. Create a stored procedure, Suitable_Locations, that has a single argument— seating capacity. Suitable_Locations should print out the first three buildings and rooms whose seating capacity exceeds the specified seating capacity.

Here is a stored procedure that will satisfy the requirement:

```
SQL> create or replace procedure Suitable_Locations
  2      (arg_Seating_Capacity IN number) is
  3
  3  cursor Get_Locations is
  4  select class_building, class_room, seating_capacity
  5  from Class_Location
  6  where
  7  Seating_Capacity >= arg_Seating_Capacity
  8  order by Seating_Capacity desc;
  9
  9  begin
 10
 10  --
 11
 11  dbms_output.enable;
 12
 12  for Get_Locations_Rec in Get_Locations loop
 13
 13    exit when Get_Locations%rowcount > 3;
 14    dbms_output.put_line('Building: ' ||
      ➥Get_Locations_Rec.Class_Building ||
 15    '  Room: ' || Get_Locations_Rec.Class_Room || '  Capacity: ' ||
 16    to_char(Get_Locations_Rec.Seating_Capacity));
 17
 17  end loop;
 18
 18  exception
 19    when others then
 20      null;
 21
 21  end;
 22  /
```

Procedure created.

To test the stored procedure, you can use an anonymous block that invokes it:

```
SQL> declare
  2
  2 Status        number;
  3
  3 -- Main block.
  4
  4 begin
  5
  5 dbms_output.enable;
  6
  6 Suitable_Locations (30);
  7
  7 end;
  8 /
Building: FLUGLE HALL    Room: 100    Capacity: 200
Building: FLUGLE HALL    Room: 150    Capacity: 120
Building: NARROW HALL    Room: 200    Capacity: 90

PL/SQL procedure successfully completed.
```

3. Write a before-delete trigger on the Instructor table that will raise an exception if an instructor is scheduled to teach a class.

Here is the script for creating the trigger. In line 7, a query is used to determine how many classes the instructor is teaching; that value is stored in counter. In line 11, counter is evaluated; if it is greater than zero, the trigger raises an application error, preventing the deletion of the instructor:

```
SQL> create or replace trigger Instructor_BD
  2     before delete on Instructor
  3     for each row
  4
  4 declare
  5
  5 counter number;
  6
  6 begin
  7
  7 select count(*) into counter
  8 from Class
  9 where
 10 Instructor_ID = :old.Instructor_ID;
 11
 11 if counter > 0 then
 12   raise_application_error (-20800,
 13                       'Instructor is scheduled to teach a
                           ➥class');
 14 end if;
 15
 15
 15 end;
 16 /

Trigger created.
```

To test the trigger, you can try deleting an instructor who is currently teaching a class. As you can see, the trigger raises the application error—20800—preventing the DELETE statement from successful completion.

```
SQL> delete from Instructor
  2  where
  3  Instructor_ID = 'E405';
delete from Instructor
       *
ERROR at line 1:
ORA-20800: Instructor is scheduled to teach a class
ORA-06512: at line 9
ORA-04088: error during execution of trigger 'FLUGLE.INSTRUCTOR_BD'
```

However, if you try to delete an instructor who isn't teaching class, the trigger will not raise the application error:

```
SQL> delete from Instructor
  2  where
  3  Instructor_ID = 'P331';

1 row deleted.
```

Day 12, "Developer/2000: Introduction to Oracle Forms"

Quiz

1. True or false? Oracle Forms Runtime will only execute an .fmb file.

   Answer: False. Oracle Forms Runtime only executes an .fmx file, not an .fmb file.

2. Name the three types of modules that the Forms Designer can create.

   Answer: The three module types are forms, menus, and libraries.

3. True or false? The Forms Designer can only save a form to an Oracle database if it contains a base table block.

   Answer: False. The Forms Designer can save a form to either the database or the file system, regardless of the form's contents.

4. True or false? You can create a block based on the contents of a table owned by another Oracle user.

   Answer: True. You can create a block based on a table owned by another Oracle user as long as you have been granted the appropriate privileges for that table.

Exercise

Create a form for the Instructor table. Specify an ORDER BY clause so that the records retrieved by a query are ordered by department ID, instructor last name, first name, and middle initial. Test the form.

Answer: Please refer to the Instructor.fmb file in the Day 13 folder on the CD-ROM.

Day 13, "Developer/2000: Developing a User Interface with Oracle Forms"

Quiz

1. True or false? A master block cannot be based on a view; it must be a table.

   Answer: False. A master block *can* be based on a view.

2. True or false? You can modify display characteristics of an item with the Layout Editor or by modifying the item's properties.

   Answer: True. You can modify the display characteristics of an item—for instance, its position or font—by selecting the item with the Object Navigator and right-clicking Properties.

3. How can the tab order of a group of items be changed?

   Answer: You can change the tab order of a group of items by changing their order with the Object Navigator.

Exercises

1. Create a master-detail window for entering Schedule_Type and Schedule_Type_Details.

   Answer: Please refer to the Schedule_Type.fmb file in the Day 14 folder on the CD-ROM.

2. In the Department_Class form, create an LOV for Schedule_ID that will validate user input.

   Answer: Please refer to the Department_Class.fmb file in the Day 14 folder on the CD-ROM.

Day 14, "Developer/2000: Application Development with Oracle Forms"

Quiz

1. True or false? An item-level trigger in one block cannot refer to items in a different block.

   Answer: False. There are no restrictions on the ability of an item-level trigger to reference items in a different block.

2. How are block items referenced in a trigger?

   Answer: To reference a block item in a trigger, use the nomenclature `:block-name.item-name`.

3. If you create an item-level trigger to validate user input, what exception should be raised if the user enters an invalid value?

   Answer: `FORM_TRIGGER_FAILURE`.

Exercises

1. Modify the Instructor form so that it has the same width and height as the MDI_Frame form.

   Answer: Please refer to the `Instructor.fmb` file in the Day 15 folder on the CD-ROM.

2. Create a menu item for the Browse menu that will invoke a form that displays Instructors in a tabular format, ordered by Instructor last name, first name, and middle initial.

   Answer: Please refer to the `menu15.mmb` file in the Day 15 folder on the CD-ROM.

Day 15, "Developer/2000: Developing Reports with Oracle Reports"

Quiz

1. True or false? You can store your RDF files in a source code control system such as PVCS.

   Answer: False. An RDF file is a binary file. Instead of trying to maintain version control on your RDF files, you should generate REX files, which are text files that can be kept under version control.

2. Name the four elements of a report layout.

   Answer: Header, footer, body, and margin. Almost every report has a body layout.

3. True or false? A report cannot have more that two queries linked together.

Answer: False. You can have multiple queries that are related. For instance, you could have a report based on three queries: a query of departments, a query of instructors in each department, and a query of the classes that each instructor is teaching.

Exercise

Create a master-detail report that lists each classroom and the classes that are scheduled for that room, regardless of meeting time (for example, all of the classes that are scheduled to use a particular room).

Answer: Please refer to the `Classroom.fmb` file in the Day 16 folder on the CD-ROM.

Day 16, "Developer/2000: Using Oracle Graphics and Procedure Builder"

Quiz

1. What are the two file types used by Oracle Graphics?

Answer: An `.ogd` file—which stands for Oracle Graphics Designer file—contains the definition of a chart or display. Using the Graphics Designer, you generate an `.ogr` file (Oracle Graphics Runtime) from an `.ogd` file.

2. Name three chart types that can be specified with the Graphics Designer.

Answer: Line chart, bar chart, and pie chart.

3. True or false? You can use the Stored Program Unit Editor to modify a package specification but not a package body.

Answer: False. The Stored Program Unit Editor can be used to modify either a package specification or package body.

Exercises

1. Create a bar chart that displays the number of courses offered by each department at Flugle College.

Answer: Please refer to the `Courses_by_Department.ogd` file in the Day 17 folder on the CD-ROM.

2. Modify the trigger on the Student_Schedule table so that it only records changes to the Student_Schedule table if the value of the Grade column is A, B, or C.

Answer: Please refer to the `Student_Schedule.sql` file in the Day 17 folder on the CD-ROM.

Day 17, "Introduction to Oracle Power Objects"

Quiz

1. True or false? A Power Objects application connects to an Oracle database through an application transaction object.

   Answer: False. A Power Objects application connects to an Oracle database by specifying a database session object.

2. Name three types of objects that you can place on a form.

   Answer: A text field, a radio button, and a repeater.

3. Give an example of a container object.

   Answer: An example of a container object is a repeater. A repeater may contain one or more text fields.

Exercises

1. Build a form for displaying and modifying information about each instructor. Display the number of classes, if any, that the instructor is scheduled to teach.

2. Modify the Student form to display the GPA of the current student.

   Answer: Please refer to the `Flugle.poa` file in the Day 18 folder on the CD-ROM.

Day 18, "Developing an Application with Oracle Power Objects"

Quiz

1. True or false? A report's `RecordSource` property must reference a single table or view; it cannot join two or more tables.

   Answer: True. The `RecordSource` property is limited to a single table or view. To construct a master-detail report, you must either create a view or add a subform to a report which contains a detail report that can be linked to the master report.

2. True or false? Power Objects supports a maximum of three levels of inheritance. In other words, you can create class A, add an instance of class A on class B, and add an instance of class B on class C.

   Answer: False. Power Objects will support many levels of inheritance. However, you should be judicious about how many levels you construct because too many levels of inheritance can have an adverse effect on performance.

3. If you can validate user input in a Power Objects application with the Validate method, why would you need to use database constraints and triggers to enforce data integrity?

   Answer: You'll always want to create database constraints and triggers to enforce data integrity, even if the same business rules are enforced in a Power Objects application. The reason is that database constraints and triggers represent the first line of defense for data integrity. Because a single database could support many different applications, each constructed with a different tool or by a different developer, you can't assume that all applications implement the full set of business rules.

Exercises

1. Power Objects includes a number of predefined classes. If you examine the contents of the Classes folder, you'll see a class named clsMeter. Add an instance of it to MyForm. See if you can figure out how to link the meter to the X position of the mouse on the form.

2. Use Power Objects to build a report which contains a list of the instructors that belong to each department. Add a lookup field to each instructor line which indicates if the instructor is not teaching any classes for the semester.

   Answer: Please refer to the Flugle.poa file in the Day 19 folder on the CD-ROM.

Day 19, "An Overview of Oracle Database Security and Tuning"

Quiz

1. True or false? A database role can be granted to both users and other database roles.

   Answer: True. You may want to create certain generic roles that have some basic privileges and grant those roles to more specific roles.

2. True or false? Adding an index to a table always improves the performance of an application.

   Answer: False. A non-unique index should only be added if the indexed column will be frequently used in queries of the table. Also, if the contents of the table are frequently changed, the index could degrade overall performance.

3. True or false? Any Oracle user can create a public synonym as long as the synonym points to a table that is owned by that user.

   Answer: False. The creation of a public synonym requires either the DBA role or the CREATE PUBLIC SYNONYM system privilege.

Exercise

You can answer this question descriptively, without using SQL statements: If you were the DBA at Flugle College, what database roles would you create? What privileges would you grant to those roles?

Answer: You might want to create these roles:

☐ A role for student

☐ A role for instructor

☐ A role for department chairperson

☐ A role for college administrator

Object privileges are commonly referred to as Create (C), Read (R), Update (U), Delete (D), or CRUD. A matrix that defines all these privileges for each role is called a CRUD matrix.

Privileges for student role:

    Class: R
    Class_Location: R
    Course: R
    Department: R
    Instructor: R
    Schedule_Type: R
    Schedule_Type_Details: R
    Student: R (only for self)
    Student_Schedule: CRUD (only for self)

Privileges for instructor role:

    Class: R
    Class_Location: R
    Course: R
    Department: R
    Instructor: RU (only for self)
    Schedule_Type: R
    Schedule_Type_Details: R
    Student: R (only for self)
    Student_Schedule: RU

Privileges for department chairperson role:

    Class: CRUD
    Class_Location: R
    Course: CRUD

Department: R
Instructor: CRUD
Schedule_Type: R
Schedule_Type_Details: R
Student: R
Student_Schedule: RU

Privileges for college adminstrator role:

Class: CRUD
Class_Location: CRUD
Course: CRUD
Department: CRUD
Instructor: CRUD
Schedule_Type: CRUD
Schedule_Type_Details: CRUD
Student: CRUD

A

Day 20, "Using Oracle Database Designer and Oracle Designer/2000 in Application Development"

Quiz

1. True or false? One drawback to Database Designer is that it supports only Oracle databases.

   Answer: False. Database Designer will allow you to generate an RDB, DB2, or SQL Server database from your database design.

2. Name three advantages of using Database Designer instead of a text editor to create the DDL statements that implement a database design.

   Answer: Some of the advantages of using Database Designer include the following:

   ☐ Far fewer errors due to "typos," such as misspelling a column name.

   ☐ Capability to capture table and column definitions in the same file.

   ☐ Capability to pass information to Designer/2000, such as display formats for columns.

   ☐ A diagram is more easily understood than a set of SQL statements and can be presented to other project members for review/feedback.

Chapter 21, "Oracle: The Next Generation"

Quiz

1. What is the role of the htp and htf PL/SQL packages?

   Answer: The htp and htf PL/SQL packages are used to dynamically generate HTML source code.

2. True or false? The Network Computing Architecture is available only for Sun Solaris and Microsoft Windows NT Server.

   Answer: False. The Network Computing Architecture is a strategy that will eventually support a wide range of platforms.

INDEX

A V I A C O M   S E R V I C E

The Information SuperLibrary™

 Bookstore

 Search

 What's New

 Reference

 Software

 Newsletter

 Company Overviews

 Yellow Pages

 Internet Starter Kit

 HTML Workshop

 Win a Free T-Shirt!

 Macmillan Computer Publishing

 Site Map

 Talk to Us

(Note: Company Overviews icon and Site Map icon positions follow the top and bottom rows respectively)

CHECK OUT THE BOOKS IN THIS LIBRARY.

You'll find thousands of shareware files and over 1600 computer books designed for both technowizards and technophobes. You can browse through 700 sample chapters, get the latest news on the Net, and find just about anything using our massive search directories.

All Macmillan Computer Publishing books are available at your local bookstore.

We're open 24-hours a day, 365 days a year.

You don't need a card.

We don't charge fines.

And you can be as LOUD as you want.

The Information SuperLibrary

http://www.mcp.com/mcp/   ftp.mcp.com

MACMILLAN COMPUTER PUBLISHING USA

A VIACOM COMPANY

 Support:

If you need assistance with the information in this book or with a CD/Disk accompanying the book, please access the Knowledge Base on our Web site at **http://www.superlibrary.com/general/support**. Our most Frequently Asked Questions are answered there. If you do not find the answer to your questions on our Web site, you may contact Macmillan Technical Support **(317) 581-3833** or e-mail us at **support@mcp.com**.

Teach Yourself Access 97 in 24 Hours

Tim Buchanan, Craig Eddy, & Rob Newman

As organizations and end users continue to upgrade to NT Workstation and Windows 95, a surge in 32-bit productivity applications, including Microsoft Office 97, is expected. Using an easy-to-follow approach, this book teaches the fundamentals of a key component in the Microsoft Office 97 package, Access 97. You learn how to use and manipulate existing databases, create databases with wizards, and build databases from scratch in 24 one-hour lessons.

Price: $19.99 USA/$28.95 CDN   *User level: New–Casual*

ISBN: 0-672-31027-9   *400 pages*

Oracle 7.3 Developer's Guide

Lave Singh, Joe Zafian, Kelly Leigh, et al.

The power user's guide to Oracle, this combination tutorial and reference covers major database development issues, including application design, designing and printing reports, and creating client/server applications. It includes tricks to use and traps to avoid in upgrading to Version 7.3.

Price: $59.99 USA/$84.95 CAN   *User level: Advanced–Expert*

ISBN: 0-672-22794-0   *1,008 pages*

Teach Yourself SQL in 21 Days, Second Edition

Ryan Stephens, Bryan Morgan, Ronald Plew, & Jeff Perkins

Fully updated and revised to include coverage of PL/SQL and Transact SQL, this easy-to-understand guide teaches you everything you need to know—from database concepts and processes to implementing security and constructing and optimizing queries.

Price: $39.99 USA/$56.95 CDN   *User level: New–Casual*

ISBN: 0-672-31110-0   *700 pages*

Developing Personal Oracle7 for Windows 95 Applications, Second Edition

David Lockman

An update to the successful first edition, this comprehensive reference takes you through the process of developing powerful applications while teaching you how to effectively use Personal Oracle7. The CD-ROM includes current versions of Personal Oracle7 for Windows 3.1 and Windows 95.

Price: $49.99 USA/$70.95 CDN   *User level: New–Casual*

ISBN: 0-672-31025-2   *800 pages*

Add to Your Sams Library Today with the Best Books for Programming, Operating Systems, and New Technologies

The easiest way to order is to pick up the phone and call

1-800-428-5331

between 9:00 a.m. and 5:00 p.m. EST.
For faster service please have your credit card available.

ISBN	Quantity	Description of Item	Unit Cost	Total Cost
0-67231-027-9		Teach Yourself Access 97 in 24 Hours	$19.99	
0-67222-794-0		Oracle 7.3 Developer's Guide (Book/CD-ROM)	$59.99	
0-672-31110-0		Teach Yourself SQL in 21 Days, Second Edition	$39.99	
0-67231-025-2		Developing Oracle7 for Windows 95 Applications, Second Edition (Book/CD-ROM)	$49.99	

❏ 3 ½" Disk

❏ 5 ¼" Disk

Shipping and Handling: See information below.		
TOTAL		

Shipping and Handling: $4.00 for the first book, and $1.75 for each additional book. Floppy disk: add $1.75 for shipping and handling. If you need to have it NOW, we can ship product to you in 24 hours for an additional charge of approximately $18.00, and you will receive your item overnight or in two days. Overseas shipping and handling adds $2.00 per book and $8.00 for up to three disks. Prices subject to change. Call for availability and pricing information on latest editions.

201 W. 103rd Street, Indianapolis, Indiana 46290

1-800-428-5331 — Orders   1-800-835-3202 — FAX   1-800-858-7674 — Customer Service

Book ISBN 0-672-31078-3

Installing the Disc

The companion CD-ROM contains all the authors' source code and samples from the book and many third-party software products.

Windows 3.1 and Windows NT 3.5.1 Installation Instructions

1. Insert the CD-ROM disc into your CD-ROM drive.
2. From File Manager or Program Manager, choose Run from the File menu.
3. Type *drive*\\`SETUP.EXE` and press Enter, where *drive* corresponds to the drive letter of your CD-ROM. For example, if your CD-ROM is drive D:, type `D:\SETUP.EXE` and press Enter.
4. Installation creates a program named "TY Oracle DB Dev." This group will contain icons you can use to browse the CD-ROM.

Windows 95 and Windows NT 4.0 Installation Instructions

1. Insert the CD-ROM disc into your CD-ROM drive.
2. From the Windows 95 desktop, double-click on the My Computer icon.
3. Double-click on the icon representing your CD-ROM drive.
4. Double-click on the icon titled SETUP.EXE to run the installation program.
5. Installation creates a program group named "TY Oracle DB Dev." This group will contain icons you can use to browse the CD-ROM.

NOTE

If Windows 95 is installed on your computer and you have the AutoPlay feature enabled, the SETUP.EXE program starts automatically whenever you insert the disc into your CD-ROM drive.